JACOB H. SCHIFF

JACOB H. SCHIFF

A Study in American Jewish Leadership

Naomi W. Cohen

Published with the support of the Jewish Theological Seminary of America
and the American Jewish Committee

Brandeis University Press
Published by University Press of New England
Hanover and London

Brandeis University Press

Published by University Press of New England, Hanover, NH 03755

© 1999 by Brandeis University Press

Printed in the United States of America

5 4 3 2 1

UNIVERSITY PRESS OF NEW ENGLAND publishes books under its own imprint and is the publisher for Brandeis University Press, Dartmouth College, Middlebury College Press, University of New Hampshire, Tufts University, and Wesleyan University Press.

LIBRARY OF CONGRESS CATALOGING-IN-PUBLICATION DATA
Cohen, Naomi Wiener
Jacob H. Schiff : a study in American Jewish leadership / by Naomi W. Cohen.
    p.   cm. — (Brandeis series in American Jewish history, culture, and life)
Includes bibliographical references and index.
ISBN 0-87451-948-9 (cl. : alk. paper)
    1. Schiff, Jacob H. (Jacob Henry), 1847-1920. 2. Jews—United States Biography. 3. Jewish capitalists and financiers—United States—Biography. 4. Philanthropists—United States Biography.
5. Jews—United States—Politics and government. 6. United States Biography. I. Title. II. Series.
E184.37.S37C64   1999
332'.092—dc21
[B]   99-30392

FRONTISPIECE
Image of Jacob Henry Schiff.
American Jewish Historical Society,
Waltham, Massachusetts, and New York, New York.

Brandeis Series in American Jewish History, Culture, and Life
JONATHAN D. SARNA, Editor
SYLVIA BARACK FISHMAN, Associate Editor

Leon A. Jick, 1992
The Americanization of the Synagogue, 1820–1870

Sylvia Barack Fishman, editor, 1992
Follow My Footprints: Changing Images of Women in American Jewish Fiction

Gerald Tulchinsky, 1993
Taking Root: The Origins of the Canadian Jewish Community

Shalom Goldman, editor, 1993
Hebrew and the Bible in America: The First Two Centuries

Marshall Sklare, 1993
Observing America's Jews

Reena Sigman Friedman, 1994
These Are Our Children: Jewish Orphanages in the United States, 1880–1925

Alan Silverstein, 1994
Alternatives to Assimilation:
The Response of Reform Judaism to American Culture, 1840–1930

Jack Wertheimer, editor, 1995
The American Synagogue: A Sanctuary Transformed

Sylvia Barack Fishman, 1995
A Breath of Life: Feminism in the American Jewish Community

Diane Matza, editor, 1996
Sephardic-American Voices: Two Hundred Years of a Literary Legacy

Joyce Antler, editor, 1997
Talking Back: Images of Jewish Women in American Popular Culture

Jack Wertheimer, 1997
A People Divided: Judaism in Contemporary America

Beth S. Wenger and Jeffrey Shandler, editors, 1998
Encounters with the "Holy Land":
Place, Past and Future in American Jewish Culture

David Kaufman, 1998
Shul with a Pool: The "Synagogue-Center" in American Jewish History

Roberta Rosenberg Farber and Chaim I. Waxman, 1999
Jews in America: A Contemporary Reader

Murray Friedman and Albert D. Chernin, 1999
A Second Exodus: The American Movement to Free Soviet Jews

Stephen J. Whitfield, 1999
In Search of American Jewish Culture

Naomi W. Cohen, 1999
Jacob H. Schiff: A Study in American Jewish Leadership

FOR YONATAN,

WHO WAITED PATIENTLY FOR HIS BOOK

Contents

Preface

At a conference of the American Academy for Jewish Research some twenty years ago, I delivered a paper on the reaction of American Jewry to anti-Semitism in Bismarck's Germany. During the question period, the elderly widow of an illustrious Jewish scholar, who had grown up in fin-de-siècle Germany, posed a three-word query. Unconcerned with my learned explanations she asked in a thick accent: "Vere vas Schiff?" She, a younger contemporary of Schiff's, well remembered that in times of crisis American Jews looked first to Jacob Schiff (1847–1920), the head of the powerful banking firm of Kuhn, Loeb & Company, for an appropriate response.

Succeeding generations rapidly forgot. Today, for example, virtually no one can locate the street on New York's Lower East Side that was named Schiff Parkway after the banker's death. Modern scholars too showed little interest in the man. In 1988 the editors of the journal *American Jewish History* conducted a survey of American Jewish historians to ascertain their choices for the two greatest American Jewish leaders, one of the nineteenth and one of the twentieth century. Roughly of the same age as the banker's great-grandchildren, not one of the respondents voted for Schiff.[1] Even they, experts in the historical development of American Jews, ignored the man so important to Jews of his era.

That Schiff was forgotten or ignored in no way diminishes his significance or the significance of his achievements. Indeed, the wide range of his activities is so impressive that it alone may have daunted would-be biographers. This study, which aims in part to rescue Schiff from undeserved oblivion, makes no claim to all-inclusiveness. Its prime focus is on the public Schiff, the way in which he became and behaved as the foremost American Jewish leader of his day. Since American Jewish institutions have become increasingly alert to problems of communal leadership, an analysis of Schiff's objectives and methods can be of more than historical interest.

There is no fixed, satisfactory model against which one can measure what makes an American Jewish leader and what accounts for his success. Various interpretations have been offered, each recognizing a different configuration of factors like personality, ancestral traditions of the group, and the needs of the minority in relation to the demands of the larger society.[2]

None, however, readily fits Schiff. His leadership, suggestive in style of the contemporary individualistic captains of industry, differed qualitatively from that of his Jewish predecessors, contemporaries, and successors. His wealth and his status in the America of 1875–1920 set him apart, but equally distinctive was his voluntary involvement nationally and internationally in the totality of Jewish interests.

An understanding of Schiff's leadership must also factor in other considerations. For example, how was he rated as a leader by those he led? How successful was he in arousing an awareness of Jewish interests on the part of the Jewish community, the government, and American society in general? To what extent did emotional and psychological nuances of his approach— on the one side, a pride in Judaism and its cultural heritage, a genuine compassion for the needy, a hypersensitivity to the Jewish image, and a vision of a secure and united American Jewish community; and on the other, a hot temper and arrogant demeanor—govern his public behavior? Did his failures, and indeed many of his ideas did not bring about desired results, compromise his leadership?

Issues that engaged Schiff sprang from the condition of the Jewish community as he perceived it, both in the United States and in Europe, and from problems that arose when the minority group appeared out of step with American society. A constant concern, whether by itself or in tandem with a larger question, was discrimination against Jews. Although Schiff's behavior was reactive to such stimuli, the solutions he proposed were often innovative. Their application reflected the assets of wealth, a broad network of well-placed friends and acquaintances, and the executive talents he had skillfully honed in the business world. Rigidity on basic values notwithstanding, he was able to compromise on specific issues and then justify the compromise for the sake of his larger communal agenda. Where necessary he sought the advice of associates and friends on strategy; on many occasions he acted independently. Overall, he had the ability to interpret long-range economic and social trends, and the answers he came up with were often indicators of the rapid changes taking place in both the American and the Jewish communities.

How readily American Jewry accepted or rejected the dictates of Schiff, the exponent of elitist leadership, is revealed in most matters that engaged the Jewish community. As new immigrants from eastern Europe matured and acculturated, they increasingly challenged the unrepresentative rule of the established Germans. The rank and file, however, felt a genuine affection for the banker or were at least respectful and admiring. Since he readily identified with them and was accessible to them, a revolt against him specifically was usually averted. Nevertheless, the questions of who determined priorities, decided on appropriate responses, and executed strategy persisted. Meanwhile, Schiff consciously labored to keep the new arrivals in line, resorting to colorful public speeches, participation in immigrant organizations, and an adroitness in handling one-on-one situations. The irony was that he and his circle, men who demanded rapid and total Americanization of the Jewish immigrants, defended their own oligarchic and hence un-American control against cries for democratically chosen leaders.

Using the points mentioned above as its guidelines, this study examines Schiff the leader, the man who was at one and the same time the defender of Jews, the philanthropist par excellence, and the lobbyist for Russian Jewry. It traces his activities in the broad areas of charity, relief for Jewish immigrants and for Jews in Russia, Zionism, and institutions for the dissemination of Judaism and Jewish culture. His business career is discussed sketchily, and only the highlights of Kuhn, Loeb's operations are included. The purpose of that chapter is primarily to show how Schiff used his prominent position in the banking world and the profits he reaped—popular respect and influential contacts as well as money—on behalf of his fellow Jews. It also points up the businesslike traits that colored his approach to communal problems.

Schiff's leadership in all its dimensions was sui generis. In no other communal figure did the same constellation of personality and assets ever appear. Besides, the American and Jewish settings in which he labored changed dramatically after his death. The state and federal governments became increasingly involved in public welfare, America and American Jews recoiled from foreign commitments, and the managerial revolution in social institutions replaced individual leaders with impersonal organizations and professional bureaucrats. Together, the new trends made the wide scope of Schiff's interests and his hands-on style of leadership out of date. Although institutions that he launched during the formative years of the modern Jewish community lived on, Schiff and his multifaceted career were possible only in pre–World War I America.

After Schiff's death, Cyrus Adler was commissioned by the family to write a biography of his friend. The result, a two-volume work entitled *Jacob H. Schiff: His Life and Letters*, is an adulatory and uncritical account. Although historians, including myself, have dealt with many subjects that are treated here, and although some have consulted the Schiff papers for articles written about specific episodes in the banker's career, no analytical biography exists.

It is a pleasure to thank friends and colleagues who assisted me in gathering material for this book. In addition to those mentioned in the notes, I am grateful to Miriam Ostow, Robert Seltzer, Esther Panitz, Rosalie Bachana, Bruce Ruben, and my loyal research assistant, Charlotte Bonelli. Librarians and their staffs who generously gave of their expertise include Dr. Abraham Peck of the American Jewish Archives, Dr. Menahem Schmelzer and Dr. Mayer Rabinowitz, both of the Jewish Theological Seminary of America, Cyma Horowitz of the American Jewish Committee, and Suzanne Siegel of Hunter College.

Publication of the book was made possible by Dr. Ismar Schorsch and Dr. Jack Wertheimer, Chancellor and Provost respectively, of the Jewish Theological Seminary; and by the Ostow family, whose generosity is a tangible expression of our long-term friendship. I also very much appreciate the friendship and support of Mr. Robert Rifkind, formerly President of the American Jewish Committee, and his wife Arleen. The American Jewish Committee, with whom I have had a long and rewarding relationship over several decades, has understood the importance of Jacob Schiff as founder and benefactor of that organization, and generously contributed to the publication of this book. I deeply appreciate their generosity and their efforts on my behalf. I am grateful also for the encouragement I received from Mr. David T. Schiff, a great-grandson of Jacob Schiff.

Above all, I am indebted to my children, Jeremy Cohen and Judith Rosen, for their unflagging support. As usual, their aid was boundless.

JACOB H. SCHIFF

1

The Making of a Leader

From Frankfurt's "Judengasse" to Wall Street

On January 10, 1847, a second son and third child, Jacob Henry, was born to Moses and Clara Niederhofheim Schiff of Frankfurt-am-Main. A dealer in shawls who became a successful stockbroker, Moses Schiff was a stern father and pious Jew who demanded the same religious behavior from his five children. Jacob, a restless boy, did not conform willingly. He preferred playing to studying, and he especially resented parental insistence that he attend the synagogue three times daily for prayers. Although relations between father and son were strained, Jacob was closely attached to his mother, "an exceptional, well-educated woman." He once remarked to a friend that whatever success he had attained and whatever good he had accomplished were due to his mother's teaching and example.[1]

Differences with his father reinforced Jacob's desire to leave Frankfurt, but he remained loyal to both parents and to his siblings. The only one of the family to emigrate to America, he maintained close ties by frequent letters and visits to Germany; even as an adult he would kiss the photographs of his parents when he finished reciting his daily prayers. Jacob devotedly marked the anniversaries of his parents' deaths, and he frequently made donations in their memory to institutions in Frankfurt as well as New York. Despite his mild rebellion against his father's discipline, his values and behavioral traits were shaped significantly by what he had absorbed from his boyhood home. Punctuality, precision, attention to details, and especially a domineering role over his household suggest patterns of his father's Orthodox mind-set.[2]

The Frankfurt in which Jacob grew up was a bustling commercial center where the number of Jews increased dramatically in the nineteenth century—from over five thousand in 1858 to more than ten thousand in 1871.

Making its mark in finance and merchandising, the affluent Jewish community contributed generously to both civic causes and their own religious and charitable institutions. Within that community the prominent Schiff family had been rooted for several hundred years (dates for the first appearance of the family in Frankfurt range from 1370 to 1600). According to one source, almost every third Schiff was a rabbi, *dayyan* (religious judge), or *parnas* (lay head of the community). The most famous of Jacob's ancestors were the seventeenth-century talmudic scholar Meir ben Jacob Schiff (the Maharam) and the eighteenth-century *dayyan* David Tevele Schiff, who became rabbi of the Great Synagogue in London. For many years the early Schiffs shared ownership of a two-family house with the Rothschilds. Located in the old Jewish quarter, the house was marked on the Schiff side by a ship and on the Rothschild side by a red shield, symbols from which the surnames of the two families had originally derived.[3]

While the revolution of 1848 hastened Jewish emancipation and the grant of full civic rights in 1864, liberalism was also challenging conservatism on the religious scene. Here the conflict for control of the Jewish community pitted the young Reform movement against entrenched Orthodoxy. After the Frankfurt synagogue fell to Reform, Orthodox forces countered by organizing a new congregation, the Israelitische Religionsgesellschaft (IRG; Jewish Religious Association). The group, whose founders included Moses Schiff, represented the oldest and wealthiest families in the city. With its eye on "the progressive demands of the times," the IRG called for a traditional but modern synagogue, a school that taught secular as well as religious studies, and a rabbi who combined knowledge of Jewish tradition with a gymnasium and university education. An exemplar of modern Orthodoxy, Samson Raphael Hirsch was engaged by the IRG as its rabbi in 1851.[4]

The school established by Hirsch was ranked by the government as a model of its kind. Young Jacob attended classes there from 1853 to 1861 and came away with a thorough grounding in secular and religious subjects and a rare appreciation of the need to synthesize German and Jewish culture. According to his close friend and biographer, Cyrus Adler, Schiff knew Hebrew well and could freely quote the Hebrew Bible. Calling the Bible the book that had the greatest influence on him, he read biblical commentaries and kept up with developments in biblical studies. Jacob may have resisted Orthodox discipline, but Hirsch's training, in tandem with his father's influence, left him with an abiding love of Judaism and an interest in Jewish learning. Although his formal education ended when he was but fourteen years old, his serious reading and travel as an adult broadened his general knowledge. "Self-polish," one journalist explained, accounted for Schiff's familiarity with economics and history.[5]

Jacob shared the legendary pride of Frankfurt's Jews in their city. He remembered his school fondly and contributed to its upkeep over many years. Recalling the religious factionalism that had rocked the Jewish community when he was a boy, he advised school officials to strive consciously for Jewish unity. In words often repeated to American Jews, he said: "Only if we are united among ourselves can we claim the respect of our fellow-citizens and successfully ward off the attacks which are made upon our race from so many quarters."[6]

Thrust immediately into the business world, Jacob was first apprenticed to a large mercantile house. He then entered his brother-in-law's banking firm where he worked until 1865. Meantime, his desire to go to America intensified. His father confessed to a distant cousin in St. Louis that, unlike his older siblings, Jacob at age seventeen was "quite a problem because he already feels that Frankfurt is too small for his ambition." Worried about whether his son would be able to live an Orthodox Jewish life in the New World, Moses put that question to the cousin. The latter either failed to respond or answered in the negative, because the father withheld his consent to the idea of emigration. Instead he advised that Jacob himself write the cousin and ask his help in securing a position that did not require work on the Sabbath. Nothing came of that, but the son proceeded with his plans. Unwilling to risk a serious family rift, he refused to leave without his father's blessing. The rest of the family supported him. They worked on the father, and his older brother gave Jacob the money for his trip. At the last moment, when the carriage was at the door, father and son were reconciled. Armed with $500, letters of recommendation, and a package of kosher meat for the journey, Jacob left Frankfurt and reached New York in August 1865.[7]

Sources for the story of Jacob's emigration are admittedly scanty. No single push or combination of pushes, except a desire to escape his father's rigidity, explained the young man's motivation. Recent scholarship puts him in the second wave of German Jewish immigrants to the United States (1865–1914); unlike the first wave (1830–1865), the later arrivals as a group were not prompted to emigrate by either economic needs or dreams of political emancipation. Rather, many were pushed by a desire to escape military conscription or pulled to join relatives or close friends already established in America.[8] None of these reasons is hinted at in the data on Schiff. The picture emerges of a highly ambitious, obstinate, hardworking, and self-confident young man from a comfortable, if not well-to-do, home—he never was the poor immigrant boy who rose from rags to riches—who, for reasons of his own, fixed on America. An independent eighteen-year-old, Jacob was younger than most of those German immigrants who would shortly constitute a Jewish banking elite in America.[9]

Jacob's ship was met by a William Bonn, who had been told of Schiff's arrival. Formerly of the Jewish high society in Frankfurt but unknown to Schiff, Bonn, a few years his senior, took the lonely newcomer to a small hotel and at Jacob's request spent the entire night talking with him. Thus began a lifelong friendship between the Bonns and the Schiffs in spite of the later rivalry between Schiff's firm (Kuhn, Loeb) and Bonn's (Speyer & Company).[10] After a few months of unemployment, Jacob was hired as a clerk in the brokerage firm of Frank & Gans. Gans was impressed by the volume of the clerk's transactions and his ability to drum up trade, and he called Schiff "a born millionaire." Shortly thereafter but still before his twentieth birthday, Jacob became a partner with Henry Budge and Leo Lehmann in the brokerage firm of Budge, Schiff & Company. Undeterred by the fact that Budge's family firm in Frankfurt enjoyed a less than savory reputation, Schiff reportedly continued to do well. Nevertheless, the American firm was short-lived.[11]

Schiff owed his achievements to the happy confluence of his personal ability and the post–Civil War demands of a booming economy. His path was eased considerably by informal contacts with other Germans, especially men like Bonn, Budge, and Lehmann, all of whom hailed from Frankfurt. In the absence of immediate family, those acquaintances became his primary support group. Although his training in a Frankfurt bank proved to be an asset, the lack of a higher formal education was of no account. On the basis of his own experience, Schiff once advised a young man that a sixteen- or seventeen-year-old who started early in business and gained experience from the bottom up had an advantage over a college graduate who entered the business world at the age of twenty or more. For his own son, however, he followed a different track, permitting Mortimer to have two years of college before entering the firm. He, the domineering father, chose Amherst despite his son's preference for Harvard because it was smaller and less likely to snare the youth in "the many temptations a young man is subject to with so many students around."[12]

Schiff found lodging in the West Fifties, then considered Manhattan's uptown. Life in a rapidly growing city was doubtless overwhelming for a relatively sheltered young man who did not speak English. The center of America's foreign trade, New York was fast becoming a major industrial city as well as the hub of the nation's credit and banking system. Simultaneously, it was the magnet attracting tens of thousands of newcomers, both immigrants and rural Americans, who flocked to new economic frontiers. To ease the culture shock, most immigrants sought psychological if not economic reinforcement from fellow nationals. Schiff joined the company of German Jews, a group that was proud of its German heritage; its members held onto their native language in their homes, clubs, and temples for many years. (Schiff's letters to his children were also in German.) Unlike those German immigrants who rose rung by rung on the economic ladder, Schiff, by virtue of his European banking experience and personal contacts, was able to move rapidly into established Jewish circles.[13]

In 1865 the number of Jews in New York was estimated at seventy-five thousand; in the 1870s the total rose to over one hundred thousand. New York's Jews had numerous synagogues, philanthropic and social institutions, and even a hospital. Controlled mainly by German Jews who had arrived before the Civil War, those institutions failed, at least for Schiff personally, to fill a Jewish youth's serious cultural needs. He recalled in 1900, at the dedication of a new building for the YMHA for which he was a major donor: "Thirty-five years ago, when I first sought my home in this metropolis, a young man, a stranger in a great city, I drastically became aware of its great temptations and at the same time I found how limited were the opportunities for those, possessed of greater aspirations than to satisfy alone bodily wants and desires." Except for bicycling and hiking, he developed no interest in sports, and he had scant use for frivolity. The Y, he hoped, would promote Jewish life among the youth and aid in keeping young Jews loyal to their heritage.[14]

Budge, Schiff & Company was dissolved in 1873. In the meantime, Schiff had been naturalized in 1870 and had joined the New York Chamber of Commerce two years later. His plans to settle in the United States were interrupted, however, by his acceptance in 1873 of a tempting offer from the Warburg banking firm in Hamburg. He held that post for a few months, until his father's death took him back to Frankfurt to be with his mother. There he met Abraham Kuhn, who offered him a position in the New York firm of Kuhn, Loeb. According to Schiff's daughter, the offer was made by the other partner, Solomon Loeb, in recognition of Schiff's knowledge of the foreign banking scene. Loeb intimated that the young man might soon be placed in a European branch that the firm planned to establish. With his mother's blessing, Schiff returned to New York and joined Kuhn, Loeb on January 1,1875. Shortly thereafter the idea of a foreign branch was dropped. Jacob explained to his mother that "the opportunity is enormous here. . . . The coming expansion of the United States, in railroading and all that, is so large that I myself don't feel there will be a foreign branch for some time to come." As he concluded, "There is more than enough to keep us busy here."

That same year Schiff married Loeb's daughter, Therese, and the young couple moved into a house on East Fifty-third Street purchased for them by her father. Although they were unlike in temperament—he aggressive and forceful, she gentle and submissive—theirs was a loving and happy union, one that over the years earned the sincere admiration of friends. After the children were born—a daughter, Frieda, in 1876 and a son, Mortimer, in 1877—the Schiffs moved to a larger house on West Fifty-seventh Street.[15]

The firm of Kuhn, Loeb grew from modest beginnings. Abraham Kuhn had come to America in 1839 and, like many other German Jews, had started out as a peddler. Ten years later, when he was the senior partner in the wholesale clothing store of Kuhn and Netter in Lafayette, Indiana, he invited Solomon Loeb, a distant cousin and poor new immigrant, to join him. Loeb's position in the business was strengthened by his marriage to Kuhn's sister, and he soon became a partner. The business moved to Cincinnati, where it turned to general merchandising. The partners prospered; during the Civil War a boom in the clothing trade and the Union's demand for army blankets caused profits to soar. While the firm gained a name for soundness, the partners grew more knowledgeable about business credits. They returned to New York and in 1867 established Kuhn, Loeb & Company, a banking firm that dealt primarily and successfully in government bonds and later in railroad securities. Kuhn's early retirement and the refusal of Loeb's sons to make the business their career (James Loeb worked in the firm but only for a few years) would be more than offset by the arrival of Jacob Schiff in 1875.

Marriage to his employer's daughter and a partnership in Kuhn, Loeb assured Schiff of high social status. Banking then was considered by many to be the top rung of the American Jewish socioeconomic ladder, and Schiff adapted his lifestyle to that of his established peers. Like them but soon outstripping most in wealth, he lived at the correct address (in 1887 the Schiffs had a new house built for them at 932 Fifth Avenue), affiliated with prestigious Reform temples (Beth-El and Emanu-El), and sent his children to appropriate schools (Frieda to Brearley and Mortimer to Dr. Sachs's School). For recreation and for business he and his circle frequently traveled to Europe and renewed their ties to Germany.[16]

Jewish investment bankers in Schiff's day formed a cohesive group whose members worked together, socialized together, and worshiped together. Bound by blood or marriage, they created a kinship network whose importance in the business history of American Jews has been an accepted fact ever since Barry Supple published his seminal essay on German Jewish financiers. Supple demonstrated how the individual firms were built on family ties and how family ties united the separate banking houses in an "interlocking structure." Identification of family with the firm intensified "regard for the business and a continuity of entrepreneurial skill," and it strengthened the firm's unity in building a reputation for confidence and trust. Creating opportunities for Jews who, because of their Jewishness, were barred from Gentile firms, the closely tied group of banking houses collectively provided a base for cooperation in new investments. For example, Schiff's friendship with the Guggenheims, with whom he shared religious and communal interests, eased Kuhn, Loeb's investment in Guggenheim mining interests. In sum, Supple concluded, the German Jewish bankers owed much of their success to the bonds of kinship.[17]

Kuhn, Loeb had been a good example of the workings of kinship ever since the first Loeb married Kuhn's sister. Schiff was Loeb's son-in-law, and Abraham Wolff, his contemporary, was Loeb's cousin. New partners in the 1890s were Felix Warburg, Schiff's son-in-law; Louis Heinsheimer, a nephew of Loeb; and Otto Kahn, Wolff's son-in-law. Schiff did not take to Kahn, but because of his affection for Wolff and in recognition of the importance of family, he agreed to the appointment.[18] Nor was there any doubt that Schiff would groom his own son for partnership and eventual direction of Kuhn, Loeb. Mortimer's training was tailored by his father. Before he entered the firm, the young man received a grounding in American railroad work and served a stint in Europe under the tutelage of Ernest Cassel. In 1900 he became a full partner. Except for his son and son-in-law the partner closest to Schiff was Abraham Wolff, a man with whom Schiff worked for twenty-six years before Wolff's untimely death.

In 1902, Paul Warburg, later of Federal Reserve Board fame, married Therese's sister and became a Kuhn, Loeb partner. Not until 1912 was there a partner (Jerome Hanauer) in the firm who was not related to Loeb, Schiff, or Wolff, and not until the post–World War I era were there partners who were not Jewish.[19]

Supple's emphasis on the distinctive traits of the Jewish banking houses has since been modified. First, as Vincent Carosso showed, non-Jewish firms also benefited from family ties. Second, the success of a firm, whether Jewish or non-Jewish, was determined more by its "creative leadership" and its reputation for integrity. Nevertheless, despite Carosso's insistence that the differences between Jewish and Gentile bankers were outweighed by their similarities,[20] the reliance of Jewish houses on a kinship network that spanned two continents played a pivotal role in their achievements.

The importance of group cohesion notwithstanding, Jewish bankers at Kuhn, Loeb and other American firms were not insulated from the rest of the world. They consciously patterned their manners and institutions on those of the Protestant upper-middle and upper classes. Where prejudice did not exclude them, they eagerly participated in activities of the non-Jewish world. Different from their counterparts in England and Germany, they had fewer problems balancing Jewish identity with integration into the larger society. American law recognized no ethnic or religious distinctions, and a society more fluid than Europe's readily permitted Jewish economic and social mobility. To be sure, the last quarter of the nineteenth century witnessed a significant rise in social discrimination in the United States that kept Jews out of private schools, clubs, and resorts. Some Jews, like many non-Jews, blamed Christian animus on Jewish separatism. Therefore, in order to gain non-Jewish acceptance, members of the Jewish elite largely determined for themselves how far they were willing to be "dejudaized." They never forgot that they were a small group in a Christian

country, but the greater danger to Jewish survival was disappearance
through rapid assimilation rather than conversion.[21]

Schiff's Jewish loyalties were more pronounced than those of most
wealthy Jews, but he also lived in both a Jewish and a Gentile world. Active
from the very outset of his career in non-Jewish organizations like the
Chamber of Commerce and the American Red Cross, he met non-Jews
from all walks of life—politics and government, business and community
affairs, education and journalism, arts and letters. He corresponded with a
wide range of Gentile acquaintances, and over the years a considerable
number enjoyed his hospitality. Schiff rapidly became a well-known figure.
The short, erect, blue-eyed, thickly accented, and impeccably dressed
banker with a flower in his buttonhole commanded public respect by his
aristocratic bearing alone. Although he did not flaunt his wealth, Schiff
lived well. The number of servants he employed, the homes he owned,[22]
the vacations he took, and the privileges his children enjoyed were only a
few indices testifying to practices very much like those of upper-class non-
Jews. The banker did not indulge in the common pastimes of millionaires,
like yachts and racing cars, but he too collected art and appeared often at
the theater and opera. He even agreed to have the artist Augustus Saint-
Gaudens cast a bas-relief of his children, an object that he donated to the
Metropolitan Museum in 1905.[23] Schiff may have consciously aped the
Jewish elite of Frankfurt as well as the Protestant elite in America, but
whatever its origin his lifestyle conformed to that of the wealthy.

Over sixty years ago, Frederick Lewis Allen drew a composite picture of
ten wealthy American business leaders, including Schiff, at the beginning
of the century. Among salient similarities, he found that none had a college
education and that most were self-made men who "knew the merits of fru-
gality." They were a pious group who blended their Christianity with the
Puritan ethic and a belief in laissez-faire economics. Under the influence of
Progressive historians, Allen also enumerated the businessmen's faults: a
callousness toward labor and toward human suffering generally, a lack of
public responsibility, and an antagonism toward government regulation.
On the surface the pattern of the frugal and pious self-made man without a
higher education fits Schiff, but Allen's list of faults did not apply to him.
More accurate was a later study of the "Eastern Establishment," which as-
cribed to leading lawyers and financiers, including Schiff and his partners,
a belief in the Puritan tradition and the "American dream"—that is, virtuous conduct in a land of opportunity promised economic rewards.
Schooled to the importance of public service, the men of the Establishment lived by a sense of duty and strict morality in their family and business lives. They held their firms to "conservative" and "sound" behavior,
and their views on the role of government in the regulation of the economy were "moderately progressive."[24] Nevertheless, since neither study

examined the influence of Judaism and Jewishness on Schiff's principles and behavior, both analyses are for our purposes incomplete.

The growth of Kuhn, Loeb into one of the most powerful investment banking houses in New York paralleled the development of a nation rapidly becoming a modern industrialized state. The small firm on Nassau Street under Kuhn and Loeb had been content to live by its initial announcement: "We do not chase after business. . . . We do business with people who come to us." After 1875, however, it embarked on new policies and an aggressive search for clients. The change to the fast lane at a pace that overtook older Jewish firms, notably the Speyer and Seligman houses, was the work of Jacob Schiff. To be sure, there were other partners, but on Wall Street and to outside observers Schiff *was* Kuhn, Loeb until his death in 1920. Established Gentile bankers had earlier turned up their noses at small and risky ventures with the comment "let the Jews have that one"; but not too long thereafter, Kuhn, Loeb, under Schiff's drive and diligence, commanded their unqualified respect.[25]

With the help of young Abraham Wolff, who also joined Kuhn, Loeb in 1875, Schiff set the firm on a different track. Where Loeb was passive, Schiff was bold. A pioneering instinct and a faith in the economic expansion of the nation drew him to uncharted fields. Loeb's son James later criticized Jacob for some ill-advised investments, but Schiff persisted. Some twenty years later he admitted that he had grown more conservative. By then he adhered to a self-imposed rule—don't go into anything about which you know little or nothing. When the elder Loeb became aware that his younger associates were bent on change, he felt constrained to withdraw. Since Kuhn had long since left, Schiff was the acknowledged head of the firm by 1885. Business differences notwithstanding, Schiff's letters attest to an abiding respect for his father-in-law and for Therese's brothers.[26]

Schiff's hard work was matched by a great pride in the firm. According to a writer for the *Magazine of Wall Street*, the pride was warranted, because Kuhn, Loeb, he said, was known to have sold more good securities and fewer bad ones than any other banking house. Schiff's integrity and that of Kuhn, Loeb, a sine qua non for any successful banking firm, was assumed. "If that is gone," Schiff said, "our business is gone, however attractive our show window might be." The young banker built on the reputation of the modest but respectable firm of Kuhn and Loeb, and he never thought of renaming the firm for himself.[27]

Like other investment bankers, Kuhn, Loeb forged ties with suppliers of capital—banks, trust companies, insurance companies. Investment firms also augmented their limited capital by organizing or joining syndicates, devices by which a group of investors pooled their resources and shared the risks. The bankers were thereby in a position to mobilize huge sums for the railroads and industrial corporations and to reap great profits for themselves. In the course of testimony before the Pujo congressional committee in 1913, Schiff explained Kuhn, Loeb's methods of underwriting securities. With regard to syndicates he stated: "The way we do our business is, we always first contract with a railroad company, or a corporation if it is not a railroad company, that has securities to sell. When we have contracted with them and have obligated ourselves to purchase a certain amount of securities or issue of securities, we form an underwriting syndicate which shares the risk of the business with us. We take the risk first and the underwriter afterwards shares it with us." If the arrangement fell through, "the risk is ours," and Kuhn, Loeb alone carried the burden of selling the securities.

The banker discussed some distinctive features of the firm's syndicates. They were composed almost exclusively of firms and corporations rather than individuals, and they relied heavily on foreign capital: "Our syndicates are very largely made up from our foreign correspondents. We always only place a part, sometimes an inconsiderable part, in the United States. We very largely place our syndicates abroad." At times only foreign houses participated; in cases where both foreign and domestic firms cooperated, about two-thirds of the specific issue went to American participants and one-third to foreigners. Kuhn, Loeb had a list of around 75 to 125 companies that were generally invited to participate, but the firm had no "standing alliances."

Schiff also mentioned the code of business ethics that regulated the behavior of major firms. For example, it was considered inappropriate for officers of the underwriting firm to participate in syndicates, a practice, Schiff claimed, that was "hardly ever" resorted to by Kuhn, Loeb. Nor was it ethical for a firm to compete with other firms for control of a transaction or to muscle in on another's clients. As he said, "It is not good form to create unreasonable interference or competition."[28]

From 1875 on, Schiff assiduously cultivated his foreign contacts, bankers through whom Kuhn, Loeb was able to sell American securities abroad and to channel European money into America's transportation and industrial systems. Later, when the flow of capital reversed direction, Kuhn, Loeb and other Jewish banks were instrumental in underwriting and distributing securities of foreign corporations and governments in the United States.[29] Frequent vacations in Europe, long walks (one of Schiff's favorite pastimes) with associates, and hospitality to foreign bankers who visited America afforded many opportunities for informal but productive business meetings.

The use of foreign connections, which in some cases ripened into warm friendships, was not specifically Jewish; other American firms had ties with European houses if not branches in Europe. But Schiff, it was said, enjoyed "unmatched" relationships with prominent bankers, Jews and non-Jews, like Ernest Cassel of London, Edouard Noetzlin of Paris, Robert Fleming of Scotland (later London), the Rothschilds of London, and the Warburgs of Hamburg. In some cases, Kuhn, Loeb built on ties already forged by European bankers among themselves. For example, since Cassel also dealt with Fleming, a triangular connection with Kuhn, Loeb was formed. Those connections figured significantly in making the firm a serious competitor of the leading American investment houses.[30]

At the same time that European business strengthened the firm, the foreign bankers benefited from links with Kuhn, Loeb. They had in Schiff a reliable source for detailed information on changing conditions, from crops to politics, that influenced the American economy, and they respected his financial advice. In terms of potential profits, the nexus promised ever increasing wealth to both Kuhn, Loeb and its foreign friends. In the first decade of the century, when Schiff arranged a guided tour from New York to San Francisco for Cassel, Fleming, and Max Bonn, a New Orleans newspaper commented: "The aggregate wealth of the party is sufficient to buy up the whole State of Louisiana at its own valuation."[31]

Of all his foreign contacts, Cassel became Schiff's closest friend. Five years Schiff's junior, he too had left school in his native Cologne at the age of fourteen to start work in a local bank. He settled in England, where he served as overseer of American and other foreign investments in the firm of Bischoffsheim & Goldschmidt. As his personal fortune grew ever larger, he left the firm and operated independently. In his early forties he became an intimate friend and adviser of the Prince of Wales, later Edward VII. A baronetcy gave Cassel the title of Sir Ernest, but on account of his influence with the court he was informally dubbed "Windsor Cassel."[32]

Cassel met Schiff in 1879 in connection with the American investments of Bischoffsheim & Goldschmidt, and a shared interest in railroads drew the two together. Recognizing a rare opportunity for his firm, Schiff promised as early as 1880 that Cassel would be rewarded if he directed clients to Kuhn, Loeb. Cassel agreed; he brought business to the American firm, and Schiff made money for him. Frequently, the latter gave his views of a specific company and then asked if Cassel personally was interested in purchasing stock. Schiff's loyalty was boundless. Once he withdrew from a Mexican loan lest he appear as Cassel's competitor. Throughout, Schiff abided by his early advice to his friend: Don't buy trash, for good securities are safer and ultimately more profitable.[33]

In short order the men were cooperating in numerous investments both in North America and in other continents. In 1890, when Cassel rescued fourteen-year-old Frieda during a mountain-climbing expedition in Switzerland, he earned the Schiffs' everlasting gratitude. A voluminous correspondence between the friends spanned some forty years, but since Schiff

destroyed most letters he received, Cassel's opinions must be pieced together from Schiff's answers. Schiff, who often wrote several times a
month, fed his "Lieber Freund" a running commentary on the state of the
American market. Supplementing their occasional meetings in America
and Europe, the friends exchanged gifts and shared news and gossip, not
only on economic conditions but on family matters, vacations and travel,
people they knew, and Jewish affairs. Although Schiff was the austere Puritan and Cassel the cavalier bon vivant, a sense of mutual trust and devotion
pervades the correspondence.[34] The letters suggest that Schiff confided
more than Cassel did, and indeed, on the subject of his secret conversion to
Catholicism, Cassel kept silent.

Bankers and Railroads: The Union Pacific Affair

By the turn of the century Kuhn, Loeb ranked second only to the House
of Morgan.* The firm owed its phenomenal success principally to its business with railroads. Assisted by European capital, it participated in the development and expansion of the nation's arteries from 1875 on. Like other
bankers, Schiff managed securities issues for individual roads and advised
with them on financial matters. In a very short time, by the process of reorganization, his firm came to share in the management of individual railroad lines.

The reorganization of the Union Pacific Railroad and its dramatic consequences catapulted Schiff into national prominence. The sequence of
events that climaxed in the Wall Street panic of 1901 underscored the
workings of finance capitalism, in this case the bankers' control of the
northwestern roads. Involving Schiff with the House of Morgan and with
two railroad giants, James J. Hill and Edward H. Harriman, the Union Pacific affair illustrated the rivalry of both railroad owners and the bankers
who backed them. In the end, the affair set Kuhn, Loeb permanently in the
American financial elite.

Intrigued by the possibility of economic expansion in the territory west of
the Mississippi, Schiff showed a keen interest from the start of his career in
the burgeoning railway system. As early as 1870, Budge, Schiff & Company

*The manifold operations of Kuhn, Loeb lie outside the scope of this study. Only
several outstanding episodes—the Union Pacific affair, the Equitable insurance case,
involvement in the Far East—will be discussed. Together with questions of how
Schiff related to businessmen and other bankers, where he stood on the issues of
government and the economy, and what character traits he displayed in his business
dealings, they provide a necessary background for his activities as a Jewish leader.

represented a German syndicate that invested $6 mllion to $8 million in Northern Pacific bonds.[35] Upon joining Kuhn, Loeb, Schiff plunged the firm into the business of financing new or expanding railway systems. The boom in railroad construction reached its peak in the 1880s, but Kuhn, Loeb had raised funds even earlier for the Chicago & North Western Railroad. The transaction was followed by many similar ventures that eventually involved the firm in the affairs of more than a dozen major lines. The volume of business grew by leaps and bounds. Kuhn, Loeb's dealings with but one old and valued client, the Pennsylvania Railroad, amounted, over a period of twenty-six years, to more than half a billion dollars.[36]

The ties between bankers and the railroads grew closer when the depression of the 1890s exposed the financial irregularities of the roads. Since many had reached the verge of collapse, if not actual bankruptcy, the bankers stepped in with plans of reorganization. Developed into an art by the House of Morgan, reorganization, or "Morganization," attempted to establish and maintain the solvency of a particular railroad and to devise sound ways for railroad fund-raising. To tighten up management and administrative policies, representatives of the banking firms responsible for reorganization were usually placed on the railroads' boards of directors. Not only did reorganization bring the bankers enormous profits, but the rate of railroad consolidation rose dramatically.[37]

Kuhn, Loeb became prominent in reorganization some years after Morgan had. In testimony to the Pujo committee, the firm admitted to its reorganization of six major roads, four completed and two pending, and to seats for Kuhn, Loeb partners on the boards of the first four. Credited for originating the phrase "directors who don't direct" (the idea behind the phrase became an issue in the 1905 investigation of insurance companies [see below]), Schiff usually refused directorships for himself unless he could supervise policy making. But over the years he sat on more than a score of boards—of industrial corporations as well as railroads—that allied him at times with Morgan and other bankers in a grand scheme of interlocking directorates.[38]

By the mid-1880s, Schiff had established ties to James J. Hill, whose control of the Great Northern Railroad made him a serious competitor of Schiff's earlier client, the Northern Pacific. A warm friendship developed between the banker and the railroad man. Hill, a frequent guest at the Schiff home and a bearer of lavish gifts, valued Schiff's "unparalleled entree" into European investment circles, and he found a trusted ally in the banker. Schiff in turn admired Hill—a "great genius," he said. The banker was elected to the board of the Great Northern, and he sent his son to be trained by Hill.[39] Schiff was a critic of wasteful competition among railroads, and with the backing of European associates who were heavily invested in the northwestern lines, he mobilized pressure on Hill in 1894–95 for the consolidation of the Northern Pacific and the Great Northern. Nothing came of that idea until Morgan stepped in. The "Colossus of Wall Street," or "Jupiter" as some called him, offered his plan of reorganization to remedy the serious financial straits in which the Northern Pacific found itself after the panic of 1893. Since he also wanted cooperation between the lines, a "permanent alliance" of the two roads was agreed to in 1896. Hill was now working with Morgan instead of Kuhn, Loeb, and the Schiff-Hill friendship quickly cooled. On Hill's initiative it was renewed later but not before Kuhn, Loeb had allied itself with Hill's archrival in the Northwest, Edward H. Harriman.[40]

In the meantime, Schiff had undertaken the reorganization of the Union Pacific. A reorganization committee of 1893 that included Morgan had attempted to solve problems of solvency and indebtedness, but it gave up the seemingly hopeless task less than two years later. When Kuhn, Loeb was asked to direct the reorganization, Schiff withheld consent until he cleared the matter with Morgan. Banking ethics frowned on attempts to wean clients from another firm, or as Schiff once put it, he wouldn't do anything that looked "as if we attempted to play in Morgan's backyard." Moreover, a note of awe and fear always tinged his regard for Morgan's power, and he preferred to behave as a respectful junior rather than a brash interloper. An early biography of Harriman by George Kennan, who consulted Schiff before publication, told of Schiff's meeting with Morgan. The latter stated emphatically that he wanted nothing further to do with the Union Pacific and that Schiff was free to proceed as he pleased. Kennan and others have pointed out that Morgan's failure to see the potential of the that line proved to be a grave miscalculation.[41]

Schiff formed a reorganization committee that included the National City Bank and thus Rockefeller money, but he assumed the all-consuming task of hands-on manager. "He could conceive financial transactions of gigantic lines," a partner and intimate friend observed, "but at the same time, no business detail escaped his attention." Always one who had difficulty in delegating authority, Schiff sacrificed his vacation pending reorganization lest his responsibilities to his fellow committeemen be overlooked. A year later his reorganization plan faced serious obstacles. Rumor had it that Morgan had undergone a change of heart and was causing the problems. Again Schiff called at 23 Wall Street, and again Morgan disclaimed any interest. Shortly thereafter, Morgan came up with the name of the culprit, Edward Harriman. The latter openly admitted to Schiff that he had blocked Kuhn, Loeb's plan. He intended to reorganize the Union Pacific himself, he said, because he wanted to add the railroad to his other lines. Willing to cooperate with Schiff, he stated that his price was the chairmanship of the railroad. Since Harriman enjoyed easy access to credit reserves that surpassed Kuhn, Loeb's, Schiff compromised. He put Harriman on the executive board but not as chairman. If Harriman proved his strength, he could most probably win the chairmanship.[42]

Schiff had known Harriman only slightly, but the Union Pacific affair began a close relationship. Harriman dreamed of making the line a weapon for capturing control of western commerce, and Kuhn, Loeb became an able partner. Until 1900 only Schiff saw Harriman's intensive study of the line—then known on Wall Street as the Kuhn, Loeb railroad—and his prodigious and ultimately successful labors to build it up. Soon the compromise that Schiff formulated redounded to the banker's benefit as well. In 1898, Harriman assumed the chairmanship; the Union Pacific, also in control of the Southern Pacific, prospered; and both Harriman and Kuhn, Loeb made millions. After Harriman's death, Schiff credited him for having turned the Union Pacific, "a rusted streak of iron," into one of the greatest lines on the continent.[43]

While Harriman carefully nurtured a railroad empire that continued to expand and that would enable him to challenge Hill's interest in the Northwest, another obstacle surfaced. Since the Union Pacific had been subsidized by public as well as private monies, successful reorganization depended on purchase of the railroad's debts to the government. Negotiations began during Cleveland's administration and continued into McKinley's. Although the reorganization committee promised the government a handsome profit, opposition to the sale and a demand for government control developed in Congress. In contact with his foreign investors, Schiff attributed the lack of progress to "Populistic agitation," a sensationalist press, and the jealousy of those who had failed to get "their finger in the pie." He lobbied strenuously with the secretary of the treasury and with the attorney-general for a settlement in favor of the railroad. In one lengthy memorandum he reviewed the steps taken by his committee to satisfy the government's demands, and he urged an end to the delay. The government finally agreed, and in November 1897, for the sum of $81 million, Schiff's group took full possesion of the Union Pacific. It was a daring move, and Schiff spent a sleepless night worrying about whether Kuhn, Loeb had reached beyond its means. Nevertheless, within a matter of weeks the banker assured Cassel that the railroad's bonds were attracting the "best" investors.[44]

Harriman and Hill locked horns in a battle over the acquisition of the Chicago, Burlington & Quincy Railroad.[45] Each wanted a line that linked his western roads to Chicago and thus assure control of the carrying trade west of the Mississippi. Each was also driven by naked ambition and self-aggrandizement. Behind the railroad magnates stood the bankers, the Morgan group for Hill and the Schiff group for Harriman.

Schiff believed that for sheer survival the Union Pacific needed to own the Burlington[46] or at least to prevent it from being swallowed by Hill. He and Harriman conferred with the directors of the road with an eye toward purchase, but the talks collapsed in the spring of 1900. An alternative tactic—control of the Burlington by a concerted purchase of its stock— was adopted, but that too failed. The story continues in a lengthy letter from Schiff to Cassel:

> Early in February [1900] it became evident that somebody [else] was buying Burlington stock quite largely, and it was then said that the Great Northern and Northern Pacific people . . . had, upon Mr. Hill's instigation, set about to get control of the Burlington; evidently for no other purpose than aggrandizement. When this situation developed, I, with others of the Union Pacific people, went to Mr. Hill and asked him whether the reports were true . . . to which he replied that these reports were utterly unfounded, as he had no direct or indirect interests in Burlington.[47]

The Schiff group soon realized that Hill had lied, that he was in fact a serious competitor for the Burlington, and they sought him out again. He now said that he regretted having misled Schiff, but aware of his former friend's concern for the Union Pacific, he feared that the banker would interfere in his plans. Harriman's forces stood firm. They warned that they would not let the Burlington fall into rival hands that "could, and in time would, use it to sap the life out of the Union Pacific." "[Hill] answered with platitudes," Schiff told Cassel, "and we thereupon turned to Morgans."[48] The Morgan bankers dismissed the Union Pacific's offer to participate in the acquisition of the Burlington, and the road went to Hill.

Thereupon the Harriman-Schiff camp plotted aggressive strategy. They would gain control of the Burlington by secretly buying its new owner, the Northern Pacific. The move was hailed in retrospect for its courage and boldness. In Schiff's words, "we . . . cleared the deck for [drastic] action, and went about to accumulate sufficient Northern Pacific stock to control the Company. . . . We succeeded, in the course of some weeks in accumulating about forty per cent of the total capital stock of the Northern Pacific Company." According to the Hill group, Schiff's confidence was misplaced. They argued that what ultimately mattered was not the *total capital stock* but the *common stock*, of which the Schiff-Harriman forces had but a minority.[49]

Hill had deceived his rivals, and they felt justified in surprising him. Not only were Harriman and Schiff out to best Hill and Morgan, but the Rockefeller–City Bank interests, also supporters of Harriman, had their own scores to settle with the formidable Morgan. A major battle seemed imminent. Schiff, a man who usually shrank from confrontation, especially with those more powerful than he (in this case the House of Morgan) suggested a negotiated peace:

> I went to Mr. Hill [during the first week in May 1901] and told him what we had done, at the same time informing him that we preferred peace and harmony to strife, and that if he and Morgans would appreciate the situation, there would be no effort on the part of the Union Pacific to displace the existing Board and management, or even to get representation, but that under all circumstances we must have a controlling voice in the Burlington lines and the policy of the Burlington management in Union Pacific territory. Mr. Hill thereupon assured me that he, on his part, would do everything to bring about what we wanted.

At a second meeting with Schiff that same day, Hill repeated his assurances, but instead of working out a reconciliation "he evidently went to the Morgans and induced them to go in the market in a frantic effort to secure enough stock to restore the control, which they had permitted to slip from them."[50]

Now on full alert, the Hill group began an intensive search to locate and buy up Northern Pacific stock. An uneasy Harriman placed an order with Kuhn, Loeb to continue buying for their side, but it was countermanded by Schiff. He might have been persuaded had Harriman reached him before the noon closing of the stock exchange on Saturday, but Schiff was at the synagogue. A junior partner at Kuhn, Loeb, Otto Kahn, recalled that Schiff was unmoved by the arguments of Harriman and Kahn for the purchase of additional common stock. Adhering to the interpretation that the total capital stock, not the common stock, determined control, Kuhn, Loeb bought only a modest amount of additional preferred stock. Despite Hill's deception, Schiff confidently believed, at least according to Kahn, that his former friend would turn cooperative.[51] Instead, the struggle was magnified on the floor of the stock exchange.

The story of the panic of May 9, 1901, has often been recounted—how the price of Northern Pacific common stock began to soar as soon as Hill's side rushed to buy significant lots; how the public, without any inkling of the Hill-Harriman rivalry, eagerly followed the principals; how the brokers who sold "short" (without the stock in hand and unable to deliver unless the price fell) faced financial ruin; how buyers who dumped other stocks in order to join the wild spree thereby depressed the market in general; how on Blue Thursday, May 9, the price of a share of Northern Pacific reached $1,000, roughly a tenfold increase in a week; and how the Wall Street conditions adversely affected European markets.[52]

During that hectic week, Kuhn, Loeb was more spectator than participant. To be sure, Otto Kahn suggested that the firm buy up depressed stocks. He reasoned that such purchases were good investments and would help to steady the market. But, as Kahn recalled, "Mr. Schiff replied icily: 'If you want to buy stocks personally, you are free to do so. But Kuhn, Loeb & Company will not, with my consent, make one dollar's worth of profit out of this calamity.'" Although Kahn was not particularly enamored of Schiff, he respected the senior partner's decision. "He foresaw that if the other side was really determined to go ahead and buy every obtainable share of Northern Pacific Common, an alarming if not critical situation would be created, and he wanted to be able to say, if such a situation did come, that he and those with and for whom he acted had no hand in bringing it about."[53]

A quick end to the panic came on the afternoon of May 9, when the two sides called a truce. Schiff also suggested that they deliver enough Northern Pacific shares at $150 each to rescue the "shorts." He explained his strategy to Cassel: "Notwithstanding Morgan's refusal, we immediately came to the relief of the legitimate arbitrage dealers, and the next day also to the relief of the shorts—in both of which steps Morgans very unwillingly followed." Meanwhile, "we took good care to accumulate so considerable an amount of the Preferred Stock, which could be more easily had, that our interests now hold what we believe to be an absolute majority of the entire capital stock of the Company." He still disputed the claim that common stock would determine the outcome, but he sought to achieve a financial coup without alienating Morgan. "Believing . . . that we now control the situation, we feel that a settlement on large, and not on small, lines should be made, especially in a manner, not to hurt Morgan's pride and prestige."[54]

New York newspapers called the panic "the most severe in the history of Wall Street" and "without precedent in this country or in any other." While each side disclaimed blame for the panic, the public clamor for curbs on the giant railroads grew louder. Morgan's cavalier remark, "I owe the public nothing," only exacerbated the tension. Schiff, whose health suffered under the strain, took comfort in the thought that "the mad race" had ended before it could damage America's vital interests. In an obsequious tone that he adopted with no other businessman, he sought to convince Morgan that both the Union Pacific and Kuhn, Loeb were ready to accede to any reasonable suggestions for a permanent agreement with the Hill group. He added: "We have at all times wished, as we continue to do, to be permitted to aid in maintaining your personal prestige, so well deserved."[55]

The temporary truce between Hill and Harriman did not resolve the serious issues at stake, and the two sides faced drawn-out litigation or a negotiated settlement. Opting for the latter, they reached an "understanding" by the end of May 1901. The Burlington remained in Hill's hands, but a new board for the Northern Pacific, to be chosen by Morgan, was to include Harriman and a few of his allies. In addition, Harriman gained certain

rights over both the Burlington and the Union Pacific. Of greater signifi-
cance, the rivals agreed to combine the three major lines (Union Pacific,
Northern Pacific, Great Northern) under a holding company, and in No-
vember the Northern Securities Company was duly incorporated. The set-
tlement satisfied Schiff, who, like Harriman, was put on the boards of the
Northern Pacific, the Burlington, and the Northern Securities.[56] He told
Cassel that the outcome vindicated his earlier efforts to safeguard the
Union Pacific against Hill:

> The result is that the Burlington Railroad, the real point in dispute, will
> come under the mutual control of the Union Pacific . . . and the Northern
> Pacific–Great Northern. . . . Although the Union Pacific is in the minority in
> this Holding Co. it will nevertheless exercise a potential influence upon the
> management of the two Northern lines. . . . In addition, the Union Pacific
> has made a territorial agreement with these two companies which protects it
> against an invasion and opens to it extensive use of important lines on the
> Northern Pacific Coast.[57]

The public was less sanguine about the outcome. Many regarded the holding company as but another example of the giant combinations out to
fleece the consumer. In 1902 the attorney-general advised Theodore
Roosevelt that the Northern Securities Company violated provisions of
the Sherman Act (1890) forbidding restraint of trade. Eager to affirm the
government's power over big business, the president thereupon ordered a
suit against the company.

Schiff did not share the mounting popular resentment of the major railroad lines for their abuses, the arbitrary rates in particular. Nor did he see
anything ominous in the railroad-banker connection brought about by reorganization. In testimony before the Industrial Commission of 1901 he
was primarily the defender of the status quo. He spoke out against government ownership of the railroads; and although he acknowledged government's right to regulate businesses that were its "servants," he refused to
say that railroad owners would welcome public supervision. "I believe that
the silent laws of nature are better correctives than any written laws can
ever become." More forthcoming on the subject of railroad competition
versus railroad cooperation, Schiff advocated what he called a "community
of interest." It meant neither mergers nor absorption of certain lines by
others but rather cooperation between competing lines by the purchase of
each other's stock. He said that only by a "coming together of the railroad
interests," which he thought was developing quite naturally, would economic benefits accrue to labor as well as to producers and shippers. He
added confidently that if the public was correctly informed, it would welcome the suggestion.

The banker evaded most questions on the operations of specific railways. When asked about the Northern Pacific and the recent panic on Wall Street, he refused to admit to any contest between Hill and Harriman or their railroads. Gamblers or speculators, he said, particularly those who had sold short, were to blame for inflating the price of Northern Pacific stock. The commission tried again: Was it true or only a rumor in the financial markets that a western railroad sought to establish control over two transcontinental lines? "I never listen to rumors," Schiff replied, nor did he know anything about the matter. The commission circumspectly refrained from challenging Schiff, and it complimented him on his testimony. One member later charged, however, that Washington had advised the panel to "soft-pedal" its inquiry of the banker.[58]

As soon as he learned of the government's intention to prosecute the Northern Securities Company, Schiff expressed to the president his strong opposition. He explained that his concern went beyond the issue of the particular holding company. A suit that attempted to block the natural trend toward combinations put the government in a no-win situation. "If the Courts should decide against the Government, the President's prestige cannot but suffer." Quite probably, harsher laws than the Sherman Act would be passed and would do even "greater mischief." If the courts decided for the government, the result would be even bleaker. "The decision sought by the Administration . . . will . . . strike with vehemence at almost every Railroad Company in this country. . . . [It] will call forth a disorganization and a chaos such as never have been known before in our history, and it will shake the structure, upon which our existing prosperity rests, to its very foundations." A situation would be created "such as has not existed since after the attack of President Jackson upon the Bank of the United States." When Schiff met with Roosevelt and Attorney-General Philander Knox, he told TR that he was "playing with fire" on a path that could lead to rampant radicalism.[59]

While the case was pending, Schiff's fears were exacerbated. To be sure, it was better for the Northern Securities Company to know sooner rather than later where it stood with the government, but that was scant comfort. He predicted that a decision in the government's favor boded ill. It would mean that if a company had any power to restrain trade, that power, even if not acted upon, was illegal. Moreover, "almost anyone for the purpose of blackmail or sinister purposes, has it in his power to open fire upon and harass most of the large railroad and industrial combinations." He explained to Cassel that since all major railroads controlled competing lines, all would be affected by a government victory. If Roosevelt continued on a reckless course, Schiff predicted utter ruin for the country's prosperity and commercial supremacy.[60]

Despite his opposition to the suit, Schiff carefully refrained from attacking the president. Indeed, his letters about Roosevelt's action usually contained expressions of confidence in TR's sagacity and his sincere concern for the nation's economic welfare. The tone may have jarred with Schiff's warnings about the government's legal action, but the banker could not have afforded to do otherwise. At the very same time that the case was pending, 1902–1904, Schiff was pleading with Roosevelt for official condemnation of anti-Jewish persecution in Romania and Russia (see below). Unlike Morgan, who usually kept his distance from politicians, the Jewish banker needed to cultivate allies in government for the sake of fellow Jews in Europe. As a businessman he could disagree with TR's trustbusting, but as a Jewish leader he didn't have the luxury of damning Roosevelt publicly. The president willingly accepted Schiff on those terms and consulted him on various economic issues. He did not seek out the company of "the big-moneyed men in New York," but he respected their power.[61] Moreover, in Roosevelt's political calculations, Schiff could and did prove to be a valuable asset in attracting the Jewish vote.

The Supreme Court's decision in 1904 upheld the government's charges and outlawed the Northern Securities Company.[62] (Both the Hill and Harriman sides disagreed on the disposition of the company's stock. Since Schiff was the only one to suggest that that the two parties settle the dispute themselves, the issue was finally resolved by a court order.)[63] Although the highest court's ruling boosted Roosevelt's popularity, it did little to change the northwestern railroad situation or to restore competition. Schiff had expected an adverse court opinion, but he confidently believed that Hill, one of the "ablest railroad men this generation has produced," would find a way to preserve the unified management of the separate lines. Once the decision was reached, the banker kept his gloomy forecasts on its harmful effects to himself. In one interview he found something about the ruling to praise. He explained that it would prevent the formation of other combinations that in turn would lead to more stringent legislation by the federal government and the states.[64]

The Roosevelt administration wasn't done with the Union Pacific. With the president's blessing the Interstate Commerce Commission (ICC) began an investigation of Harriman's railroads and the holdings of the Union Pacific early in 1907. Enemies of Harriman, called by his biographer the "Harriman Extermination League," looked to TR to lead a campaign that would destroy the railroad magnate. Compounding the charges against Harriman's "pirate-like" activities in the past was the private dispute between him and Roosevelt. Harriman claimed that an "understanding" with the president, relating to an entirely different subject, had been reached after the railroad man contributed to Republican coffers in the 1904 election. When he charged that Roosevelt had not lived up to the agreement, friendly relations between the two were broken off. A hostile president now referred to Harriman as "an undesirable citizen."[65]

In the matter of the ICC's investigation, Schiff was strongly critical of the administration. He told Roosevelt directly that Harriman's methods were admittedly "reckless," but TR's sensationalism and the way in which the investigation was conducted only increased the tension. Instead of trying to make political capital out of the investigation, the president should have worked for harmony between the public and the railroads. Roosevelt's determination to break Harriman, Schiff confided to Cassel, was sending the message to business that success brought enmity, that "large fortunes are prohibited, and that the influence and power which wealth brings are considered dangerous to the state and are therefore constantly open to attack." The banker thought that the president had gone much too far, but Roosevelt's antibusiness stance hardened still further during his second term.[66]

Since Kuhn, Loeb had been and still was Harriman's fiscal agent, several partners were summoned to testify before the ICC. How much did Schiff and the other Union Pacific directors pay for the stock that they later sold to the railroad, the *New York Times* wanted to know. While the newspaper reported on Harriman's "unlimited power" and the far-reaching "tentacles" of his empire, Schiff defended his firm to Roosevelt: Should it be disclosed that Kuhn, Loeb profited considerably in its dealings with the Union Pacific, it had to be remembered that "the risks connected with the various transactions, made under difficult conditions, have been exceptionally great." Moreover, when compared to profits usually made in large transactions, Kuhn, Loeb had earned only a moderate return.[67]

The banker, who was also concerned about his European friends' sizable holdings in the Union Pacific, was doubtless relieved by Cassel's reassurance that federal intervention in railroad affairs was no great evil. A few months later the ICC's report, which ended the official case against Harriman, satisfied Schiff. He found a parallel in the biblical story of Balaam— "I have come to curse, and I must bless." Nevertheless, in deference to public opinion, he persuaded Harriman to divest the Union Pacific of some shares that it held in other lines.[68]

Although Schiff opposed rate fixing by the ICC, he preferred "reasonable" regulation by the government—to which he thought the major railroad men would agree—above uncertainty and distrust. Such conditions, he advised Roosevelt in 1907, not only impeded the sale of securities but presaged dire results for the general economy. Hoping to avert drastic legislation, Schiff suggested a meeting between representatives of the railroads and the ICC to deliberate possible solutions to abuses by the roads. He urged Roosevelt to consider the idea. In an "I told you so" letter, he said that had the president followed his earlier advice and followed a more "prudent" course against the Northern Securities Company, a difficult situation could have been avoided. Schiff's proposal was endorsed by Morgan and by several important railroad owners. Far better, they believed, to be regulated by federal legislation than to be subjected to many state legislatures. The ICC also appeared interested, but Roosevelt, who could not understand why Wall Street regarded him as a "wild-eyed revolutionist," dismissed the suggestion.[69]

Second to Morgan

Reorganization of the Union Pacific and a major role in the Hill-Harriman struggle raised Kuhn, Loeb to the top rank of investment bankers. On Wall Street, respect for the Jewish firm rose. Since popular periodicals featured the senior partner of Kuhn, Loeb, the public too learned about Schiff. Highly laudatory articles told the story of his German backgound, his business acumen, and his outstanding successes. The *World Magazine* saw a combination of "German carefulness and American enterprise." An account in the *Philadelphia Press* traded accuracy for emphasis when it hailed Schiff "the new money king," who had surpassed Morgan and was "captain of [the] largest financial resources" in New York. Some articles commented on the behavioral traits and personal life of the banker—his philanthropies, the way he ran his office, his mode of exercise, and the way he romped with his grandchildren. The picture emerged of a devoted family man who led a simple daily life at the same time that he was immersed in all the details of his firm's national and international transactions.

Curious readers were also treated to estimates of Schiff's private fortune; figures ranged from $50 million to $100 million. The *World* ranked him among the twenty richest of New York, the twelve most charitable and public-spirited, and the three with the greatest financial power. *Cosmopolitan* predicted that if Morgan ever failed, his mantle would fall on Schiff. To some Americans the banker doubtless appeared as the immigrant who had reaped the promise of American life. Others may have bitterly contrasted their own lack of success with Schiff's achievements. One poor Jew was known to have said: "I came to this country in the same year as Jacob Schiff and look what God gave him—and look what He gave me."[70]

The nature and volume of its work brought Kuhn, Loeb into close contact with the leading banking houses. Speyer & Company, the only other major Jewish firm on Wall Street, was usually a rival despite personal ties with Kuhn, Loeb. The National City Bank, on the other hand, often aided and cooperated with Kuhn, Loeb. Schiff's friendship with James Stillman, the president of the bank, and his seat on the bank's board of directors linked him, albeit peripherally, to the Rockefeller interests. It was with the House of Morgan, however, that Schiff and Kuhn,

Loeb were often compared. Schiff disliked the practice, but since he was the runner-up to the powerful Morgan after the Northern Pacific episode, comparisons were inevitable. Some studies have emphasized the similarities between the firms and the respect that each had for the other's ability and integrity. Pointing to the transactions in which Kuhn, Loeb and the Morgans cooperated, they concluded that the two men enjoyed a good relationship. Schiff himself corroborated that opinion when he wrote Cassel, to whom he could have easily criticized Morgan, on the latter's death: "He was an eminent man who always tried to do the right thing, and was free from arrogance. . . . He was always very obliging and considerate towards me, especially since the Northern Pacific affair."[71]

Yet one searches in vain for any hints of real friendship. To be sure, Schiff flattered Morgan rather shamelessly in private and in public, and he tried repeatedly not to antagonize him. But the manner in which he deferred to the "Colossus of Wall Street," over and above the civility required by the bankers' code of ethics, reflected awe rather than warmth. Never did he act as if he was Morgan's equal. For his part, Morgan didn't consider Schiff "an ally without reservation." Nor was he prepared to concede equality to a man whom he called "that foreigner." He had to tolerate Kuhn, Loeb if only for its access to European investors, but like bankers in other old, established houses he did not suffer Jews readily. A recent book suggests that Morgan was forced consciously to suppress a deep-seated anti-Semitism when he needed Schiff for business purposes. He refused, however, to cross the business line or to permit Schiff to cross it. In the manner of those who excluded Jews from their social activities, Morgan said: "You can do business with anyone, but only sail with a gentleman."[72] An immigrant and a Jew, despite his wealth, could not make the grade.

Meanwhile, Kuhn, Loeb continued to prosper. Railroads were still the heart of its business; according to one account, Kuhn, Loeb in 1901 controlled a railroad system of 22,000 miles and stock worth $321 million. But in the beginning of the century the firm became increasingly involved in industrial companies like American Beet Sugar, Western Union, and Westinghouse Electric. Schiff also showed a strong interest in mining enterprises, and with Cassel and other contacts in Europe he handled sales of stock for Guggenheim ventures.[73]

Business had expanded beyond expectations, a satisfied Schiff told Cassel in 1903. A building that the firm had erected in 1893 no longer sufficed and was replaced ten years later by a twenty-two-story edifice at the corner of William and Pine Streets. The firm may not have enjoyed the impressive sleekness of Morgan's offices, but it was the first private banking firm in the city to install its own system of vaults. In a short time "52

William Street" became synonymous with Kuhn, Loeb and with Schiff, just as "New Court" in London was the abbreviation for the Rothschilds. Schiff's fame spread, and his circle of acquaintances widened. To friends and the press he became a barometer and forecaster of economic conditions, and he frequently aired his views before the Chamber of Commerce and in occasional articles for journals. So influential were Schiff's opinions that a warning from him on how an inelastic currency could bring about a panic of major proportions triggered an immediate decline of the market. Secure in his power after the reorganization of the Union Pacific, he shared his opinions, solicited or unsolicited, with successive presidential administrations.[74]

Schiff's family expanded too. Frieda married Felix Warburg in 1895 and by 1907 had given birth to five children. Mortimer married Adele Neustadt in 1900, and two children, Dorothy and John, were born to them. A loving grandfather, Schiff gathered the family together on Friday nights; Frieda's brood often shared long vacations with Jacob and Therese in their summer homes. Since Morti was given 932 Fifth Avenue as a wedding present, the parents moved to 965 Fifth Avenue. When Frieda and Felix built their mansion on Fifth Avenue and Ninety-second Street, the entire family lived within a few blocks of each other.[75]

The Insurance Scandals

Less than a year after the Northern Securities decision, Kuhn, Loeb was again in the public eye. In the heyday of the muckraking era, when insurance companies were attacked for mismanagement, for undemocratic procedures that denied policyholders a say in management, and for links with bankers that jeopardized the safety of their funds, Kuhn, Loeb too was under fire. As public hostility led increasingly to a clamor for government regulation, the firm's involvement in the companies, specifically the Equitable Life Assurance Society, brought it unwanted notoriety.

Ties between the companies and investment bankers like the House of Morgan and Kuhn, Loeb were commonplace. Just as much as the companies needed bankers for investing their funds in securities, so did the bankers need the companies to supply them with ready capital. But unlike the Northern Securities case, where the correct boundary between the two parties (in that case the railroads and the banking houses) was not an issue, New York's probe of insurance companies in 1905 focused specifically on the evils of the company-banker connection. Kuhn, Loeb had long done business with Equitable as well as with the other two major insurance companies, Mutual Life and New York Life, and Schiff had been a director of the Equitable Society since 1893. The banker claimed that he had sought legal advice on his rights under insurance laws and was told that Kuhn, Loeb was free to sell securities to companies in which he held a directorship.[76] But as he learned from subsequent developments, that defense carried little weight. Both his personal integrity and the good name of his firm were on the line.

In January 1905 news of a bitter in-house struggle for control between two of Equitable's officers, James Hyde and James Alexander, compounded public concern. Schiff, who sided at first with Hyde, served in February on a committee of two that attempted to reconcile the rivals. The committee's report was rejected by the board, and shortly thereafter the state superintendent of insurance announced an investigation of Equitable. Newspapers and journals had a field day. Rumors flew thick and fast about the company's malpractices and the shady schemes of its officers. Some articles and cartoons singled out Schiff in particular. One source said that the banker was asked to resign; another told how Schiff and a few others were working underhandedly to give control of Equitable to the Rockefellers. At the beginning of June, Schiff washed his hands of the dispute and resigned from the board. After new disclosures of Equitable's misconduct, he blamed both the Hyde and the Alexander sides for the affair.[77]

From February through July the banker busily defended himself. Not one to suffer such attacks in silence, he lashed out at others while protesting his innocence. He faulted Alexander for seeking to discredit him, but he put most of the blame on the yellow press for a willingness to sacrifice reputations for headlines. He wrote long letters to friends and journalists and to important public figures, including Roosevelt and ex-President Cleveland. One letter went to Adolph Ochs of the *New York Times* with the comment that the banker wanted the "conservative" press to know the true story. To a German journalist, Schiff added that Kuhn, Loeb had done as much if not more business with Mutual Life and New York Life. Rationalizing that those active in public life had to cope with jealousy and other "low" forms of behavior, he denied that he was upset. But the time and energy he expended on fence-mending revealed his true state of mind.

The banker confided to his son that the "troublesome affair" was "like a wet blanket over everything." In his own defense he claimed that he and Kuhn, Loeb were singled out for criticism in order to draw attention away from the real culprits. He said that he personally had no interest in the fight between Hyde and Alexander and that he had sided with Hyde for the sake of the company against Alexander's "scheming ring." On the major charges—that Kuhn, Loeb had acted improperly with regard to its sale of securities to Equitable and that Schiff, a director, could not be both a buyer for Equitable and a seller for Kuhn, Loeb—he explained that he never had served on the executive committee, the body that authorized transactions. On rare occasions, Kuhn, Loeb had bought and sold securities for Equitable but he himself never had. Moreover, since the value of the securities in question had risen far above the price of purchase, the firm had not robbed the company. His hands were clean and his conscience clear: "I know I have been a conscientious and good director of the Equitable Society, as Kuhn, Loeb & Co. have had no dealings with it which were not entirely legitimate."[78]

Although Schiff assured policyholders and others that the Equitable Society was solvent and safe, he called for stricter regulations over insurance companies. Moreover, he wanted directors with the power to direct; otherwise they "must not be held responsible for the selfish methods of the executive officers, of which we knew nothing until the investigation into the affairs of the Society brought these methods to light." The lesson to be learned from the episode, he told a junior partner at Kuhn, Loeb, was to handle corporations with special care.[79]

The Equitable affair turned the public spotlight on life insurance companies generally. In September the New York legislature began an investigation of the big three—New York Life, Mutual Life, and Equitable. The hearings of the Armstrong committee drew national attention, and the counsel, Charles Evans Hughes, won public acclaim. The well-prepared Hughes interrogated a parade of witnesses. Among those from the ranks of the rich and the famous were George Perkins (a Morgan partner), E. H. Harriman, and Jacob Schiff. Just because of Kuhn, Loeb's long-standing relationship with Equitable—from 1897 to 1902 alone, Equitable's transactions with the firm amounted to some $30 million—Schiff was a key witness.[80]

Hughes carefully questioned the banker on two central issues, the financial transactions of the Equitable Society and its relations with Schiff and Kuhn, Loeb. Intent primarily on clearing his own name, Schiff bitterly described what he called the society's manipulative, irresponsible, and power-driven executives. Management had made the board of directors and the finance committee, on which he also served, into mere figureheads, and neither body was significant in the purchase or disposal of securities. The finance committee, for example, never initiated but could only react to transactions that the executive chose to report. It followed that he, Schiff, neither advised purchases through Kuhn, Loeb nor was automatically apprised of transactions that involved his firm. Denying that he ever heard reports at meetings of the finance committee that proved the society's irregularities, he explained at one point that he had a hearing problem! Again the banker stated that he had received legal advice on the rectitude of serving as a director.

Hughes persisted. Without bullying Schiff or purposely antagonizing him, he labored diligently to prove the banker's full knowledge of Equitable's dealings, particularly with Kuhn, Loeb. Using different ways to extract the information, he questioned Schiff at length on the manner in which Kuhn, Loeb divided allotments to participants in its syndicates, on what it charged for commission, and on its links through individual partners to certain banks and trust companies. Usually, Schiff answered willingly, but in many instances he said he couldn't remember specific dates or names. When Hughes proved that Hyde had been siphoning off the company's money and receiving payments from Kuhn, Loeb to his private account, Schiff readily blamed Hyde but denied any underhanded arrangements by his firm. Nor was he aware, he maintained, of how the society channeled funds to accounts not in its own name. In a dramatic peroration to his testimony he forcefully asserted that he personally had received no favors from the society and that in no way did "favoritism" or "undue influence" color the Equitable–Kuhn, Loeb connection.[81]

Schiff's protestation of innocence was not entirely convincing, and not all were convinced. When the manager of Equitable's securities department testified to the numerous payments made to Kuhn, Loeb and its employees separately, he underscored the unlikelihood of Schiff's ignorance. One Anglo-Jewish weekly commented that the banker's admirers were forced to admit that the man who could have made himself the virtual dictator of American Jewry was "no better than other mortals." More than a year later the *New York Sun* still sneered at the "singularly debilitated condition" of Schiff's memory at the Armstrong hearings. Indeed, from one who was always known for a careful mastery of details, Schiff's so-called memory lapses during the hearings (and similarly in the later Pujo investigation) were open to question. The best explanation is that the banker was resorting to a tactic used by businessmen since the Gilded Age. Resentful of investigative bodies, they showed their defiance by claimimg a loss of memory.[82]

The report of the Armstrong committee indicted the insurance companies for financial and political misconduct and led shortly thereafter to legislative reforms. Although Schiff believed that his testimony had vindicated him, Kuhn, Loeb did not escape unscathed. The report pointed to considerable loans made by Equitable to Kuhn, Loeb, and it also told of how Equitable, using Kuhn, Loeb, connived at falsifying accounts. The committee may have been skeptical about Schiff's professed ignorance of Equitable's transactions, but the banker personally was not attacked.[83]

Government and Business

Schiff voted his business interests in the presidential election of William McKinley. The businessman's creed had as its primary objective a stable and rational economic order, one in which investors had confidence. In the eyes

of business those goals dictated support of the Republicans. After the tur-
bulent events of the early 1890s—Populist agitation, Coxey's army, the
Pullman strike—that climaxed in the election of 1896, Schiff rejoiced in
McKinley's victory: "Would the grass look as green, the sky as blue, the
people as pleasant" if the Republicans had lost? With little attention to the
changes demanded by Progressives, he stayed loyal to the party in the elections of 1900, 1904, and 1908. In 1912 he left the Republicans and deserted
Roosevelt, the Progressive candidate. A supporter of Woodrow Wilson,
largely because of his stand on the abrogation of a Russo-American treaty
(see below), he was unafraid of the Democrat's agenda. Wilson was a moderate and unlikely to upset national prosperity, he assured a European associate. As for the campaign promises of the candidate's New Freedom that
could affect business, well, "the soup is never eaten as hot as it is cooked."[84]

An outspoken opponent of cheap money and of an immoderate tariff at the
mercy of political influence, Schiff long harped on the necessity of banking
and currency reform. Since the National Banking Act of 1863 that had
governed the economy until 1913 was hopelessly unsuited to modern conditions, he called for an elastic currency that contracted and expanded according to changing economic needs. Toward that end, as he explained in
an article prepared for the American Academy of Political and Social Science, he advocated the establishment of a central bank—an idea put forth
by his partner and brother-in-law, Paul Warburg—or a "central association" of banks to be constituted by the banks themselves.[85] In 1912, shortly
after his election, Wilson sought the support of Kuhn, Loeb on behalf of a
new banking system. Allegedly aimed at Morgan's power, banking reform
was a key ingredient of the New Freedom agenda, and Wilson's advisers
consulted with Paul Warburg as well as Schiff. At first, Schiff thought that
government control might "revolutionize" the banking system, but he approved the passage of the Federal Reserve Act (1913).[86]

On the subject of the rights of labor, Schiff's business views were tempered by other considerations. (With respect to the needle trades or "Jewish" labor, as discussed below, he worried about the public's reaction to
workers' demands and industrial strife.) To be sure, Schiff feared the possibility of widespread social unrest at the turn of the century; and he, like
others of his class, deplored the increasing pressure of labor, which he described as "arrogant" as corporations. Nevertheless, for humanitarian reasons he strongly supported child labor legislation and the improvement of
working conditions. At the same time that the Supreme Court was whit-
tling down the weapons of organized labor, he readily accepted "proper"
and "responsible" labor unions. Before the Industrial Relations Commission of 1915 he stated: "I believe that the proper organization of employees

for their own benefit, which is the benefit of the State, ought to be encouraged in every way." The "benefit," he explained, meant the "moral and economic betterment" of labor. The banker preferred independent union policies that were separate from citizens' organizations or the government, and only in 1919, a high point in labor unrest, did he advise legal regulation of unions.

The clash between Schiff the businessman and Schiff the humanitarian was also reflected in the matter of strikes. Although he opposed strikes on principle, he contributed on occasion to the relief of strikers' families while the job action lasted. For the settlement of industrial disputes the banker counseled mediation and arbitration instead of strikes and blacklists, and in some cases he acted as an arbitrator. Schiff opposed the Adamson Act of 1916, not for its imposition of an eight-hour day for railway workers but for the pressure tactics of organized labor.[87]

The prospect of organized labor's advances seemed not to have worried Schiff. "We are all of us something of Socialists nowadays," he said about his pro-labor stand in an early meat-packing dispute. He also thought that increased taxes on capitalists were perhaps justified. In 1910 the banker predicted quite calmly that the coming decades would "belong" to labor; the wealthy would take a back seat, and labor's representatives would sit on boards of corporations.[88] Since Kuhn, Loeb was affected by industrial labor disputes only insofar as they influenced the stock market or the companies financed by the firm, Schiff could be more detached than corporate executives from the demands of workers.

More troublesome was the issue of government regulation of business during the Roosevelt and Taft administrations. In accord with mounting public condemnation of trusts, government suits against large industrial combinations multiplied. Although Kuhn, Loeb was compelled to take note of public opinion, Schiff found little merit in the antibusiness mood. Politicians played on the trust theme in order to build up a following. "Unfortunately it is human nature to . . . get something for nothing, or for little, than to pay its proper value, and any demagogue can easily make a success on that line." He complained that businessmen were caught between harassment by the government on the one hand and pressure by labor on the other. Unsure of the legality of their practices, they needed guidelines from the Supreme Court or preferably a more explicit Sherman Antitrust Act in order to conduct their affairs. The major decisions by the Supreme Court in 1911 on Standard Oil and the tobacco trusts were therefore beneficial insofar as they eliminated uncertainty and instructed the combinations on how to reorganize.[89]

The panic of 1907 brought charges from big business that Roosevelt's regulatory policies were to blame. Speaking usually for the railroad combines, Schiff disagreed. To be sure, the president had acted in a spirit of "vengeance" against Harriman and the roads, but hard times would have come even without his antitrust actions. He explained to Fleming in London that investors had become discouraged when the government, labor, and the people dug in their heels. The prospects were gloomy if the situation persisted, because it was "easier to conjure up ghosts than to lay them." He believed, however, that Roosevelt could still speed up the return of confidence were he to adopt a protective attitude toward the railroads. Meantime Schiff, like Morgan, worked for cooperation among banks to prevent a total collapse of the market. The initiative was Morgan's, and again Schiff praised his former rival. No one else could have accomplished what Morgan had despite his "autocratic" manner.[90]

Nonetheless, the panic fueled public outcries against Wall Street. As Vincent Carosso has explained, fear of a conspiracy involving a few international bankers for control of the nation's economy, if not the nation itself, grew from early antebellum roots. Now, in the first decade of the new century, muckrakers and others urged federal curbs on the "money trust" and its alleged abuses. In 1912 the House of Representatives authorized an investigation of the most prominent Wall Street banks by a subcommittee under the chairmanship of Arsène Pujo. The Pujo committee engaged able counsel in the person of Samuel Untermyer, a multimillionaire and corporation lawyer turned critic of big business. All understood that in the legal sense no money trust existed, but the term was used to describe the consolidation and concentrated control of industry by the major bankers. Under the glare of the public spotlight, Untermeyer questioned leading bankers on their business methods, their stock holdings, the control they exercised over the companies whose stock issues they had underwritten, and their ties to one another. The House of Morgan was the prime focus, but Kuhn, Loeb was targeted as well.[91]

Like the other banking houses, Kuhn, Loeb was required to complete a detailed questionnaire for the committee, but the firm stated in its covering letter that it was under no legal obligation to furnish most, if not all, of the information requested. The testimony of two other bankers shed a bit of light on the practices of Kuhn, Loeb; but Schiff, resentful of the investigation, was a reluctant and even a hostile witness. If he didn't answer Untermyer's questions with "I do not remember," his best responses were "I believe," "I think so," or "it may be." A sparring match developed when counsel reiterated that the banker hadn't answered the question. Tempers flared; to Untermyer's "Will you not answer the question?" Schiff snapped back, "I shall answer . . . in my own way." Nor was the latter forthcoming on the investments and directorships of his partners and of Kuhn, Loeb. He was especially vague when asked about the practices of other firms, like

Morgan and City Bank—"I do not look into other people's business"—and about joint transactions between Kuhn, Loeb and the others.

Untermyer led his witness through various aspects of financial concentration—alliances of bankers with other firms and underwriters, interstate ties, and bankers' control over smaller firms and industrial companies. Schiff straddled certain issues. He favored interlocking directorates, but he supported the requirement that banks publicize their assets. He agreed to "proper supervision" of banks by the government, but "you can crush the life out of a bank by too much law." He termed monopolies "odious," but he meant only those established by corporations. Those of individuals were harmless; if they overreached themselves, they would collapse under their own weight. Overall, he grudgingly admitted that he was aware of the trend toward concentration of control but that it did not concern him. Shying away from labels of right and wrong with respect to banking practices, he preferred to emphasize what he thought was "prudent" or "practical."[92]

The Pujo committee's findings were never in question. Concentration and control of the nation's banking and credit were thriving under Morgan's direction. Kuhn, Loeb, although not a member of Morgan's "inner group" of firms, was guilty at least by association, since it was "qualifiedly allied" with the culprits. Congress took no action on the Pujo report, because the Taft administration was winding down. Nevertheless, the report was kept alive by a scathing critique of the money trust by the "people's attorney," Louis Brandeis. Among other things, his book *Other People's Money* rehashed the Union Pacific affair and told of the huge fees and commissions collected by Kuhn, Loeb.[93] Since the public became more sensitized to the power of the investment bankers, it was not surprising that Kuhn, Loeb drew attention when hearings were held in 1914 on the appointment of Paul Warburg to the Federal Reserve Board. Then rumor had it that if Warburg was confirmed he would use the post on behalf of his firm.[94]

The Far East

The international dimension of Kuhn, Loeb's transactions had begun early on. Interest in foreign investments sprang initially from the firm's ties to European bankers. Since it was dependent on the Europeans for much of its capital and since Schiff's associates in England and on the Continent were eager to fund industrial growth in Europe and to tap the resources of underdeveloped countries, Kuhn, Loeb willingly followed suit. In the 1880s, years before the United States emerged as an imperial power, the firm was involved in business with Mexico and Canada. Within a short time it widened its focus to include Central America and, as the firm continued to expand, the Orient and the Ottoman Empire as well. Although Schiff at times thought that opportunities in America were more attractive, Kuhn, Loeb's investments in European industrial corporations and governments also multiplied before World War I.[95] Schemes for investments abroad brought an important side benefit. Impelled to steep himself in contemporary European politics and international diplomacy, Schiff cultivated personal contacts around the world; their cooperation proved useful in business and in Jewish communal affairs.

Schiff personally was attracted to ventures in far-off fields. As early as 1872, when still affiliated with Budge, Schiff & Company, the twenty-five-year-old banker and his friend James H. Wilson, a railroad man and a former Union general known for his capture of Jefferson Davis, attempted to secure a share of a Japanese bond issue. The effort failed despite aid from the English banking house of Bischoffsheims, but Schiff remained alert to financial opportunities in the Far East.[96] At such times he displayed the same boldness and tenacity of purpose that underlay much of his business success.

In the last quarter of the nineteenth century the interest and influence of the Western powers in Japan and China intensified. Japan took readily to modernization as preached by the Westerners, and its victory over China in the Sino-Japanese war of 1894–95 made it the foremost power in the Far East. During the same decade the major European nations, together with Japan, carved up parts of China into spheres of influence. As rivalry among the powers for Chinese concessions (e.g., to build railroads, to develop mines) increased, the United States, for strategic and economic reasons, stepped in with the Open Door policy. Formulated by Secretary of State John Hay in two notes (1898 and 1900) that were circulated among the powers, the policy bound the signatories to respect both equal access to trade with China and Chinese territorial integrity. Roosevelt and Taft, each with his own interpretation of the Open Door policy, encouraged American economic penetration into China, and both looked to bankers for investments that would strengthen the American presence in the Far East.

Without any prodding from the government, Kuhn, Loeb undertook its most ambitious and aggressive foreign venture when it funded Japan in its war against Russia (1904–5). Although Schiff sided with Japan largely because of Russia's anti-Semitic policies, loans also promised financial gains. European and American investment firms had initially turned a cold shoulder on what was perceived as too risky a venture, but after Schiff's negotiations with Cassel and other English bankers early in 1904 they were persuaded to cooperate. The first two war loans were underwritten in New York and London; the second two, in New York, London, and Berlin; the fifth, an immediate postwar loan, in New York, London, Berlin, and Paris. With Kuhn, Loeb as the hub of American action, Schiff effectively mobilized the participation of leading firms, like the insurance companies as well as Rockefeller and Morgan interests. Japanese bonds generated lively activity in the United States, and the pace of the sales forced Schiff to engage personally in the tiresome task of countersigning tens of thousands of bonds. The American share of the five loans combined amounted to over $196 million, a sum that was said to set a record for large-volume financing before World War I. In 1905, Schiff advised Japan to accept the peace terms worked out at Portsmouth, New Hampshire, but he pledged Kuhn, Loeb's continued aid irrespective of the outcome.[97]

Not only was Kuhn, Loeb's aid to Japan a critical component in bringing about Russia's defeat, but it was a major victory for Schiff. Like the Union Pacific affair, it boosted his reputation nationally and internationally. Having eclipsed the House of Morgan in the enterprise, Kuhn, Loeb was now the primary manager of American accounts held by the Japanese government. Schiff visited Japan in 1906, and in the course of what the Yiddish *Forward* described as a triumphal tour, he was decorated by the emperor with the Order of the Rising Sun. Schiff's contributions to the war effort left a double-edged legacy in Japan. On the one hand, his friendship was long remembered; on the other, as *the* all-powerful Jewish banker, he and his firm fed the later currents of Japanese anti-Semitism.[98]

Out of the war a warm relationship developed between Schiff and Japanese banker Baron Korekiyo Takahashi, a financial representative of his government in 1904 in London and New York. Takahashi sent his young daughter back to New York with the Schiffs to live with them for three years while she furthered her education. Through Takahashi and others, Schiff maintained a keen interest in Japanese economic and political affairs. He also kept alert to any signs of anti-Semitism in Japan. As a friend of Japan and informal adviser on financial matters, he worked to maintain good relations between Japanese and Americans. In 1908, for example, he invited forty of America's top financial and educational leaders to a dinner for a high Japanese official. In his speech he emphasized the close ties that bound the two nations, and he tried to minimize the tension generated in Japan by prejudice in California and by the voyage of the American fleet around the world.[99]

After the Russo-Japanese War, business reasons and anti-Russian sentiment led Schiff to continue his support of Japan. (He temporarily abandoned that policy in 1910 when Japan allied itself with Russia.) He fully realized that he was dealing now with a more aggressive Japan. During his visit he had become convinced of Japan's determination to establish firm control over Korea and Manchuria and to dominate China. At that time he tried but failed to secure Japanese consent to E. H. Harriman's control or partial control of the South Manchuria Railway.[100] Understanding full well where the country was headed, he planned to use an expansionist Japan to further his own opportunities in China.

Since his goal was stability in the Far East, the banker believed that Japan was in the best position to maintain safe conditions for business. If that necessitated Japan's domination of China, so be it. When, during World War I, Japan presented twenty-one demands to China that would have made that country a virtual protectorate, the banker readily agreed. He told Takahashi that both countries would benefit: Japan needed China's resources, and China needed Japan's administrative talent. The Open Door policy notwithstanding, he dismissed considerations of Chinese territorial integrity and showed concern only for a guarantee of equal access to Chinese markets for other nations.

Schiff pressed his opinions on the State Department. In 1916 he wrote the counselor of the department that Japan had to expand to solve its problem of surplus population. Furthermore, "Japan, because of her nearness to China, . . . understands better than perhaps China herself, and certainly better than any other nation, the needs of China and the manner in which it will be possible to organize China into a modern state." Therefore, American opposition to Japan's policies could well lead to an explosion. Concerned that the United States had overly offended Japan, the banker thought it wise to supply Japan with the funds for "the labor of modernization." He repeated his opinion to Secretary of State Robert Lansing in 1917, when the Japanese envoy to the United States, Viscount Kikujiro Ishii, sought American recognition of Japan's "paramount" interest in China. Whether the United States liked it or not, Schiff said, Japan will dominate in China, and American influence would be felt only if it operated alongside Japan. [101]

Schiff looked to China as another promising area for investment before the turn of the century. In 1891 he discussed Kuhn, Loeb's possible participation in a Chinese bond issue. During the Sino-Japanese War he was approached by John Foster, a former secretary of state and one long concerned about China. His interest aroused, Schiff suggested to James Wilson in 1895 that Foster, then in China, should "keep his eyes open and not lose any opportunity to secure financial and railroad negotiations." He was confident that, with Cassel's aid, Kuhn, Loeb could handle investments. While Morgan stayed aloof, Kuhn, Loeb secured a modest share of loans that were handled largely by Europeans.[102]

Dependent on capital from Europe, Kuhn, Loeb could not venture further. Moreover, like other American houses, the firm was well aware of the difficulties business faced in China. The country was disorganized and

heavily in debt; the European powers, competing for economic concessions, backed their own bankers. Since the American government had not
joined the mad scramble, its support was uncertain. In 1895 a group of
bankers organized the American China Development Company for the
purpose of securing concessions and industrial privileges in China, and
both Schiff and Morgan participated. The plans for a railroad failed, and
despite pleas from Roosevelt, who promised official backing, the bankers
dissolved the company in 1905. After the Boxer Rebellion and the stiff in-
demnity that the European powers exacted of China, Schiff believed that a
large loan was possible only if the country overhauled its taxation and rev-
enue systems and agreed to an international commission to supervise re-
payment. Since the loan would necessitate American participation, it
would also increase American influence in the region.[103]

Two stimuli reactivated Schiff's interest in China. The first came in the
person of Willard Straight, a young man who had served short terms with
the American diplomatic staff in Korea and Manchuria and who was
brought to the State Department in 1908. Straight urged large-scale capital investments by the United States in China and Manchuria. He claimed
that railroad building and development of Chinese natural resources were
to serve a dual purpose: the enhancement of American economic strength
and the protection of Chinese territorial integrity. Straight met Harriman
when the latter traveled to the Far East to push his plan for acquiring a half
interest in the South Manchuria Railway. He impressed Harriman, and
Harriman passed him on to Schiff. The banker spoke several times with
Straight and was similarly taken with his point of view. To be sure,
Straight's design was poised against an aggressive Japan, but Schiff believed
that he could successfully juggle investments in China with his friendship
for Japan. Indeed, in 1908, Schiff tried once more to gain consent from
Japan for Harriman's designs on the South Manchuria Railway. This time
he described the proposition in terms of Japanese self-interest—that is, it
would lift the burden of financing the railroad from Japan's shoulders. A
few months later he told Straight that Kuhn, Loeb was prepared to consider a major loan to China.[104]

The second stimulus came from the American government. Both President Taft and his secretary of state, Philander Knox, supported the policy
of dollar diplomacy. Preaching "dollars not bullets," the administration
was bent on directing American capital abroad. Investments in underdeveloped countries would ensure America's influence over those countries at
the same time that they contributed to the economic and political stability
of the targeted nations and of the world at large. Not too different from
Straight's point of view, it meant, in the case of China, procuring an equal
share for Americans in ventures of the rival nations. The policy called for a
close alliance between the government and the bankers and, if necessary,

pressure by the government to keep the bankers in line. Success depended as well on the willingness of the European powers, secure in their own concessions, to make room for the Americans.

Ironically, the same administration that brought suit against industrial combinations at home used consolidation and concentration of banking houses in pursuit of diplomatic objectives. Knox and Straight persuaded Morgan, Schiff, and two large New York banks to form an "American group," headed by Morgan, through which the government planned to implement its Chinese policies. Straight was hired to serve as the group's representative, and he, like the State Department, encouraged the bankers to push American demands aggressively. Under close and ongoing surveillance by the State Department the group handled American negotiations throughout Taft's administration.[105]

Although the bankers acceded to the government's pressure, they resented Knox's interference and his saddling them with "dangerous and ambiguous responsibilities." It was one thing to enjoy the government's protection but quite another to permit the government to set business policies. Preferring not to alienate their business associates abroad, the group well understood European hostility to attempts by Americans to pressure their way into arrangements already concluded. Schiff told Cassel that the American bankers were willing to compromise with the Europeans but that the State Department would not permit them to accept anything but an equal share. Given the obstacles, negotiations were protracted. For example, American participation in the Hukuang railroad loan for the construction of railways in southern and central China began in 1909, but the loan was not finalized until 1911. The more complicated "neutralization" plan, which aimed at international support of the Chinese purchase of Manchurian railways, was never implemented. In that instance the bankers thought that the State Department had bungled. Since many variables were involved—the political problems of China, the aims of European governments and bankers, shifting lineups in the diplomatic arena—specific projects like railroad and currency reform loans and a reorganization loan to postrevolutionary China were also doomed. Conflicting views among the bankers occasionally surfaced within the American group. Kuhn, Loeb, for example, was displeased by Russian participation in the banking consortium of the United States, England, France, and Germany.[106]

Morgan's offices in New York and London represented the American group in negotiations with their European counterparts, but Schiff was not a passive spectator. Both before and after the group was formed, he consulted informally with important contacts—Straight in Washington, Cassel in London, Takahashi in Tokyo. In that fashion he served as a source of information, free of political and diplomatic jargon, for the interested parties.

He openly described the tension between the group and the State Department, and he told Harriman and others that "there was more patriotism, than money, in Chinese business." Nevertheless, "I feel it but right for those who, like you and me and Morgans, who occupy prominent positions, [to] do something to vouchsafe American preponderance and influence in the Far East."[107]

Collective action by the group notwithstanding, Schiff guarded the interests of Kuhn, Loeb. He asked Straight quite candidly to remember "our own readiness to deal with Manchurian and Chinese matters." When the group met with European representatives on the Hukuang railroad loan, he secured permission for his partner, Otto Kahn, to participate in the deliberations. The purpose was simple: "in order not to make a Morgan group of the affair and to protect our own position and prestige."[108]

An important part of Schiff's self-assumed activity was to maintain friendly relations with Japan while the American group operated. He could thereby prove his importance to both Japan and the State Department. Before Knox took up the idea of neutralization (which in fact originated with Straight at a meeting with Schiff), Schiff sounded out Takahashi. Assuring the latter that the Americans desired only what was satisfactory to Japan, he urged Japan to sell its railroad interests in Manchuria. When he learned that Japan refused, he was impelled to advise that the plan be dropped.[109]

Takahashi believed, correctly, that Schiff was alienated by Japan's refusal. Schiff was primarily enraged, however, by the Russo-Japanese entente (1910) on Manchuria. He had financed Japan's successful war in 1904–5, and the temerity of Japan to join Russia was tantamount to rank ingratitude, if not betrayal. Informing Takahashi that Americans were amazed by the entente, he proceeded to attack Japan publicly: "I was greatly mortified," he said in a speech to the Republican Club, "to learn that Japan had joined hands with Russia—Russia the enemy of all mankind" for the purpose of keeping China "in a state of vasselage." Endorsed by England, "perfidious Albion," the alliance presaged "a mighty war," which would involve the United States. The story made the headlines, and in a lengthy editorial in support of the Open Door and neutralization the *New York Times* reported that Japan had reacted with "surprise."

At this point Schiff backed down, and he rushed to explain to Takahashi that his remarks had been distorted by the press. He had not prophesied war but rather commercial rivalry; his aim was to protest the effect of the Russo-Japanese alliance on Manchuria and China; his warm attachment to the Japanese prompted his warning that their action would in the end prove disadvantageous. Takahashi accepted the explanation, and Schiff showed his goodwill by supporting Japan's demand for inclusion in the international banking consortium on a loan to China.[110]

While Schiff worked out his private differences with Japan, the American group increasingly wearied of the China affair. The frustrated American bankers began to talk seriously in 1910 of dissolving the group. At a crucial meeting on September 1, opinion divided. Schiff and Henry Davison of Morgan argued against dissolution, and only strong appeals to patriotism by Davison and the State Department kept the group alive. In the last days of the Taft administration, Kuhn, Loeb reversed its stand and told Morgan that it was "unbusinesslike" for the group to continue. Schiff believed that negotiations weren't going anywhere and that Chinese business had become a "bottomless pit." Others agreed, and when Woodrow Wilson repudiated dollar diplomacy as soon as he took office in 1913, the group was effectively dissolved. The Chinese affair had profited neither the bankers nor the government, and the group's efforts had succeeded mainly in evoking European antagonism.[111]

Schiff reached the pinnacle of his career in the decade before World War I. Neither his power nor that of Kuhn, Loeb suffered lasting damage because of official investigations and hearings. His weak showing at the Equitable hearings was more than canceled out by his role that same year in the Russo-Japanese War. Simultaneously, he was expending countless hours on philanthropy and on the defense of his fellow Jews, activities that spread his fame throughout the world. His ability to engage in communal affairs at the same time that he ran an active business—in effect two fulltime positions—testified to his energy and to his skills as a meticulous organizer and able administrator.

The banker enjoyed his work. Adhering to a rigorous self-imposed regimen—it was said that he answered every piece of mail—he continued to drive himself even after the age of retirement. His business acuity and judgment earned wide respect. European bankers who worked with Kuhn, Loeb attested to his courage and his "unusual grasp of problems." One said that "he often rushed in where others feared to tread [but he] almost never made a mistake in business judgment." A writer for a popular magazine meant it as a compliment when he said that Schiff had "the mind of his race, which is essentially a realistic mind."[112]

Those who had dealings with Schiff saw various facets of his character. His co-workers at Kuhn, Loeb knew him to be serious, formal, if not straitlaced, and a highly self-disciplined employer who held them to high standards. Clients commented on his legendary self-confidence in business dealings. (A director of the Pennsylvania Railroad recounted how Schiff would listen to a discussion and then say: "I have had a long experience, and I have come to this conclusion, and I think it is right!" And that, the railroad man said, generally ended the matter.)[113] Friends praised his humanitarianism, but they saw in addition his obstinacy and quick temper.

None pointed out, however, that Schiff was surprisingly thin-skinned. He shrank from personal confrontations, and his protests to the contrary notwithstanding, he was troubled by criticism or opposition, especially by those whom he respected or feared. As he showed in the Equitable affair, he did not accept blame easily, no matter what the merit of the evidence against him. Rather, he looked for excuses or for other culprits in order to exonerate himself.

Despite his self-assuredness, the banker thought of himself as a modest man who shunned publicity and public accolades. (Once he asked a journal not to refer to him as "the greatest living Jew.") Yet he would have appreciated the many tributes that poured in from European bankers after his death. The most glowing came from Gaspard Ferrer of Baring Brothers in London: "No one on Wall Street stood on a higher plane than Schiff; in character, ability, and humanity he was in the very foremost rank, and that in a generation which grew the biggest kind of men—Mr. Morgan, . . . Mr. Hill, Mr. Harriman, . . . and many others. Those were the days when the individual had full scope for his energies and abilities [and] Mr. Schiff certainly made the most of his opportunities."[114]

The banker kept his Jewish life distinctly separate from his business. He never hid his involvement in Jewish matters, but he discussed them only with a few of his banking associates—Maurice de Hirsch, Ernest Cassel, and Max Warburg. In the United States his closest friends outside the firm were Jews who shared those concerns. Nevertheless, the same skills that he honed to a fine art in business—bold initiative and meticulous administration—characterized his handling of Jewish affairs as well.

The man who built up Kuhn, Loeb to its awesome heights enjoyed an unrivaled reputation as the foremost American Jewish leader. His power as a leader rested mainly on his prominence in the financial world; his wealth alone permitted him to support a vast array of civic and Jewish institutions and, if he so desired, to direct their policies. Respect for the banker's economic status allowed him to ask favors for Jewish causes from Gentiles as well as Jews. Impressed by the influence that Schiff wielded in the larger society and proud that he readily identified with them, his fellow Jews were usually prepared to follow his lead.

2

Leadership and Philanthropy

Elitist Leadership

While Schiff built up his financial empire, he was simultaneously establishing his position as the foremost leader of American Jewry. It was an unprecedented feat, particularly notable in a country where the forces of individualism, localism, and pluralism militated against communal cohesiveness. Equally impressive was the breadth of his goals: the defense of Jews and Judaism, the unity of American Jews, and the integration of Jews into American society. Together they generated a myriad of issues encompassing virtually all of Jewish life. But more than an ethnic broker or one who tried to mediate the differences between the Jewish community and the host society,[1] Schiff had a larger purpose. He labored to shape a collective Jewish identity in tune with the modern era, an identity predicated on Jewish continuity even as it broke from ghetto life. How he approached communal matters reflected his vision of the optimal survival of a religioethnic and voluntaristic minority in a democracy. How well he succeeded depended largely on the influence he wielded with the fragmented Jewish community and with American decision makers. His unique strengths and tactics set him apart from his contemporaries and in short order made him a pivotal figure in world Jewish affairs as well.

For the better part of the nineteenth century, American Jewish leadership was roughly divided between religious and secular agencies. On one side were the prominent rabbis. Wielding power through prestigious synagogues, combined at times with an influential periodical—Samuel M. Isaacs of New York and the *Jewish Messenger,* Isaac Mayer Wise of Cincinnati and the *American Israelite,* Emil G. Hirsch of Chicago and the *Reform Advocate*—they spoke for their members and commanded community-wide recognition. On the other side, fast gaining the upper hand over the

synagogues, stood the philanthropic, fraternal, and cultural institutions directed by lay volunteers. The Americanized leaders of those organizations,
usually affluent businessmen or professionals of German extraction, addressed problems within the community as well as those relating to Jewish
rights in the larger society. Their economic status and dedicated communal service earned them the confidence and respect of their constituents.
Equally important were their associations with prominent Americans that
enabled them to enlist Christian champions for specific Jewish causes.
How steeped they were in the Jewish heritage or even the present-day
needs of their community rarely influenced their acceptance as communal
representatives.

Since the United States never mandated Jewish identification, religious
or otherwise, neither side could claim exclusive authority. Nor were the
lines between the two spheres hard and fast. Rabbis and religious organizations freely engaged in secular matters. The organization of Reform rabbis, the Central Conference of American Rabbis, pioneered on behalf of
church-state separation; and laity, as in the case of Reform's Union of
American Hebrew Congregations (UAHC), governed the Hebrew Union
College, Reform's rabbinical seminary. Individuals who served simultaneously in both spheres made for some coordination, but overall communal
unity was sporadic, limited usually to times of crisis and taking the form of
parallel rather than joint activities by sectors within the community. After
the 1880s, unity was further diluted when the waves of eastern European
immigrants, in a world separate from the German Jewish establishment,
created their own organizations.[2]

The layman's authority in civil matters, the modern *keter malkhut* in
Daniel Elazar's cogent analysis, was self-assumed. "Schiff never claimed
leadership," a younger associate wrote; "he just naturally exercised it." A
close friend, Louis Marshall, called him "a natural leader." The banker
once gave his own definition of an American Jewish leader. "Jews do not
elect their leaders," he told a mixed group of Jews and Gentiles; "one becomes a leader among them." When asked how that happens, he answered:
"One needs to have God in his heart. An ethical figure before whom the
people stand in awe and to whom they will listen with deference even
though they may not like what he has to say—such a person is naturally a
leader."[3] (Ethical behavior was the point of a story found in a biography of
Dorothy Schiff, Mortimer's daughter. It tells of a banker who sat with
Schiff on the board of Mount Sinai hospital. When Schiff learned that the
man had declared bankruptcy, he left a board meeting, announcing that he
wouldn't work with someone who didn't honor his debts.)[4]

Called a hero worshiper by his friend and biographer, Cyrus Adler,
Schiff admired the position and power that went with leadership. As Ernest
Cassel once told him, dictatorship was not the issue. One can be a dictator,

Cassel said, "but be a good one." Although Schiff functioned as a steward rather than an absolute dictator, leadership to him meant elitist control. To be sure, greatness often came "from accident or favors," and it carried with it "the realization of greater responsibilities on our part toward others." But at the same time, it "lifts us above the multitude." In many ways similar to the behavior of the Gentile American establishment, elitist leadership was nurtured in Schiff's case by a family tradition of public service, a sense of noblesse oblige, and a forceful personality. Wealth certainly validated his assumption of power, but his voice would have been heard, admittedly to a lesser degree, even without his personal fortune. After all, neither Marshall nor Cyrus Adler, leaders in their own right, was considered wealthy.[5]

No matter how naturally leadership came to Schiff, the man depended on the cooperation of friends. His most important ally was Louis Marshall, a prominent attorney who was equally committed to Schiff's agenda. Marshall planned policy and strategy with the banker, and he was the principal resource for questions of law. Another trusted and respected adviser was the scholar and communal worker Cyrus Adler. Used by Schiff for his knowledge of Judaism and Jewish history, Adler often suggested which educational and cultural institutions deserved the banker's support. Despite strict formality—it was always "Mr. Schiff," "Mr. Marshall," and "Dr. Adler"—the three worked closely together. There was never a question of who was most important, and Marshall and Adler consistently deferred to Schiff. They watched his moods and learned how to best couch any differences of opinion that they might have entertained. Their loyalty, the trait that Schiff valued most in associates, was boundless.

Besides Marshall and Adler there were other Jews on whom Schiff relied for their particular strengths or expertise: Oscar Straus, three-time envoy to Turkey and secretary of commerce and labor under Theodore Roosevelt, who enjoyed entrée into government circles; Judah Magnes, the young rabbi who was trusted by the masses and who often bridged the gap between the uptown Germans and the downtown eastern Europeans; Mayer Sulzberger, a Philadelphia judge, who combined a broad knowledge of Jewish affairs and a personal interest in Jewish learning with a common sense approach to issues. If Schiff was the "heart" of American Jewry, Israel Zangwill once wrote, the wise Sulzberger was "at its head."[6] Still others called into service were Jewish journalists, congressmen, and social work experts. The banker was usually acquainted with those he tapped; if he wasn't, he made it his business to learn about them.

Schiff's authority developed independently of any power base, such as an organization or a synagogue. Independence in turn strengthened his belief in control of the community from the top down. Unconcerned with the problem of democratic leadership before 1900, he and his friends ignored issues like popular representation in policy making, open deliberations between leaders and constituents, and accountability. They alone were responsible for what amounted to Jewish public policy. To be sure, elitist leadership could not be absolute in a democratic America. Despite secret planning sessions, leaders did communicate with their constituents through public speeches and through the columns of a watchful press. But generally, the undemocratic methods went unchallenged.

Control by the stewards was eminently palatable to the German-American Jews at the end of the century. Despite local and regional differences, the Germans were essentially a homogeneous group that shared Schiff's emphasis on Jewish integration into American society. Within the expanding eastern European immigrant community the centrist elements also looked to the German leaders as models to be emulated. The newcomers, particularly labor leaders and Yiddish journalists, occasionally chafed under elitist control, but at the same time they expected and desired the establishment's protection. Over both camps the stewards wielded what has been described as "the authority of confidence."[7]

Schiff too recognized communal restraints on the leader. Secure in his own decisions, he was, however, well aware that even elitist leadership depended at bottom on the support it commanded from the rank and file. Only a leader with an impressive following could set policy for the community and, equally important, ask favors of Gentile power brokers for that community. Although his style frequently resembled that of the premodern "court Jew," Schiff objected to the label *Hofjude* and its connotation of irresponsible action or neglect of group interests. He stated publicly: "I am by no means so narrow as to believe, because a man expends part of his means for public or philanthropic purposes, that he owes responsibility to no one but himself."[8] In practice, however, responsibility meant that he acted for the good of the community as he interpreted it without sharing plans or strategy with more than a small number of friends.

The banker and his close allies firmly believed in the leader's need of Jewish credentials. Orthodox religious observance and a Jewish education were not essential, but communal service and some sort of religious faith were. When Schiff recommended Marshall to the Supreme Court in 1909, his praise for his friend, "the highest and best type" of Jew, meant the proper credentials. On the same grounds, Schiff and Marshall withheld their approval when Woodrow Wilson, looking for a Jew in his administration, considered the appointment of Louis Brandeis to the cabinet (1913). One critic of Brandeis called the Jewish attorney an agent of Schiff(!), but the latter let it be known that he did not consider Brandeis to be a "representative Jew." The argument was no longer relevant four years later in connection with Brandeis's appointment to the Supreme Court. Although Brandeis had included Kuhn, Loeb in his attack on the money trust, he had nevertheless won national recognition as the leader of American Zionists.[9]

Proper credentials were also required for less significant posts within the Jewish community. In 1908 the trustees of Temple Emanu-El, under Marshall's prodding, called for the resignation of a board member whose daughter had been married in a Catholic ceremony in her father's house.[10]

Schiff devoted countless hours to communal service. He faithfully attended meetings of all sorts, of both the established Jews and the post-1880 immigrants—his rabbi once met him on the crowded "el" on the way to three downtown meetings.[11] Since his philanthropy or endorsement touched numerous groups, sometimes diametrically opposed, he gained access to all religious wings—Orthodox, Reform, Conservative—and to most secular movements. His fingers on the community's pulse, he carefully read the daily press and major journals; pertinent articles in Yiddish were translated for his attention. Concomitantly, by speeches, interviews, and articles of his own, he labored to mold Jewish public opinion. His letters and articles and especially his speeches were colorful and dramatic. On sticky issues he knew how to finesse his remarks to fit the point of view of his audience.

Despite his claim that duty, not a craving for leadership, drove him, the banker enjoyed power. Nonetheless, his objectives outweighed any thought of exclusive control over the community. Unlike many of his contemporaries he understood that progress demanded stable and uninterrupted leadership. When he reached the age of fifty, he purposely sought out younger men to be trained in the needs and direction of American Jewry. He acknowledged early on that the masses of the new eastern European immigrants would inevitably change the face of American Jewry. It was therefore incumbent on the Jewish establishment to school the newcomers in proper communal values and to instruct them in the ways of group responsibility. "We should prepare them for the position they will occupy," he said in 1895, "for in years to come they will be the ones to support our institutions."[12] Schiff envisioned a process of aristocratic assimilation whereby the established German Jews would admit the eastern Europeans gradually into the policy-making councils. How readily he relinquished power in specific instances was another matter, but his intuitive grasp of the responsibilities of leadership in a democratic society added an unusual dimension to his public record.

Schiff's devotion to individual Jews and to Jewish causes won him the loyalty and admiration of the masses of Jews. On receiving a very small favor from Schiff, one young friend wrote: "You are, in a sense, the Head of the Jewish community, and all of us feel safer to know that you are dwelling in our midst." Accolades came from the Jewish press, too. The influential *American Israelite* wrote that Schiff's qualities were unimpeachable. He "stands for . . . warm loyalty to all Israel. If ever American Israel should organize, Jacob Schiff should be our leader." Among his fellow Jews, both the older German element and the newer Russians, the banker carved out a unique position. In his later years, according to a longtime associate in philanthropic affairs, "this benevolent looking, soberly dressed, mild-mannered yet very dignified . . . gentleman" commanded a respect unmatched by others. "His appearance at a board meeting invariably caused a quiet stir and a sudden hush in the conversation, in deference not merely to his great wealth . . . but because of an aristocratic quality in his personality that palpably, yet subtly, distinguished him . . . from them."[13]

Not that the banker escaped criticism; that was the price of leadership, he philosophized. His quick tongue and temper tended to exacerbate any friction. True, some of his primary goals, like unrestricted immigration and relief for Russian Jewry, won overwhelming Jewish support; but other undertakings and his methods in particular were subject to attack by some of his social peers as well as the rank and file. Department store mogul Nathan Straus, for example, often said that Schiff's pretensions to leadership were predicated on the philosophy of "rule or ruin" and did damage to Jewish interests. Louis Ginzberg the talmudist, who knew Schiff from his association with the Jewish Theological Seminary, was another bitter critic. Calling Schiff a "great financier and small man," he commented on Schiff's "stupidity" in believing that his large contributions to Jewish institutions made him "the rightful owner of American Jewry" and the matching stupidity of American Jews for seeking advice on major Jewish issues from a Wall Street banker. Ginzberg's close friend, Henrietta Szold, shared those sentiments even though she acknowledged that Schiff's intimate associates thought of him "as a truly large- and warm-hearted man."[14] Stubborn but sensitive, Schiff defended himself at times to his critics, especially those whom he respected or whose influence he feared, but he never apologized.

By the 1890s, Schiff was recognized in Europe not only as a powerful banker and leader of American Jewry but as a major participant in deliberations concerning world Jewry. His frequent business trips to England, France, and Germany and an active correspondence with prominent European Jewish leaders provided opportunities to be seen and heard on Jewish affairs. In 1890 an international conference on Jewish immigration met in Paris at his suggestion; in 1897 he addressed the Anglo-Jewish Association in London. His reputation in Europe soared, particularly after his support of Japan in the Russo-Japanese War. Edward VII received him in 1904, and the German kaiser granted him an audience in 1911.[15] The banker's Jewish network widened, encompassing rabbinic along with lay figures and extending to eastern Europe and Palestine, and Jews throughout the world learned his name.

Schiff's foreign contacts were primarily individuals like the Rothschilds of London, Sir Samuel Montagu, and Baron Maurice de Hirsch, men whose power transcended specific organizations. The American became a member of that informal and unstructured fraternity; and although surpassed in wealth by the Rothschilds, he was accepted as an equal. Cooperation among the Western Jewish leaders focused on crises, usually on Russian persecution and the flood of emigration unleashed by czarist anti-Semitism, whose impact on Jews transcended national boundaries. The leaders also dealt with problems of Jewish security and rights in the Balkans, Morocco, and Palestine, as well as in Russia. They subscribed to an unspoken rule: intervention was permissible in "backward" countries but not, unless specifically called for, in lands west of Vienna. Although accountability to the Jewish masses was hardly an issue (and Schiff listened sooner to his European peers than to the American Jewish masses), each leader was sensitive to the political pressures of his own government.

Schiff fit easily into the circle. Despite his German sympathies, which fed his preference for the German Hilfsverein der Deutschen Juden (and its co-founder Paul Nathan) over the French Alliance Israélite Universelle, he generally advocated international unity. The volume of letters from Europe to 52 William Street increased, and representatives of foreign organizations on missions to the United States made their way first to Schiff.[16] Reform Judaism taught that Jews constituted no more than a religious group, but it failed to weaken the ethnic bonds that propelled a man like Schiff to the defense of fellow Jews abroad.

The spokesman of American stewards to their European counterparts, Schiff held fast to an American agenda as well. Repeatedly, he defended his government against European criticism that the United States could have done more on behalf of persecuted Jews. Sensitive to American popular opinion, he usually advised against meetings of Western Jewish leaders lest they exacerbate the negative image of the powerful "international Jew."[17] With respect to American Jewry, he aimed to hasten its acceptance as an equal partner in world Jewish affairs, heretofore dominated by English and French leaders. Toward that end he lectured the Europeans time and again on the special responsibilities borne by American Jews in matters of Russian relief and emigration. Schiff's role on the world scene, a role that no other American Jew ever played, enhanced the status of American Jewry while it simultaneously added to his personal influence at home.

The Leader as Defender

The radical transformation of the Christian majority–Jewish minority relationship in the nineteenth century made the tasks of Jewish leadership more complicated. In the pre-Emancipation communities where Schiff's ancestors had won renown as scholars and communal authorities, firm boundaries set off the Jews from their Christian countrymen. In everyday life the Jew and the Christian moved in separate orbits that rarely intersected. Ghetto Jews lived largely according to Jewish law; short of outright conversion they could not even dream of unconditional Christian acceptance. Emancipation changed the rules by incorporating the Jews into the body politic. Old boundaries grew blurred, but Jews remained a distinct minority in a Christian society. Still not fully equal, even in the United States, they were confronted by vestiges of Christianity that were legally recognized (e.g., Sunday laws, religious teachings in the public schools) and by pervasive social discrimination. Both within society and yet outside society, American Jews were forced time and again to come to grips with an ambiguous situation. How were they to react to the majority religion? How much Jewishness were they prepared to renounce in exchange for full equality? Concerned Jewish leaders like Schiff recognized the problem. Consciously or unconsciously, they offered guidance by their public actions and personal conduct as to how the group could best achieve the continuity of Jewish identity even as it fought the barriers to complete integration.

Although Schiff boasted of close friendships with Christians in both the business and social worlds, he was ever conscious of a deep and immutable religious barrier. To him, Christianity was "the other side." He professed genuine respect for Christianity and a fondness for Christians who lived up to its precepts. "I only wish," he candidly remarked to urban reformer Jacob Riis, that "some of my friends would be better Christians than they are." But he had no inhibitions about questioning the triumphal march of Christianity. Russian pogroms in the twentieth century were "horrifying," a sad commentary on the behavior of a Christian state. The outbreak of World War I evoked greater criticism: "With all my respect for every religion, I am afraid Christianity, if it after two thousand years has not been able to bring forth anything better than the conditions as they now exist, is bankrupt."[18]

Whatever their religious shortcomings, Schiff expected Christians to respect his faith. He claimed to understand the Christian doctrine of mission to the Jews, but in fact he resented missionizing, especially if done underhandedly or if targeted at unsuspecting children. For that reason he secretly underwrote antimissionary activity and supported the Hebrew Free School Association, established in 1864 to counteract the conversionary efforts of the free Christian mission schools. He worried too lest Jews in public institutions—hospitals, the armed forces, prisons, and juvenile reformatories—without recourse to rabbinical support, fall under Christian influences. It was a *hilul hashem* (literally, a desecration of the Lord's name), he said, that Blackwell's Island (where New York sent the incurably ill) had no Jewish chaplain. Since missionaries actively plied their trade among new immigrants, he offered to pay the salary of a chaplain for New York's port of entry, Castle Garden.[19]

Nor did Schiff condone Jewish attendance at Christian religious exercises in the public schools. It was inappropriate to inject religious holidays into the schools; both Christian and Jewish festivals belonged in the home. When the banker considered enrolling his son at Groton, the prestigious Episcopal boarding school, he asked up front that the boy be excused from religious exercises and instruction. He explained to the headmaster, the Reverend Endicott Peabody, that "my boy would either become an Episcopalian, a doubter or a hypocrite, and since he has been born in the Hebrew faith, I shall want him to revere and remain in the religion of his ancestors." Because Peabody made no exception, he and Schiff agreed that Groton was not the place for Morti. The banker's support of Jewish attempts in 1906 to rid New York's public schools of Christmas celebrations aroused criticism. Jacob Riis once warned: "I have just written to Mr. Schiff . . . asking him to call off the Jews who are meddling with Xmas [sic] in the public schools warning them that *that* was bad. . . . The Jews must not question it. If they do, they will precipitate trouble they will be sorry for."[20]

Schiff endorsed Jewish-Christian cooperation on matters of philanthropy and social reform, but he vehemently rejected any form of religious syncretism. Joint worship was wrong because the time had still not arrived for union on a common religious platform. "The distant future may bring even this, . . . but as long as Christianity means to a large number of our co-religionists oppression and prejudice, if not persecution, the Kingdom of God has not arrived on earth, nor has the brotherhood of man become an actuality." Accordingly, he broke with Rabbi Stephen Wise over the introduction of interfaith services at the Free Synagogue. Seeking to guard Jewish worship against any Christian influence, Schiff objected to synagogue or church choirs that employed singers of the opposite faith and even to the use of a Christian architect for building a synagogue.[21]

Particularly distasteful to the banker was the Society for Ethical Culture, whose largely Jewish membership purposefully rejected a transcendent Judaism in favor of union with likeminded Christians. He contributed to the society out of an appreciation for the social welfare activities of its founder, Felix Adler, but Schiff and other Jewish leaders denounced Adler's break from religion. All of Judaism was an "Ethical Movement," Schiff said, and the society could teach nothing that the Jewish religion hadn't already taught. The banker regretted that Adler's "great qualities have been lost to the Race and Faith we have both sprung from," and he confidently predicted that Judaism would outlive any free-floating ethical system divorced from a belief in God.[22]

The banker disapproved of intermarriage and conversion to Christianity, but his principles affected neither his relations with Zangwill, who married a non-Jew, nor with Ernest Cassel. The latter, Schiff's most intimate friend for forty years, not only married a Catholic but at her dying request in 1881 went "over to the other side" and converted to Catholicism. The conversion was a carefully guarded secret until Cassel's death. Baron Maurice de Hirsch, for one, appeared unaware of the conversion, and he appointed Cassel a founding director of the Jewish Colonization Association and an executor of his will. It is quite possible that Schiff too was ignorant of the matter. A loyal Jew who believed apostasy to be the "unpardonable deed," he would very likely have hesitated before sending his son to be trained by Cassel.[23] In no fashion did Cassel's private life change the tenor of the Schiff-Cassel correspondence. The men avoided the subject of religion, and Schiff continued to detail accounts of his activities on behalf of "our people."

Some members of Schiff's peer group thought differently. Daniel Guggenheim approved of his son's marriage to a Catholic, and Otto Kahn, Schiff's partner, was kept from converting only by Nazi anti-Semitism. To be sure, in his later years, Schiff became more accepting of Jews who had left the fold. Descendants of Samson Raphael Hirsch, he said, had converted, and who knew what our descendants would do? But the banker attempted to safeguard his own family. He stipulated that his grandchildren would forfeit the trust funds he created for them if they intermarried.[24]

In matters other than religion, Schiff and his associates frowned upon Jewish separatism. At a time when anti-Semitism predicated on racism was making rapid strides in both Europe and America, the leaders of the Jewish minority demanded rapid Americanization and unalloyed patriotism for themselves and their fellow Jews. Logically, the behavior they prescribed could make no dent in the racist argument, but Jewish stewards optimistically believed that acceptance would yet result from proper Jewish conduct. They never quarreled with the majority's definition of Americanism as long as it made room for non-Christians, but they worried constantly about the image projected by the Jews. Determinedly seeking Christian approval and respect, they tended to judge Jewish actions through the prism of "what will the Gentiles say."

Considerations of image colored manners as well as beliefs. The stewards, for example, like their American counterparts, preached against all forms of radicalism. Fearful of offending Gentile taste-makers, they, like the anti-Semites, deplored Jewish ostentation or vulgarity. On those grounds Schiff was critical of the lavish mansion built by his daughter, Frieda Warburg.[25] Similar reasons added an urgency to his calls for communal unity.

He believed that the sight of Jewish workers striking against Jewish employers tarnished the Jewish reputation, and he therefore engaged in mediation efforts during the major clothing strikes of 1910 and 1915. Although he emphasized the need for Jews to hold onto a religious faith, again a worthy American as well as a Jewish value, he sharply criticized religious divisiveness: "If anything tends to injure us in the eyes of our neighbors," he wrote, "it is this constant wrangling amongst our Rabbis of different opinions." Religion free of internal disputes helped to gain Gentile respect, and only Gentile respect could effectively lessen discrimination.

Time and again, Schiff responded when individual Jews or the group as a whole met private or government discrimination. Particularly alert to what was purveyed by Christian sermons and by the press, he answered slurs whether on "Jew bankers" or on Disraeli the "Jewish adventurer."[26] Although he operated without any popular mandate or communal power base, Schiff came well armed. His power in the business world automatically assured him a respectful hearing at home and abroad, and his service in civic causes and political parties added to his clout. For example, while his business interests justified a long association with the Chamber of Commerce, he consciously positioned himself in the organization to guard against anti-Jewish prejudice in business circles. The banker's extensive philanthropic activity—with the stroke of a pen he was able to make or break a charity—also figured in countering or at least in raising an awareness of discrimination. Equally important were the contacts he carefully cultivated with people of influence. With unfailing charm he entertained lavishly, wrote innumerable birthday and holiday greetings, and sent countless letters and gifts. Whether advising TR or Taft on remedies for rheumatic attacks or commending a politician for a constructive achievement, his words conveyed a sense of genuine personal concern. Those associations, along with loans or donations to the press—notably, the *New York Times*, the *American Hebrew*, and the Yiddish *Day*—served to augment his influence.[27]

The federal government acknowledged his position, too. It never used Kuhn, Loeb the way Germany's Bismarck used Schiff's older contemporary, Gerson von Bleichroeder,[28] but the banker's opinions on matters of banking and currency, taxes, and government regulation of the economy were carefully noted. His readiness to cooperate with all levels of government and serve on all sorts of committees cemented an easy access to officeholders. Never shy about using his influence, Schiff regularly brought Jewish interests to the government's attention; and where he sensed prejudice on the part of American officials, federal, state, or municipal, he communicated his outrage.

Nor did Schiff hesitate to recommend Jews to public office. Arguing that Jews, on grounds of numbers and merit, deserved posts in all levels of government, he skillfully marshaled his contacts and political contributions to that end. In 1896 he suggested to President-elect William McKinley that Edwin Einstein, a former congressman from New York, be appointed ambassador to Italy. The Jews had almost unanimously supported McKinley's campaign, he said, and the appointment of one who represented the "best elements of our race" would do credit to American principles. Whether or not an appointment was made (and in this case it wasn't) was less important than alerting the president to Jewish demands. Five years later, Schiff instructed Mayor Seth Low in no uncertain terms that one of Low's tax commissioners "had better be of the Hebrew faith." Although he denied the existence of a Jewish vote, he reminded Low that Jews had supported him in the recent election. Schiff warmly endorsed appointments of Jews to major national posts like those of Oscar Straus to the cabinet, Louis Brandeis to the Supreme Court—two "firsts" for American Jews—and Paul Warburg to the Federal Reserve Board. Some even said that the appointments of Straus and Warburg were made at his suggestion. In each case, Schiff was well aware that the Jewish factor figured in the selection or confirmation of the candidate.[29]

The banker and his friends consistently fought the rampant private discrimination of the early twentieth century that excluded Jews from business firms, hotels, private schools, and clubs. The fight itself was a gamble, for it could compound gentile resentment and bias. Usually, the prejudice was too strong to be uprooted, but the stewards scored an unusual victory in 1904 when they forced the resignation of Melvil Dewey, state librarian of New York. Since Dewey's Lake Placid Club barred Jews, they argued that his official position implied the state's sanction of dicrimination.[30]

At least as troubling were the negative stereotypes of Jews held by some of Schiff's Christian friends. In 1893 the stewards were stung by Andrew D. White's criticism of "medieval" talmudic practices and, by extension, Jews who lived by talmudic law. Since White was then American minister to St. Petersburg, the Jewish leaders had hoped to enlist his aid on behalf of Russian Jewry. They may have agreed privately with White, but the situation demanded a rebuttal. Furthermore, as Schiff bitterly asked, if the minister entertained such ideas, what could Jews expect of others? The stewards therefore arranged for explanatory articles by the renowned theologian Dr. Kaufmann Kohler, which they then sent on to White.[31] Another friend, Charles W. Eliot, held fixed assumptions about the power of an international and interlocking Jewish money power. To be sure, he didn't charge the Jewish bankers with conspiracy, but the myth itself fed anti-Semitism. Like White, the ex-president of Harvard had no intention of insulting Schiff. The association of Jews with money power was an age-old myth that commanded credence and acceptance by other Christian liberals as well. Neither Eliot nor White understood Schiff's sensitivity to such images nor his determination to refute them. The banker's close relations with Eliot kept his temper in check, but he did tell his friend that banking was not done on "racial" lines and that Eliot erred by suggesting that a network of leading Jewish bankers throughout the world dominated the international stock exchanges. Certainly, the banker added, Kuhn, Loeb did not behave in such fashion. Schiff corrected Eliot a second time for saying that Jews were wanting in education. Paraphrasing a verse in the *Sayings of the Fathers*, he pointed to the Jewish maxim that the world was built on education, service, and good deeds. In this instance, Eliot was quick to retract, adding that the same tenets underlay Unitarian teachings.[32] Although they were successful in isolated cases, Schiff and his circle learned from experience that pervasive stereotypes were no match for arguments based on reason and reality.

Sensitivity to discrimination was not dulled by Schiff's financial ambitions. When he was appointed vice president of the Chamber of Commerce, he particularly appreciated the fact that he was the first Jew to hold that post.[33] He never forgot his Jewishness, but if he had so desired, the banking community, like the Morgans, would not have permitted it. Never an insider, Schiff assumed a double responsibility, the protection of Kuhn, Loeb's image as both a reputable house and a Jewish one. He believed that the firm, precisely because of its prominence, was obligated to behave in ways that contradicted the widespread anti-Semitic slurs against the cunning and manipulative Jewish banker. On one occasion the prestigious Episcopal bishop of New York, Henry Potter, repeated to his good friend Schiff what he had heard about Jewish bankers: The "Hebrews" were "tricky," "untrustworthy," and the only "race" on Wall Street whose deed fell short of its word. Christian persecution may have contributed to such behavior in the past, but, Potter implied, that was no excuse in persecution-free America. Schiff hotly rebutted Potter's charges, but even if he convinced the bishop and even if Kuhn, Loeb behaved as ethically as Protestant firms, the stereotype of the unscrupulous Shylock or other myths that underlay the "polite" anti-Semitism of the older Wall Street firms, remained.[34]

Where possible, Kuhn, Loeb fought anti-Semites by refusing their business. In his early years with the firm, Schiff resolved not to deal with the Reading Railroad. Its president, August Corbin, had publicly insulted the Jews by excluding them from his real estate developments. The banker explained to Cassel: "Our self-respect forbids us to have anything to do with this man, able as he may be." A short time later, when the New York, Ontario & Western Railroad distributed an anti-Semitic pamphlet, Schiff informed the company that Kuhn, Loeb would not handle their bonds. In that instance he succeeded in securing an apology.[35]

Schiff at times was the victim of social discrimination. At the turn of the century, just because he was a Jew, he was the only prominent financial magnate not listed in the *Social Register,* or, as Frederick Lewis Allen called it, the "Gentile Register." Social exclusion of that sort probably piqued his vanity but never enough for him to compromise his pride as a Jew. He refused invitations to dine at the University Club, announcing openly that he would not enter a place that barred Jews from membership. Similarly, he promptly resigned from a country club in Rumson, New Jersey, the site of his country home, that denied memberships to his family for reason of their Jewishness. Since the banker socialized with some prominent Christians and since all of his best friends were Jews, he personally was unruffled by the "five o'clock shadow," or the prevailing custom that distanced a Morgan from a Schiff after business hours.[36]

The American Jewish Committee (AJC), which was organized in 1906, took over the open-ended duty of exposing and combating anti-Semitism. A primary task at the beginning was the defense of the eastern European immigrants, who, more than the established Jews, were the victims of discrimination. Since Schiff was never one to be inhibited by an organization, particularly one in which he was the dominant force, he continued on his own to counter charges leveled by bigots and immigration restrictionists. Nor, to his way of thinking, did the existence of a defense agency free the newcomers of their own responsibility for proper behavior.

On some occasions, Schiff acted independently when circumstances warned against group intervention. The notorious case of Leo Frank (1913–15), a northern Jew who was framed for the rape and murder of a factory employee in Atlanta, was one example. Since popular outrage against Frank testified to the frightening strength of Populist Tom Watson's anti-Semitic crusade in Georgia, Marshall and Schiff were convinced that AJC action would only fuel the charge of a Jewish conspiracy. When Frank was convicted and sentenced to hang, the two men, publicly ignoring the Jewish element and treating the case as a miscarriage of justice, acted on their own. While Marshall labored on the legal aspects, Schiff contributed money for the Frank cause and wrote to prominent non-Jews imploring them to join him in appeals for clemency. In 1915, Governor John Slaton commuted the death sentence, but thereupon Frank was lynched. Meantime, Schiff's involvement was sufficient to raise the charge that Jews, especially the banker, were spending large sums of money to pervert the judicial process.[37]

Schiff was appalled by the unprecedented act of violence. A man who bore grudges, he opposed plans by the Jewish Chautauqua Society in 1917 to send a lecturer to the University of Georgia. Since he preferred to boycott the university because of the state's "outrageous conduct," he resigned from the board of the Chautauqua Society. Four years after the lynching he still felt impelled to speak up against the appointment to the federal bench of the man who had prosecuted Frank.[38]

Minority status within a Christian society fixed the framework within which Schiff operated. Whether dealing with Jews or non-Jews on matters of defense, philanthropy, Zionism, religion, or even Jewish behavior, two constant components underlay his approach: a sensitivity to discrimination and a drive for Jewish integration. Despite a pronounced emphasis on conformity, the banker differed from German Jews in Victorian England. Whereas the latter were avidly bent on total assimilation, Schiff and his closest friends chose less extreme conduct. In Ezra Mendelsohn's words, they were integrationists rather than assimilationists, and they refused to repudiate Jewish identity for the sake of Gentile approval. Rather, they believed that it was possible to have both.[39] Nevertheless, their behavior and what they demanded of the community were often marked by ambiguities and inconsistencies. In the long run they failed; over time, the majority of American Jews succumbed to the forces of total assimilation.

Principles of Giving

An account of Schiff's philanthropic activities and the vast array of causes that he supported can easily become a panegyric. His compassion and sensitivity to individual and social needs were genuine and impressive. Nor did he limit his contributions to the garden variety of charities, like hospitals and poor relief. In his case, philanthropies included cultural enterprises, both Jewish and non-Jewish. Schiff, however, was not a saint. His drive for power and public approval, his overwhelming self-confidence, and the way in which he dominated his subordinates and the beneficiaries of his gifts were equally apparent. His very choice of beneficiaries showed an awareness of philanthropy as social control, or the means of shaping the behavior of both organizations and individuals. The institutions he supported reflected his civic and social values, and the institutions in turn disseminated those values among those they serviced. A blend of both the humanitarian and the quasi-dictator, Schiff's behavior was essentially that of a benevolent despot.

Like other Jews, Schiff entered the ranks of leaders by way of philanthropy, an area in which he worked both independently and through established organizations. Forging ahead of his predecessors and contemporaries with regard to service as well as donations, he chalked up a record of accomplishments that won him national and international acclaim. Philanthropy drew him closer to the American non-Jewish establishment. As a Jew he was never fully accepted, but on the subject of help to the needy or to communal institutions none could fault him. An article in *Forbes Magazine* put it this way: "Mr. Schiff spends almost as much time giving away money as making it." The sums Schiff disbursed set standards for giving, and the causes he supported won him popular commendation.

Generous with his time and his money, Schiff was quickly absorbed into the governing councils of numerous communal agencies. In many instances his voice became the decisive one. His influence spread to larger matters of Jewish public policy; and before long, Schiff the New York philanthropist had become Schiff the defender of both American and European Jews. As early as 1901 a visitor from the Alliance Israélite Universelle in Paris reported that the banker was at the center of all that transpired on the Jewish scene.[40]

In the last quarter of the nineteenth century, a time when organized charity still depended on the private sector and was usually linked with specific religious groups, the network of Jewish philanthropic agencies in New York rapidly expanded. Scores of synagogue-affiliated and secular Jewish institutions for the needy—the poor, the orphan, the sick, the aged, and the unemployed—took root, largely in response to the swelling tide of eastern European immigration. Mandated by age-old religious teachings that had withstood the inroads of assimilation, philanthropy was a norm of proper Jewish behavior that promised the givers both worldly and spiritual rewards. For some it served as a surrogate for religion; for others, a path to social status. How well the community cared for its own instilled group pride. Non-Jews commented enthusiastically, especially since the same donors contributed to non-Jewish relief drives as well. According to one estimate, American Jews in the mid-1880s gave $2 million in charity annually, of which one-third went to non-Jewish causes. Twenty-five years later the overall expenditures of Jewish philanthropic agencies had risen to $10 million. Thus, while philanthropy permitted Jews to act out their separate ethnic identity, it simultaneously added luster to the Jewish image.[41]

Until the 1880s the numbers and problems of the Jewish needy were comparatively modest. "A few private gentlemen," Schiff recalled, "were able to deal with [them] with the help of only a few paid workers." Although the flow of immigrants in the last two decades of the century stretched the resources of the community to a virtual breaking point, institutions both new and old remained private ventures that depended primarily on the largesse of the wealthy. Donors had their pet charities, but for the most part they all contributed to numerous agencies. The same men who sat on the board of Mount Sinai Hospital were more than likely to run the Hebrew Orphan Asylum, the United Hebrew Charities, and the YMHA as well. A self-constituted interlocking directorate, they often included members of the same family. They exacted time and effort from themselves and each other, and they made philanthropy a requisite component of communal leadership. Jews of means who failed to live up to that behavior did not escape criticism. Why, the *American Hebrew* asked on the occasion of Schiff's $10,000 gift to the Sanitarium for Hebrew Children, did the burdens fall only on a few committed ones? The banker too complained of American Jews whose apathy in response to relief needs was "shocking and discouraging." He also criticized those who did give for often limiting contributions to hospitals and poor relief and ignoring schools and cultural institutions.[42]

During the period corresponding roughly to the Progressive era in American history (1890–1916), the scope and methods of Jewish charities were undergoing major changes. Not only did the number of new agencies mushroom (close to 1,200 by 1909) but they took on more specialized activities. There was one bureau that focused on wife desertion, another that provided day care for children, and still another that dealt with juvenile delinquents. As in general American circles, the movement for "charity organization" was spreading. Among other things, it sought to put relief operations on an orderly and rational basis and to encourage coordination among separate agencies. Attuned to the Progressive emphasis on efficiency, experts such as social scientists and trained social workers increasingly urged a scientific approach to the multiple facets of charitable institutions.[43]

Ultimately, the new approach prevailed, usually weakening the influence of individual patrons. The latter continued their contributions, but their personal leadership and involvement waned. Not so in the case of Schiff. Self-confident and domineering and a man praised by contemporaries for his commitment to social betterment,[44] he made use of scientific experts, but he was hardly likely to abdicate control to trained technocrats. His years of philanthropic service spanned the transitional period between the old and the new approaches; but even as he incorporated modern ideas and methods into his activities, the banker took old-style paternalistic leadership to a dramatic climax.

A young Jacob Schiff joined the ranks of Jewish philanthropists before he established permanent residence in New York. In perhaps the earliest notice of the man by the press, the *Jewish Times* of 1871 recorded his contribution to Mount Sinai Hospital. Other sources for the 1870s reveal his support of the Hebrew Benevolent and Orphan Asylum, the newly founded United Hebrew Charities, the YMHA, and the Hebrew Free School Association. One friend recalled the banker's personal association with the free schools: "[Schiff] offered prizes for essays that were read at the anniversary of his parents' death, and at these times he usually visited the schools and said *Kaddish*, the anniversary prayer for the dead. Often he himself read the evening service [in Hebrew]." On the lighter side, he became active in the Purim Association, whose annual masked charity balls brought out the city's Jewish elite. Early on, appearing unrecognized at functions, Schiff earned the reputation of one who learned about an organization before he supported it.[45]

A generous giver, the banker supplemented customary donations with special gifts marking occasions in his life and in the lives of his family. Signing checks was but a small part of his philanthropic activity; in most cases it worked in tandem with an active involvement in the operations of particular agencies. As he himself said, those who gave of their time and thought were more important than mere contributors. The number of meetings he attended multiplied, and so did the number of boards on which he sat. Fast making himself known to communal leaders, he was named treasurer of the relief committee formed in 1878 to alleviate the plight of Ottoman Jews during the Russo-Turkish War. The position of treasurer, which he subsequently held in many Jewish and non-Jewish ventures, testified to more than his personal donations and a close watch over disbursements. It also connoted his ability to advance sums before their actual receipt and to transmit them safely to their destination. His fund-raising skills drew praise too, and he became known as a master canvasser.[46]

The banker's philanthropic interests burgeoned within the next two decades, indicating, among other things, Kuhn, Loeb's steadily rising profits. His wide range of charities prompted Bishop Henry Potter to call Schiff the greatest philanthropist of New York. Ranked alongside outstanding European Jewish communal leaders, he was known to American Jews by the mid-1880s as "the Montefiore of New York," a reference to the internationally renowned and respected Sir Moses Montefiore of England. Some thirty years later, Louis Marshall, never given to effusive compliments, summarized his friend's lifetime of philanthropy: "There are many who give generously out of their abundance. There are fewer who give unstintingly of their time and of their energies. There are but a very few who ponder and plan creatively for the amelioration of conditions that call for improvement. But Mr. Schiff is one of those rare men who combines in himself all of those virtues."[47]

B. C. Forbes, a financial reporter and admirer of Schiff, once wrote that the banker's emphasis on the responsibilities and obligations of citizenship dictated his choice of beneficiaries without regard to religion or race. Another account added: "It was because he ranked citizenship above Judaism that he put his hand into his pocket as readily to help a poor negro or a poor gentile as any member of his own race." The reports were not quite accurate. The banker's impressive support of numerous non-Jewish institutions notwithstanding, his involvement in Jewish charities transcended all others. Nevertheless, Schiff consciously did use philanthropy to prove that his identity as a Jew and his abiding attachment to Germany, which was also reflected in his donations, in no way conflicted with his loyalty to America. For example, he said that one of his reasons for establishing a foundation for German culture at an American university was to demonstrate publicly that despite his preoccupation with Jewish problems, he had forgotten neither his "birthland" nor his adopted country.[48]

Schiff bequeathed $1,350,000 in his will to charitable causes, but more impressive were the millions he distributed during his lifetime. On his seventieth birthday alone, friends estimated that he gave away half a million dollars.[49] Well aware that charitable giving added to his importance, he enjoyed the praise of prominent Christians. With some, notably Charles W. Eliot of Harvard and Andrew D. White of Cornell, philanthropy led to genuine friendships. Meanwhile, his circle of Jewish associates, some of whom (like Julius Rosenwald of Sears, Roebuck) also became close friends, expanded. Hardly any person of substance involved in Jewish affairs anywhere in the country was unknown to him.

There were other rewards as well. Philanthropy was a challenge for Schiff, affording him the way to test new approaches and institutions. Not all his ventures succeeded, but he courageously explored unfamiliar territory. Genuinely moved by the plight of the needy, he also reaped the inner satisfaction that philanthropy brought. Contemporaries commented on his distaste for public acclaim, and he often stipulated that his gifts not bear his name. Most important, philanthropy was for him the fulfillment of an ongoing responsibility. When his doctor once ordered him to reduce his workload, he relinquished some of his business obligations but refused to cut back on charitable commitments. The banker trained his children in the duties of giving. Only by fulfilling the social demands imposed by wealth could they live up to the standards that their father set for a conscientious American Jew.[50]

An Orthodox religious upbringing had instilled in Schiff a fierce loyalty to biblical and rabbinic teachings on philanthropy. Explaining to non-Jews that the Bible spoke not of charity but only of *zedakah*, or justice, he said that he objected to the word *charity*: "The ancient Hebrew lawgiver . . . knows no such word as charity; to him even giving to the poor is only an act of justice, and justice is the expression he solely applies, when he urges his people to their duty to the needy and dependent." He told *Forward* editor Abraham Cahan only half-facetiously that his emphasis on justice—"justice to the lowly, justice to the delinquent, justice to every member of human society"—meant that Schiff the arch-capitalist wasn't so distant from Cahan the Socialist.[51]

In line with the teachings of premodern Jewish sages, Schiff believed that true philanthropy meant providing a job for the unemployed. It was "something terrible," he said, for a person to want honest work and not find it. He applauded attempts at self-help and mutual aid, ideas that Jews brought from the Old World, and he gave generously to several free loan societies. In 1900 his $5,000 donation enabled the United Hebrew Charities to create a self-support fund. Schiff set the terms: loans to those deserving poor who had the chance of making themselves self-supporting. He established another fund, aptly entitled the Self-Respect Fund, which gave temporary assistance to working families never before on charitable lists who had been hit by unemployment in the wake of the 1907 panic.[52]

Schiff's Frankfurt origins resonated too in his philanthropic activities. The affluent nineteenth-century Jews of that city took pride in their communal traditions, particularly the commands of tithing and noblesse oblige. Indeed, so strong was the "Frankfurt tradition" of philanthropy that Jews of German origin still remember it today. In America, Schiff followed the same guidelines. Since God gave him more than his share of opportunities, he bore "a responsibility . . . which sometimes is overwhelming" to provide for the needy. His belief in the stewardship of the wealthy derived from noblesse oblige and Jewish religious precepts: "Men of means acknowledge the duty imposed upon them to permit their fellow beings to benefit . . . through the large wealth which a kind Providence has allotted to them. . . . The surplus wealth we have gained, to some extent, at least, belongs to our fellow beings; we are only the temporary custodians of our fortunes." In 1903 an article in the popular *Munsey's Magazine* lauded the banker, whose annual contributions to Jewish and nonsectarian causes exceeded $100,000, for living up to the "Hebrew precept" of tithing.[53]

Considerations of a strictly defensive nature figured prominently in Schiff's giving. Although Americans frequently complained about Jewish separatism, they preferred not to take the Jewish needy under their wings. In an early speech, Schiff said that Jews were looked upon in many quarters as "a foreign element." "The fact will ever remain that, as Israelites, no matter how high a position we may have, we are held responsible one for the other." In 1655 the Dutch West India Company had grudgingly permitted Jewish settlement in New Amsterdam on the condition that the Jews take care of their own, and both the minority and majority still abided by that contract. Nor did Schiff dismiss Jewish resistance, born out of group pride or fear of missionaries, to the acceptance of Christian or public aid. He himself said that "a Jew would rather cut his hand off than apply for relief from non-Jewish sources." All such reasons dictated that men like Schiff shoulder a double burden and contribute to general as well as specifically Jewish organizations.[54]

Schiff was well aware of the ways in which he could make philanthropy a weapon in the defense of American Jews. First, as an advocate of nonsectarianism in institutions he dominated, like the Montefiore Home and the Henry Street Settlement, he knew that Jews who opened their charities to all creeds scored high marks for civic virtue. Second, philanthropy permitted him to undertake new ventures for building bridges between the Jewish and Christian worlds and, in particular, for enhancing the respectability of Jews and Judaism in the larger society. Finally, handsome giving provided him with a tool for attacking anti-Jewish discrimination within the non-Jewish agencies he supported.

Like most respectable Americans of his day, Schiff preferred to limit his gifts to the "deserving poor," industrious men and women who, through no fault of their own, were unable to earn an honest living. Indiscriminate giving, on the other hand, was not only demoralizing but, by rewarding those whose moral deficiencies accounted for their poverty, only fostered pauperism. To weed out the deserving from the non-deserving the banker insisted on careful investigation of all applications for relief. His attitude on encouraging independence among the poor was well summed up in his idea for bicycle clubs on the Lower East Side. When Lillian Wald preached about the ghetto dwellers' need of fresh air, Schiff encouraged a favorite pastime of his own, bicycling. He was prepared to purchase equipment—some one hundred bicycles—for clubs in the tenement district. The users, however, were to be charged a small fee for maintainance costs. As Schiff reasoned, they "must not feel that they get the enjoyment and benefit through anyone's philanthropy, which is too apt to be construed as charity, but they should rather feel that the small dues . . . give them a sense of proprietary interest in the proposed affair."[55]

Striving to inject a businesslike approach into philanthropic undertakings, Schiff emphasized balanced budgets and efficient operations. Requests from agencies on the matter of new equipment, for example, required considered judgment. (For a frugal man who, it was said, used the backs of envelopes in order to save paper and who made his family list every phone call they made, nonessential expenses in budgets were unjustified.) The banker once lectured the president of the Baron de Hirsch Fund on how to authorize payments. If the proper business form was not observed, Schiff, a vice president and trustee, disclaimed responsibility.[56]

Since he endorsed emerging trends to rationalize charitable operations, the banker supported the study of philanthropy as a scientific discipline. For the training of experts on social welfare he endowed a chair of "social economy" at Columbia University. At the same time, however, he refused to sacrifice the individuality of the recipient or for that matter the donor on the altar of scientific giving. Aware that the deserving poor were often humiliated by charitable handouts, he sternly reminded the director of the United Hebrew Charities to serve all applicants in a "kindly fashion." The needy deserved respect and compassion; those who were treated as beggars were likely to sink to that level. For his part, if moved by the plight of particular persons who caught his attention—an art student, a physician, a barber, the family of a murdered peddler—he operated outside channels. On behalf of individual cases he tapped friends for favors, he contributed anonymously, and he kept a confidential pension roll. Once, when an unknown correspondent invited him to a bar-mitzvah celebration with the promise of a $100 donation to a charity designated by Schiff, the banker considered it his personal duty to attend.[57]

As a rule, Schiff preferred constructive philanthropy and social reform to narrow charity. The many exceptions that he made with respect to individual beneficiaries showed, however, that he still retained features of the old philanthropic approach. In 1904, Schiff, usually the forceful individualist, came out in favor of the federation of charities. A union of Jewish agencies had been tried with the United Hebrew Charities, but federated fund-raising was something new. A Jewish first, it had been instituted in cities like Boston, Cincinnati, and Philadelphia, but it was not implemented in New York until 1916. His favorite institutions notwithstanding, Schiff argued persuasively that united fund-raising would net higher contributions from the Jewish community. But although he admitted the need for separate agencies to relinquish an essential independent function, he continued to insist that the individuality of institutions not be overlooked.[58]

Mayer Sulzberger once wrote about his friend Schiff: "In perfect innocence and good faith" the banker "opposes all suggestions but his own, then ponders over them, and finally produces a new thing indistinguishable from that which has been suggested to him." Sulzberger exaggerated, but Schiff was in fact an administrator more than an idea man. Impatient with unsolicited advice on how to spend his money,[59] he willingly entertained ideas on the desirability of various charitable, educational, and cultural schemes from friends and social welfare experts. He responded with hours of meetings and consultation, subventions, and frequently advice on how to invest the institution's funds. Since he disapproved of having an agency dependent solely on one donor and since he tried to prod other wealthy individuals to a recognition of their proper responsibilities, he often qualified large donations with the condition that the agency obtain matching gifts. Unabashedly, he used his contacts in the business world and with government officials on behalf of his pet charities.

As in business, Schiff preferred not to be identified with institutions where he had no say on policy making. Implicit in all his ventures was a growing awareness of philanthropy as social control and a preference for undertakings that gave free rein to his views. Often he was attracted to the innovative and experimental: a place for the chronically and incurably ill (Montefiore Home), agencies for distributing Jewish immigrants from the eastern seaboard to the interior of the country (Industrial Removal Office, Galveston project), settlement houses in ghetto neighborhoods (Lillian

Wald's house on Henry Street), and active social service outreach by synagogues (Stephen Wise's Free Synagogue). Further afield he encouraged
and underwrote scientific research, both medical (at Montefiore) and archaeological (excavations in the Near and Far East). The larger goal of
such contributions, he would have said, was to benefit society as a whole.
Similarly, as a patron of the arts he meant his gifts for public enrichment.[60]

Schiff's views on philanthropy fit well his American surroundings. Merle
Curti has shown how the country's emphasis on individual achievement,
self-help, and private initiative, as well as its acceptance of the Judeo-
Christian doctrine of stewardship, were woven into the tapestry of American philanthropy. Schiff shared those ideas as well as the American pragmatic outlook. Others, like his contemporary, John D. Rockefeller, also
used the tactic of matching gifts.[61] But different from many among the
wealthy, Schiff did not wait until he had amassed his fortune before turning
to serious philanthropic projects. Nor did he believe in leaving his entire
fortune to his family. On observing that wealthy people with descendants
rarely made contributions, especially for educational purposes, Schiff said:
"If some of these people could only foresee how frequently the very wealth
which they . . . so carefully guard for their descendants becomes the very
means through which these grow degenerated, they would not hesitate to
direct part of their wealth during a lifetime into channels where lasting
benefits are to accrue from it."[62]

Schiff once referred publicly to Carnegie's principles on the uses of
wealth, but there is no evidence that he was consciously prompted by the
famous article, "Wealth" (1889), that Carnegie wrote. There are, however,
striking similarities between his views and Carnegie's "Gospel of Wealth."
Schiff too believed in "laws" of individualism, private property, and competition, and he too talked of the responsibilities of stewardship over surplus wealth. He also insisted that inequities resulting from the concentration of wealth in the hands of a few did not justify any radical redistribution
of wealth. Rather, the remedy lay in the obligations of the wealthy. When
his gift of a new building to the YMHA was dedicated in 1900, he explained: "The chief value of wealth consists in the opportunities it creates
to make others contented, to expend it freely in an endeavor on the part of
its possessor to equalize the accidental differences in human life." At the
same time, he claimed that the philanthropist benefited, because his was
the privilege of doing good. In answer to "An Open Letter to the Rich"
that once appeared in the *New Republic*, Schiff argued that if a man like
Rockefeller was stripped of his resources, he would hardly be able to function as a philanthropist![63]

Both Carnegie and Schiff talked of the allocation of surplus wealth during the lifetime of the owner. The two men also agreed on the value of endowing institutions of a permanent social value like museums, universities, and libraries. The salient difference between the steel magnate and the banker was that Carnegie argued in secular terms and Schiff drew from a God-given directive. Their solution to social problems raised charges of arrogance and heavy-handed paternalism, but neither one was the purist, rapacious social Darwinist. Indeed, Schiff once said: "There is, perhaps, no more cruel principle . . . than . . ., as Herbert Spencer has expressed it, 'the survival of the fittest.' "[64]

Schiff never rejected a role for government in public welfare, whether through housing reform or municipal aid to settlement work, libraries, and public lectures.[65] Nor did he think that the principle of church-state separation militated against state appropriations to institutions under denominational control. When the threat of prohibiting the use of public funds for sectarian institutions came before a New York constitutional convention in 1915, he and Marshall worked to avert the "great blow" to Jewish charitable agencies. In Schiff's scheme of things, ideas tested in the private sector that proved of use or value deserved government support.[66]

How Schiff applied the principles that underlay his philanthropy is reflected in the following account of his activities on behalf of certain institutions and causes. His labors similarly show how he interpreted the behavior of a Jewish leader, specifically in the area of philanthropy, toward Jews and non-Jews in the America of his day. Most important, his very choice of philanthropies testifies to the priorities generated by his vision of a secure and vibrant American Jewry.

The Montefiore Home and Hospital

Of all his many charities, the Montefiore Home was Schiff's favorite. His earliest major project, it was, he said, the one that gave him "greater satisfaction . . . than . . . anything it has been my privilege and good fortune to accomplish in my life." "I have reared it as I would my own child," watching its growth "fondly and proudly."[67] But also a stern and domineering parent, he ruled the institution for thirty-five years as a virtual fiefdom. In large measure it was the mirror of the man—his character, values, and methods.

The home was created to fill a specific void. The care of the Jewish incurably and chronically ill—sufferers of cancer, tuberculosis, syphilis, drug addiction, or melancholia—had no place in most private hospitals. Mount Sinai, the first Jewish hospital in New York, sent incurables to Bellevue and then Blackwell's Island. The hospital had considered the problem of long-term care in the 1870s, but it soon realized that it could not meet the widespread need without impairing its regular functions.[68] Meantime, the urgent need for a new facility grew stronger. The mass immigration from eastern Europe had not caused the problem, but as the number of immigrants steadily increased, so did the numbers of the incurables and the chronically ill.

The idea of a new institution took root, but it was not acted upon until 1884, when the community made plans to mark the one-hundredth birthday of Sir Moses Montefiore. The English philanthropist had gained renown in the United States as well as in Europe, and members of the Jewish elite discussed various suggestions for a proper tribute. All practical men, they considered social needs, not monuments: a model tenement (Schiff's idea), a reformatory for delinquents, and a home for incurables. The last won out, and in October (the month of Sir Moses' birthday), the Montefiore Home for the Incurables, a small gaslit house on Eighty-fourth Street with accommodations for some twenty-six patients, was formally opened.[69]

New York's Jews warmly welcomed the home. Contributions large and small poured in, and a Ladies' Auxiliary Society and a Young Ladies' and Gentlemen's League were organized to provide entertainment and other nonmedical services for the patients. In 1886 a gala fair for the benefit of the home netted close to $160,000. A leading figure behind the fun-filled event, Schiff too reportedly shed his customary formality. Ten years after the home's birth the *American Hebrew* hailed Montefiore, one of the youngest of Jewish charities, as one that ranked among the community's top favorites. Schiff, who was the financial angel of the home from its inception, became president in 1885. During his tenure the institution expanded rapidly, and in 1913, under the new name of Montefiore Home and Hospital for Chronic Diseases, it relocated to its present site in the Bronx.[70]

The banker plunged wholeheartedly into the work of the home. He liked the challenge of a new institution, especially if his power was unquestioned. To be sure, he had served on the board of Mount Sinai until 1885, but there he was still subordinate to his elders and those who had been in America longer. Montefiore offered him the chance to demonstrate how a charity, specifically a Jewish charity, should be run properly. It provided him and his staff with the setting for innovation and new directions, like medical experiments in hydrotherapy, tuberculosis, and radium treatment. One physician observed that Schiff's interest in the scientific departments, "the chemical, bacteriological and pathological," matched his grave concern for the patients. For serious causes like cancer research, the banker tapped contacts in London and Berlin that could lend expertise and practical assistance. Only after his death was a personal concern of Schiff's added to the experimental agenda. Since the banker had suffered many years from impaired hearing, he left Montefiore $300,000 for research that included "the constant study of and searching for ways and means by which it may become possible to permanently alleviate or cure deafness."[71]

Montefiore also related to Schiff's broader vision on how to ameliorate the living conditions of the new immigrants. Appalled by the squalor of the Jewish tenements, he valued the home for reducing the number of chronic invalids and thereby the prevalence of disease in the overcrowded quarters. Since he often preached the salutary effects of moving immigrants from the factories and shops to the land, he warmly supported the home's sanitarium in Westchester, where farming and fresh air were integral components of therapy for mild tuberculosis cases. As a way of improving ghetto life or of showing the benefits of agricultural labor even to a few, the home served as a social as well as medical laboratory.

Control of the home rested in the hands of an executive committee of the board, which was charged with the review of applications, purchase of supplies, and weekly inspections of routine operations. Schiff's devotion exceeded that broad mandate. Associates knew that he was never available on Sunday mornings, which were reserved exclusively for meetings of the Montefiore board. At 52 William Street matters of the home frequently took precedence over business affairs. On May 9, 1901, the day that the war over the Northern Pacific Railroad sent the stock market reeling, Schiff was anxiously sought on Wall Street. When he was finally located at Montefiore, he explained: "I thought that the poor people up there needed me more than you people down here." According to a friend, Rabbi Samuel Schulman of Temple Beth-El, the banker's greatest joy was in leading Sabbath services in the home's Orthodox synagogue.[72]

A hands-on administrator in philanthropy as in business, Schiff read and reacted in writing to countless applications, financial statements, medical and staff reports, and complaints from donors. He made frequent rounds of inspection, consistently refusing to be accompanied by staff. Injecting himself personally into the lives of the patients, he learned their names and medical progress. He chatted with them on his weekly visits to the wards, he donated Yiddish books and newspapers for their use, and he and his wife took them out on annual excursions. Patients well enough to be discharged were helped to make fresh starts, and if a patient died at the home, he was assured a decent burial. Perhaps most important to the hospitalized, Schiff made provision for families impoverished by a breadwinner's illness.[73]

The patients responded to his warmth and compassion. The president of a non-Jewish hospital told a moving story to the *American Hebrew* of a visit to Montefiore's wards in Schiff's company: "We . . . saw many of [the] patients, and finally Mr. Schiff opened the door of a small room the only occupant of which was a young boy lying upon a bed from which he had not the strength to rise. When the door was opened and the boy saw who was the visitor, a smile came over his face, and when [Schiff] moved up to the bedside and took him by the hand, and said a kindly word, his eyes gleamed, and all sense of pain, of stress, and of anguish gave way to an angelic sweetness."

Working tirelessly to build up the financial resources of the home, Schiff tried various methods of fund-raising. Montefiore was the chief institution for which he personally solicited funds, and every donation was personally acknowledged. Because Schiff *was* the home, it attracted contributions from non-Jews as well as Jews. Doubtless some donations came in as a result of Schiff's gifts to the pet charities of others, and in that way Schiff dollars funded Montefiore indirectly as well as directly. The only donation the banker refused was a $10,000 check from August Corbin, president of the Manhattan Beach Company, who in 1879 had announced the restriction of Jews from his resort development on Coney Island. Schiff told Corbin that Jews didn't want his gifts; but in order not to deprive Montefiore, Schiff made up the $10,000 out of his own pocket.[74]

While Schiff kept a tight rein on salaries—don't spoil a man by making too much of him, he advised—and other expenditures, he was alert to all sources of money that the home could tap. Montefiore charged small fees of those patients in a position to pay, and it received an allotment from the Hospital Saturday and Sunday Association, a nonsectarian agency that allocated money to private hospitals in accordance with the number of non-paying patients they treated. Schiff, a director of that association, was in a position to insist that the home get its fair share. Similarly, he worried about Montefiore's share when federations and united fund-raising took over.[75] Beyond the private sector, the home received token amounts from the city that were measured in pennies for each patient by the day. Soliciting higher municipal subsidies, Schiff looked as well to the state and federal governments for minimal assistance. He maintained that the use of public funds for sectarian institutions like Montefiore should not be prohibited, and he called for state help to advanced tubercular patients. The needs of the home were also paramount in his pressure for tax exemptions for charitable gifts. He believed that without such an exemption the home would have died or at best vegetated.[76]

Schiff drove himself, and he expected similar dedication from the staff and directors. Happiest when captain of the team rather than a mere player, he had free rein at Montefiore. No detail, not even the size of postcards to be mailed, escaped scrutiny, and errors by staff members incurred impatience if not anger. Nor did he, a man who held onto many traditional religious observances, permit employees to miss work on the second day of

Jewish holidays. Citing a talmudic precept, albeit out of context, he maintained that it was better even to work on the Sabbath than to depend on charity. The board too was kept in line, underscoring his dislike of "directors who don't direct." To ensure attendance at meetings, Schiff picked up board members on their street corners to ride with him, and he encouraged them to visit with the patients. On one occasion a director jokingly referred to the banker as a despot, a remark that hurt Schiff, but the label of "hard taskmaster" stuck. Nevertheless, the board ran harmoniously. The "entente cordiale" among the directors, as the *American Hebrew* called it, was often cited as a reason for Montefiore's success. Schiff rewarded faithful associates with tokens of personal interest and, in the case of the staff, with monetary gifts.[77] Overall, the wonder is less his despotism than the time he spent on myriads of details.

The patients too felt Schiff's firm hand. Rules were set and noncompliance punished. At his suggestion a sign was posted in English, German, and Yiddish that read: "Officers and nurses must be implicitly obeyed. Complaints can be made to the House Physician or to the Superintendent. Failure to comply with this rule will cause immediate discharge for the offender." Patients grumbled about various matters—the food, lack of fresh air—and once some fifty of them staged a walkout. Nevertheless, Schiff stood firm. When some Orthodox patients complained about his rule forbidding them to wear yarmulkes except at prayer, he answered that for reasons of cleanliness and "good manners" no exceptions were allowed. A stickler for regulations, he bent them on rare occasions, as in the case of a young polio victim who but for Schiff's compassion would have been denied admission.[78] Overall, however, the banker ran a highly disciplined and businesslike operation.

Schiff publicly called the home "a monument to Jewish benevolence and generosity," but he saw it also as an American institution, one that proved his contention that Jews were no different from other Americans except in matters of religion. The yarmulke incident was one example. Like his suggestion that citizenship be a condition of admission, it testified to his insistence on the rapid acculturation of his fellow Jews. Three years after the home opened, the board made it nonsectarian. All religious ceremonies were Jewish and the Orthodox synagogue and kosher food stayed, but patients could ask for clergymen of different faiths. Not all Jews agreed with the move, for some still feared Christian missionizing among the most vulnerable.[79] Nevertheless, Schiff felt amply rewarded when the policy drew the praise of his Christian friends. Carl Schurz, the featured speaker at the dedication of the home's second building in 1888, called nonsectarianism the answer to anti-Semitism. At Montefiore's tenth anniversary celebration other prominent non-Jews spoke of the lesson to Christians in Jewish generosity and evenhandedness. The fact that the celebration fell on Thanksgiving also underlined the harmony between Jewish philanthropy and American values. Several years later, at the dedication of Montefiore's sanitarium, Vice President Theodore Roosevelt again applauded the good citizenship of the Jews.[80] On Schiff's scale of a proper Jewish image the home had more than paid for itself.

Schiff marked his seventieth birthday with large charitable gifts. Having reached the biblical age of three score and ten, he thought of curtailing his close involvement in certain institutions, including Montefiore. In 1918 he yielded to pressures from the trustees to remain president, but two years later he made his retirement official. The need, he said, was for younger leaders who could better adapt to changing times. The Montefiore family paid warm tribute to his years of service, and the reference by his successor to the period of 1880–1920 as the "Schiff era in Jewish philanthropy" lived on.[81]

Breaking the Barriers

Schiff spread substantial sums of money among non-Jewish beneficiaries. With respect to Christian enterprises, nonsectarian agencies, and public or quasi-public institutions he acted according to self-made guidelines. Reflecting more than his interpretation of civic responsibility, the guidelines testified to an ongoing concern for Jewish equality and for Jewish integration into society. On occasion personal motives, whether genuine compassion or a desire to draw closer to non-Jewish leaders—as in the case of the YMCA or the American Red Cross—also played a part. His choice of beneficiaries influenced others in the Jewish community. To his satisfaction and doubtless at least in part under his influence, the partners of Kuhn, Loeb contributed individually to both Jewish and non-Jewish causes.[82]

American Jews had donated money for the erection of churches as early as the colonial period, but Schiff usually turned down appeals for Christian religious needs. He saw no reason to curry favor with the churches, and besides, he thought it equally inappropriate for Jews to seek Christian help in matters like synagogue building. On occasion, however, he was inconsistent. Once, when a circular letter to Catholics reached him by some error, he answered: "I have the advantage of being a Jew," but he sent a donation nonetheless. Similarly, he supported the YMCA although it had been founded for a religious purpose.[83]

The banker was less ambiguous about two related matters. First, despite Christian prejudices, he frequently defended the need to keep Jewish charities open to Gentiles. Second, with regard to the public sector, equal treatment for Jews and Gentiles by the government was nonnegotiable. Private agencies that claimed to represent a public constituency were also bound by that requirement if they hoped to elicit a generous response. Schiff gave only a small amount to the New York Juvenile Asylum because it planned to serve only Protestant children; and when he contributed to the Prison Association of New York, he stipulated that "prisoners of my faith" receive the same benefits as others. That condition also obtained during World War I, when he professed a readiness to support the distribution of Christian Bibles to servicemen only if the Jewish Bible was issued to Jewish men.[84]

Among his beneficiaries, Schiff counted nonsectarian agencies, notably the Charity Organization Society, in which he long served as vice president; and he publicly urged Jewish aid to such institutions. A means of gaining Gentile goodwill, such undertakings promised to integrate the Jews more rapidly into American society by breaking down barriers between Christian and Jew.[85] At the same time, Schiff believed that the label "nonsectarian" imposed certain rules of conduct on an institution. An agency like a settlement house that claimed to be nonsectarian could not disseminate Christian teachings or exclude "representative" Jews from its directorate. It even erred when it solicited funds from Jews on grounds that it served Jews, because those very words betrayed an ongoing distinction between Christian and non-Christian.[86] Schiff neither hesitated to lecture errant nonsectarian agencies nor to use his position within charitable circles to attack rank discrimination. After the panic of 1907, when the number of Jewish needy escalated and forced the temporary closing of the United Hebrew Charities, he sparked the establishment of an employment agency underwitten by private donors. Not only would it put social service above profit making, but one of its principal objectives was to "ignore and thereby counteract" discrimination against Jews in employment. Concerned primarily with the Jewish unemployed, he invested heavily in the resultant National Employment Exchange, which was open to all.[87]

A few years later, when the prewar crusade for Americanization hardened prejudice against Jews, Schiff was inundated with complaints from job-seeking Jews. They brought charges of discrimination on the part of the exchange just because they were Jews. The banker conducted his own investigation and was appalled by the findings: "I discovered that the forms applicants had to fill out contained a space requiring a statement of the applicant's religion—this in an American social service society!—and that applicants who stated their faith as Jewish were treated with scant courtesy and discouraged from returning for further aid and information." The manager of the agency justified the discrimination on the grounds that many employers, including Jews, refused to hire Jewish applicants. Besides, the "better class of Jews" didn't use the exchange, and the charge of discrimination came only from some of the "lower grade." Schiff retorted that liquidation of the exchange was preferable to yielding to such pressures; but since the directors held firm, he resigned from the board.

When Schiff recounted the story to a friend and co-founder of the agency, Robert De Forest of the Charity Organization Society, the latter maintained that the wishes of the employers had to be met, and he pointed to similar discrimination faced by other ethnic groups. The banker answered sharply. Jews were not a separate nationality, and to be a Jewish citizen in the United States "means to be an American of the Jewish faith," a faith to be ranked in accord with the standards applied to any other religious denomination. The wrangling continued for the better part of 1915–16. Insisting that it was a matter of principle and for himself one of self-respect, Schiff wanted a categorical refusal by the exchange to service employers who called specifically for non-Jews. The agency, on the other hand, insisted that its very existence depended on deference to the clients' specifications. Eventually, De Forest was worn down, and as the intermediary between Schiff and the exchange he engineered a compromise. A form letter would tell prospective employers of the agency's nondiscriminatory policy, and the organization's staff would be similarly instructed. If the exchange decided on a Jewish applicant for a position but the employer continued to ask for a non-Jew, the agency would urge him to interview the Jew before making his decision. Schiff could do no more, but his objections put the exchange on notice that his disaffection might well be communicated to other supporters. Although there was little change in the daily policy of the exchange, Schiff's reputation as the fighter against discrimination in employment was solidly entrenched within the Jewish community.[88]

The banker's choice of non-Jewish charities included Blacks as well as Whites. His correspondence with Black leaders reveals a commitment to Black education, notably to Booker T. Washington's Tuskegee Institute. Washington's moderate agenda and his primary emphasis on training for his fellow Blacks were calculated not to alienate the White majority. So impressed was Schiff with Washington that he made the educator his personal almoner for schools in the South. The banker also spoke up against racial discrimination and for "justice to the negro." He predicted that so long as Blacks were treated unfairly, "the problem will come back to plague us and make us feel ashamed of ourselves." One of his two requests of Woodrow Wilson during the latter's first term as president called for the removal of the color line in government offices.[89]

The widespread exclusionary practices against Jews on the part of business or social establishments at the turn of the century troubled Schiff less than the discrimination of elitist cultural institutions and opinion molders. With great passion he explained to Bishop Potter: "When prejudice flows from the fountain-head, the effect must necessarily make itself felt wherever the stream touches. And this flow from the fountain-head is the spirit which, as by a tacit understanding, excludes the Hebrew from the Trustee-room of Columbia College, of the public Museums, the public library, and many similar institutions of influence upon the public mind." The masses were not the principal culprits, for "the river cannot rise higher than its source." Rather, the blame for prejudice lay upon "those who have the influence and power to counteract it, but decline even to make an effort in this direction, though they may mourn for the guilt of its existence."

Schiff revealed much about himself in that letter. Just as he believed that the wealthy bore a distinct obligation in matters of philanthropy, so did he ascribe to American communal leaders a responsibility for social tolerance. Unafraid to lecture the highly respected cleric, Schiff had no patience for Christian hypocrisy or for those who piously condemned anti-Semitism at the same time that they abetted its persistence. He was disturbed by Potter's earlier comment that Jewish resentment of social discrimination was surprising—didn't Jews too look askance upon intermarriage, the bishop had asked—and he saw no reason to blunt his customary forthrightness.[90]

Focusing on the "fountain-head," Schiff showed a special sensitivity to anti-Jewish prejudice in private schools that was manifested in discrimination against Jewish students, faculty, or directors. Generous gifts to various universities, including Harvard, Columbia, and Cornell, enabled him to monitor the situation at different seats of higher learning. When he heard that his brother-in-law, James Loeb, was not appointed to Harvard's board of overseers because he was Jewish, he brought the matter to the attention of his friend and president of Harvard, Charles W. Eliot. The latter told him that the report was inaccurate; but although the president's evidence was rather weak, Schiff seemed eager to be reassured, and he dropped the subject.[91] At Columbia, suspecting an anti-Jewish bias in faculty appointments, the banker asked anthropologist Franz Boas, then in the sociology department, to investigate. Boas found no evidence for the report, but Schiff was not convinced. He also acted when accounts of bias against Jewish students reached him. He replied to a Cornell student who had complained of prejudice on campus that discrimination unfortunately was "inherent" in the student body and therefore not easily eradicated. Nevertheless, he was prepared to seek corrective measures from a Jewish trustee and from the president of the university.[92]

Schiff was not so naive as to believe that philanthropy constituted the perfect antidote to discrimination; social anti-Semitism, he once said, could not be controlled. But he made use of his wealth and contacts to combat its manifestations. Similar prejudice in Germany called forth a similar response. When he promised to endow a chair in Semitic studies at a university in Frankfurt, he stipulated that religion not be a consideration in the appointment of faculty.[93] Only in the Harvard matter, probably apprehensive lest it jeopardize his friendship with Eliot, was he reluctant to take a strong position.

On the question of whether separatism by Jewish students on campus was the correct answer to "polite anti-Semitism," the banker differentiated between social and cultural student societies. Opposed to the organization of Jewish fraternities at Harvard and Cornell, he said that separatism merely strengthened the stereotype of the clannish Jew who shunned Gentile company. On the other hand, he approved the creation of the intercollegiate Menorah Society, which offered a serious type of Jewish program. He was confident that the society would "raise the respect for the Jewish College man . . . and preserve his own dignity in a better way than if he seeks admission, which is so often denied him, into the Greek letter societies."[94]

Schiff pressed long and hard for securing a Jewish seat on the board of trustees of Columbia University, a prestigious body in which no Jew had participated since 1816. (Gershom M. Seixas, rabbi of New York's oldest synagogue, Shearith Israel, had served until his death in 1816. His appointment was in accordance with the early charter of the university, which called for clerical representatives of the various denominations.) In that episode, Schiff learned firsthand that philanthropy even in the grand manner could not topple ingrained prejudice. Despite generous gifts and financial advice to Columbia and despite a close relationship with President Seth Low, who himself was an opponent of anti-Jewish discrimination at the university, the banker's wish was ignored. When he raised the matter in conversation with Low, the latter brushed it aside. Nor was a follow-up letter from Schiff, warning that exclusion alienated "wealthy Hebrews," any more successful.[95] Low and his successor, Nicholas Murray Butler, who was less favorably disposed to Jews, put him off with the vague promise that, when the opportunity arose, a Jewish graduate of Columbia would be considered. Schiff thus understood early on that he was out of the running, and his own suggestion for the seat was Isaac N. Seligman. Indeed, Schiff the individual was not the issue. As E. Digby Baltzell has written, the castelike behavior of the upper-class WASPs kept the control of cultural institutions beyond the reach of all others.[96]

On principle, Schiff kept the matter alive. Increasingly impatient, he turned to Butler more aggressively in 1907. For over fifteen years, he wrote, he had argued for a Jewish appointee, claiming that "a class, comprising probably twenty-five percent of the population of the Borough of

Manhattan, and representing a very considerable portion of its intelligence, wealth and producing capacity, furnishing, moreover a very considerable part of the students of the University should be entitled to representation in the University's governing body." His letter, similar to the earlier one to Potter, went on to indict the prejudiced custodians of American culture: "So long as . . . citizens of Jewish faith are, by a tacit understanding, kept out of the Government of Columbia University, the Metropolitan Museum of Art, the Museum of Natural History and other leading communal corporations, prejudice is being kept alive against the Jewish population, which those who lead public opinion should do everything in their power to eliminate. It cannot be expected that the stream run pure, so long as its source is contaminated." When the board refused to alter its discriminatory policy, the banker seriously curtailed his sizable contributions.[97]

Not one to accept defeat lightly, Schiff kept up the pressure. In 1912 he gave Cornell $100,000 for a program in German studies. The choice of Cornell, he explained to friend Max Warburg, was a "quiet protest" against Columbia's unjust discrimination. Schiff aired his grievance when he spoke in Ithaca: "I have directed my benefaction toward Cornell as a sort of protest against the narrow spirit which, I am sorry to say, has taken hold of a certain college of this State." When asked if he meant Syracuse, he gave a broader hint: it was a university much nearer to him. At Cornell, however, which he ranked second to Columbia as the greatest university in New York, Jews did serve on the board of trustees. Schiff's agitation may have contributed to the eventual relaxation of Columbia's barriers, but the "blot," as he called it, on the university's record continued to rankle.[98]

Meanwhile, the philanthropist continued his long attachment to Barnard, where he served for several years as its first treasurer. In 1915 he was approached by George Plimpton, a longtime acquaintance and his successor as treasurer, for an endowment of a student hall. A sympathetic Plimpton agreed that Columbia's behavior was an "outrage," but he implied that Columbia's sister college should not suffer the consequences. He argued persuasively that since Barnard had closed down social groups discriminating against Jews, there was a need for a center where students could mingle freely. Aware of Schiff's habit of marking personal milestones with gifts, he pointed out the timeliness of an endowment in 1915, both Barnard's twenty-fifth anniversary and the fiftieth anniversary of the banker's arrival in the United States. He finally succeeded in persuading Schiff to pledge $500,000 for the erection of a women's student hall "for social and ethical activities." Schiff spelled out his conditions in advance: no preference would be shown to any religious group in the building's activities, and an advisory committee of five would include one Catholic and one Jew. Dean Virginia Gildersleeve later recalled Schiff's special interest in Jewish students at the college, an interest that was matched by a determination to investigate all complaints of prejudice.[99]

Schiff failed to scale the walls of the Metropolitan Museum and the Museum of Natural History, the two other institutions he had mentioned to Butler. He made donations to both, but neither tapped him for its leadership circle. In this instance he embraced a novel legal solution. Since New York City contributed to semiprivate institutions like the museums and the state gave funds to the city, why couldn't the state make its aid conditional on the right of the mayor to appoint some of the trustees? (The assumption was that the mayor, an elected official, would recognize the Jews and their vote.) It was "monstrous," he stated, that Jewish taxes went for the support of discriminatory institutions.[100] Generally conservative on matters of big government, the banker looked for government involvement in the fight against discrimination.

Schiff never behaved obsequiously in his battle against discrimination. Indeed, his bluntness and candor irked some Columbia trustees who may have preferred timid or fawning Jews. Rather, when faced with institutional anti-Semitism or slurs against Jews, he abided by a private rule: Even if you can't abate prejudice, don't swallow it in silence, because self-contempt is the "lowest degradation" to which a human being can sink.[101]

A Heritage Affirmed

Insistence on acceptance and respect for *Jews* was matched on Schiff's part by an equally strong insistence on acceptance and respect for *Judaism*. Educated Americans of the late nineteenth century read little and studied even less about Jewish culture or religion. The knowledge of Hebrew and the Hebrew Bible, not uncommon among the learned of colonial America, was increasingly confined to Protestant divinity schools. A survey of 1897 found fifteen colleges and universities that offered programs in Semitics, and only four of those included Jewish studies.[102] Were Americans, however, to learn about Jewish influences on Western culture, Schiff thought, it stood to boost Jewish group pride as well as non-Jewish respect. His emphasis on preserving the Jewish heritage suggested that Judaism meant more than religion to him and that that there were limits to the path of total acculturation.

Proof of Jewish contributions to civilization in general and to America in particular appeared particularly desirable at the end of the century, when anti-Jewish discrimination had become an accepted fact of life. How better to answer anti-Semitic charges against the "alien" or "un-American" Jews than to show that Jews and Jewish thought had influenced the development of American culture and indeed of modern civilization? Imbued with a faith in enlightened public opinion as the answer to irrational bigotry, prominent Jews considered ways to disseminate "scientific" knowledge of the significance of Judaism and Jewish history.

Two of Schiff's friends took important steps in that direction. In 1885 Oscar Straus published the *Origin of the Republican Form of Government in the United States*, a historical work that emphasized the Old Testament roots of the American government. Three years later, Cyrus Adler, along with several others, broached the subject of an American Jewish historical society, an institution that would document the uninterrupted involvement of Jews in the development of the United States. As Americans made plans to mark the four-hundredth anniversary of Columbus's voyage, ideas of legitimating American Jewish belonging assumed greater attractiveness.[103] Sympathetic to such ideas, Schiff became interested at that very same time in securing a niche for Judaic studies in universities and libraries. The venture had a pioneer quality about it, and here too philanthropy provided the wherewithal for achieving his purpose. When he underwrote the acquisition of Judaica by the Library of Congress, he wanted a "dignified" collection that would honor both the library and Jewish "literature and civilization."[104]

More unusual was the university project that enjoyed his greatest support, the Semitics Museum at Harvard.[105] Brothers of Therese Schiff attended Harvard, and through one, James Loeb, the banker was introduced in 1888 to Professor David Gordon Lyon of the university's newly enlarged Semitics department. Lyon fired the philanthropist's imagination and secured his endorsement of a program in Semitics and a Semitics museum. Schiff too looked forward to 1892, which was also the four-hundredth anniversary of the expulsion of the Jews from Spain, and he sought an appropriate way of vindicating Jewish honor. Before any money changed hands, he was invited to serve on the visiting committee to the Semitics department, a post that he held for twenty-five years. In short order he gave $10,000 and the promise of more toward the acquisition of a Semitics collection, as well as $25,000 for the construction of a museum. He envisioned the museum as "an honor to our race," something "to convince Christendom in general that its adherents are indebted to the Jewish people for more than at this time the Gentile world is ready to acknowledge." Ideally, the first step in reaching that end required involvement by non-Jews, and Schiff made his $25,000 donation contingent upon the receipt of a matching sum. In no way was the venture to be known as a "Jewish enterprise," nor were Jews to predominate on the visiting committee. Only if Protestants, New Englanders and Harvard backers specifically, lent their support could the purpose be realized. Their acknowledgment that both

Christianity and many American institutions and concepts of government derived from the Hebrew Bible promised to awaken Christian respect for Jewish history and literature. In the end, since only a meager sum was raised, Schiff covered the costs of construction and furnishings in addition to underwriting Lyon's travels and acquisitions.[106]

The banker spoke openly of his motives when the collection was installed in 1891. Jews were proud of their origin, he said, for Israel had been the birthplace of monotheism. Today, "anti-Semitism in Europe [and] social prejudice and ostracism in free America may for a time be rampant. . . . To combat . . . these unsound currents in an efficient manner, opportunities should be created for a more thorough study and a better knowledge of Semitic history and civilization, so that the world shall better understand and acknowledge the debt it owes to the Semitic people." Just as anti-Semitism in Schiff's mind referred only to Jews, so did Semitic studies mean Jewish studies. Twelve years later, the museum, the first of its kind, was formally opened. At the dedication ceremonies some of the speakers echoed Schiff's sentiments. Professor Charles Norton dwelt on the Hebraic foundations of Puritan New England, and Lyon voiced the hope that the museum would serve as a corrective to anti-Semitism. Probably most meaningful to Schiff was a personal letter he received from Harvard president Charles Eliot that expressed a strong sympathy with the banker's purpose. Eliot, who claimed that the "extraordinary injustice" to Jews was the result of pagan distortions of Christian teachings, wrote: "What we need at Cambridge, and what is needed in the Christian world, is recognition of the great part which Semitic literature has played in all historical time throughout the civilized world. The centuries-long antagonism of the Christian church to the Jewish race has obscured . . . the immense obligation of civilization to the Hebrew race. . . . You are availing yourself of American freedom to reconquer for the Jewish race the intellectual and moral respect of mankind."[107]

Deepening his involvement with the Semitics Museum, Schiff subsidized Lyon's plans for archaeological expeditions to Samaria. Perhaps there, under the layers of later ages, the remains of an ancient Jewish city would be unearthed. As was his custom with respect to all investments, Schiff expected detailed reports of developments. Negotiations for an archaeological permit from Turkey dragged on, and Schiff grew impatient. As it turned out, the results of the digs were minimal. A disappointed Schiff explained to Mayer Sulzberger that he had known before the work started that "nothing of great moment" would be found, because the Jewish religion forbade the creation of any art comparable to that of the Egyptians or Greeks. Nevertheless, he had hoped that "something would be laid bare, which would give to the world new light upon the life and accomplishments of our ancestors in Palestine." Sulzberger, known as "the most scholarly layman among us," comforted his friend by pointing out the value of displaying the few unearthed artifacts along those of other ancient peoples. Like Schiff he believed that the Jewish position would be strengthened by intensifying public awareness of the historical importance of Jews.[108]

The Harvard venture netted Schiff close friendships with Professors Lyon and Crawford Toy and a warm and lasting association with President Eliot. Outwardly, Schiff and Eliot were a study in contrasts—the immigrant and the descendant of the early Puritans, the businessman and the academic, a Jew and a foremost WASP. Yet they genuinely enjoyed each other's company. On long walks in Bar Harbor, Maine, where Schiff vacationed near Eliot's house, and in a rich correspondence they discussed all sorts of matters, from business ethics to conservation, from world diplomacy to infant feeding. In the unfortunate James Loeb incident neither man thought it inappropriate for Eliot to investigate on behalf of his friend.

Eliot won Schiff's respect and affection for his liberal principles and for his laudatory public pronouncements on Jews. Harvard's president stressed the values of individualism and diversity, he welcomed all religions to Harvard, and unlike most of his class he held no brief for the total assimilation of immigrant groups. According to one writer, Eliot "was almost unique among philo-Semites in advocating the eternal [religious] separateness of the Jew," another view that jibed with Schiff's. When Eliot became a strong ally in championing unrestricted immigration, some said it was Schiff who influenced him toward that position. To be sure, Eliot harbored some fixed negative images—for example, on the international power of Jewish banking firms—but that marred neither his treatment of individual Jews nor his ties to Schiff. The relationship was such that Eliot could criticize Jews and just as easily listen to Schiff's rebuttal.[109]

For his part, Eliot admired Schiff's way of thinking: "I have . . . never found any benefactor's mind more interesting". And he respected the banker for his loyalty to Judaism and his fellow Jews. Schiff represented a world different from Eliot's, but the two shared common values. The academician once wrote: "Your experience and your field of observation has been so different from my own, that talk with you is always instructive and enlightening to me; and I have often found close resemblance between your ideals, hopes, and anticipations and my own." Doubtless, Eliot's friendship prompted the banker to make other gifts to Harvard, and although Schiff contributed to several universities, he proudly identified himself as "somewhat of a Harvard man."[110]

Eliot's resignation in 1909 marked a change in the fortunes of the Semitics department. No encouragement was offered by his successor, A. Lawrence Lowell, who was hardly a philo-Semite. Distressed by the decline in enrollments, Schiff pushed, but to no avail, for renewed interest by the administration. Although the department was like "a child" to him, an unhappy Schiff resigned from the visiting committee in 1914. During his twenty-five years of service he had donated over $250,000 to the Semitics program and library, and in his will he left another $25,000 to the museum. The short-term failure notwithstanding, the desire to legitimate Jewish studies in American universities as a means to combat prejudice lived on. In 1895 one prominent Chicago rabbi put it this way: "One Jewish professor, especially if he teaches Jewish science and teaches the history of Judaism and the philosophy of Judaism, does more for the generations to be than all other movements to combat prejudice combined."[111]

Some five years after Schiff's death, Harvard appointed Harry Austryn Wolfson to the Littauer chair in Jewish literature and philosophy, thereby inaugurating a university program in Jewish studies. Coincidentally, it was Schiff who had underwritten stipends for Wolfson when the latter was a bright undergraduate. But because Schiff disapproved of the young man's plans to pursue a teaching career in Palestine, he gave the assistance grudgingly. The whole point of Judaic studies was to cultivate an appreciation of the Jewish heritage in American non-Jews and Jews, and the talents of Harvard-trained scholars were needed in the United States.[112]

"I welcome with my entire heart every work and every movement that will tend to demonstrate to the world the debt it owes to Semitic civilization," Schiff wrote in 1891. Often, as a self-appointed missionary, he gave his Christian friends Jewish books or books about Judaism. He also distributed copies of Rabbi Kaufmann Kohler's magnum opus on Jewish theology, a heavy work explaining the fundamental beliefs of Reform Judaism, among Christian clergymen and public libraries. No undertaking was too insignificant if it promised to raise non-Jewish consciousness about the riches of Judaism. When a faculty member at City College of New York asked for material on Jews and Judaism, Schiff gladly supplied it. In 1905, at the celebration of the 250th anniversary of Jewish settlement in America, Schiff chaired the ceremonies in New York. It was a fitting occasion, he thought, for publicly singling out the share of both Judaism and Jews in the country's development.[113]

At the same time, Schiff directed a sizable portion of his donations to Jewish education. Jews too had become woefully ignorant of their tradition and, in a society largely barren of major Jewish cultural institutions, were rapidly drifting away from their religion. Constantly deploring the preference of philanthropists for institutions like hospitals and orphanages, he contributed to a wide variety of schools—from Talmud Torahs for young-sters to seminaries and institutes for the training of rabbis and teachers. The Jewish Chautauqua Society, which popularized the knowledge of Judaism through home reading courses and summer assemblies, also received his blessing. He appreciated its work, especially for Jews who lived in small communities without the benefits of synagogues and schools. Schiff believed that the dissemination of a knowledge of Judaism, whether to large or small audiences, was essential for inculcating high moral standards and for assuring the survival of Judaism in America. Nor did Judaism conflict with Americanism: "The Jew of the future will be as good a Jew as he is an American and as good an American as he is a Jew."[114]

Schiff was hardly a learned Jew, but his respect for Jewish learning, instilled by his Frankfurt upbringing, underlay his efforts to root the scholarly tradition in American soil. Alert to suggestions for worthwhile publications, he assisted individual scholars who wrote in Hebrew and Yiddish as well as English. He also supported the Jewish Publication Society (JPS) and the publication and distribution of the monumental, multivolume *Jewish Encyclopedia*, ventures that would keep alive both Jewish writings and the story of the Jews in history. His subventions helped make possible two major undertakings of the JPS, a new English translation by Jews of the Bible and the Library of Jewish Classics, a series of postbiblical literary works. The classics in English, Schiff said, "would open up to the Jew his great inheritance, of which unfortunately present Jewry knows so little." Calling that project a "great gift" of the Jews to the English-speaking world and second only to the Bible, he optimistically foresaw a revival of Jewish literature in America that would eclipse the golden age of Spanish Jewry.[115]

A Reform Jew by affiliation, the banker cared little for denominational labels or whether the scholarly and educational projects he endorsed were under Reform, Conservative, or Orthodox auspices. When he learned in 1886 of plans to establish a Conservative rabbinical seminary, he asked if he could participate. He wished to contribute to the library and thereby aid in the development of Jewish scholarship. Nor did he object when the Orthodox Uptown Talmud Torah accepted his donation on condition that it would in no way alter the school's religious policy. In that case, Schiff stipulated that in exchange for his taking over the mortgage the school would modernize and Americanize (i.e., include physical development, hygiene, and pedagogy in its curriculum). On a visit to the school he was surprised to see that Jewish history, for example, was not taught. What he observed and objected to—how young boys of ten to fourteen argued abstruse talmudic passages—convinced him that the youth would eventually revolt against Judaism. Impatient with resistance to educational change, he also made his support of the Orthodox Rabbi Isaac Elhanan rabbinical seminary conditional on the modernization of its methods and program of studies.[116]

Modernized education and scholarship for the survival of Judaism, but survival toward what end? Schiff generally ignored questions of theology, but on one occasion he supplied an answer in line with classical Reform's concept of the Jewish mission: Providence had dispersed the Jews among the nations so that they might labor for universal acceptance of the unity of God and brotherhood of man. To achieve that mission its bearers needed a sound knowledge of Jewish history and a loyalty to the Jewish religion, conditions that would permit the continuity of the religious heritage. "If we, as American Jews, . . . have really the wish to take up the work . . . and carry forward the mission for which Providence appears to have destined us, our first and never ceasing effort must be to promote among the members of our race a thorough knowledge of its history that the foundations of our faith . . . may . . . be kept alive and handed down to our children and to coming generations."[117] That formulation validated the importance of Jewish education and Schiff's ideal of a religiously and culturally vibrant American Judaism. Since he explained Judaism only in those terms: (i.e., religious and cultural), he comfortably squared his Jewish and American loyalties.

3

The New Immigrants

For over thirty years the problems of eastern European immigrants to the United States eclipsed all other philanthropic concerns of Jewish communal leaders. The problems themselves were abundantly clear; the solutions were less apparent. Never before had the established Germans been confronted by a tidal wave of newcomers whose physical and cultural conditions begged for immediate attention. Schiff, for one, undertook the added responsibilities with least unwillingness. Working on various fronts simultaneously, he seized on multiple ideas that harbored any glimmer of success. The agencies through which he addressed the immigrants' needs were largely untried and experimental.

Certain principles remained unchanged. The banker's assumption and exercise of leadership powers, although more pronounced, were not new. Neither was his sensitivity to government and non-Jewish popular opinion that always attended his choice of approach. Two new factors, however, colored his activities. One, the relation of American to European Jews in directing and supporting the eastern Europeans gave rise to complications in matters of international policy making even as it hailed the coming of age of American Jews. A second, the steady maturation of the immigrant constituency, a Jewry that increasingly resented the established leaders, added obstacles to the purposes and practices of elitist control. The breadth of Schiff's expanded operations enhanced his importance among American and European Jews. At the same time, situations arose that ultimately threatened his leadership and adumbrated radical changes in communal governance.

Baron de Hirsch Steps In

The mass emigration of eastern European Jews in the wake of pogroms and czarist economic and cultural restrictions cast 200,000 on American shores in the 1880s, 300,000 in the 1890s, and another 1.5 million between 1900 and World War I. American Jews were neither prepared for nor overjoyed by the seemingly incessant flood. Communal leaders reacted at the beginning with marked ambivalence. On the one hand, worries about new economic burdens and fears of the newcomers' impact on the status of the established Jews bred resentment and hostility. The Union of American Hebrew Congregations (UAHC) candidly warned in 1891: "If there should grow up in our midst a class of people not imbued with American ideas . . . , prejudice and ill judgment will hold us responsible for evils of which we none may be guilty." To mitigate the fallout, some spokesmen called for selected immigration, or the weeding out of those who failed to measure up to physical and characterological standards. On the other hand, humanitarianism and an overriding sense of responsibility dictated a positive if grudging reception of the immigrants. One active contributor to immigrant relief explained: "We did not invite them, but they came, they came for the reason that America is the only country that is willing and able to receive these hounded people. . . . We look upon the reception of these people as the first and highest duty, a duty that one human being owes to another, and by that law that one Jew owes to another." So long as Russian policy remained unchanged, Western Jews—which meant primarily American, since England, France, and Germany were too limited in resources or fettered by restrictive immigration laws—had little choice but to cope with the consequences. Schiff and his friends aptly described the situation after 1890: America had become the "center of gravity" of the Russian Jewish question.[1]

Between 1880 and 1900 voluntary relief committees in western Europe sprang into action, assisting in the transport and physical care of the emigrants. International conferences were hastily convened in efforts to regulate and direct the transcontinental exodus and to divide the burdens equitably among Western Jews. Nevertheless, the work of those ad hoc bodies, which betrayed a woeful lack of planning and coordination, was too little and too late. The enormity of the task failed to impress American Jews, but the Europeans, for their part, often ignored American desires. An efficient central agency might have better heeded conflicting demands, justifiable or not, regarding the numbers that could be absorbed, the preferred type of immigrant, and the need to distribute refugees throughout the United States. But persistent persecution doomed any ongoing plans for orderly emigration. Propelled by its own momentum, the human tide swelled out of control. Most emigrants in search of a haven fixed upon the United States and on New York City in particular. In 1892 a cartoon in the popular magazine *Judge* called the city the new Jerusalem.[2]

Tens of thousands of immigrants poured into one square mile of New York's Lower East Side. To be sure, the Lower East Side was not the first

area of settlement of all the immigrants; some made their way to Harlem
and to the other boroughs. But the section of Manhattan south of Four-
teenth Street became the quintessential ghetto and one that horrified the
Jewish stewards. A "worse hell than was ever invented by the imagination
of the most vindictive Jew-hater in Europe," said Leo Levi, president of
B'nai B'rith; "a disgrace to the name of Jew," said Schiff. The appalling
conditions of the ghetto, which have been described countless times, altered the scope and direction of Jewish philanthropy beyond recognition.
Any previous guidelines on what the community had to budget annually in
the way of relief were rendered totally useless by the magnitude of the situation. The representative of the Alliance Israélite Universelle reported in
1901 to his organization in Paris that there were more needy Jews in New
York than there were Jews in France and England combined.[3]

The needs of the newcomers, largely impoverished and drained of material and emotional resources, became evident immediately upon their arrival at Castle Garden and later (1892) Ellis Island. To counteract the
blandishments of zealous missionaries and to protect young women who
were lured into prostitution rings, the immigrants had to be met; decisions
by local officials who frequently denied them entry had to be monitored
and, if need be, contested. When the immigrants found their way to the
squalid ghetto tenements, cases of the hungry, the homeless, the deserted,
the sick, the orphaned, and the unemployed assumed first priority. Besides
those elemental needs, the ghetto spawned problems of social deviancy.
Jewish crime, for example, emerged for the first time as a major problem. It
was "horrifying," Schiff wrote in 1901, to find that 23 percent of delinquents in reformatories were Jewish, especially when Jews constituted only
14 percent of the city's population.[4]

The burden of the new immigrants fell most heavily on the established
German philanthropists. They expanded existing agencies and created new
ones. Duplication was unavoidable, but in some areas a rough division of
labor emerged; for example, the National Council of Jewish Women
worked to shield women from prostitution, and the Board of Delegates of
the UAHC kept tabs on cases of unfair or illegal deportations.[5] Although
the costs were lightened somewhat by subventions from the Baron de
Hirsch Fund and by the eastern Europeans who quickly established their
own self-help organizations, the perceived horrors of ghetto life continued
to plague communal leaders until World War I. Jews, as traditional city-
dwellers, would hardly have shared established American beliefs about
urban centers as the root of social decay. But ironically, the same indictments of the city's nefarious influence and its need of moral uplift resonated in German Jewish charges against the urban Jewish ghetto. Jewish
critics went even further and insisted that the ghetto problem could not be
measured in physical terms alone. First of all, it lent "proof" to immigration

restrictionists who ranted about the responsibility of immigrants for the spread of pauperism, disease, and crime. Second, it stoked the fires of American anti-Semitism. The immigrants did not cause Jew-hatred. Admit it, Schiff once said, in many quarters Jews in general were regarded as foreigners and outsiders. But the "peculiarities" of their manners and customs could conceivably exacerbate it. A symbol of the alien and hence un-American Jews who by sheer force of numbers warned of the ultimate "judaization" of New York, the ghetto appeared to threaten the security of the older settlers as well as the newcomers.[6]

The eastern European immigration catapulted Schiff the local Jewish philanthropist to national and international renown. While still a young man, he became enmeshed in the immigrant problem, and for over thirty years he grappled with many of its ramifications. Not only did he personally overcome the typical German aversion to the immigrants, bearers of what to them was an alien and inferior culture, but a sense of duty and a concern for the American Jewish image drove him to new activities. So too did the conviction that the problems, if not properly addressed, would influence America to close its doors to future immigration. His logic dictated that he employ his resources in ways calculated to turn the newcomers into productive and loyal citizens as quickly as possible. More than ever he used philanthropy as a calculated instrument of social control, in this case the remaking of the immigrants. Always the heavy-handed benefactor, he played the tutor and guardian to his wards, the eastern Europeans. Confident of the remedies he prescribed and the counsel he proffered, he epitomized paternalism in the grand manner. Yet another side emerged too, that of a man who was receptive to new ideas and for whom the challenge of the immigrant question proved a personal learning experience.

Schiff plunged with his usual intensity into relief activities for eastern European refugees. In the thick of ad hoc committees and new societies that sprang up after the 1881 pogroms, he subscribed to the Russian Emigrant Relief Fund and served as treasurer of the Russian Refugee and Colonization Fund. When refugee relief was largely absorbed by the Hebrew Emigrant Aid Society, an organization that resolved to aid and advise immigrants "in obtaining homes and employment, and otherwise providing means to prevent them from becoming burdens of the charity of the community," he again responded. The banker donated $10,000 through that society in 1882 for the renovation of an immigrant shelter on Ward's Island. A sort of halfway house, the shelter accommodated immigrants until suitable employment was found for them. (The "Schiff refuge," as it was known, may have had good intentions, but its inadequacies bred immigrant unrest.) The ever loyal *American Hebrew*, praising "a noble triumverate" concerned with the plight of the eastern Europeans, ranked the thirty-five-year-old Schiff alongside two European philanthropists roughly twenty years his senior, Frederick Mocatta of England and Maurice de Hirsch of Germany.[7]

The Russian problem joined the American one directly with a fellow member of the "triumverate," Baron de Hirsch. The story began in 1887 in Constantinople where Hirsch, scion of a wealthy banking family and builder of railways, met the American minister, Oscar Straus. By then the baron's original plan to raise the status of the Jews in Russia through the creation of elementary and agricultural schools had failed. Convinced now that any future for the eastern Europeans lay in large-scale emigration, he envisaged the physical and moral regeneration of the Russian Jews as productive citizens, primarily farmers and craftsmen, in Western countries. He was prepared to establish a relief fund in the United States, and he asked Straus to recommend individuals to serve as trustees and to apprise him of their ideas on assistance to immigrants. At Straus's request, Michael Heilprin, a well-known literary figure in New York who had been engrossed in the immigrant problem since 1881, suggested a plan that jibed with the baron's views and was endorsed by Straus, his brother Isidor, and Schiff. Serious negotiations began, and in 1891 Hirsch signed over $2.4 million for a relief fund controlled by nine American trustees.[8]

Several months later the baron gave $10 million for the creation of the European-based Jewish Colonization Association (ICA). Through the ICA, whose purpose was to establish Jewish settlements in various parts of the world, major attempts were made to develop Jewish colonies in Argentina. Since the American trustees refused to take shares in the organization or participate in its direction, they were promised a portion of ICA's income. The arrangement, however, often bred resentment, for control of the purse strings permitted the Europeans a decisive vote on many American relief policies.[9]

The stimulus from Hirsch and Heilprin forced Schiff and his circle to face a question larger than immediate relief giving: How could the immigrant masses be absorbed most efficaciously in ways that balanced the needs of the country, the established Jewish community, and the immigrants themselves? The Jewish philanthropists knew what they did not want—congested ghettos seemingly impervious to Americanization, dependent groups converted into a pauper class by charitable handouts, the image of the Jew as unproductive and unassimilable—but they were vague about the remedies. Hirsch's endowment steered them to the implementation of specific ventures, an agenda prompted by their perceptions of what Americans expected of the immigrants: (1) classes in English and the duties of citizenship, (2) training in mechanical and agricultural skills, (3) encouragement of agricultural settlement, and (4) dispersal of the immigrants throughout the country in order to relieve the ghetto and hasten the assimilatory process. The trustees agreed to earmark a portion of the fund for temporary relief, but their prime focus was on aiding those who showed promise of economic independence. Embarking on untried experiments, they set out to chart the paths of the new arrivals. Problems worsened and expenses mounted in direct relation to the immigrant tide. Where we formerly needed hundreds of thousands of dollars, we now need millions, Schiff wrote in 1909. "I am still wondering that we have not been crushed under the weight of these problems."[10]

Schiff, who was involved from the beginning in the establishment of the fund, began a private correspondence with the baron. The two men met in London in 1890, and common business interests as well as the Russian question cemented their association. The American served as one of the original trustees of the fund, and he actively cooperated in many of its enterprises. Although its work paralleled that of some agencies he supported, Schiff never scaled down his independent activities. Publicly he called on wealthy American Jews to support the fund, but privately he worried about the wisdom of accepting European money for American philanthropy. To be sure, it was desperately needed, and he frequently urged the ICA to lighten the American load. But immigrant relief from foreign sources could be interpreted by the American government and public as a form of "assisted" and hence illicit immigration.[11]

The heavy immigration that placed unusual burdens on the established Jewish community magnified the role of American Jews in international Jewish affairs. Baron de Hirsch's endowment was, among other things, a signal of a new respect on the part of Europe for American leaders. Until then, according to Schiff, the Europeans had shifted the burden of the immigrants onto the Americans and, in the case of English Jewish leaders, responded only with "contempt" and "abuse."[12] After the fund was established, the American trustees grew restive under the domination of the baron's advisers in the ICA and the Alliance Israélite Universelle who sought to control the entire emigration process, from the selection of emigrants to relief budgets. A sparring match developed between the two sides that lasted some twenty years. While the Americans complained that the Europeans largely ignored their appeals for financial support, the Europeans retorted that since they funded Jewish rehabilitation in Europe, it was the Americans' responsibility to raise their own money.

Schiff, who in short order became the unofficial solicitor of funds and protagonist of the Americans, was openly resentful, particularly of the French Alliance. Despite his personal contributions to charitable institutions in Europe and Palestine, the banker wondered at the gall of the Europeans who appealed for American aid on behalf of their own projects. They had to realize, he asserted, that no more than a dozen American Jews were in a position to be dunned for significant contributions, and those men were already overburdened. Besides, since Americans disapproved of Jewish money leaving the country, why incur additional ill-feeling? Furthermore, how could the Europeans, who understood neither the American scene nor the specific American projects, decide which emigrants to send or which projects of the fund to support? After all, the Americans bore the brunt of the Russian exodus, and, as had been arranged, they had been promised a share of ICA's income. Since the Europeans had also reneged on their promise to keep the degenerate and the utterly destitute from immigrating to America, the Americans would have no recourse but to oppose free immigration.[13]

Schiff frequently vented his anger at the "Paris Gentlemen" (his term) for their seeming callousness to American sensibilities. He once warned that if American demands were not treated seriously, "self-respect" and "self-preservation" would force the severance of ties with Europe and curtailment of American work. Then, he concluded darkly, the world would judge which side was to blame. Schiff wanted no less than an equal partnership with the Europeans. "I am unwilling," he wrote to Judge Myer Isaacs, first president of the Hirsch fund, "to permit the Paris Gentlemen to address us and deal with us in the dictatorial spirit and tone, which they have assumed. We *are* doing the work, not *under* them, but as their peers, and if they are not satisfied with what we are doing, they can take the responsibility."[14] Since the Europeans were less tractable on the idea of equality, ill-feeling erupted sporadically before World War I.

In 1915, when Schiff testified before the Commission on Industrial Relations, part of the discussion dealt with the Baron de Hirsch Fund. Like the Rockefeller, Sage, and Carnegie funds, the Hirsch Fund's wealth had aroused the curiosity if not uneasiness of the commission. The banker summarized the work of the fund, which by then had grown to $4 million and of which he was still a trustee and vice president. Affirming his unshaken belief in "preventive charity," he spoke with special pride of the fund's training schools and of its "tremendous" success in reducing poverty. A defender of private philanthropy under elitist control, he adamantly opposed the notions that democratizing the choice of trustees or involving the government in its administration could improve the fund's operations.[15]

Relief for the Ghetto

Schiff believed that the purpose of philanthropy in the ghetto transcended temporary physical relief. Both individually and together, the various charities constituted the building blocks in his overall design for remaking the immigrants into proper citizens indistinguishable from other Americans except for religion. As he told his fellow philanthropists, their endeavor should be "to give the poor Jews on the East Side a moral education."[16] Downtowners showed less enthusiasm about institutions that assumed their need of a moral education, but the stewards usually ignored the criticism.

For the sake of their own image among non-Jews just as much as for the immigrants, Schiff and his associates crusaded determinedly for the Americanization of the newcomers. As observers noted, no other ethnic group, not the Slavs nor the Italians, shared the same intense concern. To Jewish leaders, Americanization signified a veritable cure-all. In tune with the environmentalist ideology of the Progressive era, it connoted optimism and a belief in progress. Established Jews employed terms like "moral uplift" to describe the process that would transform the eastern Europeans into clean, healthy, educated, and patriotic Americans. If the ghetto could not be emptied physically, at least its "state of mind" or psychological stranglehold could be broken. Once free of the ghetto's alien way of thinking, the new Americans would be readily acceptable to the larger society.[17]

Recognizing the key role of the public school in the Americanization process, Schiff raised his voice to municipal officials on behalf of adequate schools in the tenement districts. In 1895 he sought to "compel" the mayor and Board of Education to assure enough classroom space for the overcrowded neighborhoods. If the immigrant children were not Americanized through the schools, he warned, they would become "a lasting menace" to society. Similarly, when calling for public funds for free libraries, he stressed the need of educational facilities for the poor and unlettered immigrants.[18] In his eyes the rapid integration of Jews into American society did not conflict with the preservation of Jewish learning. Acting on his own blueprint, he strove to mold an American Jew who was knowledgeable about both American and Jewish culture.

Hardly a single Jewish institution on New York's Lower East Side escaped Schiff's notice. Among the numerous charities that clamored for his support, the banker took a special liking to a few. One, the Hebrew Free Loan Society, differed from most of the others. Founded in 1892 by the eastern Europeans themselves, it was financed largely by dues and donations. The Free Loan made modest non-interest-bearing loans requiring no collateral; the loans were repaid in weekly installments, and losses proved minimal. Gaining a reputation for not humiliating the newcomers, the agency became a source of justifiable pride to the Eastsiders. "I used to attend meetings of the organization," Philip Cowen, publisher of the *American*

Hebrew wrote, "and they were worth going to. The auditorium . . . would be crowded with bearded men and bewigged women who came to the meeting of 'inser society' for they were proud of it, as well they might be. Half of those who were there had themselves benefited by the loans at one time or another and then joined the society out of gratitude that others might be helped."[19]

The popular society, based on biblical precepts, was a "natural" for Schiff's aid and respect. In accordance with the banker's own principles, it encouraged self-help and group responsibility while it steered recipients on the road to independence. Since it protected borrowers against loan sharks, it also reduced Schiff's concern about swindlers who preyed on immigrants. Convinced by the first director of the society that his patronage would draw additional capital donations from affluent Russian Jews, Schiff responded enthusiastically and soon earned the name of the society's "guardian angel." A regular participant at each annual meeting, the banker was unstinting in his praise: "No other society in this city was conducted with such care, such efficiency, and such economy." While other agencies "degenerated" the poor, the Free Loan "regenerated" them. Schiff influenced others of his circle, including Baroness de Hirsch, to aid the society, and he personally donated over $50,000 to the Free Loan's "perpetual loan fund." Over the years his contributions and those of his son amounted to more than $100,000.[20]

Schiff broached a variation of the Free Loan's theme in 1893, a year of economic depression, when he suggested that the Charity Organization Society open pawnshops in the tenement districts based on philanthropic as well as business principles. The suggestion resulted in the establishment of the Provident Loan Society, an ambitious undertaking, supported by wealthy businessmen like J. P. Morgan, James Speyer, and John S. Kennedy, that planned to lend money at minimal interest rates. When Schiff was approached for a $5,000 subscription for the capital fund, he promptly remitted his share as well as subscriptions from two of his partners. Jewish borrowers also made use of this nonsectarian agency, and the Provident like the Free Loan enjoyed tremendous success. Schiff took pride in both agencies, but he thought the Free Loan did better work.[21]

Far different in purpose was the establishment in 1884 of the Hebrew Technical Institute, a vocational school headed by Schiff's brother-in-law, Morris Loeb, that trained young men in crafts and mechanics. The *American Hebrew* proudly reported in 1887 that twenty of the institute's graduates were employed in fields like carpentry and ironwork. "It has been amply demonstrated," the paper boasted, "not only that the Jew *is* fitted for manual labor, but that when he takes hold of it he can teach his Christian neighbor, who has been accustomed to work, new methods and better ones." In this case Christian opinion more than immigrant help appeared to be the major consideration. For Schiff, too, the school was primarily an exercise in image building. He, like other emancipated Jews, had internalized Christian criticism of the unproductive Jew unfit for honest labor, the Jew whose lack of skills and resulting lifestyle threatened to "develop only the baser instincts of mankind." Although they never applied the lesson to their own vocational choices—banking certainly lay outside the accepted meaning of "productive" labor—the established Jews sought to disprove the negative stereotypes via the immigrants. To be sure, they recognized the eastern Europeans' bias against vocational training. "In Russia," a report of the institute noted, "the work of a carpenter is looked down upon as one of the lowest." But pateralism was as determined as it was benevolent, and the German leaders pressed ahead, at times overemphasizing the school's success.[22]

Schiff became an eager advocate of industrial training that would guide young men into "respectable" employment, that is, jobs other than in small shops or in the Jewish and often maligned needle trades, and raise their image among Americans. Calling the typical graduate of the school "an enobling agent . . . , a producer among those who, by inclination and training, have for generations been consumers only," he thought that molding immigrants into skilled workers would both Americanize them and counteract the popular image of Jews as a "foreign element" in society. The banker and his fellow trustees of the Baron de Hirsch Fund put vocational training high on their list of priorities; and using the institute as a model on which to expand, they increased the number of training classes, supplied tools for mechanics, and ultimately found employment for several thousand outside the larger eastern cities. Such efforts, they happily concluded, relieved the ghettos while creating "productive Americans."[23]

Image building, albeit on a much smaller scale, also involved Schiff in encouraging young immigrants whose dreams of a higher education had gone unfulfilled in Europe. Learning of such cases, he and a few others—Michael Heilprin, Rabbi Gustav Gottheil, and Professor E. R. A. Seligman—privately assisted individuals who were likely candidates for professional or intellectual careers. Here the purpose was to counteract the stereotype of the Jew who lacked cultural and aesthetic tastes.[24]

Of all his charities on behalf of the Lower East Side, Schiff's favorite was the Henry Street Settlement and Visiting Nurses' Service. The agency, so different in concept from customary relief giving, was the brainchild of Lillian Wald. A third-generation American from an affluent Jewish home, who had trained as a nurse, Wald dedicated herself to a singular mission—

to live among the immigrant poor and minister to the sick. In 1893 the banker met Wald, then in her mid-twenties, and was impressed by her self-less idealism. He understood that personal nursing care, especially if focused on people generally fearful of hospitalization, offered a wide range of advantages. Above all, it promised to address one of his paramount concerns, the health of the children trapped in the overcrowded ghetto and vulnerable to epidemics. The banker and his mother-in-law, Betty Loeb, agreed to pay the salaries of Wald and a co-worker, but they stipulated that their names not be attached to the service. In short order, Schiff secured the cooperation of the United Hebrew Charities (which permitted Wald to call upon their physicians), the "moral support" of the Board of Health, and within two years a house for the nurses on Henry Street. The nonsectarian pioneering venture that coped with problems of sanitation and personal hygiene as well as sickness drew immediate acclaim. "I envy you the paternity of so admirable a work," Bishop Henry Potter told Schiff after a visit to Henry Street in 1895.

Work in the tenements broadened Wald's sights. Convinced that recreation and the arts, as well as education, were essential components of preventive medicine, she expanded the nurses' service shortly after its inception into a settlement house for the ghetto neighborhood. Nursing remained a central component, but the house on Henry Street gradually added a kindergarten, a playground and gymnastics, classes in art, house-keeping and vocational training, clubs for teenagers, and a dramatics group. Prominent visitors of all stripes flocked to the settlement to observe its activities and participate in its open discussions; many were sensitized to its philosophy of reform. The idea of settlement houses grew increasingly popular in the United States during the 1890s, and Henry Street and the others became, in Allen Davis's words, "spearheads" for Progressive reform.[25]

Schiff took an active interest in Wald's burgeoning enterprises. Responding to her graphic descriptions of tenement hardships, he often added contributions for individual cases or special conditions. A wire to Wald in the summer of 1906 read: "If you can do anything for relief populace tenement from suffering excessive heat, shall gladly place five hundred dollars [not a small sum in those days] at your disposal." The banker funded excursions for children to his summer home in New Jersey, and he enlisted the sympathy and services of his wife and children in the settlement. On one occasion he called on his brother-in-law, a professor of chemistry, to advise on water and heating arrangements! His generosity extended to the staff too, and separate funds were earmarked for the welfare of the nurses. By 1917, Wald's nurses, operating from Henry Street and district offices, were serving close to thirty thousand patients annually. On their behalf, Schiff appealed to Mayor John Mitchel and Comptroller

William Prendergast for municipal aid. In the public interest, he argued, it was wrong to classify Wald's effective medical service in the home as outdoor relief and thereby deny it city assistance. During the last year of his life he also secured a significant contribution for the nurses' service from John D. Rockefeller.[26]

As in the case of Montefiore, benevolence was accompanied by a strain of despotism. Schiff appreciated Wald's hard work, but he demanded efficient accounting and balanced budgets. At the very beginning she reported to him daily about the individual cases she treated—the feverish Goldberg baby, the consumptive Hattie Isaacs, Baby O'Brien's whooping cough, and frail Mrs. Gittelman, who worked as a peddler to support five children and an old mother.[27] The banker carefully watched Wald's expenditures. Cautioning her against running up deficits, he even criticized a phone bill that he thought was excessive (although he proceeded to pay it). Wald cleverly and silently swallowed his criticisms, and her relationship with the Schiffs blossomed into a warm friendship. They exchanged gifts, and she visited them socially. The salutations remained formal—"Miss Wald" and "Mr. Schiff"—but in a voluminous correspondence that lasted for the rest of his life, the friends discussed family matters, travel, and books, as well as Henry Street.[28]

The friendship proved mutually rewarding. Under Schiff's tutelage, Wald grew more worldly, learning from his business acumen and administrative talents. He provided valuable contacts for her in business and government circles; at her request he arranged for Jane Addams of Chicago's famous Hull House to meet with prominent men like Carnegie, Hill, and Harriman. He encouraged many of her ideas—excursions for children, plans for enlarged parks (a popular reform idea), a "respectable" social hall for the Lower East Side—and where necessary he picked up the tab. As she broadened her skills from nursing to social work, she profited from his constant sympathy.[29]

For his part, Schiff found in Wald a trusted sounding board for his views on subjects like Russia, immigration, and social issues. He enjoyed his frequent visits to Henry Street, which soon became an "old haunt," where he mingled comfortably with the Eastsiders. Labor matters, a favorite topic at the settlement, engaged him, the archcapitalist, in spirited but friendly discussions with union sympathizers. The story goes that on one occasion the banker and an Eastside labor leader traded biblical quotations in Hebrew. Wald later recalled that his visits apprised Schiff of the appalling conditions under which the immigrants worked. On one occasion he tried, through the settlement, to bring together management and labor in the garment industry. At times Wald's pro-labor sympathies clashed with Schiff's views. However, she stood her ground and at least once succeeded in changing his opinions. The house on Henry Street exposed a side of the ghetto world that Schiff hadn't known, and it gave him a keener insight into the area and its residents.[30]

Schiff and Wald agreed on the nonsectarian and nonracial character of the Visiting Nurses' Service and the settlement. "One God has made us all," he assured her when she informed him that she was treating Blacks. He disapproved generally of settlements with a religious purpose, and accordingly, the Henry Street house made no provision for marking Jewish holidays or customs. Schiff even proposed on one occasion that a non-Jew be chosen for president, reasoning that an emphasis on nonsectarianism would broaden the base of public support. That comment alone, besides Wald's accounts of the participants in the house's activities, indicated, however, that the settlement was known as a Jewish agency.[31]

His emphasis on nonsectarianism notwithstanding, Schiff drew the line at the celebration of Christmas. The substitution by Jews of Christmas for Hanukkah was "both thoughtless and faithless." Worse still, it exposed Jewish youngsters in the settlement to a religion that they might come to regard as superior to their own. One year he ordered Wald to remove the tree that she had set up for the nursery, which then included only Jewish children. If Jews were a minority in the nursery, it might be different, he said, "but it is both unpardonable and unjustifiable to tempt little children into the customs of a religion foreign to theirs, innocent as this may appear to be, and this must not be tolerated." His personal feelings aside, the banker was well aware of rampant immigrant suspicions of Christianizing influences in settlement houses.[32]

The quarrel over Christmas celebrations exposed a deeper problem. To be sure, the settlement houses, even those without formal classes in English or civics, worked to Americanize the immigrant, but did Americanization include acceptance of or conformity with Christian practices? Most Americans would have said yes. At the turn of the century they did not acknowledge religious or cultural pluralism, and despite the rapid strides of secularization, the United States was still very much a Protestant nation. Thus, if Christian usages were American as much as Christian, why shouldn't Jews celebrate Christmas too? Wald obviously did not find the prospect offensive, but Schiff did. Yet he and his fellow philanthropists failed to come up with guidelines for balancing the needs of both Jewish identity and Americanization. The issue strained uptown-downtown relations, and it continued to haunt Jewish philanthropies for many years.

Wald and her work, more than anything else, drew Schiff closer to the environmentalist approach to reform. Reformers like Wald believed that ghetto conditions rather than the residents created the social and moral problems. A champion of the causes of women, children, and organized labor, Wald and her eyewitness reports of housing and factory conditions that called for legislative remedies elicited her patron's compassion. His support of housing reform and child labor laws, his aid to strikers rendered hungry by their strikes, and even his gift of a public fountain in the heart of the ghetto—an attempt to lighten the oppressiveness of the tenements— bore her imprint. Wald did not convert the conservative banker into a Progressive, but she deepened his sympathy for the have-nots and for government intervention on their behalf. At the celebration marking the twentieth anniversary of the settlement house he spoke like a true reformer: "The time is long past when the proposition that that Government was the best which governed least."[33]

Money alone did not solve all ghetto problems. Delinquency and prostitution, for example, usually required cooperation with the authorities. The stewards, however, could not afford to ignore those matters, since the image of the entire Jewish community was on the line. Schiff never agreed with his friend, Mayer Sulzberger, who said that Jews had as much right to their share of criminals as any other group, and he was horrified by Jewish crime and by the widespread existence of prostitution in the Jewish quarter. "Prostitution in our city, one almost can say, has become Semitic," he wrote to leaders of the ICA in 1901. "We Jews, who have hitherto boasted of the moral purity of our people, must hang our heads when the question is raised." The *American Hebrew* spoke for Schiff and other leaders when it wrote that "the vile traffickers in this awful trade are mainly persons of Jewish parents, who have used Jewish young men as their debased agents to debauch Jewish girls." Our "paramount duty," the paper insisted, was to "hound" these "contemptible wretches" who polluted "the virtuous Jewish home" out of the community.[34]

Exposés of Tammany-protected prostitutes and pimps led to a municipal crusade against vice at the turn of the century. To the chagrin of Jewish leaders, the Lower East Side had earned the dubious distinction of being a flourishing red-light district. In an effort to combat the evil a non-partisan committee of fifteen prominent citizens, including Schiff, investigated the increase of prostitution in the city and considered appropriate legislation (1900–1901). Although Jewish leaders would have preferred to deal with the matter privately—to clean house before non-Jews learned how filthy the house was—it had become a full-blown public issue by the time of the mayoral election of 1901.

The campaign pitched a reform ticket headed by Fusionist candidate Seth Low against the Tammany machine. Taking their cue from the Jewish stewards, the reformers stressed the issue of prostitution in their appeals to downtown Jews. One campaign leaflet in Yiddish, which included endorsements of Low by Schiff and several others of his circle, was typical. Entitled *Hilul Ha-Shem* (literally, "desecration of God's name"), it painted in lurid terms why the Jewish quarter was blamed for immorality, and it exhorted voters to vindicate Jewish honor by supporting the reformers. Low and his ticket won the election, and although some spokesmen for the ghetto blamed "a few German Jews" for charging that downtown was the source of immorality, both eastern Europeans and Germans celebrated the Fusionist victory.[35]

The election adumbrated significant changes in Jewish behavior and in communal leadership. Not only did it show cooperation between uptown and downtown, this time as equals in the polling booth, but it taught uptown that it could cast off its habitual reluctance to parade Jewish interests publicly in elections.

Public exposés as well as counterefforts by Jewish agencies increased during the decade, but prostitution on the Lower East Side persisted. Behind closed doors organizations individually and collectively grappled with the problem of Jewish vice, now broadened by the charge that Jews ran international white slavery rings. Quietly, Schiff too continued his personal efforts, purportedly sanctioning the use of detectives and raids to stamp out prostitution. In 1906, Therese Schiff made a $10,000 donation enabling the National Council of Jewish Women to support a home for "wayward" girls.[36] Again the stewards demonstrated that social issues feeding anti-Semitism and immigration restrictionism and indirectly besmirching the name of the established Jews could not be left to the newcomers alone.

Rabbis as Missionaries

Americanization did not stop with the public school or settlement house. Acculturation was a two-sided process: adoption by the immigrant of American manners and behavior and, simultaneously, his renunciation of alien separatistic habits. Since Schiff and his circle viewed the religious customs of the newcomers as obstacles to full integration, their crusade for Americanization invaded the synagogue. Undeterred by the religious (or indeed irreligious) sentiments of the eastern Europeans, the stewards, many of whom were Reform Jews, had two goals. They sought to reconcile Jewish traditionalism with American modernity, and they hoped to stem the inroads of secularization within the community. Their answer to both problems lay in the reorganization of a Conservative institution, the Jewish Theologial Seminary (JTS). Here too the leaders had no qualms about prescribing for the new immigrants, and never did they sound out representatives from the ghetto. The fact that the seminary needed eastern European acceptance for its survival was at best a minor issue.

The support of a Conservative school by wealthy Reform Jews gave rise to questions that immediately or over time would plague the institution.

Did the blueprint of the stewards mean the school to be merely transitional, that is, until proper Americanization was achieved and the eastern Europeans were made ready for Reform? Where did ultimate power lie, in the hands of the donors or in the faculty and academic heads? How long would or should Reform Jews, unconcerned and uninterested in the development of a Conservative religious movement, support a seminary that competed with theirs, the Hebrew Union College (HUC)? Schiff and his associates, all practical men, did not anticipate future problems. Their primary concern, at least for their own generation, remained Americanization.[37]

Although the German stewards preached to the immigrants on the blessings of integration, they never called for a renunciation of religion. Schiff, for one, maintained that Americanism and Judaism were inseparable, that the Jewish religious faith supplied the "moral stamina" necessary for outstanding citizenship. The banker and his associates feared the secularists and atheists—or worse still, the socialists and anarchists—as much as they despised the eastern European brand of Orthodoxy. A secularized Jewry of any sort reduced Jewishness to an ethnic or racial category that challenged their belief that religion was the core, if not the sole meaning, of Judaism. It also threatened to confirm the teachings of anti-Semites, for whom a Jew, with or without religion, remained a Jew. Since Americans accepted religious distinctions but frowned upon radicalism and ethnic separatism, the stewards felt justified in judging the modern religious Jew unquestionably preferable to the secular Yiddish culturalist, socialist, or atheist.[38]

When labor leader and Zionist Joseph Barondess once asked Schiff to support a Jewish National Radical School, the banker flatly declined. Bristling at the words *national* and *radical* as well as at the idea of a Yiddish education, he offered a rare explanation of his beliefs:

The Jewish Nation, hardly any one will deny, was called into existence for the express purpose of becoming the bearer of a great religion and later became dispersed among the Nations . . . to carry the Word of God into the wide world. Those who deny the dogma of the Jewish religion . . . should be the last to have any justification for seeking the reestablishment of a Jewish Nation [in Palestine]. . . . Nor is it, in my opinion, justified to seek to perpetuate the use of the Yiddish language in this country, . . . and the proposition that there is wanted a new type of school, "National instead of religious, Yiddish instead of English or even Hebraic," is too unreasonable to deserve consideration. I do not know what is meant by a "radical" school. I do not like radical measures. Social justice must be reached by evolutionary and not by revolutionary methods. I have every respect for the honest and serious socialist, but if the creed of the Jewish Socialist includes a denial of the Jewish religion and seeks to supersede the Public School by Yiddish instead of English schools, . . . then I shall prefer to have none of it.[39]

To preserve a Judaism palatable to Americans and to shield immigrant youth from dangerous "isms," the German Jews had to co-opt rabbis and teachers—"missionaries," Schiff and others called them—in their drive for Americanization. For several years the banker toyed with the idea of establishing a People's Synagogue on the Lower East Side. "I felt that the younger element of the Eastside down-town population were losing their moral hold," and, alienated from Old World Orthodoxy, they became "ready adherents of every other 'ism' rather than of Judaism." He sought a rabbi, preferably one who would live among the Eastsiders, who was "a thorough Jew" and "thoroughly American"—and who was "neither an extreme orthodox, nor extreme reformer"—to teach religion and a modern form of worship. He was prepared to invest heavily in the project, but neither of his candidates, the young and charismatic rabbis Stephen Wise and Judah Magnes, was willing to assume the responsibility.[40]

Although many of the stewards were Reform Jews, the goal of Americanization transcended denominational loyalties. They understood that Reform temples, which showed a blatant distaste for the newcomers and which highlighted the socioeconomic differences between the old and new Jewries, were utterly alien to the eastern Europeans. The latter, whether observant or not, usually perceived Reform as the penultimate step to total assimilation. They could swallow neither Reform's wholesale disregard of custom and ritual nor its repudiation of Jewish ethnicity. In time, acculturation and economic mobility would prepare the eastern Europeans for Reform rabbis trained at HUC, but the Americanizers were unwilling to wait a generation or more. Those who, like Schiff, realized that control of the community would soon pass to the more numerous newcomers, sought through Americanization to perpetuate their own values and communal vision. If a compromise between Reform and shtetl Orthodoxy was necessary to produce religious leaders, modern but sufficiently traditional for immigrant tastes, so be it.

From its inception in 1886 under the leadership of Rabbis Sabato Morais and Alexander Kohut, JTS focused on Americanization and on the spiritual needs of the eastern Europeans. An appeal for support from the first president of the seminary's lay association declared that the immigrants "need ministers who will also be missionaries, to refine their lives, elevate them and maintain that high standard of moral character which has always been the boast of our race." However, since the school would also serve to counter the tide of Reform, its attraction for Schiff, an affiliated Reform Jew, was all the more interesting. He gave money for a new building and for the library, and he gave time, even serving as judge of student debates. If not for his donations, Schiff said, the institution would have been ruined. Nonetheless, the school rapidly declined. At the turn of the century, when plans were laid to reorganize JTS and invite a world-renowned scholar, Dr. Solomon Schechter, to be its head, the banker's involvement escalated. He became a major fund-raiser for the seminary as well as its largest contributor. To Schechter he was identified as "*the* Yehudi of New York."[41]

Why a Conservative seminary became a favorite project of a Reform Jew, second only to Montefiore in his affection, sheds light on both the man's social vision and his personal conduct. Americanization was always a primary impetus. "The solution of the Jewish question in this country," Schiff said, "depends largely on the success of the Educational Alliance [the major settlement house on the Lower East Side, of which he was a founder and one-time president] and of this seminary." The mission of its graduates was to harmonize the religion and the "often peculiar" habits of the eastern Europeans with American customs. Since the main stumbling block was to find rabbis acceptable to the Russians, an appropriate seminary had to be created. In the words of one JTS supporter (and the syntax strongly suggests Schiff), "if to the seminary there can be attracted young men from the tremendous colony, who will be educated up town, and then return to the Ghetto, it is believed Russians there will accept them for guidance."[42]

There were other reasons, too. First, Schiff desired the seminary to be the fountainhead of a vibrant American Jewish scholarship. He always hoped that the United States would become a flourishing center of Jewish religious and cultural creativity. His friend Mayer Sulzberger explained that *am-harazim* (ignoramuses—and Sulzberger included himself) needed to support schools. Second, as one who wished that the United States would be the melting pot for different forms of Judaism, Schiff entertained hopes for an institution that might reduce denominational wrangling. What really was the difference among believing Jews, he once asked, as long as their watchword was *Sh'ma Yisrael?*[43]

On both scores the banker thought that HUC, the Cincinnati-based Reform seminary and one to which he generously contributed, fell short. Most important, it had produced no prominent scholars or teachers like the Reform pioneers of nineteenth-century Germany. Moreover, its very location was wrong, for Cincinnati lacked "an academic atmosphere." Instead of growing into "a high seat of learning," HUC merely "vegetates," he wrote to the chairman of the board in 1900. Moreover, by the mid-1880s the college, originally planned for the training of all American rabbis, had become a partisan Reform institution that alienated non-Reformers. Schiff continued to support HUC, but he defended the existence of Orthodoxy as well as Reform on the American scene. Reform, a "healthy liberalism," saved many Jews from leaving the fold, while Orthodoxy preserved the heritage that nourished Reform. Like Solomon Schechter, with whom he worked closely on the reorganization of the Conservative school, he preferred the concept of "Catholic Israel" to denominationalism. A seminary that taught "reasonable" Orthodoxy yet, "with tolerance to all views," permitted its graduates to fashion their own religious behavior was his ideal. He explained to one graduating class that while he rejected an Orthodoxy that isolated itself from modern conditions, he looked to JTS to produce well-trained traditionalist rabbis.[44]

Personal sentiments also attracted Schiff to Conservative Judaism. Raised by his parents as an Orthodox Jew, he admitted to "a certain Orthodoxy in me." He confessed to Israel Zangwill that "the familiar words of the Orthodox prayer book have . . . the peculiar charm for me, which the reminiscences of one's early references and surroundings are so apt to call forth." A man who was equally at home in an Orthodox synagogue as in a Reform temple and one whom Mayer Sulzberger called a "conservative reformed" Jew, he often said that a good Reform Jew first had to have been an Orthodox Jew. Publicly, Schiff described himself as a Jew who was much attached to tradition and who would "do naught to help to destroy the reasonable fences, which have been erected in order to maintain the integrity of our faith."[45]

Like his friend, the Reform theologian Kaufmann Kohler, Schiff abandoned the teachings of Samson Raphael Hirsch, their Orthodox mentor in Frankfurt, but he was never as extreme as Kohler or as ready to slough off traditional observances and ritual. He wrote despairingly to one Reform rabbi: "Unfortunately, the large mass of American Israelites have become a law unto themselves, doing what appears right in their own eyes without reference to the Law of Moses and tradition." Not an indifference to tradition but social reasons had led Schiff to affiliate with Temple Emanu-El, the "cathedral" of Reform, and Temple Beth El, where Kohler officiated. His friends and associates were members, and he doubtless was well aware that Reform symbolized Jewish affluence and social status.[46]

A close associate and biographer, Cyrus Adler, concluded that Schiff's religious behavior was as much a product of his own judgment as of Reform influences. A Jew who knew some Hebrew and who liberally peppered his remarks with biblical and rabbinic verses, Schiff recited the daily morning prayers, and he regularly attended Sabbath services. His observance of traditional Sabbath rules grew more lax over time, but since he regularly abstained from work on that day, J. P. Morgan was once forced to cancel an important business meeting scheduled for Saturday. On Friday evenings, always a family occasion at his home, prayers were said, candles were lighted, and, according to tradition, the children were blessed. Schiff did not keep the dietary laws, but he fasted on Yom Kippur, conducted the family seder on Passover (once even in Japan), and lighted Hanukkah candles.

Visitors to his home saw a mezuzah on the door; non-Jews were impressed by the recitation of grace after meals. Younger members of the family found his religious code too rigid for their tastes, but his friends recognized a God-fearing man who discerned the finger of Providence in the lives of individuals and nations.[47]

Schiff had rebelled as a youth against the Orthodox discipline of his home, but as he matured away from his father's influence, he was able to relate more sympathetically to traditionalists. His willingness to accept "reasonable" in place of what he called "uncompromising orthodoxy" may have reflected his German background, at least in part. Professor Gotthard Deutsch of HUC, a contemporary who traced Schiff's antecedents, wrote that the banker was understanding of Frankfurt Orthodoxy, an Orthodoxy that signified "men of good secular education, of high standing in the community, and perfect social manners" who were at the same time strictly observant Jews. It was Schiff's belief, Deutsch continued, that the eastern Europeans could develop into the Frankfurt type. There is no evidence that the banker tried consciously to replicate the Frankfurt experience, but some similarities surfaced in his American Jewish agenda. The statement on objectives formulated in 1850 by the Frankfurt Israelitische Religionsgesellschaft (IRG), for example, called not only for the protection of Judaism as it developed but for a synagogue, school, and other institutions that combined reverence for tradition with "a sensitivity" to the "progressive demands of the times." Moreover, thanks to his upbringing, Schiff was mindful of Orthodox sensibilities. He disapproved of Saturday meetings for Jewish communal agencies, and he refused to attend if written notes were taken on the Sabbath.[48]

An officer for many years of the UAHC, the lay arm of the Reform movement, Schiff loyally supported Emanu-El and Beth El. Nonetheless, he missed a religious vibrancy and a knowledge of Judaism in those citadels of Reform. It was "mortifying," he said, that Emanu-El's members were unequipped to use the Judaica library that the congregation owned. For a while he tried, albeit futilely, to foster a "renascence of Judaism" at the temple that might spark a deeper religious commitment among the young adults. Schiff also missed learned congregational rabbis. After one Yom Kippur service he confided to fellow congregant Marshall: "Fortunately, I understood little of what Dr. [Joseph] Silverman said in the pulpit." Nor did Reform temples satisfy him when he commemorated the deaths of his parents. On those occasions he sought out traditionalist settings for reciting the *Kaddish* prayer.[49]

Like post-Emancipation Jews in general, Schiff fashioned a personal eclectic code of religious behavior that drew from both traditionalism and Reform. His ethnic sentiments differed from classical Reform, but he never clearly defined how much ethnicity or Jewish "groupness" was inherent in his religious faith. At times the issue of Jewish peoplehood as opposed to Jewish religion, particularly with regard to Zionism, generated contradictions and ambiguities in his words and actions. Nor did he successfully instill loyalty to religious faith or ritual practices in his children and grandchildren. Lacking both his Frankfurt training and a serious Jewish education in America, Frieda and Mortimer were given only private lessons in Bible readings, which neither enjoyed, and Morti celebrated his bar mitzvah at Temple Emanu-El.[50] Their father's own religious conduct also failed to impress them. Ritual observance as defined by Schiff was the enforced norm for the household, but to the untrained it was bound to appear unintelligible and unappealing.

In 1900 the *American Hebrew* ran a symposium on whether HUC and the pre-Schechter JTS should merge. The time seemed ripe; both institutions were in desperate need of funds, and neither had appointed a suitable replacement for its first president (Morais of JTS and Isaac Mayer Wise of HUC). Schiff favored a merger, and he made public his criticisms of HUC. Again he urged unity. A seminary need not be either Reform or Orthodox, "especially not in this country, with its constant shifting movements, and where the orthodox Jew of to-day is to-morrow found in the reform camp." Far more important was "how can Judaism be maintained as an active force in the daily life of our people, so that they may not become swamped by materialism and indifference, as is seriously threatened." In that effort Orthodox and Reform "can, should and must join hands." Schiff may have correctly assessed currents on the Jewish religious scene, but he underrated the genuine ideological commitments that doomed the idea of merger.[51]

A few months after the symposium, at an informal gathering of friends, Cyrus Adler happened to remark that New York's Jews were allowing the Conservative seminary, the city's only Jewish institution of higher learning, to die. Schiff was struck by the comment and its implicit challenge. In short order, with the help of Adler and Louis Marshall, he mobilized a few wealthy Reform laymen, like Leonard Lewisohn and Daniel and Simon Guggenheim, to establish an endowment of $500,000 for reorganizing the institution.[52] The venture appealed to other individuals as well, traditonalists and reformers alike, who were drawn principally by the call for Americanization. Some, again irrespective of religious affiliation, also intended that "this institution is . . . to be the seat of Jewish learning and scholarship in this country." Their stand reflected a deep respect or even a personal commitment to Jewish studies. Marshall, for example, the attorney, communal worker, and president of Temple Emanu-El, devoted leisure time to the translation of Hebrew prayers and to the study of the Book of Job.[53]

Enthusiasm mounted when Schechter arrived in New York—in Schiff's words "eine grosse Acquisition" for America. The banker took an instant liking to Schechter, an academic who fused eastern European roots and Western scholarship and who preached against religious extremism of both left and right. Just as Schechter illustrated Schiff's ideal of an American seminary, so did the charter of the newly incorporated JTS spell out objectives that the banker had long endorsed: "the perpetuation of the tenets of the Jewish religion . . . the pursuit of biblical and archaeological research; the advancement of Jewish scholarship; the establishment of a library, and . . . the education of Jewish rabbis and teachers." To complete the framework, Schiff purchased land near Columbia University and erected a building for the school and its library. A literal and figurative symbol of the upward move from the ghetto, the choice of Morningside Heights, along with tighter requirements for admission and for faculty appointments, testified to his expectations of a scholarly institution. An appreciative Mayer Sulzberger, a fellow director of JTS and himself a devotee of Jewish scholarship, congratulated his friend with the biblical verse "How goodly are thy tents, O Jacob!"[54]

The theme of a seminary dedicated to a Judaism transcending denominational differences echoed in Schechter's inaugural address of 1902. Schiff picked up the same idea a year later at the dedication of the new building. Again he talked of "an institution which should appeal to all desiring to prepare for the Jewish Ministry." It wasn't long, however, before vicious attacks on the school from both the Reform and the Orthodox aired in the Jewish press. Schiff comforted Schechter, encouraging him to stand firm and disregard the attacks, while he, Schiff, pressured representative religious leaders to call off the more outspoken critics. The "very undignified and very unjustifiable jealousy and intolerance" on the part of HUC supporters "will and must cease," he warned Kaufmann Kohler, president of the Reform college. And with an appropriate verse from the Book of Exodus he reminded Orthodox rabbi H. P. Mendes that God's blessing applied to the seminary too.[55] Nevertheless, under the weight of the opposition the dream of an all-inclusive seminary evaporated.

Schiff became a familiar figure at JTS, and as with Montefiore he expected frequent visits by other directors. Board meetings were held at his home and the school's investments were handled in his office, but students and faculty met him at social affairs and at the annual commencements. With Schechter he discussed issues of all sorts, and despite occasional clashes, notably over Zionism, the two quick-tempered men enjoyed each other's company. Schiff's Reform affiliation aroused little reaction. To be sure, Dr. Mordecai Kaplan, dean of the school's Teachers Institute, mocked Schiff's plea for Jewish religion after he saw him at a non-kosher dinner, but Kaplan's jaundiced comments about JTS figures were not unusual. For his part, Schiff respected the seminary's traditionalist conduct. When he attended holiday or Sabbath services, his driver let him off two blocks away;

all knew that he rode, but he would not spoil the traditionalist ambience. At Montefiore Schiff passed on all policies, but he stayed clear of religious rules and customs at JTS. At one commencement he charged the graduates to hold fast to the spirit of the Torah, "which fundamentally must not be altered." The Law must never become "a sterile letter."[56] Such remarks, however, could have come as easily from Reformers as from Conservatives.

The seminary took its Americanizing role seriously. It required applicants for the rabbinate to hold a B.A. degree and to be well grounded in secular subjects. Courses in homiletics, elocution, and pastoral work taught the students how to deliver sermons in English and conduct decorous services. Although Schiff worried lest the faculty show too little of an "American spirit," the men appointed by Schechter imparted a Western, scientific approach to scholarship. Schechter himself urged that the seminary give heed to American ideals. He advised that in a country so loyal to the Bible, the school pay greater attention to biblical studies than was customary in Europe. Schiff, who knew of Schechter's fascination with Lincoln, bought a bronze tablet of the Gettysburg address for display at the school, perhaps to inspire the men to become "self-reliant, dignified Americans." Meantime, the directors continued to stress the aim of Americanization in appeals to students as well as potential donors. Pushing for the Americanization of the Russians, members of the board, like Schiff, assumed that Americanization did not require shortchanging Judaism.[57]

The major benefactor of JTS, Schiff underwrote the school's training program for teachers.[58] His purchase of famous private collections as well as individual books for the library was equally impressive. The library would have been still richer had World War I not cut short his plan to buy the vast collection of books and manuscripts amassed by Baron David Guenzburg of St. Petersburg. But although Schiff and his fellow directors carefully watched the seminary's endowment and investments, the returns did not cover operating expenses. Repeatedly, the board was called on to find additional money for faculty salaries, needy students, and pensions for the widows of Schechter and Professor Israel Friedlaender. Schiff, the treasurer and the wealthiest, despaired of what he called a hand-to-mouth existence, but he responded to most requests. When he agreed to loans for rabbinical students, he stipulated only partial aid; he insisted that the young men had to learn to make sacrifices for the sake of their careers. Deficits were attacked in a straightforward Schiff-like manner: "He would compute the sum, and on his own pad, with a pencil, write out: 'I agree to give $—— to meet this deficit,' the amount he named usually being one half of the total. Then he would pass it around to such of his fellow directors as he thought would join him, and hand the slip back to the chairman, with the sum generally completed."[59]

Financial considerations led Schiff and others to consider a merger with

Dropsie College in Philadelphia, a postgraduate school that offered advanced courses in Judaic studies. Incorporated in 1907, Dropsie was a better endowed school and looked like a serious competitor. Schiff was prepared to move the seminary to Philadelphia, but legal obstacles prevented any serious negotiations. The directors also sought financial aid from the Orthodox of the Lower East Side. It was a logical move, since most of the students were of east European origin and their training at JTS was to be used on behalf of the immigrants. Schiff and Marshall personally canvassed the synagogues in the ghetto, asking for one dollar from each member, but the response was chilling. The Eastsiders were suspicious of a seminary sponsored by Reform Jews, where English had supplanted Yiddish as the language of instruction and where the old ways of training rabbis had been discarded. The Reform *American Israelite*, amused at the spectacle of wealthy American Jews appealing for aid, correctly pointed out that if the Eastsiders responded they would demand a say in the seminary's governance. Opposition from the secularists as well as the Orthodox, however, precluded any grass-roots support and made the issue of governance a moot point. Attempts at popular fund-raising, except for appeals by the school's graduates, were soon abandoned, and the anomaly of a Conservative institution supported largely by Reform donors persisted.[60]

One appeal by Schiff to the Lower East Side drew criticism from Henrietta Szold, a close friend of the seminary circle. Although she too opposed rigid Orthodoxy, she thought it in "abominable" taste, as well as inaccurate, for the banker to have claimed that more "true" Judaism had existed in New York City before the immigrants arrived. Furthermore, who was he to urge Jews to renounce Orthodoxy? Even if Szold's opinion of Schiff and "Schiffian Judaism" was overly harsh, her words were doubtless voiced by many immigrants.[61] Schiff ignored such criticism; a school accredited by him was beyond reproach. Neither he nor the East Side deemed the issue important enough to test his leadership by a vote of confidence.

The firm foundations set by Schiff and his associates enabled the seminary to outlive most other institutions for Americanizing the new immigrants. In time, as the suspicions of the Eastsiders were allayed, the school's appeal to the children of immigrants grew. JTS turned out rabbis and teachers who mediated the extremes of Reform and Orthodoxy and, in opposition to secularism, offered the second generation a comfortable way of blending traditional faith and ethnic loyalties with American life. Fast becoming a pillar of Zionism cast in religious terms, the seminary in turn subtly influenced men like Schiff and Marshall to a more positive stand on Jewish nationalism. At the same time, the school developed into the source of Jewish scholarship that the directors envisioned. Schiff did not live to see the institution's steady progress, but there is little question that he would have judged his work for JTS to have been a sound investment.

Uptown/Downtown

Downtowners made good use of agencies endowed and run by uptowners—Nathan Straus's pasteurized milk stations, the United Hebrew Charities, the Henry Street Settlement, or the Educational Alliance. Acculturating to their new surroundings with or without the stewards' help, most newcomers showed that their aspirations did not differ radically from what the German Jews preached. The Eastsiders also wished to Americanize rapidly; they too aimed at economic independence, if not affluence; and they too sought to escape the confines of the ghetto. Bearers of the same Jewish heritage as the Germans, they also labored to meet their philanthropic obligations. Soon after their arrival they organized their own network of charities, thereby challenging the monopoly of the uptowners. The influential centrist elements within the Jewish quarter (i.e., the middle class or would-be middle class) were the ones most in accord with the stewards. Even those in the nascent Zionist movement, as Arthur Goren has cogently observed, chose their leaders "in the patrician image."[62] When uptown and downtown later joined forces in other communal endeavors, like relief drives, the *kehillah*, and the first American Jewish Congress, downtown cast its votes for leading uptowners.

To be sure, genuine and profound differences in matters of religious belief, social and cultural behavior, and Jewish identity separated the immigrants and the established Jews, but the wide chasm that developed was nurtured as well by emotional reactions to the steward/ward relationship. Downtowners were afraid of their affluent uptown patrons, who, as one Yiddish article put it, regarded the eastern European as a "schnorrer, a tramp, a good-for-nothing." In the offices of the German-run philanthropies, the article continued, the immigrant was "questioned like a criminal. He trembles like a leaf, as if he were standing before a Russian official." Although downtowners expected uptown's aid and protection, they smarted under the often humilating treatment dished out by the German "yahudim," who ignored immigrant sensitivities and never tired of faulting their "improper" behavior. For their part, uptowners resented the financial burdens thrust upon them. While they chided downtown to pull its weight, they feared the damage their alien brethren might work on the image of American Jews. Each side had a list of grievances, bluntly summarized by the president of B'nai B'rith, an eminent member of the Jewish establishment:

The Western Jew treats his co-religionist from Eastern Europe as an inferior. He considers him ignorant, superstitious, bigoted, hypocritical, cunning, ungrateful, quarrelsome, unclean, and in many other ways abominable. In the eyes of the Eastern Jew, the Western Jew is a cad. His education is superficial and flashy; his philanthropy ostentatious, and insincere; his manners a cheap imitation of the Gentiles upon whom he fawns; his religion a miserable compromise in which appearances count for everything; his assumption of superiority another proof that "every ass thinks himself fit to stand among the king's horses."[63]

The German-Russian rift drew from European roots and flourished in the United States from the beginning of the mass immigration. Established Jews aired their complaints at organizational conventions, in lectures and sermons, and through the Anglo-Jewish press. The eastern Europeans launched counterattacks, usually by writers in the Yiddish press, who discussed specific grievances (e.g., the lack of Jewish content in Jewish institutions and on occasion the basic issue of elitism versus democracy).[64]

In 1903 two indictments of the German stewards rocked the New York Jewish community. The first, a biting satire by the Yiddish playwright Jacob Gordin, was entitled *The Benefactors of the East Side*. Caricaturing the overbearing philanthropist, his schemes for Americanizing immigrants, and his retinue of sycophants that included an unctuous, hypocritical Reform rabbi and a matron who feared physical contamination from the new arrivals, Gordin mocked the arrogance and pretentiousness of the established leaders. Schiff was obviously the model for the wealthy philanthropist, Ashley Jefferson Joske. In the play, Joske convenes a meeting at his home of a few uptowners, one labor leader to represent the Lower East Side (the only decent character), and a reporter who will give the philanthropist the publicity he desires. The philanthropist outlines his concern for downtown in flowery terms: Lincoln freed the slaves, and we are like Lincoln; true, the downtowners are neither Blacks nor Ethiopians, but they are (almost as lowly) Russians and Romanians; since we are human beings, we need to make them—the beggars, idlers, radicals—into worthy citizens; all this in the name of truth, love, humanity, progress, civilization. Schiff doubtless knew of the parody, but he stayed aloof from the spirited discussion of the play in the press.[65]

A second critic was Dr. Isaac Rubinow, a Russian-born and American-trained physician and economist, who wrote a strong defense of ghetto life. He said that concentration in cities was natural; since opportunities for employment were better, other nationalities, not only the Jews, followed the same track. Questioning the strongest boast of the philanthropists, Rubinow also claimed that the newcomers helped themselves, without aid from the outside, to achieve economic independence. Nor did he have patience for the belief that the ghetto exacerbated anti-Semitism. The social status of the Jewish immigrants was higher than that of many other nationalities, and besides, the newcomers were Americanizing rapidly. A second and much longer article by Rubinow, for a Russian Jewish journal, doubtless had few American readers, but it too expressed some of downtown's feelings. Here Rubinow again soft-pedaled the issue of anti-Semitism: there was no "Jewish Question" in New York. As for the contempt of the Germans for the eastern Europeans, he denied the insults hurled by uptown at the newcomers in the antiprostitution campaign of 1901.[66]

Efforts at conciliation—reminders to the Germans of the prejudice they had met at the hands of the early Sephardim, calls to remove the barriers that separated the two groups, even an article on the children's page of the *American Hebrew* on the evil of prejudice—had little effect on the antagonism of uptown and downtown. Compounding the bitterness, downtown did not care to acknowledge the role of the Germans as their defenders against hostile elements (immigration restrictionists, missionaries, dishonest ticket agencies, hoodlums) in the non-Jewish society, while uptown held back on sheer human understanding. Marshall, quoting a downtown spokesman, admitted that the latter's words rang true: "The difficulty with the new Russian immigrant was that . . . he was looked after, so far as his material wants were concerned, by his German brethren, but they nevertheless held themselves aloof and refrained from giving him the brotherly advice which he required more than he did the material assistance."[67]

Projects in which Schiff was involved, like the Baron de Hirsch Fund, settlement houses, and the JTS, received a fair share of criticism from downtowners,[68] but personally the man escaped virtually unscathed. His wealth and status commanded the immigrants' deference and respect; his generosity, their gratitude. Most important to them were his accessibility and genuine concern. More than a donor who mailed out checks from his Fifth Avenue mansion, the banker became a familiar and trusted figure on New York's Lower East Side, one who, contrary to popular lore, didn't hold his nose in the company of immigrants. Although he despised their "enslavement" to Yiddish, he participated in their meetings, listened sympathetically to individual tales of hardship, supported their schools and libraries, and even attended funerals of prominent downtowners. The masses were largely ignorant of his work against Jewish crime[69] and Christian missionaries, but they did know that they could turn to him to combat discrimination in employment and on the campus or to ask their employers to excuse their absence on the Jewish high holy days. Downtowners appreciated Schiff's encouragement of their efforts for economic independence and mutual self-help as well as his work with their independent philanthropies like the Free Loan Society. They also saw a man who publicly touted the virtues of the new immigrants. Within fifty years, the banker predicted optimistically before World War I, the amalgamation of the German and Russian "was destined . . . to produce the finest Jewish type of all time."[70]

Downtown responded to Schiff's warmth and reciprocated with loyalty and affection. Known as "unser Yankele" (literally, "our little Jacob," a Yiddish term of affection)[71] rather than as the heavy-handed patron, Schiff was able to expand his control over a broad constituency. The theoretical issue of elitist direction of the Jewish community in a democratic host country had yet to be tested.

The first test was not long in coming. It was foreshadowed in the 1903 episodes, and it was abetted by the immigration after the Kishinev pogrom (1903) of a younger and more radical element of Russian Jews unwilling to bow to elitist leaders. When a wave of Russian pogroms erupted in 1905, the stewards organized the National Committee for Relief of Sufferers by Russian Massacres (NCRSRM), a nationwide relief drive under their direction. Downtown was aroused too; it staged a mass protest march of more than 125,000 in what the *Times* called "one of the largest parades this city has ever seen."[72] Barely had operations of the NCRSRM begun, when a clamor for a permanent national Jewish organization arose in different quarters. Neither the repeated failures of nineteenth-century American Jews to create a viable union nor the reality of a more fragmented and heterogeneous group at the beginning of the twentieth century were seen as insurmountable obstacles. Furthermore, the success of the NCRSRM in mobilizing the community was totally ignored.

Believing that the 1905 pogroms would probably not be the last, and swept up by the Progressive faith in the curative powers of democratic organization, many Jews called for a representative communal agency to handle such emergencies. Under the leadership of the Jewish Self-Defense Association, a body whose purpose was to arm Russian Jewry in its own defense, twelve national organizations representing the immigrant stratum endorsed the idea of an elected congress. The older national bodies, like B'nai B'rith, which were jealous of their power, resisted the eastern Europeans' stab at democratic leadership.

Not just downtowners asked for a representative organization. The staid and conservative Cyrus Adler offered one such plan. The *American Hebrew* too, usually the unquestioning supporter of the stewards, insisted that efficiency was less important than a committee responsible to the community and able to command undivided support. "Let us once for all have faith in the rank and file of Jewry," the paper implored. "The democratic spirit should prevail, and if there are dangers in free popular discussions, our smothering the voice of protestants will only make matters worse." Arguing for an American Jewish congress, the paper opened its columns at the end of 1905 to supportive opinions from readers across the land. The relief work of the NCRSRM was not the issue, but control by a self-constituted national committee was. When the World Zionist Organization called for an international conference of all Jewish organizations on the Jewish situation in Russia, the American Jewish press advised the creation first of a separate body in each country.

The call for a democratic congress reverberated in downtown New York under the leadership of Judah Magnes. The popular young rabbi, who enjoyed easy access to both the Jewish establishment and the new immigrants, headed the Jewish Self-Defense Association. Successfully mobilizing thousands of supporters, he broadened the Association's aim of supplying arms to Russian Jews to that of toppling elitist rule by a democratic national organization. His indictment of the modern "court Jews" summed up his reading of popular discontent:

> Whenever anything confronts the Jews, some excellent gentlemen, . . . in the name of the Jewish Community, devise plans for the Jewish community to relieve them. These gentlemen do not represent the Jews of the United States at all, or a greater part of the Jews of the United States. It is simply another instance of persons who are respected at court, and who have the ear of those in power, and because of having the ear of those in power have the means of representing the Jewish community. It is necessary that the Jewish people itself have a voice in the conduct of its own affairs. There is no people in all the world that has not a voice in the conduct of its own affairs, that is no people which calls itself civilized, or democratic.[73]

Disaffection with the power wielded by Schiff's circle was also fed by geographical and organizational jealousy. Midwestern Jews chafed under domination by New York based-stewards; their jealousy, Schiff said, was "ever present." B'nai B'rith too resented being overlooked or underrepresented in leadership councils, and an International Jewish League in California threatened to take independent and more drastic action on the Russian situation.[74] With signs indicating serious communal divisions, Schiff and his associates were faced with the gravest challenge ever made to their leadership. It would have been understandable had they washed their hands entirely of time-consuming and unrewarding communal service. The fact that they didn't testifies both to an instinct to preserve their power and to the depth of their Jewish commitment.

The issue of an American Jewish congress involved more than power distribution. At a meeting of the Judaeans, a prestigious club where established Jews discussed topics of current interest, arguments were raised against a permanent Jewish body. Why shouldn't Jews want to assimilate, two speakers asked, instead of validating the anti-Semitic canard that Jews, the stereotypical aliens, constituted a nation within a nation? Implicit in those remarks was the assumption that since Jews were protected as citizens of the country, a defense organization was tantamount to a show of no confidence in America. Inevitably, the discussion led to Zionism. The Zionist participants, who favored the congress idea, clashed with antinationalists, who maintained that Jews were no more than a religious group. Clearly, the ramifications of a congress, which was initially understood as a means of serving beleaguered foreign Jews, could not ignore the elemental question of American Jewish identity.[75]

Schiff and his associates bowed to the inevitability of a permanent organization and staged a preemptive strike to avoid any wildcat action. Louis Marshall candidly admitted: "Although we all felt the danger of such a movement, it was the consensus of opinion that inasmuch as such an organization was in the air, and would undoubtedly be formed by somebody, in order to avoid mischief it was desirable that we should take the initiative." Accordingly, a small conference of prominent men (including Magnes) from different cities was arranged to consider the feasibility of a central agency and the basis of representation. Important Jewish newspapers criticized the unrepresentative character of the invitees, but the plan held and deliberations began. The word *congress*, which smacked of nationalist assertiveness, was quickly dropped. Although a few objected to domination by religious congregations or by the immigrant element, the plan put forth by Schiff and Marshall called for an organization whose members were elected by congregations. Designed to raise the fewest objections, it defined Jews as a religious group, it accepted democratic elections, it undercut claims to national leadership by powerful organizations like the B'nai B'rith and Reform's UAHC, and, officially at least, it broke the oligarchy of the New York stewards.[76] It is unlikely that either Schiff or Marshall feared that he personally would be displaced, since years of communal service had won them the confidence of both German and Russian Jews. Indeed, Schiff went beyond the acceptance of a democratic body and spoke on the need to reach out to Jews unaffiliated with synagogues. He said that a new Jewry had arisen in the United States since 1881 and their confidence was necessary for any general representative body.[77]

In the end, however, after months of wrangling and compromises, democracy received only token recognition in the establishment of a permanent defense organization, the American Jewish Committee (AJC). In a gesture aimed at broadening the base of leadership, the constitution provided for district advisory councils to elect the sixty-member committee, which in turn would choose an executive committee of thirteen. But since the idea of participatory advisory councils never materialized, leadership rested in the hands of a handpicked, all-powerful executive committee, virtually the same group that directed the NCRSRM. Although spokesmen for the eastern Europeans ranted against the oligarchic structure, the stewards and their tactics of quiet personal diplomacy won hands down. Since the new agency was also a victory for the New York group, Marshall felt compelled to placate the other organizations with a public offer of cooperation. At least for the moment, the readiness of the Schiff circle to compromise succeeded in preserving rule by a few. Disaffection did not evaporate, but the episode underscored the need of reconciling uptown and downtown. Judge Mayer Sulzberger faulted both sides—uptown's belief in the superiority of the established Jews and downtown's "arrogant assumption . . . that mere numbers give wisdom."[78]

Schiff, who saw the new organization as a means for uniting American Jewry, briefly considered not joining the executive committee. "The monopolizing of leadership by a few," he said, "should gradually be made to cease." He had not changed from an elitist into a proponent of democracy, but overburdened by communal tasks, he thought it might be wiser to leave the field to younger men. Nevertheless, a national defense organization without Schiff would have been a contradiction in terms. He was persuaded to serve, and for a time he acted as chairman of the agency's finance committee. Sulzberger was chosen first president, but policy, now covering domestic as well as foreign matters, was set principally by Schiff and two of his loyal associates, Marshall and Cyrus Adler. As in prior years the banker's forte lay primarily in linking American Jewish leaders with their European counterparts. More often than not it was Schiff rather than the AJC who decided on American cooperation with the Anglo-Jewish Association, the Alliance Israélite Universelle, and the Hilfsverein der Deutschen Juden. His foreign contacts served him well, especially when he tackled international issues like Russian Jewry and emigration from eastern Europe.[79]

The New York stewards faced a more serious challenge to their leadership in 1908. When Police Commissioner Theodore Bingham charged that Jews, the new immigrants in particular, accounted for 50 percent of the city's criminals, both uptown and downtown felt challenged to respond. At first uptown, more worried than angry, held back. They could not honestly deny Jewish crime, and they preferred to avoid public controversy. But since their reputation, both with downtown and with non-Jews, was at stake, they decided to act. As Schiff explained, uptown wasn't responsible for the vice and crime among the immigrants, but since Americans held them responsible, they had to do something. Downtown spokesmen, bitter over the stewards' delay in responding to Bingham, not only lashed out at the commissioner but embarked on a plan to create an all-inclusive *kehillah*, or Jewish community, for the management and defense of their interests. In accord with the Progressive emphasis on broadening popular participation in the political process, they aimed for a representative body, one that would unite the vast array of Jewish agencies—synagogues, fraternal lodges, federations, and professional societies. The very idea was a vote of no confidence in the AJC insofar as defense of the ghetto was concerned.

Ironically, democratization required elitist participation. From the start, downtowners knew that the success of their plan depended on the AJC's cooperation. Only a partnership with the established Jews could provide the funding and prestige essential to their task. The key objective was a *partnership* in place of the existing steward-ward relationship. The Yiddish *Tageblatt* explained: "There is not a single Jew on the East Side who does not recognize the importance to American Jewry of a Jacob Schiff and a Louis Marshall. . . . But we wish self-recognition as well. . . . We want to give our famous Jews their honored place in an American Jewish organization . . . but we we wish them to work with us and not over us."[80]

Schiff and Marshall reacted positively. Schiff wrote: "To me and also to others it was a question whether we should keep aloof and permit the [*kehillah*] to be anyhow organized and represent New York Jewry, or whether the element represented by the German Jews had not better secure a potent voice in the proposed community and exert the conservative restraining influence which, without the co-operation of the German element, might be wanting." Whereas participation might allow the retention of some form of control over roughly one million new immigrants and substantiate the committee's lip service to democracy, a refusal to cooperate could unleash a democratic monster. Moreover, here was an opportunity to establish order out of downtown's chaotic affairs and to relieve the stewards of some of their burdens. Since Judah Magnes led the *kehillah* movements, his ties to uptown (he was a member of the AJC, a former rabbi of Temple Emanu-El, and Marshall's brother-in-law) assured a hearing of their views. Other possible gains looked attractive to Schiff. Not only would organization aid in Americanizing the new immigrants, but a *kehillah* could help turn the dream of a united Jewry into a reality. The banker also recognized that the eastern Europeans by sheer numbers would ultimately wrest control of the community from the established Jews. Cooperation therefore provided the soon-to-be minority with the means of perpetuating the stewards' communal values for future generations of American Jews.[81]

The committee discussed the merits of the proposed *kehillah* at its 1908 annual meeting. Marshall led the defense, and Schiff argued the need to encourage the eastern Europeans to greater independence under AJC supervision. Pointing to the delight with which Jews greeted the proposal for a *kehillah*, he added:

These gentlemen who have started this movement come to us and they say "here we are; we do not want to have it thrown in our mouths that we are agitators for power; we want to have the guidance of intelligent men, and we want you to cooperate with us." . . . Shall we repel these men and say oh we do not want any of them? What will be the consequences? It is a mighty stream which we have an opportunity to keep in these waters, and the boats are swimming on it, and it is a good opportunity to start them right.[82]

Negotiations between the two sides led to an arrangement whereby the *kehillah*'s executive became the committee's advisory council for New York. Its jurisdiction was limited to local matters, leaving all national and international issues to the committee. Although Schiff at first had cautioned against hasty action, he cheered on the joint deliberations. At one organizational meeting where his presence was loudly acclaimed by the downtowners, he moved the adoption of two articles in the proposed constitution of the *kehillah*. One defined the purpose of the *kehillah* in religious terms—"to further the cause of Judaism" in New York City—and the second stipulated that the *kehillah* would not engage in any political activity. The motion was adopted unanimously, and since all delegates were required to be citizens, the banker was assured that the new organization would not be secularist, nationalistic, or political but eminently American.

When the founding convention proceeded to elections for the *kehillah*'s executive, Schiff received most votes, an indicator of downtown's respect and appreciation. The AJC won ten places on the twenty-five-man body, thereby allaying any fears the stewards may have harbored of being cast aside. Downtown wanted independence in 1909, but it wanted the tried leadership of the established Jews just as much. In turn, men like Schiff and Marshall showed an awareness of the inappropriateness of oligarchic rule in a democratic society and were sufficiently flexible to yield a share of absolute control. Schiff declined to serve on the *kehillah*'s executive, but he had great hopes for an organization that would keep communal management out of the hands of "disconnected, uncontrollable elements" and under the AJC's thumb.[83]

Under Magnes's dedicated leadership, the *kehillah* created an umbrella-like structure of bureaus that dealt with education, social morals, philanthropy, industrial relations, and religion. Magnes appealed repeatedly to Schiff to fund *kehillah* activities, and the banker was usually responsive. Indeed, donations from Schiff and his son-in-law, Felix Warburg, were largely responsible for the innovative educational work of the Bureau of Education under the direction of Dr. Samson Benderly. The banker did not approve of the Zionist leanings of Benderly's teachers, but he valued more the need to revitalize moral values and religious and cultural training through a modern Jewish education. Contributing also to the *kehillah*'s efforts at fighting crime and mediating labor disputes, Schiff shored up his leadership of the new immigrants. As one Yiddish newspaper put it, "He who picks up the bill has the final say."[84]

Schiff had shown an interest in the problems of the needle trades as early as 1897, and in cooperation with the *kehillah* he continued to work for industrial peace. His largely benevolent opinions on organized labor as discussed above applied here too, but in the case of the clothing industry, where Jews predominated as manufacturers, workers, and union leaders, he had an additional reason for involvement. Always sensitive to the public image that his fellow Jews projected, he sought to avoid the spectacle of class warfare within the Jewish community. Furthermore, divisiveness of any sort threatened his larger goal of a unified American Jewry. The chances of mediation and arbitration in the garment industry looked good; all parties shared a common ethnic background and a tradition of arbitration. As members of a vulnerable minority they too were concerned about public opinion, and they too preferred not to sully the Jewish image by exposés of deplorable working conditions.

Schiff and other influential Jews had interceded in 1910 to bring an end to the "Great Revolt," a strike of over fifty thousand workers in the cloakmaking industry. The famous Protocol of Peace that followed labor's victory set new guidelines for the needle trades, but it failed to prevent recurrent unrest.[85] When in 1915 the manufacturers abrogated the protocol, another major strike loomed. The National Civic Federation, an organization that stood for the peaceful resolution of industrial strife, urged Schiff's intervention. Since he was agreeable to both capital and labor, he was the logical choice for working out a settlement. Relying on the advice of Magnes and Lillian Wald, the banker agreed to intercede. He refused, however, to become a member of the *kehillah*'s Committee on Industrial Relations; he thought it wiser to appear as a neutral and thus avoid the charge that the "moneybags" (his term) controlled the *kehillah*. Along with Magnes and three other friends in the AJC, Schiff publicly called the manufacturers to a meeting in his office. While the war raged in Europe, the stewards said, it was imperative to avoid "an appalling economic and moral waste to the entire community." The manufacturers yielded to the pressure, and for the time being a strike was averted.[86]

Schiff used the opportunity to mend his fences with downtown. At a time when the AJC's fight against Louis Brandeis and his followers over an American Jewish Congress was heating up, the banker suggested to Magnes that Brandeis be asked to serve as "final arbitrator." The popular Zionist leader was fully knowledgeable about conditions in the needle trades, and in no way should he think that the AJC planned to "crowd" him out or "to make capital against him with the working people." To the contrary, "we should show him that we at least are unprejudiced and want unity among our people." Neither side in the dispute, however, pushed for Brandeis, and he was not approached.[87]

Less than a year later trouble arose again in the same industry when the owners threatened to impose a lockout on thirty thousand workers. The mayor's efforts to avert drastic action were disregarded, and Schiff called the manufacturers to a last-minute meeting. This time he failed. The owners put the lockout into effect and criticized Schiff for meddling into affairs about which he lacked sufficient knowledge. The banker resented the snub, and although he resolved to interfere no longer, he came out publicly on the side of the "masses" against the "classes": "I say to the workers, fight the good fight, for you are fighting the fight of good citizenship." Paraphrasing a verse from the prophet Zechariah, he added, "Your fight must win, not by might, not by power, but by the spirit of God and of social justice." Schiff cheered on the workers throughout the fourteen-week strike, and so did the public. An agreement between the employers and the union was finally reached. The Protocol was not resurrected, but since the strike had been presented as the workers' struggle for peace through collective bargaining, the vindication of the union's action was labor's victory.[88]

The *kehillah* drew criticism from some Jews, particularly the extreme Americanizers, who looked upon it as a state within a state. Some years later that charge was embellished in a scurrilous attack by the *Dearborn Independent*, the mouthpiece of the rabid anti-Semite, Henry Ford. Calling the *kehillah* the center of Jewish world power, the paper charged that it had forged a Jewish union based on hatred of non-Jews and that it had captured control of New York. Nevertheless, the leaders of the AJC believed that the early years of the *kehillah's* existence had justified their cooperation. Louis Marshall publicly defended the experiment, praising the accomplishments of the bureaus of education, religion, and philanthropy. Above all, the *kehillah* deserved commendation for its labors to bring order into the fragmented ghetto. Schiff agreed; he called the *kehillah* the "most important undertaking that has ever been launched by the Jews of the City of New York." Nevertheless, downtown's stab at independence, attesting to the rapid acculturation of the newcomers and their readiness to Americanize the Jewish legacy of community, was only short-lived. The *kehillah* quickly declined with the outbreak of war, when hyper-Americanism questioned forms of ethnic expression and when concern for the war-ravaged Jewish communities in Europe eclipsed internal issues. Hastening the *kehillah's* demise was downtown's support of an American Jewish Congress. Although uptown had willingly pacified the masses with partial autonomy, it held the line at a congress that joined Zionism with a push for democracy. Since differences over the degree of democracy could no longer be masked, the carefully constructed alliance between uptown and downtown fell apart.[89]

Removal from the Ghetto

The successive waves of eastern European immigrants magnified the ghetto's problems and appeared to harden its resistance to charitable and Americanizing enterprises. Aside from any personal aversion they may have harbored to the newly transplanted shtetl Jews, concerned philanthropists reasoned that if the problems could not be solved in the ghetto, they could perhaps be mitigated or avoided entirely by distributing immigrants to other parts of the country. Hadn't their own families, the mid-nineteenth-century immigrants from central Europe, spread out through the length and breadth of the country? Distribution stood to benefit the immigrant, the established Jews, and, by supplying manpower where it was needed, the country as well. It promised fewer burdens on New York Jews, more rapid Americanization of the immigrants, and a less conspicuous "alien" Jewish element to incite popular suspicions. Most important, certainly for Schiff, distribution seemed the surest guarantee for keeping America's doors open to refugees. Thus, from the beginning of the mass eastern European exodus the stewards seriously discussed ideas of settling the newcomers in the South and West.

Of the various options, the idea of agricultural settlement was the perennial favorite. The oft-touted myths of agrarian virtue had resonated in American Jewish circles since before the Civil War and were revived with greater intensity in the last decades of the nineteenth century. The *Jewish Messenger*, a New York weekly that often ranted about the "leprosy of the ghetto walls," reminded its readers that "Paradise was a garden, not a city." As a path to physical well-being and "moral elevation," a back-to-the-soil movement presaged a healthy diversification of the traditionally urban people while it simultaneously refuted the image of the nonproductive or parasitic Jew.[90]

How well the Jewish farmer undid the negative stereotypes about Jews was quite another matter. In 1904 the *Springfield Republican* described the reclamation of old New England farms by Jewish settlers. The paper praised the industry and productivity of the farmers, but it went on to add: "These Jews . . . have an eye ever open for business, and are very sharp in a trade or bargain. In fact, they represent the typical Jew of Baxter street,

New York."[91] Clearly, even as homesteaders Jews failed to erase anti-Jewish stereotypes.

Schiff readily lent his support to early relief organizations that endorsed schemes for turning Jews into farmers. Even before the creation of the Baron de Hirsch Fund, he served for a short time on the Committee of Agricultural Pursuits of the UAHC, whose purpose was to subsidize would-be independent Jewish farmers. Toward that same end he urged Baron de Hirsch to establish agricultural credit banks, an idea that later blossomed into the Jewish Agricultural and Industrial Aid Society. Through the Hirsch Fund, he pushed for the establishment of a colony in Woodbine, New Jersey, one that he optimistically envisioned as the model for a string of settlements in various states. Well aware of the lack of American Jewish funds for such undertakings—in essence New York money—he repeatedly pleaded with ICA to support colonization and agricultural training for the new immigrants.[92]

Schiff cheered on the farmer, and so did other established Jews. When the Federation of American Jewish Farmers held its second convention in 1910, the *American Israelite* pointed admiringly to the "good color," "firm step," and "independent air" of those who had declared "their emancipation from the thralldom of city life."[93] The objective observer might well wonder why the same established Jews had totally ignored their own urban "thralldom."

Colonization in the West was especially exciting to Schiff. The potential of the yet unknown hinterland for immigrant settlement meshed with his expanding business investments, and the banker communicated his enthusiasm to railroad magnate James Hill. Hill was not only a sympathetic friend, but, like Schiff, he understood that settlements in the northwestern states would increase the profits of his lines. When Schiff asked him in 1891 to consider the practicality of a colony in Minnesota, Hill responded immediately. He planned out a settlement of forty families under the supervision of a small committee of prominent Jews from the Twin Cities on land that he owned in Milaca. A grateful Schiff promised that the Hirsch Fund, which gave him and Hill carte blanche on arrangements, would send only the "best" Russians. "These Russian emigrants," he assured Hill, "are, in the main, a sturdy race, thrifty, and anxious to work, and if they are only started in the right manner, they are sure to become successful." Hill set the plans into motion: forty small houses were built and a supervisory committee was organized. But the venture was abandoned midstream after a critical investigative report by the fund.[94]

Despite his business acuity, Schiff failed to acknowledge at the outset that colonization was a losing proposition. Many of the sites were unsuitable, and capital was scarce. The newcomers were neither ripe for recruitment nor willing to become, as one critic put it, "a contented Jewish peasantry." A small number of idealists found the idea of colonization appealing, but the overwhelming majority, inexperienced and unaccustomed to the rigors of agrarian life, stayed aloof. The new economic frontier that lured American farmers as well as the foreigners was the rapidly industrializing city. There, despite the hardships of the ghetto, the immigrants found a way of cushioning the trauma of uprooting in a place where they could comfortably speak their language, practice their religious customs, and find familiar companionship. In 1905, looking back at twenty years of experimentation, Schiff finally admitted that the meager results of colonization did not warrant the expense. He never repudiated the agrarian ideal, but he shifted his support to independent farmers and particularly to Jewish agricultural schools. Only those "fit" to be farmers would be so trained. Over time, Schiff grew dissatisfied with the agricultural school at Woodbine, the first such attempt by the Hirsch fund (1894), and thirty years later he looked for a fresh start. In 1916 he and Chicago millionaire Julius Rosenwald each offered $150,000 for relocating the school to Peekskill, New York, but both the plan and the fund's commitment to a separate agricultural school were abandoned after America entered the war.[95]

Schiff seized on other ideas for relieving congestion in the eastern ghettos. A consistent champion of immigrant distribution, he held fast to a statement he had made in 1890: "The city of New York . . . can scarcely digest large additional numbers of Jewish emigrants, and if serious results in many respects are to be obviated, more efficient means must be found to distribute the new arrivals over the less densely populated parts of the country." He and like-minded champions of unrestricted immigration argued that the country could well absorb an ongoing flow of new arrivals as long as the immigrants were more evenly directed. The banker assured Baron de Hirsch that "if we had the ways and means to distribute the arrivals over the country, I think it fair to say that the United States are in a position to absorb successfully and cheerfully between 1.5 and 2 million more Russian emigrants within the next ten or fifteen years."[96]

"Ways and means" meant primarily financial aid from Europe for helping immigrants settle in the interior of the country, but European cooperation in the form of advice to prospective immigrants and supervision of the emigrant flow also was required. To be effective, distribution had to be designed *before* the eastern Europeans arrived. Above all, emigrants had to learn that America was not synonymous with New York. "I wish to God it were different," Schiff wrote, but since over 70 percent of the immigrants disembarked regularly in New York, that impression was well nigh ineradicable. When he traveled to Europe in 1890, he suggested a corrective: officers of an international organization in charge of emigration would give each person a certificate indicating his destination. If he were directed to the interior but refused to leave New York, he would forfeit his claim to any aid intended for immigrants. The idea went no further, but at a conference that year of leading French, English, and German Jews, convened at Schiff's request, the participants agreed to take on supervisory roles in the emigration process. Addressing both the issues of distribution and of staggering the number of arrivals, they promised that those Russian Jews not severely oppressed would be induced to stay put. The others, whose destinations would be fixed, would be persuaded to postpone their departure as long as possible.[97] From the point of view of Schiff and his associates progress had been made, but vague promises quickly evaporated as the plight of Russian Jewry worsened.

A new wrinkle in the settlement of Jewish immigrants surfaced the next year, this time involving the American government. Restrictionist sentiment was on the rise, and in 1891, Congress passed a new immigration law that barred entry to those "likely to become a public charge" (LPC). Assisted immigrants (or those whose passage had been paid for by foreign individuals or organizations) could be detained by local immigration authorities until they proved that they didn't fall into the LPC category. Strictly speaking, Russian Jews whose passage was funded by others or who had money but no guarantee of employment in the United States were liable for detention or deportation. Again distribution offered a way out. When Simon Wolf of the UAHC's Board of Delegates pleaded with Secretary of the Treasury Charles Foster for a lenient interpretation of the law, Foster consented, albeit grudgingly, on condition that American Jews successfully disperse the immigrants to places outside the congested industrial centers. To be sure, the law placed new responsibilities on both the European and American Jewish leaders. As Schiff reminded Hirsch, the Europeans had to remember to exclude prospective emigrants who would become public charges. On the American side the situation was far stickier, since the actual disposition of cases depended on local officials, and each adverse decision necessitated a separate appeal. (On that score, Schiff confided to Cassel that banker Jesse Seligman, whose firm served as fiscal agent of the Navy Department, successfully influenced the government to ignore certain open violations of the law.) But Foster's interpretation of the LPC law added strength to the case for distribution.[98]

More than any idea of immigrant relief, distribution by whatever device bespoke the assumed superiority of the stewards toward their eastern European wards. A carryover of Old World patterns of prejudice, the German Jew, who chose to forget that he had been the victim of Sephardic discrimination, generally looked down on his "unenlightened" eastern brethren who were seemingly incapable of self-direction. One communal worker candidly explained how the philanthropists regarded the immigrant: "The immigrant was a child who must be carefully kept in his place. His benefactors knew better than he what was good for him. These benefactors had made substantial business successes and, therefore, felt they were the competent guardians of the newcomers, . . . distant relatives whom one must look after carefully lest they do things that might bring the family to shame." Schiff may have been more sympathetic and accepting, but he too found nothing wrong in deciding for the immigrants where they should settle: "We have not only the right, but the duty to properly direct this immigration, and we *can* properly and justly say to the Russian Jew, who wants to leave his own inhospitable country and come to the United States 'you must settle there where we think it best and proper for you to found your new home.'"[99]

Distribution was neither a new nor an exclusively Jewish idea. Broached by urban reformers in the 1850s, it was endorsed after 1880 by Italians as well as Jews who were confronted with the arrival of vast numbers of fellow ethnics. Both sides of the distribution idea, removal from the ghetto and resettlement in the hinterland, became increasingly popular with American charitable and civic organizations and with state and federal officials.

The Baron de Hirsch Fund experimented with several forms of distribution in addition to agricultural settlement—suburbanization, removal of industries to outlying districts, and job placements for immigrants in smaller cities around the country. The last was handled by the Industrial Removal Office (IRO), an agency that matched immigrants with job listings garnered from committees in outlying cities. More in tune with immigrant tastes than rural ventures were, the operation also illustrated a way of effectively channeling workers to meet the specific labor needs of different geographical regions. As part of a vigorous campaign, the IRO even stationed representatives at Ellis Island to persuade new arrivals to set their sights on places outside New York. Although some feared that the IRO could be seen as a strike-breaking agency, Schiff remained a staunch supporter. He used his railroad contacts in attempts to secure lower rates for transporting immigrants, and he gave his personal attention to individual cases handled by the organization. IRO in turn became the model for the short-lived Division of Information (1907) in the Department of Commerce and Labor. Here again, innovative philanthropy on the part of the private sector directly influenced public policy.[100]

Distribution became a favorite topic of the Anglo-Jewish press. At conventions of Jewish organizations prominent established Jews and their invited speakers dwelt on the advantages of removal from New York and other large cities. Conducting a vigorous propaganda campaign, the IRO won the endorsement of national Jewish organizations like the UAHC,

B'nai B'rith, and the National Conference of Jewish Charities and of non-Jewish observers. Nevertheless, the agency was hardly cost-efficient. The considerable sums of money and effort that it required succeeded with fewer than 6 percent of the immigrants (some 79,000) during the twenty-year lifetime of the agency. Many of the eastern Europeans had relatives or friends in New York; others refused to face the hardships of a second voyage.[101] In 1903 a spirited debate on the merits of removal and distribution appeared in the pages of the *American Hebrew*. Dr. Isaac Rubinow, the foremost critic, dismissed distribution as the "new patent medecine." In a strong defense of the economic and cultural advantages of the urban ghetto, he argued that "a well-meaning member of the Jewish 'better classes,' a generous contributor to every cause, a man beyond any suspicion as to his motives" (Rubinow probably had Schiff in mind) lost sight of those assets when confronted by the congestion and filth. For different reasons non-Jewish Americans also criticized the idea of distribution. Some said it was a device to send pauper Jews to the United States; labor leader Samuel Gompers and economist John Commons called it a subterfuge for evading outright restriction. In the words of Prescott Hall, spokesman for the influential Immigration Restriction League, distribution was "a bluff of the Jews and steamship companies to throw dust in the eyes of the ignorant and prevent proper legislation."[102]

In 1909, while the restrictionist tide continued to swell, Schiff endorsed distribution in a speech to the Jewish Chautauqua. He repeated his stock ideas: the United States could and should absorb more immigrants, but the problems of immigrant congestion in the eastern cities menaced both the cause of free immigration and the status of the American Jew generally. Those were the issues, he confessed, that gnawed at him "in the small hours of the morning when responsibilities weigh particularly heavy, when burdens often appear almost unbearable." He added privately that "because I feel that this country for long years to come must continue to form the great outlet for Russian emigration, I am the more anxious to place myself and my means into accomplishing all that can be done to open the wide territory beyond the Mississippi to a large Jewish immigration."[103]

The American press commented on the Chautauqua address, and this time the Hearst papers joined the critics. "Well Meant, But Not Entirely Sound" read the headline in the *Boston American*. Density of population gave Jews a political voice, the paper said, and hence the wherewithal to counter prejudice. As for those who feared that Jews might become too powerful, well, that could happen only if Jews proved abler than other Americans, and in that case they deserved the power. While Hearst nurtured his political ambitions by pandering to the immigrant masses, criticism failed to shake Schiff's convictions. He repeatedly explained to downtown audiences how free immigration depended on proper distribution.

The immigrants, he said, had made New York a great communal center. Nevertheless, since the city's absorptive capacity had peaked, they should advise their friends in Europe to avoid New York in favor of the South and West. Ironically, the same new immigrants who generally balked at the idea of distribution greeted his remarks with warm applause. On these and other occasions it made little difference what he said. His very appearance was sufficient to trigger a positive reaction, proof yet again of the esteem he had won and of his control over the rank and file.[104]

4

Captivity and Redemption

At War with the Czar

Despite his grand vision of relocating millions to places west of the Mississippi, Schiff admitted time and again that the Russian Jewish question had to be resolved in Russia. Relief for Russian Jews at moments of major crisis was imperative, but it was at best a patchwork device of temporary value. Only a radical change, indeed nothing less than equal rights for Russian Jews, could break the pattern of persecution and suffering, and toward that end Schiff waged a private war against czarist Russia from the 1890s until 1917.

Schiff's war, which developed over time into an all-consuming passion, was prompted by motives far deeper than any wish to be freed of responsibilities for victims or immigrants. The banker repeatedly drew analogies between the Russian situation and the biblical story of the Jews in Egypt; subconsciously, he doubtless saw himself as another Moses. Insisting that the Russians, like the Egyptians, feared the Jews, he read a modern meaning into a verse from the Book of Exodus: "Here are a people abler than we; let us take heed and suppress them lest they become our masters." Like the early Hebrews the Russian Jews were in bondage and cried for redemption. Since Jewish law mandated the ransoming of captives and because Providence had wrapped him in the mantle of leadership, he keenly felt the duty to rescue the modern-day captives. "I am grateful to God," he wrote to Baron Horace Guenzberg of Russia, "that He so placed me to be able to be of some help to our coreligionists." He empathized closely with the persecuted, "those who, of my own flesh and blood, are being plundered, tortured and murdered for no other cause, than that they are Jews."[1] Indeed, the struggle for Jewish liberation in Russia took on the emotional overtones of a personal crusade, almost as if the czar were hounding him, Jacob Schiff. The banker often quoted the Psalmist's promise of divine help, and Schiff took the Bible seriously, but for a man who was loath to admit helplessness in any situation, the biblical promise did not consign him to passivity.

Although American Jews had risen to the defense of their foreign brethren ever since the Damascus Affair of 1840, their early methods reflected an immature community whose occasional appeals to the government were timid if not obsequious. The Jewish establishment had become more sophisticated by the last quarter of the nineteenth century, when Germany considered the rescission of Jewish rights in 1881 and when France tried and convicted Captain Alfred Dreyfus of high treason in the 1890s. In those instances, however, Jewish leaders chose to stay aloof. Still the junior partners in the relationship with western European Jewries, they would not intervene unless requested to by their fellow Jews abroad. Furthermore, the "new" anti-Semitism in western Europe confounded the Americans as much as it disturbed them. It belied their optimistic faith that Jewish history had turned a corner with the Enlightenment and that prejudice and bigotry would fall before the inevitable progress of mankind. Preferring to interpret the eruptions as isolated aberrations, they sensed that intervention on their part would be tantamount to an admission of spiritual bankruptcy. In the Dreyfus case, Schiff and other prominent Jews opposed protest meetings and, attempting to deny that race prejudice was involved, looked to the civilized world for expressions of resentment. Privately, Schiff fumed at French injustice and could not bring himself to visit Paris during those years, but he held his tongue.[2]

Czarist oppression, however, which was seen as a carryover of medieval barbarism, elicited a markedly different response. The American stewards believed that modern Jews fought the good fight by challenging the reactionary forces in Russia that blocked the advance of civilization and with it the well-being of Jews. Intervention was unlikely to worsen the lot of the Russian Jews, and since the latter were hardly the equals of their emancipated western co-religionists, their consent to such intervention was unnecessary. Just as Schiff played guardian to the new immigrants on the Lower East Side, so did he and his associates adopt the Jews in Russia as their wards.

Schiff harnessed his wealth and political influence on behalf of Jewish liberation in Russia. Making good use of his far-flung network of European contacts—from his brother Philip in Frankfurt to Ernest Cassel in London, from sources in Russia to officers of the Anglo-Jewish Association (England), the Alliance Israélite Universelle (France), and the Hilfsverein der Deutschen Juden (Germany)—he became the virtual nerve center of all news relating to the Russian situation. The banker functioned as lobbyist and diplomat as well as philanthropist, and he fast gained universal recognition as the champion of eastern European liberation. A Jew from Russia once recalled that as a youngster he had known of Schiff. "He belonged not only to the American Jewry but to the Jewry of the entire world."[3]

Schiff's tasks were self-assumed, and he plotted strategy with only a handful of trusted friends. The creation of relief committees in aid of pogrom victims and even the subsequent work of the American Jewish Committee (AJC) in defense of foreign Jews neither lessened his importance nor cut down his image. Behind the scenes he still called the signals and passed on all important plays.

Schiff wondered at Russia's self-defeating policy of anti-Semitism. Once given their rights, Russian Jews were certain to become productive and patriotic assets to their country.[4] But as long as the czar's government persisted in its course, only pressure from outside sources could effect a change. Prepared to consider any suggestion that offered the slightest glimmer of amelioration (Schiff alternated between optimism and pessimism about the plight of Russian Jewry) he tried numerous ways, usually simultaneously, of generating that pressure. To be sure, some methods, like the mobilization of public opinion and appeals for government intervention, had been utilized by American Jews as far back as the Damascus Affair. Radically new, however, were Schiff's independent efforts to isolate Russia in the diplomatic arena, notably through international financial pressure. Different too, precisely because Schiff directed the protracted campaign against Russia, was the style of Jewish protest. The earlier timidity of Jewish supplicants was gone. Now the American Jewish establishment had in Schiff an aggressive spokesman who pursued the objective with little fear of incurring disfavor.

The anti-Russia crusade brought Schiff to the height of his communal powers and to a position never before attained by an American Jewish leader. The rank and file of American Jews knew little of his anti-Russia efforts and were consulted even less. Since he operated independently and without a power base, he saw no reason to change his belief in control from the top down. From his point of view, unleashing an inchoate and politically immature immigrant community was sure to generate noisy, disjointed, and irresponsible actions that could undermine the tried techniques of quiet, personal diplomacy.

After the pogroms and the restrictive May Laws of 1881, Schiff and a few other American Jewish stewards closely monitored the Russian Jewish situation. In 1890, despite denials by the American minister to St. Petersburg, they learned from their counterparts in western Europe of new impending restrictions that included expulsions from Moscow and other cities. On the initiative of Oscar Straus, who maintained his contacts with the State Department after his first tour of duty as minister to Turkey, and Jesse Seligman, whose firm served as fiscal agent for the Navy Department, they presented their case to Secretary of State James Blaine and President Benjamin Harrison. They had two objectives: to expose the misinformation of Minister Charles Emory Smith and to ask for an American protest against Russian policy.

The stewards gained a respectful and even sympathetic hearing. Influential Jews like Straus, Seligman, and Schiff could not be easily dismissed, especially since Blaine admitted the falsity of Smith's reports. Moreover, the Jewish leaders shared the secretary's aversion to public protest meetings and were willing to keep the Jews in line. In tried accommodationist fashion, they made their case an American rather than a Jewish issue by arguing that the persecution swelled the volume of immigration into the United States. If America could prove that Russian policy caused the mass entry of destitute refugees, its national interest justified a rebuke of the czar. At a time when the country was testing its wings in international diplomacy, no overriding economic or strategic reasons dictated appeasement of Russia.

Meanwhile, to show their own good faith the stewards pressured European Jewish leaders to exercise greater control over the emigrant flow. At one international conference in 1890, Schiff pushed the need for proper distribution. The next year, foreseeing a major catastrophe in Russia, he suggested that the United States join with the major European countries in asking Russia for a hearing on the subject of staggered Jewish emigration over a period of years. The administration shied away from any direct confrontation with the czarist regime, but Harrison agreed to appoint a commission, headed by John Weber, to investigate the conditions that led to emigration. Hoping for at least an indirect slap at Russia, Schiff and the others arranged for friends in Europe to brief the commissioners.[5]

Blaine's instructions to the American legation for informal representations to Russia and the pro-Jewish report by the Weber commission were small but significant victories, showing Russia that the United States had taken an interest in the problem. Jewish diplomacy scored another victory with the appointment of Smith's successor. Determined now to secure a representative in St. Petersburg who was alert and sympathetic to the Jewish plight, Schiff, Straus, Seligman, and Myer Isaacs (president of the Baron de Hirsch Fund) successfully pressured Harrison into giving the post to Andrew D. White, a former president of Cornell University. They followed up the appointment by maintaining contact with the new minister and feeding him relevant information. Doubtless, White also read the *American Hebrew*, the newspaper of the Jewish establishment; because of Russian censorship, the paper was delivered to him by diplomatic pouch. A cooperative minister was a significant asset, and since White was retained in Russia after the election of 1892, he was pivotal in easing the stewards' approach to the Cleveland administration. The Russians usually influenced American diplomats to take the side of czarist policies, but White proved to be the exception.[6]

Events in the early 1890s underscored the urgency of disseminating accurate and sympathetic reports on Russian Jewish suffering. Nineteenth-century Jews looked upon the cultivation of "enlightened public opinion" as the prime weapon against anti-Semitism. Children of the Enlightenment, they genuinely believed, before World War I, in the power of reason to advance mankind along the paths of progress and justice. Hence, the stewards aimed at a loud non-Jewish outcry, contradicting the erroneous diplomatic reports, that might successfully ameliorate the Russian situation or at least add weight to the argument for diplomatic intervention. Publicity also dovetailed with the search for non-Jewish allies. Although the stewards argued for humanitarian diplomacy (i.e., that the the mission of America, the beacon of liberty to the world, obligated the country to champion the cause of the persecuted) they were sufficiently astute to recognize a minority's need of political support. When news syndicates deliberately purveyed misinformation and when influential journals like the *North American Review*, the *Nation*, and *Century Magazine* opened their columns to respectable writers who blatantly attacked Jews or blamed persecution on Jewish behavior, countermeasures for reaching the American public through a sympathetic press commanded top priority.[7]

Schiff sought the cooperation of Oswald Garrison Villard of the *Nation* and George Jones of the *New York Times*, and he sent articles from the European press condemning Russian persecution to Horace White, editor of the *New York Evening Post*. It was high time, he said, that American newspapers took similar action. How was it that the press was quick to condemn Russian atrocities in Siberia but showed no interest in what Russian Christians were doing to Russian Jews? The banker arranged for the publication of "enlightening" books, and he looked for occasions—for example, a dinner in honor of Jesse Seligman—where his remarks on Russian conditions would receive press coverage.[8]

The public relations campaign was largely a hit-or-miss operation that called on editors and publishers to report Russian persecution and that thanked those who did. In one instance, Schiff and a few others took the initiative by underwriting a trip to Russia by *New York Times* correspondent Harold Frederic. The latter's accounts of conditions were circulated by various papers and shortly thereafter published in book form. Seeking allies, Schiff also lent support to the Friends of Russian Freedom and its publication, *Free Russia*. The move sparked a warm friendship between the banker and George Kennan, the man who had exposed the Siberian labor camps.[9] Association with Kennan and his group alerted the stewards to a cause larger than the Jewish question—the downfall of the Romanov empire. To be sure, Jewish liberation under czarist rule remained Schiff's immediate focus, but subsuming that goal under the movement for a Russian democracy became a possible strategy, worthy at least of minimal support.

More daring were Schiff's attempts to stand by the anti-Russia campaign even in the face of American favors to the czarist government. In 1890 he advised against Jewish participation in festivities honoring a Russian warship in the New York harbor lest the impression arise that "New York Jews are wanting in self-respect." He explained: "Have we a right to ask sympathy . . . in behalf of our Russian coreligionists and the condemnation of their oppressors if we hasten to do honor to those who come here officially representing the Czar's government?" A more delicate situation arose less than two years later in connection with a severe famine in Russia. The American government turned down a Russian request for foodstuffs, but members of the cabinet suggested that it would be good policy for New York's Jews to send a private relief ship. The stewards were caught in a bind. Not to undertake the project might annoy the government or tarnish the Jewish philanthropic image. On the other hand, the supplies could be used by Russia as proof that American Jews were unconcerned by the Jewish situation or that Jewish suffering drew money into the country. Either way, Russian Jewry stood to lose. Although Baron de Hirsch advised against Jewish relief, Schiff and Oscar Straus took a middle course. They turned down the cabinet's suggestion, but they supported the relief drive of the Chamber of Commerce. By that move they lent a Jewish presence to the general campaign and simultaneously positioned themselves to avert any potential harm to the Jewish cause. In a speech before the Chamber of Commerce, Schiff defended Jewish charity with great passion, but he warned against supplies falling into the hands of corrupt czarist officials. He went on to challenge the popular belief that Russia was a friend of the United States. Would a friend, he asked, force its exiles upon America?

To avert Jewish criticism of American appeals for famine relief, Schiff reminded his fellow Jews in a letter to the *American Hebrew* that their quarrel was neither with the Russians nor with the American government but solely with the czarist regime. True, Christian America had been less than forthcoming in relief for Jewish refugees from Russia, but the country had done more than any other nation by keeping its doors open to the immigrants. Besides, as a small minority, Jews could not afford to ignore American appeals. Therefore, it behooved them to help the famine sufferers but, he insisted, only if they had first contributed generously to Jewish relief.[10] Obviously concerned lest Jews incite an adverse public reaction, Schiff was unafraid to call attention to specific Jewish interests. In an age when most Jews preferred not to admit publicly to such interests, his was a refreshing voice.

Within some twenty years, Jewish leaders had fixed on several strategies for securing the rights of Russian Jews. They lobbied with Republican and Democratic administrations, cultivated public opinion through the press, and quietly encouraged non-Jews arrayed against the czar. (At times Schiff also thought of underwriting a pro-Jewish press in Russia itself.)[11] Gradually, as the Russian situation deteriorated, what had begun as Jewish reactions to specific crises became fixed patterns.

By the turn of the century, Schiff was embarked on yet another approach, that of closing America's and perhaps even the world's money markets to Russian loans. Radically different from the other strategies, it changed the Jew from the seeker of goodwill into an active adversary who relied on his own power. The banker mustered sound business reasons for his stand: Russia's distasteful political conditions repelled American capitalists; it was unwise to tie up American capital in loans unattractive to investors; Russia's huge indebtedness in European money markets boded ill for its creditors. Above all, however, was the banker's aversion to dealing with Russia. "I should not participate in any business with the Russian Government so long as it maintains and so ruthlessly enforces its special legislation against the Jews," he pledged. It mattered little to him, he told Paul Warburg, that some important European Jewish bankers behaved differently. Rather, he took pride in having successfully stymied Russia's dealings with American bankers after 1900.[12]

Acknowledging Schiff's financial power early on, Russia wooed the American banker for many years. Around 1900 the government sent Adolf Rothstein, a baptized Jew who was director of the St. Petersburg's International Bank of Commerce, to offer Kuhn, Loeb the position of favored financial agent for the marketing of Russian treasury notes. In addition to large profits, Rothstein promised that the minister of finance would work for the repeal of the anti-Jewish May Laws. "This we flatly refused," Schiff related to Lord Rothschild, "telling Mr. Rothstein that promises were cheap, and that action would have to precede Russia's application to the American money markets before our cooperation could be had, and that until then we should bring all the influence we could command to bear against Russia getting a foothold in the American money markets."[13] Bleeding Russia financially became Schiff's personal weapon and one that he wielded most effectively during the next decade, a period that witnessed recurring pogroms and a Russian empire in turmoil.

"One of the Most Dangerous Men . . . against Us"

When Theodore Roosevelt assumed the presidency in 1901, Schiff's role as lobbyist with the government expanded significantly. His reputation in the business world had reached a high, and after the Northern Pacific affair he

was ranked as second only to J. P. Morgan. Increasingly, the banker became
a familiar figure in Washington, often invited to discuss issues of railroads,
banking, and regulation of corporations with the president and members
of the cabinet. Clearly, he was not a man to be ignored.[14]

Schiff in turn made ready use of his entrée into government circles for
Jewish interests. During one business conference in 1902, for example, he
alerted TR to the severe restrictions then suffered by Romanian Jews. That
move was followed up by Straus and Congressman Lucius Littauer and resulted in the famous note issued by Secretary of State John Hay protesting
Romania's policies.[15] Frequently, Schiff corresponded directly with TR's
secretaries of state, Hay and Elihu Root. They resented his pressure, but
his messages received their personal attention, and on occasion their letters
to him were unsolicited. Like the president, they recognized him as the
most important, if irritating, Jewish spokesman. Jesse Seligman had died,
and Straus, a close presidential adviser who, in fact, tried to soften Schiff's
bluntness, was far less demanding. At the president's invitation, Schiff was
one of three Jews who passed on the portion relating to Russian-American
relations in Roosevelt's letter accepting the 1904 presidential nomination.
And if the popular story is to be believed (although both TR and Schiff denied it), it was Schiff whom the president consulted before appointing
Straus as secretary of commerce and labor.[16]

Now able to approach the government independently of his Jewish colleagues, Schiff found in Roosevelt a man to admire. Like the banker, the
president was hyperenergetic, a natural and forceful leader, and a man who
enjoyed power. Schiff had certain reservations about Roosevelt's regulation
of big business, but he shared the president's beliefs in absolute morality,
noblesse oblige, and elitist leadership by moral, selfless men. He called
Roosevelt a person of "spotless character," and the latter in turn considered
him a "genuine friend." Schiff well understood that Roosevelt was concerned about Jewish votes, and in 1904 the banker did his part by urging
Jewish support of the president's bid for reelection; but he believed that
TR's horror at anti-Jewish atrocities was genuine. Roosevelt's stand against
discrimination—the way in which he, when police commissioner, had
mocked the notorious German anti-Semite Hermann Ahlwardt, and his
willingness to see a Jew in the cabinet and perhaps even in the presidency—set him apart in Jewish eyes from his fellow WASPs. As long as
Roosevelt was president, Schiff confidently told Paul Nathan, he would defend the persecuted Jews.[17]

Schiff's admiration, however, did not becloud his determined campaign.
Up to a point he behaved in good diplomatic fashion; he thanked the administration warmly for its interest, and he carefully defended Roosevelt
against European Jewish critics.[18] But, different from most minority peti-
tioners, he was blunt in voicing his requests and equally candid in criticizing

government answers that he found inadequate. Never did he accept any limits on the number of times he could approach the administration.

Pogroms had become almost an annual rite of the Easter season since the 1880s, but the one in Kishinev in 1903 shocked the Western world. The American Jewish leaders responded immediately. Following the receipt of a cable from the Alliance Israélite Universelle on the government-instigated riots, a meeting was hastily called in Schiff's office, a relief committee was formed, and urgent appeals went out to Roosevelt and Hay for American action. Schiff wrote candidly to Hay that he understood the latter's annoyance with many letters on Kishinev, but he asked that the secretary try to understand the feelings of Schiff's fellow Jews. Again the American representative to St. Petersburg, Ambassador Robert McCormick, denied the atrocities in Kishinev, and again Schiff, but in words less polite than those used against Smith in 1890, expressed his "disgust" with the way in which the ambassador served as the "messenger" and "whitewasher" of Russia. Claiming that the czarist ministers could not have improved on McCormick's reports, Schiff told the president that "what we particularly need, are Ambassadors . . . who shall not sacrifice, to their social comfort, the representation of the true [American] spirit."[19] Privately, the banker admitted that an American protest would have little effect. The Russian government could easily deny responsibility while it made reassuring but worthless promises for the future. But Jewish outrage demanded a response. He himself helped inflame Jewish opinion by publicly denouncing Russia's use of a Jewish scapegoat.[20]

Hay opposed official action—wasn't it merely an internal Russian affair, and couldn't Russia point accusingly at mob violence in the United States? But in the end a more sympathetic Roosevelt agreed to forward a petition, circulated publicly and condemning Russian conduct, to the American embassy in St. Petersburg. Even if Russia refused to receive the petition, which in fact it did, the substance would be made known and thereby indirectly convey America's sentiments. Schiff doubted the petition's positive value. He preferred Christian protests, and he dreamed, albeit in vain, that TR might suspend relations with Russia in order to command a hearing. To be sure, the Russian Jewish problem soured relations between the two countries, but neither Schiff nor the fear of Jewish votes could move the administration further.

Americans responded generously to the Kishinev relief fund, outstripping the Germans and French combined almost tenfold. The public also expressed its horror over Kishinev at mass protest meetings, and this time the Jewish stewards made no attempt to restrain the Jewish community. Schiff helped to plan one such meeting, and he arranged that it be called by non-Jews and feature non-Jewish speakers.[21] Relying primarily on the government and on Christian public opinion, he and his associates never thought of mobilizing a community-wide Jewish effort in response to Kishinev.

Barely had the uproar over Kishinev subsided when concerned American Jews were angered by a series of articles on the Russian situation by a British journalist, Arnold White. Inspired by his anti-Semitism and by pro-czarist motives, White presented a blend of anti-Semitic imagery—how the western Jews controlled the press and world finance; how the eastern Jew, the ubiquitous usurer, differed racially from his countrymen—with suggestions on how to solve the Jewish question. On the premise that Jewish emigration increasingly troubled the Anglo-Saxon countries, he suggested that an international conference of Russia, England, and America discuss his plan for keeping the Jews in Russia. According to his proposal, Russia would find land for the distribution of the destitute Jews who were rapidly multiplying in the Pale of Settlement, and the Western countries, relying on Christians but principally on wealthy Jews, would supply funds for rehabilitation.[22]

Not all American Jews, even if they condemned White's Jew hatred, dismissed his plan of population transfer out of hand, but Schiff did. Angered by White's belief that heavy Russian immigration would create a serious Jewish problem in the Western world, Schiff decided to answer the journalist publicly. He was eager to expose White's anti-Semitism, and he also feared that an international conference would exacerbate worldwide Jew hatred. White was wrong on several counts, the banker contended. First, the immigrants constituted no problem in America; Jewish newcomers who quickly became self-supporting and Americanized were exemplary citizens. Second, the answer to the Russian Jewish plight lay *not* in pouring money into Russia for the erection of a larger Pale. Baron de Hirsch (whom White had once advised) had at first allocated funds for the rehabilitation of Jews in Russia, but his plans had failed. Not only did the Russian government refuse to cooperate, but it was said that they used the baron's money to build churches. Schiff insisted that the only proper answer had to come from Russia itself in the form of equal rights for Jews. To forestall any serious mischief by White, Schiff shared his views with TR, who quickly reassured him that there was no thought whatsoever of an international conference.[23]

A second postscript to Kishinev took on a longer-lasting significance. In the summer of 1903, Russia hardened its policy of refusing visas to American Jews. As long as the United States raised no objection, it was in effect participating in Russian discrimination, this time against its own citizens. Schiff remonstrated with Roosevelt, but the latter considered official objections useless. Although Schiff was reluctant to thrust a Jewish issue into politics, he felt forced to seek support from the two major parties.[24] Over the next few years, however, the Jewish stewards found a way of turning the insult against American Jews into a campaign to liberate the Jews of Russia (see below).

The Russo-Japanese War of 1904–5 gave Schiff the opportunity to flex his financial muscles in a grand manner, and as one American diplomat put it, he "went out of his way to help Japan." Years later, Cyrus Adler recalled a meeting of Jewish communal leaders in February 1904 in Schiff's home. There the banker stated: "Within 72 hours war will break out between Japan and Russia. The question has been presented to me of undertaking a loan for Japan. I would like to get your views as to what effect my undertaking of this would have upon the Jewish people in Russia." The consensus must have been favorable, because Kuhn, Loeb became active early in 1904 on Japan's behalf. Since TR and American public opinion also sided with Japan, Schiff had no compunctions about damage that he might cause the Russian regime. Japan was totally right and Russia totally wrong, the banker said. His contributions during the war earned him Japan's lasting gratitude and Russia's lasting anger. Interviewed in 1911, the Russian minister of finance said to journalist Herman Bernstein: "Our government will never forgive or forget what that Jew, Schiff, did to us. . . . He alone made it possible for Japan to secure a loan in America. He was one of the most dangerous men we had against us abroad."[25]

As the war progressed, Schiff saw Japanese gains redounding to the benefit of the Jews. Czarist officials would become convinced, he said, that changes in Jewish policies were necessary in order to strengthen Russia's international position. "Plehve [minister of the interior] and his colleagues are finally beginning to realize that they have made a complete mess of things . . . and I believe the Russian Government would now go very far to gain the good will of international Jewry." The banker confidently believed that Jewish action made a telling difference in the Russian situation. The ever growing influence of American Jews had altered the long-held pro-Russian sympathies of their compatriots, and his private war was showing results too. Jewish pressure on the American government and the press continued unabatedly, and the banker confided to Paul Nathan of the Hilfsverein that many other things, which he couldn't put in writing, made him feel optimistic. The fear of some Russian Jews that too much was being demanded of their government was of no consequence. "It is simply one more case of the experience which Moses had in Egypt when he intervened for Israel and tried to stir them up, 'but they hearkened not unto him, for anguish of spirit and for bondage.'"[26]

More determinedly than before, Schiff renewed efforts to block Russia's access to funds from abroad. At a private conference of leading New York bankers he dramatically announced that he had instructed Kuhn, Loeb to adhere to the policy of no loans to an anti-Semitic Russia even after his death. But his strategy could succeed only if other banking houses followed suit and remained impervious to Russian offers of three or four times the normal profit. He threatened to resign from the board of the National City Bank if it floated a Russian loan, and he argued with the Morgans, albeit in vain, that doing business with Russia was financially as well as morally unsound. Jewish houses fell into line more readily. Isaac Seligman of the Seligman firm reported in 1905 that as a unit they refused to handle Russian bonds as long as the country's Jewish policy remained unchanged.[27]

European Jewish bankers posed more of a problem, for some houses did aid Russia. In Schiff's words, "Jewish high finance" had the wherewithal to pressure Russia in the 1890s "but instead closed its eye to make a despicable profit, and rendered service to the Russian Government selling her Jewish subjects for a few pieces of silver." Lord Rothschild assured Schiff in 1904 that his London firm had not handled a Russian loan since 1875 and that Russia had no chance in England with either Jewish or, for that matter, non-Jewish houses. He was less sanguine about the firms on the Continent. Although the Paris Rothschilds were anti-Russia, former Jewish firms in Berlin were now either Christian or religionless. Besides, he reminded Schiff, the Continental bankers were under greater pressure from the shifting diplomatic maneuvers of their governments.[28]

Neither Rothschild nor Schiff was deterred by the possibility that their loan policies might provoke Russia still further against its Jews. Nor were they constrained by considerations of Jewish image. When the stakes were so high, it mattered less what non-Jews might say about international Jewish money power. Besides, two of Schiff's Christian friends, Andrew D. White and Charles Eliot, wondered why Jewish bankers did *not* exert unified pressure on Russia. Assuming the existence of an international banking combine, they turned the old stereotype around and used it to criticize Jewish inaction. The behavior of the Jewish bankers as a group, they charged, sabotaged the cause of Russian Jewish liberation. Ironically, Schiff and his associates were now called upon to explain why the nonexistent international combine of Jewish bankers had *not* mobilized its resources!

Schiff's hope for a united boycott of Russian loans never materialized. The condition of Russian Jews was not improved, and the efforts of Schiff and Rothschild only fed the myth of Jewish political machinations. Nevertheless, Schiff's intransigence on the matter of loans was significant enough to elicit special attention from the czarist regime.[29]

Wartime needs impelled Russia to try again to win over Schiff or at least to neutralize him. In 1904, von Plehve let it be known that he desired to confer with Schiff. The banker was amenable but only on two conditions:

(1) the minister had to invite him directly and not merely imply that Schiff would be received, and (2) restrictions on Jewish visas had to be abolished, for Schiff refused to visit Russia by special favor. Although equal rights for Jews were not mentioned, Schiff had not yielded. He believed and the Russian government also understood that "when foreign Jews are equally entitled to cross the Russian border with other foreigners, then the Russian Government will not long be able to insist on maintaining the scandalous restrictive laws against her own Jews." If Russia agreed to his terms, he would take on the mission as "the noblest task of my life."

Von Plehve's assassination a few weeks later, which Schiff explained as inescapable "divine justice," cut short the negotiations. Nevertheless, the banker reiterated his readiness to help Russia if the visa policy was changed. "If Czar Alexander II, with one stroke of a pen, could free millions of Serfs, who had certainly not attained to the cultural level of the Jews in Russia, there should be no difficulty in giving the Jews the same civic rights as are accorded to other Russian citizens." At this point, Schiff momentarily retreated from his original terms. Now prepared to accept a compromise that smacked of his American experience with immigrant distribution, he suggested a law permitting Jews to move freely about the empire but with certain restrictions—no further movement into regions where a large percentage of the population was Jewish and no settlement in new areas if the number of Jews would exceed the general proportion of Jews in the entire population.[30]

Russia continued to seek Schiff's financial help in America through Gregory Wilenkin, a privileged Russian Jew, who was a financial attaché in Washington and a distant relative of Schiff's brother-in-law, Isaac Seligman. Schiff gave Wilenkin his standard response: Russia had lost American money markets and goodwill by its "barbarous" treatment of the Jews, and only a complete reversal of policy (i.e., Jewish equality) could regain support among Americans and American Jewish bankers. Wilenkin persisted in his overtures for many years. In 1908 he invited Schiff again to St. Petersburg to confer with the minister of finance, but the banker cynically dismissed Romanov promises unaccompanied by concrete evidence of Jewish rights. Wilenkin also sounded out Schiff on a possible railroad deal in Manchuria between Russia and Japan. The banker agreed to pass on the suggestion to Baron Takahashi, perhaps to show Wilenkin his readiness to be of service to Russia if his conditions were met.[31] As discussed above, however, Schiff sided with Japan after the Russo-Japanese War in its competition with Russia in the Far East.

Direct negotiations with Russia, perhaps more than any other episode, revealed how far Schiff's power extended in Europe as well as in the United States. Equally striking was his characteristic independence. The Jewish community was neither alerted to nor asked to pass on his terms for dealing with Russia. He, the foremost Jewish leader, had the self-assumed right to lobby as he saw fit with the agents of the czar. Had it been otherwise, he doubtless would have declined any involvement.

The Russo-Japanese War allied Schiff with George Kennan in a venture to spread revolutionary propaganda among Russian prisoners of war held by Japan. The operation was a carefully guarded secret, and not until the Russian Revolution of March 1917 was it publicly disclosed by Kennan. He then told how he had secured Japanese permission to visit the camps and how the prisoners had asked him for something to read. Arranging for the Friends of Russian Freedom to ship over a ton of revolutionary material, he secured Schiff's financial backing. As Kennan told it, fifty thousand officers and men returned to Russia ardent revolutionists. There they became fifty thousand "seeds of liberty" in one hundred regiments that contributed to the overthrow of the czar.[32] Thus, just as the Russo-Japanese War changed power configurations on the international scene, so did it generate new strategies for Schiff to employ in his private war for Jewish liberation.

Diplomacy and Relief

An opportunity for the American stewards to plead the case of Russian Jewry directly to a high czarist official arose in the summer of 1905. When Sergius Witte led a Russian delegation to Portsmouth, New Hampshire, for the peace negotiations ending the Russo-Japanese War, Adolf Kraus of B'nai B'rith arranged for the Russian envoy to meet with five leading Jews. At first Schiff was reluctant to take part in a conference that he thought would prove futile. Nor did he want it said that he went to discuss Russian finances or, now that the war was over, to be in the position of a supplicant without any bargaining chips. Jews had to remain firm: "To give as hard knocks to Russia as we can, . . . to accept no promises in return for our aid, when this is asked for, and to do nothing for Russia until she has *actually* given civil rights to her Jewish subjects."[33] He was persuaded, however, to join Oscar Straus, Isaac Seligman, Adolph Lewisohn, and Kraus for a meeting with Witte and the Russian ambassador to the United States. A bold exercise of elitist leadership, the episode also illustrated the virtual impossibility of forging a consensus within the amorphous Jewish community.

Reporters who were closely monitoring Witte's doings met the Jews on their arrival at Portsmouth. The committee spoke guardedly. Schiff denied that the mission was concerned with financial matters; rather, the Jews wanted to show Witte that emigration in response to discrimination had become an international issue. Russian Jews were good citizens, he added, and the charge that their revolutionary activities were responsible for any persecution was utterly false. As a reminder of Schiff's status, the press noted that he was the first of the committee to enter Witte's room.[34]

At the three-hour conference the Jews reviewed the Russian situation in detail. Loans were not officially on the agenda, but the implication was clear enough when the stewards repeated Schiff's stock formula: Russian goodwill in America was endangered if Jews did not receive their rights. Witte, who was sensitive to popular dislike of Russia caused by the Jewish question, agreed in principle to equal rights. Unlike the Americans, however, he insisted on gradual rather than immediate emancipation. (According to one prominent American Jew who had not participated in the conference, Witte attributed anti-Semitism to racial, not religious reasons. But since the statement was loaded with harmful innuendos for all Jews, it was not divulged by either side.) A loyal supporter of the autocratic system, Witte had come to realize the necessity of political reforms. The Jews were impressed by him, and they in turn thought they had impressed him.[35]

Participants reported that only Schiff behaved antagonistically. When, for example, Witte urged the stewards to use their influence to keep Russian Jews out of the revolutionary camp, Schiff denied that the Americans had that power. Besides, "is it not probable that the young men became revolutionists in the hope that a republic will grant them just laws which are denied under the rule of the Emperor?" Four years later, Witte described Schiff's behavior: "I have never met such a Jew as Schiff. Proud, dignified, conscious of his power, he declared to me solemnly that so long as the Tsar's government would continue its anti-Jewish policy, he would exert every effort to make it impossible for Russia to get a copeck in the United States. He banged the table with his fist and declared that a government which indulged in massacres and inhuman persecution on religious grounds was not to be trusted."[36]

In the end, Schiff said that the conference had been worthwhile, perhaps just because he had irritated Witte. The president also heard that Schiff had prejudiced Witte against the Jewish cause, but outwardly the Russian official remained conciliatory. He dared not risk any offense to Kuhn, Loeb, and he privately assured the banker of his positive assessments of American Jewish sentiments. Publicly, Witte promised to seek amelioration of the Russian Jewish condition.[37]

The meeting aroused widespread comment. Secretary Elihu Root sneered at "certain Jews in America [who] were merely striving for notoriety,"[38] and secular papers talked of Jewish ultimatums or deals. On the other hand, leading Jewish periodicals commended the stewards, as did banker Samuel Montagu in London. Some hopefully noted reports from St. Petersburg that certain classes of Jews would be permitted to stand for election to the Russian Duma, but they wondered if Witte, no matter how

well-intentioned, could effect any meaningful change. When a serious pogrom occurred that very same month in Bialystok, doubts about the success of the meeting began to multiply. The Baltimore *Jewish Comment*,
which on August 18 had hailed the conference as "the most important Jewish demand for rights in Russia ever made to a responsible representative
of the Russian Government," admitted four weeks later that "so far as the
Jews are concerned, the visit of M. Witte was largely thrown away."

The episode reflected the state of communal disarray. Some Jews worried about the image of Jewish power projected by the press, others warned
of harmful consequences to Russian Jewry, and still others feared that
Witte's real achievement was a turn in American public sympathy toward
Russia. Jewish radicals in particular condemned the conference, arguing, as
did Abraham Cahan of the Socialist Yiddish *Forward*, that only a revolution
in Russia would bring about Jewish liberation. A good number of critics
denounced the *hofjudische* diplomatic approach that assumed the right of a
few powerful men to speak for the community. Some Russian Jews interrupted a synagogue meeting in Chicago, tossing around handbills that de-
rided the stewards as scheming politicians. The Zionist *Maccabaean* ranted
about the unrepresentative character of the Jewish delegation. Had the
Jewish people been consulted—and that should have included Jews in Russia as well as America—they most likely would have shunned an interview
with Witte. Feeding the growing indictment of elitist leadership, the journal stated: "We should be only too glad to see Mr. Schiff and Mr. Oscar
Straus elected to carry out a Jewish policy—but it must be a policy that has
the sanction of the people who elect them to bear their messages to the nations." Even the loyal *American Hebrew* saw the persistence of "mediaeval
practices" in the absence of a modern representative body. One Jewish
newspaper concluded that Jewish complaints about the meeting had vi-
tiated the chance to make a strong impression on Witte. If the Russian sur-
veyed the gamut of reactions, "he will probably come to the conclusion
that the Jews do not know what they want themselves; how, then, can Russia be expected to give it to them."

Criticism failed to goad Schiff into a public debate. Only to Paul Nathan, who also complained that the Americans should have linked the Jewish question with the larger issue of radical changes in the Russian government, did he defend the strategy of asking solely for Jewish equality. "If the
Russian population is not satisfied with its Government . . . it is obviously
for the whole Russian people to take such steps as may bring about a
change." Financial support of societies like Kennan's Friends of Russian
Freedom was rather harmless, but Schiff probably reasoned that it would
have been highly irresponsible for the stewards to behave as if international
Jewry was fomenting a revolution against the czar. On the issue of democratic versus elitist leadership he had no comment at all.[39]

Whatever hopes Schiff entertained of Jewish liberation by the revolutionary upheaval of 1905 in Russia were dashed by the wave of reaction that
swept the country in the fall of that same year. From mid-October to the
end of November, 690 pogroms erupted, leaving close to 900 Jews killed,
between 7,000 and 8,000 injured, and property damage estimated in millions of rubles. "One must almost lose one's faith in mankind," Schiff wrote
to Cassel, "if such horrors, beside which even a Bartholomew's night pales,
can be perpetrated at this day." Since the outbreaks continued into 1906,
the number of casualties mounted even higher. Witte was then prime minister, and Schiff accepted his explanation faulting local authorities for the
atrocities. The banker neither blamed Jews for siding with the revolution-
aries, nor did he believe that rights for Jews would spark new pogroms. At
the same time he sought comfort in a spiritual explanation. There was a
higher purpose to Jewish suffering, he said. Jews had been sacrificed
throughout the ages in order for mankind to enjoy better things, and "so it
is now in Russia where the Jew must die so that freedom and liberty may
become living facts." The sorry events presaged Russia's doom: "As sure as
there is a God who looks down on all mankind, bitter vengeance will some
day be wrought."[40]

The victims could not wait for divine retribution. Since the American
ambassador, like his predecessors, ignored the atrocities and since the Red
Cross erroneously claimed that it provided generous relief to the sufferers,
help lay only with fellow Jews. A flurry of cables between Schiff and leading European Jews greeted the news of the first pogroms. A few days later,
in tandem with European relief activities, the stewards established the first
national organization for the relief of foreign Jews, the National Committee for Relief of Sufferers by Russian Massacres (NCRSRM). Whereas relief efforts for Kishinev in 1903 had been handled locally, the NCRSRM
was a centralized national body. At an emotional community-wide meeting
at Temple Emanu-El, Oscar Straus was elected chairman; Schiff, treasurer;
and Cyrus Sulzberger secretary. Although opinions clashed on whether relief should go to Christians as well as Jews, the same downtowners who
were quick to find fault with aristocratic leadership readily yielded in the
emergency to the dictates of the stewards. Headed by a small executive
committee of ten (Abraham Cahan was the sole representative of the
downtown element), the NCRSRM immediately launched an ambitious
and highly successful campaign. If the Portsmouth meeting with Witte
epitomized elitist highhandedness, the relief committee proved the organizational skills and tireless efforts of the same elite.[41]

Over Schiff's signature wires appealing for funds went out to Jewish
communities throughout the land. The committee enlisted the aid of rabbis
and congregations, social societies, fraternal orders and lodges; businesses

and trades were mobilized, and so were university students; Talmud Torahs were canvassed, and banks on New York's Lower East Side were authorized to accept donations. Although no direct appeal was made to Christians, the press was alerted, and some churches and clergymen added their contributions.[42] The NCRSRM's sole competitor was the Jewish Self-Defense Association, which aimed to provide arms for Russian Jews. A movement that symbolized Jewish independence and self-reliance, it had a distinct antisteward ring. Bemoaning the passivity of his fellow Jews, one Zionist criticized dependence on the steward "who cringingly sought the favor of the ... mighty ones, generally mingling his voice of wailing with the ringing sound of precious metal." Schiff himself contributed to the defense fund; but doubtless worried by reports that the fund was used for revolutionary purposes instead of defense, he stayed aloof from managing the fund.[43]

The popular response to the NCRSRM was almost deafening. In addition to contributions, all sorts of letters were received, from those inquiring about the fate of relatives in Russia to those from entertainers offering their talents on behalf of the cause. Within less than a month the NCRSRM raised close to $1 million from 690 localities and 399 lodges and societies. New York City's share came to almost one-half of the total, but responses from far-flung cities and towns—often less than $5 and sometimes accompanied by a note in Yiddish, Hebrew, or ungrammatical English—testified to the committee's extensive and efficient labors. Each donation was recorded and acknowledged by Schiff's office. The banker personally thanked Christian leaders and prominent public figures (like J. P. Morgan) at the same time that he advanced sums to Europe before their actual receipt.

Overall, Schiff's supervision guaranteed a strictly businesslike campaign. The unprecedented success of the relief drive, successful enough to permit withholding a portion in reserve for future emergencies, proved that American Jewish unity was soonest attained in response to the needs of fellow Jews abroad. Ironically, a successful relief drive of this kind could be self-defeating. Some stewards noted bitterly that they were creating a "Pogrom Endowment Fund,"[44] assuring Russia that Jewish money would enter the country whenever pogroms occurred.

Schiff's role encompassed more than that of treasurer. For all intents and purposes he was the linchpin or cohesive element that bonded the American and European Jewish leaders. Since he was the powerful banker who enjoyed access to President Roosevelt as well as to Witte, it was natural for the Europeans to turn to him first. With Rothschild and Montagu of London, Nathan of Berlin, and Baron Horace Guenzberg in Russia, who was authorized by his government to supervise the distribution of funds, Schiff was pivotal in the planning and execution of strategy. The joint labors of this handful of men dealt with all facets of the relief problem: they shared news reports on daily developments from private, reliable sources; they arranged the complicated logistics of safely transmitting funds so that the money would not fall into the hands of Russian officials; they carefully monitored collections while urging an equitable response from all Western countries; they sent Paul Nathan and two others on a fact-finding mission to the stricken areas; and they considered provisions for children orphaned by the pogroms. Seeking a united Jewish front, Schiff criticized the Alliance Israélite Universelle, which, out of frustration that it could not control operations, remained aloof. The spectacle of even partial international unity was impressive, but Schiff and the NCRSRM never forgot the American pressures on them. Sensitive to popular restrictionist sentiment, they turned down participation in an international conference lest it raise the specter of a significant wave of refugee immigrants. And although victims appealed directly for funds with which to immigrate, they refused to countenance induced or assisted immigration.[45]

Schiff's British associates simultaneously pressed him to seek Roosevelt's intercession. On December 5, Montagu wired: "Do you think your President would . . . initiate identical notes of great powers asking for equal rights for Jews so as to prevent outrages in the future?" Both Schiff and Oscar Straus were in touch with the State Department and the White House, but whereas Straus was determined to shield Roosevelt from what he considered impossible demands, Schiff knew no such limits. He agreed that a joint international remonstrance was impossible, but as he wrote the president, something had to be done to prevent further slaughter. Hinting at the use of force against Russia, he reminded Roosevelt of American humanitarian intervention in Cuba: "If you personally then felt so strongly in this regard that you willingly took your life into your hands to help to prevent the oppression of the Cuban people . . . is it not in the face of the horrors now occurring in Russia, and which its very Government declares it is powerless to prevent, the duty of the civilized world to intervene?" Terming Schiff's request "hysterical," Roosevelt dismissed it out of hand. Not only was diplomatic pressure useless when a country was gripped by revolution, but the United States could not be the policeman for the rights of ethnic groups like Armenians or Jews. Empty threats without a readiness to go to war had no effect; as the saying went, "Never draw unless you mean to shoot." Perhaps impressed by reports on Russian Jewish revolutionary activity from his friend the British ambassador to St. Petersburg, Sir Cecil Spring-Rice (never a philo-Semite), Roosevelt also warned that a show of force could boomerang against American as well as Russian Jews.[46]

Independently, Schiff carried American Jewish protests to high Russian quarters. In communication with Witte, he reminded the prime minister of his assurances at Portsmouth and warned of a mass exodus from Russia if Witte's government failed to emancipate the Jews. In that event, he predicted, Russia's fate would be sealed. Although not fully convinced of the prime minister's goodwill, he refused to stage an endrun around Witte by purchasing the help of the high Russian nobility. Until the end of 1905 he continued to hope that liberal reform would crush the reactionary forces.[47]

Reaction and recurring pogroms continued to sweep Russia in 1906. No help for the Jews came from the Duma, and Witte was removed from power in April. Verbal prodding from TR helped to avert pogroms during Easter, but in June the Jews of Bialystok were again badly hit. Schiff called Bialystok the last gasp of a dying regime, but he too lost his usual optimism. Tried stratagems—pressure on the administration, attempts to influence public opinion through the press and periodicals, efforts to block Russian loans—had little telling effect. He turned yet again to the president, but Roosevelt refused to rebuke Russia publicly. Undeterred by the TR's mounting impatience, Schiff enlisted his son, the president's neighbor in Oyster Bay, to relay his messages and the grim cables from Europe. I know you can't help, he admitted to TR, and only the horror of the situation prompted his requests. To feel powerless was "maddening." Grasping at straws, he mentioned a report that the French might send ships to evacuate the victims. If they did, it would be "the greatest act of humanity" by any government. On another occasion he suggested that Roosevelt write directly to the czar. Nevertheless, his appeals to Roosevelt's humanitarianism failed.[48]

The appointment of Oscar Straus to the cabinet (1906), which Schiff, like TR, held up as a lesson to Russia on how Jews should be treated, made no impression on the czarist regime. In those trying days other approaches were equally unsuccessful. Despite Jewish counterefforts, Russia succeeded in floating a loan through French banks and the Baring house in London. And since the Associated Press, under the biased management of Melville Stone, kept up the distribution of pro-Russia reports to the press, appeals for enlightened public opinion became empty rhetoric.[49]

Schiff confessed to a friend that his mind was occupied day and night with the Russian situation. Loath to admit utter helplessness, he tried to mobilize non-Jewish allies; he met with the representative of the Russian Peasant Party, and he supported Jan Pouren, whose extradition was demanded by Russia. Out of desperation and out of character, he also canvassed associates for ideas on what to attempt next. Although he felt that he should scale down his activities when he turned sixty, he refused to admit defeat in his war against the czar.[50]

Sir Ernest Cassel, now the close associate of Edward VII, offered a new approach. He told Schiff that "Nature has not endowed me with the capacity which has enabled you to become one of the foremost leaders to fight against an enormous power," but he was prompted by Schiff's work during 1905–6 to try his hand at the improvement of the Russo-Jewish situation.

Now he suggested a policy of "friendly persuasion," by which he meant loans to Russia, which he thought would redound to the benefit of the Jews. He also believed that the international realignment after the Russo-Japanese War that led Russia to seek a rapprochement with England augured well. In contact with high Russian officials, Cassel told them that "fair play" for the Jews would aid immeasurably in their country's economic development. Schiff, however, preferred diplomatic isolation of the czarist regime. He was never convinced that the carrot, be it money or England's friendship, was more efficacious than the stick. "Die Botschaft hör ich gerne, aber mir fehlt der Glaube," he answered his friend.[51] According to Schiff, England's shameful support emboldened Russia to drop even the pretense of promising Jewish rights in exchange for loans. He himself demanded proof of a changed policy toward Jews when Wilenkin again urged him in 1908 to meet with the Russian minister of finance. On that occasion, the Russian gave no promises. Rather, he advised that the timing was wrong for a discussion of the Jewish question.[52]

The story goes that Cassel consulted Schiff about another tactic, a personal interview with the czar. Two oral accounts, both attributed to Schiff and resurrected after his death, related that Cassel attempted in 1909 to see the czar on behalf of the Jews. (A letter from Schiff to President Taft's brother in August 1909 also hinted mysteriously that the idea of a meeting between a certain "individual" and the czar was under consideration.) But although the czar liked Cassel, he refused to discuss the Jewish question with him.[53] Since all tried roads appeared blocked, Schiff and his associates fell back on one last idea, the use of the passport issue as the means for effecting the liberation of Russian Jewry.

Schiff versus Taft

The campaign orchestrated by the AJC and its spectacular success in forcing the government to terminate a treaty with Russia, the source of the passport impasse,[54] was a significant first in the annals of American Jewish stewardship. It differed from the usual tactics of quiet diplomacy in three essential ways: an ambitious *public* effort, it aroused popular opinion and Congress to a near "wave of hysteria"; it injected a Jewish issue squarely into the political forum; and it put a Jewish organization in an adversarial position vis-à-vis the incumbent administration. It was a gamble fraught with many dangers; failure would have meant a loss of influence with the government and possibly an anti-Semitic reaction to open Jewish agitation. On the scale of communal leadership the stewards also scored well. Here too they alone fixed strategy and worked out the details of a tight, well-coordinated campaign. The larger community went unrepresented, but the same complaints against elitist control that accompanied the meeting with Witte, the NCRSRM, and the organization of the AJC and the *kehillah* were not heard. Not only did the masses share the desire to defeat Russia, but even if they understood the blueprints of the campaign, they could not help being overwhelmed by the AJC's skillful, steamrolling tactics.

Technically, the AJC ran the campaign, widely publicizing the issue and mobilizing congressmen, opinion molders, religious leaders, and the public at large to their side. Behind the scenes, however, Schiff as always took center stage. To be sure, the daily moves were executed by Marshall, Adler, and a few others, but no step was taken or decision made without the banker's clearance and consent. Nor did committee action constrain him, a leader rather than a team player, from striking out on his own. When he saw fit, he used his own contacts and issued his own statements. Angry, defiant, and obsessed with the Russian issue, he turned the campaign for abrogation into a personal contest with President William Howard Taft. Privately, the latter too felt personally challenged, and he blamed the matter on "Jake Schiff" and his vanity. At times the banker's associates feared his quick tongue and hasty actions, but Mayer Sulzberger, the respected elder statesman of the AJC, was more tolerant: "On the general principle that every successful business needs and has a wicked partner, there is no occasion for tears or regrets. Nagging and dunning are sometimes more effective than genteeler methods."[55]

By the terms of a commercial treaty of 1832 reciprocal rights of sojourn and trade were granted Russians and Americans. In the last quarter of the nineteenth century, however, Russia began to restrict American Jews seeking to enter the country, refusing even to visa passports. Sporadic protests by the United States moved Russia only to make some exceptions but not to retreat in principle. As Jewish leaders bitterly noted, as long as America accepted such practices, it was in effect participating in discrimination against its own citizens. Seeking help from both the Republican and Democratic parties, the banker also reminded TR of the importance of the issue to Jewish voters. Defining the matter as an American issue, the stewards rightly charged that Jewish equality was being compromised.

Although the sanctity of the American passport and the stigma of second-class citizenship constituted the core of the public brief for abrogation, the Jewish stewards were at least equally committed to the idea that abrogation would effect the liberation of Russian Jewry. Given the Russian premise that foreign Jews could not be treated differently from native Jews, it followed that if Russia granted full rights to foreign Jews, it would have to accord the same privileges—tantamount to civic equality—to its own subjects. Schiff had explained even before the establishment of the AJC that "when foreign Jews are equally entitled to cross the Russian border with other foreigners, then the Russian Government will not long be able to insist on maintaining the scandalous restrictive laws against her own Jews." Therefore, one of the conditions he made in 1904 for a visit to Russia was the removal of restrictions on foreign Jews. Were the United States successful in changing czarist policy on Americans, then, according to Schiff's scenario, other nations would follow suit on behalf of their citizens and thus radically alter the course of Russian Jewish life.

The Russian situation had worsened steadily after 1906. In Schiff's words, pogroms had given way to "the still more brutal method of slow extermination" that resulted from the crippling restrictions on Jewish settlement and economic life. After a trip to Europe in 1909 he reported that no major outbreaks had occurred, but "it is the quiet of the grave." Since "slow and deliberate" repression was unlikely to awaken public interest or to prompt American action,[56] the committee called for outright abrogation of the treaty. In a letter to TR the organization spelled out both purposes, the rights of American Jews and the liberation of Russian Jews. A few months later, Secretary Elihu Root told Schiff that America preferred revision to termination of the treaty and that it had so informed Russia. There matters stood when Roosevelt left office.

More encouraging was the seeming sympathy of the incoming administration. Taft had written the Republican pledge on the rights of passport holders, and he had addressed the issue in campaign speeches. Lest he forget, Schiff pointedly reminded him of its importance for Jewish voters. Arguing for American Jewish equality, Schiff added that if Protestants were denied entry, all nations would doubtless sever diplomatic relations with Russia. Taft promised that the matter had his special attention; and although the banker was unsure whether the administration would live up to its word, the stewards held their fire for the time being.[57]

During his first year in office, Taft instructed Secretary of State Philander Knox to attend to the situation, but by February 1910 the AJC had become increasingly impatient. Taft would do everything to satisfy another group of citizens in a similar situation, Schiff said at an executive meeting of the AJC. "We were simply licking the hands of the President. We do not respect ourselves sufficiently to come out boldly and demand our rights. . . . We have been fed on similar promises and assurances for many years, . . . but four more years will pass, and nothing will have been accomplished." He urged strong action: "Unless the President is made to understand what it is we want and that we want it very much, there will be a revolt on the part of the Russian-Jewish Citizens which could not be checked."

Although Schiff, a loyal Republican, professed a "warm attachment" to Taft personally, he was determined to hold the president to his campaign promises. Taft was "inclined to take things easy," and he had to understand "that we are going to see this thing through. . . . We must not let him off." Simultaneously, his differences with the administration over the Galveston movement (see below) as well as Taft's refusal to consider Louis Marshall for the Supreme Court were also straining his relations with the president. Despite two subsequent conferences at the White House, the banker was not pacified. Perhaps the time had come to "build a fire in the rear of the President" and to force Taft to act.[58]

The hyperbole and intemperate remarks testify to Schiff's belief that his personal honor was on the line. The leading American Jew of his generation, whose loyalty to the country was unimpeachable, his position demanded uncompromising resistance to a policy that violated American Jewish equality. As the would-be redeemer of Russian Jewry whose various strategems had fallen short of the desired climax, he also felt that he was racing against time. To effect the liberation of Russia Jewry, which had become the most important mission of his life, he seized what appeared to be the last chance. He directed his frustration and determination against the Taft administration, gambling that Taft was an easier mark than Roosevelt.

Schiff, whose subsequent wires to the White House went unanswered, understood that under the influence of the State Department and the ambassador to Russia, Taft had changed his mind on the need to conciliate the Jews. A submissive president now acknowledged that Russia's legal case justified restrictions against foreign Jews, and he was fully convinced that stern diplomatic measures would imperil American business interests in Russia. Moreover, since Ambassador William Rockhill maintained that Russian Jewish suffering was grossly exaggerated, the administration now warned that anti-Russian action might worsen the Jewish condition.[59] Aware of the forces arrayed against the Jewish cause in both the executive and the legislative branches of government, Schiff also knew that Russia was more resistant to American pressure, both because of Jewish aid to Japan in 1904–5 and because of its own recent rapprochement with Japan. Despite the obstacles, the banker urged Louis Marshall to discuss the case for abrogation in an address to a national Jewish audience, a meeting of the Union of American Hebrew Congregations (UAHC), in January 1911. Indeed, to ignore the matter might lead the government to infer that the Jews were less concerned than they really were.[60] A public address was the AJC's final warning. Continued inaction by the government, the organization was saying, could force it to run a public campaign that made abrogation nonnegotiable.

A turning point both in the AJC's decision to go public and the Schiff–Taft rift came in February. Marshall's impressive speech, followed by the UAHC's unanimous resolution calling for the termination of the treaty, failed to convince the president, and he invited a small group of Jewish leaders of the AJC, UAHC, and B'nai B'rith to a conference at the

White House. Taft thought that he could win the Jews to his side with the vague promise of continued reminders to Russia, but he misjudged the temper of his guests. They were in no mood to be cajoled by presidential affability; and with Schiff and Marshall as their designated spokesmen, they had resolved to stand as a unit behind abrogation. Much to their dismay, Taft began by reading a long explanation of why he had decided against abrogation. After rehashing the legal and economic arguments as well as the futility of abrogation as a corrective to Russian policy, he admitted that if he were a Jew he would feel differently. "But I am the President of the whole country," he concluded, and obligated to weigh the total picture. By ignoring the ground rules of a bona fide give-and-take—as Schiff angrily said the meeting was not a conference but merely a stage for the president to present his conclusions—and by implying that the Jewish interest was narrower than the American, Taft and his political ineptitude sorely offended the conferees. Simon Wolf of the UAHC asked him not to publish the statement, but Schiff, enraged and agitated, responded differently: "I want it published. I want the whole world to know the President's attitude."

A brief recess during which the Jews, at the president's behest, read a long and what Schiff termed an insulting, pro-Russian memorandum from Rockhill served to fuel the banker's anger further. He lashed out at Taft:

> Mr. President, you have said that you are not prepared to permit the commercial interests of ninety-eight million of the American people to suffer because two million feel that their rights are being infringed upon. My own opinion has always been that it was the privilege of the head of this nation that, if only a single American citizen was made to suffer injury, the entire power of this great Government should be exercised to procure redress for such injury, and now you tell us . . . you would not do anything to protect two million American citizens in the rights vouchsafed to them under our Constitution and laws. We feel deeply mortified that in this instance, Mr. President, you have failed us, and there is nothing left to us now but to put our case before the American people directly, who are certain to do us justice. . . . In 1861 . . . public opinion insisted that the slave must be freed and the Union remain supreme at any cost; the war for the right was thereupon fought and won. . . . To this same public opinion, Mr. President, we shall now turn, and we have no fear of the results.

The only American Jew on record who so badgered a president, Schiff alone did not shake the president's hand when the meeting ended. One conferee sadly summed up the episode with the words "Wir sind in Golus." Schiff, however, in characteristic fashion, told Marshall, "This means war" and pledged $25,000 toward the cost of a public campaign.[61]

The disastrous conference gave the green light to the AJC to make public the fight for abrogation. They planned and executed a masterful campaign that publicized Russian discrimination against American passport holders, they encouraged pro-abrogation rallies in various cities, and they labored painstakingly to garner political support on the state and federal levels. Initially, the stewards envisioned a campaign that would last until the presidential election of 1912, but the overwhelming support they received allowed them to telescope the schedule into ten months. Schiff, who threw himself enthusiastically into the campaign, guided or at least passed on all strategy concerning publicity, finances, and pressure on lawmakers. In contact with interested organizations like the Friends of Russian Freedom[62] and in constant correspondence with prominent political figures, he and the AJC displayed a keen understanding of the basic rules of minority politics: the need to present a united Jewish front, the advantages of non-Jewish allies and spokesmen, the importance of tapping individual experts or men of influence within a far-flung Jewish network, and above all, the careful definition of the cause in American rather than Jewish terms. They made the moral and legal wrong against American passport holders, not rights for Russians, the focus of attention. To pressure the government on what rightly belonged to its citizens held out a greater chance of success than to beg Russia for favors to Jews.

Schiff himself exploded a minor bombshell at a conference of leading Jews with New York's senators, Root and O'Gorman. Offended by Root's opposition to abrogation, he told how Ambassador Rockhill, supposedly working toward a solution, had stated publicly that business interests overshadowed the passport issue. He also revealed what Wilenkin had told him about Russia's negotiations with Taft's friend, businessman John Hays Hammond. Although Taft was ignorant of the entire episode, and despite Hammond's countercharge that Schiff's account was "an unqualified falsehood, a cowardly lie," the story left the impression that Hammond had influenced the president and that the administration ranked financial profit above American rights.[63]

On his own, Schiff followed up the February conference with a letter to Taft repeating his criticisms of the president's stance. Proving that the banker's verbal outburst had been more than a momentary loss of temper, the letter put the president on the defensive. His bitterness toward Schiff grew as the abrogation campaign progressed, and he spread the word among his friends that the Jewish leader was bent on destroying him politically. "[Schiff] has been consumed with fury because he could not control the Administration and sacrifice all national interests to the gratification of his vanity and that of some wealthy Hebrews," the president said. To the editor-in-chief of the *New York Tribune* he wrote that he was threatened with the "formidable" Jewish vote. "It . . . can easily be roused on such an issue and Jake Schiff is . . . spending money to rouse it, but he can't frighten me into a useless injury to our National interests, not to advance a principle but to gratify his vanity." Taft stubbornly maintained that abrogation was the wrong strategy; but in the face of the mounting public agitation that was "growing like a weed," he tried anew to press American demands on Russia. By the fall, Schiff happily commented that it had become "fashionable to be on our side."[64]

Seeking to circumvent executive opposition, the AJC pressed for a joint congressional resolution calling for the termination of the treaty. Congress obliged in December 1911, and when hearings were held on the resolution, Schiff was called to testify. The banker's flair for dramatic words came across in his presentation before the House Committee on Foreign Affairs. Leaving the legalist approach to Marshall and the others, he impassionedly invoked principle:

> Gentlemen, just think of it! If any of you who may happen to confess the Jewish faith, any American who accidentally was born of Jewish parentage, wants to go to the Far East to-day, and wants to take the shortest route, he takes the Trans-Siberian Railway. When he comes to the Russian border he is told "No thoroughfare." Just think of it, gentlemen, just think of what that means to an American. . . . Are you going to stand for this?[65]

The result was never in doubt. With only one dissenting vote in the House, Congress went on record in favor of abrogation. The issue had captured the nation's approval; few Americans understood the legal or diplomatic considerations, and even fewer had conflicting interests.

Schiff took the initiative toward a reconciliation with Taft. When he was sure of victory in Congress, he asked the president for a private meeting. He followed up his request by sending Taft medicines for his attacks of gout and rheumatism! In mid-December, a day after the government notified Russia of the termination of the treaty, he wired congratulations to Taft. But the latter was not that easily appeased. Shortly after his defeat for reelection in 1912, he bitterly commented that he had been right all along in opposing abrogation and that the joke was on Schiff and his "circumcised brothers."[66] Russian resistance to American pressure hardened during 1912, and both foreign and native Jews were threatened with added restrictions. In the United States resentment against abrogation was also heard. Henry Ford played on the theme in the *Dearborn Independent* of 1921, and his anti-Semitic tirades highlighted abrogation under the words "*Frankfort-on-the-Main had won!*"

Schiff hailed the abrogation victory in jubilant words: "For the first time,

Russia, that great Colossus, has received a slap in the face from a great nation, which act . . . must be of the greatest consequence in the history of civilization." And now, at Hanukkah time, he looked to the "Maccabaeans in Europe" to follow the American Jewish example. Much to his disappointment and contrary to what his private sources had led him to expect, supportive action from western Europe failed to materialize. Moreover, he and his associates were forced to stand guard during Wilson's administration lest discrimination find its way into any new commercial treaty.[67]

Despite customary public denials by the stewards of the existence of a Jewish vote, Schiff, like any good minority leader, understood the importance of rewarding the friends of abrogation with Jewish political support. In 1912, after four decades as a loyal Republican, he switched to the Democratic side. Alienated by Taft's behavior on the passport matter, he preferred the Democratic contender, Woodrow Wilson, a supporter of abrogation who had promised after his nomination that he would oppose any future treaty with Russia that discriminated against Jews. Since the Republican party was split between the Taft wing and the Progressives under the leadership of TR, the banker knew that the Democrats had a better than even chance. He may have reasoned too that any Democratic ambassador to St. Petersburg was hardly likely to chalk up a worse record on the Jewish situation than his Republican predecessors. Disagreeing with his staunch ally Marshall on Republican loyalty, Schiff denied that he was leaving the Republicans permanently or "running with the winning horse."[68]

The banker had no qualms about deserting the once admired Roosevelt. Although he was grateful for Roosevelt's prior help on behalf of eastern European Jews, he had been put off during the abrogation campaign by TR's proposal to arbitrate the passport impasse. Moreover, he was disturbed by the ultraprotectionist stand of the Progressive party and Roosevelt's calls for seemingly radical reforms. He perceived a lust for power in the candidate, a man who saw himself as "a Caesar." When George Perkins, one of Roosevelt's financial angels, intimated that Schiff turned to Wilson for business reasons, the banker hotly denied the charge. "I am not standing at Armageddon and battling for the Lord," he retorted in a sneer at Roosevelt's rallying cry. He told Perkins that he too could quote the Bible: "Not of bread alone man liveth."[69]

The abrogation campaign also committed Schiff to Democrat William Sulzer in New York's gubernatorial race. Although his friend Oscar Straus was the Progressive candidate, Schiff had promised to support Sulzer, then chairman of the House Committee on Foreign Affairs, on whose resolution the House of Representatives had voted for abrogation. Explaining that "vegam Harbona zachur latob!" (Hebrew for "And may Harbona too be remembered for good," a reference to a palace eunuch who befriended Mordecai in the book of Esther), he told Straus, "Mr. Sulzer saved the day for us." Straus's family, however, thought differently. Straus's sister-in-law, Mrs. Nathan Straus, commented bitterly that Oscar's election might have benefited the Jews and that Schiff's stand "has hurt the Jewish cause more than can be made good in years to come." Nevertheless, Straus and Schiff remained friends.

Never in doubt, Sulzer's victory climaxed a campaign in which he played up his aid to the Jews. Less than a year later, however, he was impeached. Since the governor had failed to report Schiff's check for $2,500 in his statement of campaign contributions, Schiff became peripherally involved in the proceedings. He testified that the gift was "unrestricted" and that Sulzer had the use of the money for any purpose whatsoever. It was at best a disingenuous answer, for a note in the banker's handwriting on the face of the check indicated that the gift was earmarked for campaign purposes. More important to Schiff, however, was the need to demonstrate to non-Jewish powerbrokers that Jews paid their political debts.[70]

Abrogation failed to bring about Russian Jewish emancipation, but Schiff and the AJC could claim at least a partial victory. Their campaign had shown that American Jewry refused to accept the government's violation of Jewish equality. More than the others, Schiff and Marshall, whom Schiff called the "real soul" behind abrogation,[71] personified a new breed of emancipated Jew, different from his cringing ghetto ancestors and unafraid to defend Jewish rights.

5

In Search of a Refuge

The American Solution: Unrestricted Immigration

As long as the persecution of Russian Jews persisted, the flow of emigrants continued to swell. Jewish leaders in the Western world were forced to admit that the alternative, the rehabilitation of Jewry under the czar, was a losing proposition. In terms of sheer economic and physical survival, the exodus from eastern Europe could not be stayed. The need for havens of refuge was imperative, and it nagged incessantly at Schiff. Although he was prepared to consider other solutions, the United States still ranked highest of all possible options.

The ambivalent and even negative attitude on the part of American Jews toward the entry of large numbers of eastern Europeans in the 1880s and early 1890s gradually changed to one in defense of free immigration. Ultimately a "constant" in American Jewish history, it mustered overwhelming support within the community. In pre–World War I days, when new arrivals customarily earmarked part of their meager earnings for the purchase of passage to America for relatives in Europe, the issue transcended religious and political differences and united Orthodox with freethinkers, Zionists with anti-Zionists, and uptown with downtown. Even Jewish Socialists, breaking with classic socialist dogma, refused to ignore Jewish problems in eastern Europe and the need for safe havens. The early arrivals themselves contributed to the change in the stewards' attitude. Their rapid Americanization, economic mobility, and assumption of responsibility toward the succeeding waves of newcomers significantly abetted the leaders' efforts at alleviating the ghetto problems. Downtown as usual was not privy to strategy formulated by the stewards, but it registered its support of free immigration in the Yiddish press and in elections. Differences with the stewards over tactics persisted. When, for example, uptown opposed the government's classification of Jews as a separate race, Zionists, who defined Jews as a discrete people with national interests, disagreed. To avoid more serious communal rifts, the stewards of the American Jewish Committee (AJC) held meetings with other groups and even consented to public rallies. Such conciliatory moves were necessary both to preserve their own leadership and to show politicians, who were becoming increasingly sensitive to the immigrant vote, the unified stand of the Jewish community.[1]

Fortified by opposition on the part of organized labor, patrician activism in the Immigration Restriction League, and the popularity of racism particularly in the South and Far West, restrictionists pushed for legal barriers to immigration, notably the literacy test. Their pressure reinforced the Jewish resolve to defend unrestricted entry. It was one thing for Jews to criticize immigration privately or to argue with their European counterparts about saddling America with a disproportionate share of the burden, but quite another when non-Jews and the government made the same points. Selected immigration presented a feasible option only if the selection was done by the Jews themselves. Were America to close its doors even partially, hope for victims of future and perhaps graver crises would be dimmed. Legally mandated restriction, particularly in a popular racist garb, not only impeded the entry of foreign Jews but threatened to set off acculturated American Jews, by association, as a less than desirable element. Thus, security for themselves as well as responsibility for their fellow Jews led the normally hyperaccommodationist minority leaders to an open challenge of regnant public opinion.[2]

Business had long defended immigration as a source of cheap labor, but Schiff approached the issue not as a businessman but as a Jew. To be sure, before the turn of the century he too supported systematized and selected immigration (i.e., a preference for the hardy and industrious), and he too was concerned with the horrors of ghetto blight. But unlike some of his contemporaries he suggested neither an end to immigration nor deportations. He once remarked that Russian Jews who were sent back for whatever reason "are sent back to hell." Nor, despite an occasional allusion to increased social prejudice spawned by the problems of the new arrivals, did he blame the Russians for causing American anti-Semitism. He constantly warned European Jewish leaders to avoid stimulated or assisted immigration that ran afoul of American law, but he sought liberal construction of existing regulations by sympathetic immigration authorities. On one occasion in the 1890s he charged the assistant secretary of the treasury, who was in charge of immigration, with obstructive and oppressive tactics against new arrivals. He called for the official's removal, and the latter's superior, Secretary Charles Foster, complied. In 1892 the banker complained directly to President Benjamin Harrison about the obstacles put in the way of immigrant admissions. His remarks applied to all immigrants, he said,

but since "I do not hesitate to admit that my sympathies are specially in behalf of the members of my own race," he wrote a lengthy defense of the
Jewish newcomers.[3]

Regarded by associates as second to none in the championship of liberal
immigration, Schiff insisted that exclusion was "un-American," in violation
of both America's best interests and its mission as a haven for the oppressed. He also decried the "narrowness" of restrictionists who had found
their opportunity in the United States but now denied the same opportunity to would-be immigrants. All Americans, they themselves or their
fathers or grandfathers, had been immigrants. "If we are going to reverse
the immigration policy which has prevailed since times immemorial, . . . we
had better first proceed to Plymouth Rock and blast it into fragments, for it
is there where the first immigrants . . . proclaimed the policy, towards
which they in fact pledged themselves and all those who were to come after
them."[4] Schiff's knowledge of colonial history may have been less than accurate, but as he presented it, the desire for religious freedom on the part
of Russian Jewish immigrants was akin to the Pilgrim spirit.

Alert to the mounting agitation for restriction in the new century, the
banker publicly reiterated time and again that the United States had ample
room to absorb those able and willing to do manual labor. Especially impatient with those Jews who sided with the restrictionists and thereby stirred
up non-Jewish ill-feeling, he warned against leading Russia to believe that
American Jews opposed immigration. An anti-immigration stand, he maintained, served only to justify czarist anti-Semitism.[5]

Certain seeming inconsistencies ran through Schiff's thinking. Harping
on the desirability of manual laborers, he opposed the entry of physical
hardship cases. Shortly after the Kishinev pogrom, however, he told the
Jewish Chautauqua Society that it was better for the strong, who could care
for themselves, to remain in Russia and for the weaker to emigrate. He explained, "I mean the weakest in the struggle for existence, such as the man
of science or the student, who is much respected in Russia, but not appreciated in the United States, where he has a hard struggle." He still called
distribution outside the eastern ports the safety valve for keeping America's
doors open and for maximizing the desirability of the immigrants. But at
the same time, he admitted that the masses of immigrants in need of assistance would remain in the large urban centers like New York and Chicago.
Schiff was ambivalent too about how many Jews in Russia could be relo-
cated. On countless occasions he stated that over five million could not emigrate, but he supported immigration to America as well as to lands outside
both Europe and the United States. Nor was his warning to Witte, after the
failure of the 1905 revolution, that Jews would be forced to leave en masse
made lightly. As discussed below, his own projections in connection with
the Galveston movement on how many could ultimately find refuge in the

United States and perhaps Canada ran into the millions.[6] Two reasons best explain the contradictions: first, they were often immediate reactions to developments in the Russian situation and in the struggle against the restrictionists, and second, they paralleled Schiff's unending search for weapons in his war against the czarist government.

For public consumption, Schiff and his associates endowed the Russian immigrants with the middle-class virtues so attractive to Americans—they were hardworking, sober, law-abiding, and family oriented. Schiff lauded in particular the "idealistic" Russians who tempered America's materialism. A rosy picture of immigrant life provided the stewards with ammunition for contesting restrictionist proposals—the literacy test, the requirement that the immigrant produce a certificate of good character from his native government, and deportation for any immigrant who conspired to overthrow a foreign government (a blow to Irish nationalists and to all Marxists). The seamy side of ghetto life—disease, crime, prostitution—was ignored as the stewards argued the immigrant contributions to the nation. Indeed, even before those specific issues caught the public's attention, the communal leaders were quietly combating health problems and delinquency in the ghetto. As previously discussed, Schiff supported Lillian Wald's nursing service and settlement house, the need for housing reform, and the political crusade of 1900–1901 against prostitution. He also defended the immigrants when Police Commissioner Bingham charged that Jews accounted for a disproportionate number of New York City's lawbreakers and when published reports revealed a high incidence of tuberculosis among the newcomers.

To men like Schiff, amelioration of ghetto conditions and even the goal of rapid Americanization were not only ends in themselves but also means to build up the image of the desirable Jewish immigrant. Every significant facet of immigrant behavior, from self-help (good) to Zionist affiliation (decidedly bad, since it smacked of questionable loyalty to the United States) was weighed for its possible impact on the cause of free immigration.[7]

From 1904 on, Schiff warned American Jews to guard against restrictionist legislation. Alternately optimistic and pessimistic about the chances of free immigration, "which should be as unlimited as the world is wide," he witnessed the growing strength of anti-immigration sentiment in Congress and the rising popularity of the literacy test. Aware of the high rate of illiteracy among Jews (roughly 25 percent of men and women over fourteen years of age), he denounced the test and even argued that in some ways the illiterates were preferable: "The immigrant who comes here to find actual work, by which to support himself and his family, and who possesses good health and physical strength, is likely, even if he cannot read or write, to become a better citizen and greater asset to this country than he who is highly trained and educated and who, because of this, assumes that the world owes him a living and who becomes a danger to society if that be not granted him in the manner he expects." Another time he stated that the literate alien was more likely to retain his own language and customs and perhaps even become a demagogue or anarchist. In 1906 the Dillingham immigration bill passed Congress without a literacy clause; merely a temporary holding device, the act provided for an investigative commission to study the entire matter of immigration.[8]

The signs were ominous for the antirestrictionists, but the Jewish stewards dug in their heels. The situation demanded that they buy time for beleaguered Russian Jews, and if they could not prevent restriction, they could at least delay or weaken legislative proscriptions. The Jewish campaign against restriction was run primarily by Louis Marshall and Cyrus Adler of the AJC and by Simon Wolf and Max Kohler of the Union of American Hebrew Congregations (UAHC) and B'nai B'rith. Schiff joined his associates in planning strategy for reaching members of Congress. In 1908 the Jews lobbied with the platform committee of the Republican party; in 1910 they formulated the Jewish presentation to the Immigration Commission; and in 1912 they approached Democratic leaders for a proimmigration pledge from that party's presidential candidate. The banker, who was tuned in to Washington gossip, particularly when Oscar Straus served in the cabinet, acted independently too. Privately, he asked Theodore Roosevelt to choose a Jew for the Immigration Commission, but the president refused, saying that he preferred persons without pronounced viewpoints. Roosevelt yielded to Schiff, however, on the reappointment of Robert Watchorn, an antirestrictionist, as commissioner of immigration. The stewards well understood the importance of the commissioner in deciding policy at the ports of entry, and they appreciated Watchorn's sympathy. Schiff also continued to apprise leading European Jews of American developments. When the Dillingham Immigration Commission took up its investigation in Europe, he directed his contacts abroad to supply the commissioners with "accurate" information. At the same time he strongly cautioned the Europeans against an international conference on emigration. A gathering that might hint at an international Jewry out to dump aliens on American shores was hardly advisable.[9]

The work of the Immigration Commission, known from the outset as a restrictionist body, spurred on Jewish efforts against a literacy test. Schiff, for example, used his personal influence with several prominent Christians. He virtually coached John Finley, president of the City College of New York, on what to say at a proimmigration rally. It was also Schiff who reportedly enlisted Charles Eliot on the side of liberal immigration. Sensitized by his friend to the plight of Russian Jewry, Eliot condemned the literacy test as a "misdirected and untimely" device for judging the desirability of foreigners. Schiff was grateful for so influential an ally, and in 1911 he distributed one hundred thousand copies of an address by Eliot on immigration.[10]

For every Finley and Eliot there were those, including liberals and progressives, who defended restriction. Since Schiff always retained a paternalistic interest in the major causes he endowed, he was especially irritated by the anti-immigration views of Edward T. Devine, the man he had nominated to be Schiff Professor of Social Economy at Columbia University. In 1911, Devine wrote an editorial for *Survey*, a journal devoted to social work subjects, in which he supported the literacy test. He contended that unrestricted immigration, which beyond certain limits produced a "degenerative race," endangered American standards and the national heritage. Schiff, who maintained that it was his duty to those "who look to me—and have a right to look to me—for the defense of the right of migration," fired off an impassioned reply:

> Are you aware that you are putting forward precisely the same arguments that were advanced by the so-called "Know Nothing" party against German and Irish immigration some five or six decades ago—an immigration which has made the United States what they are now? Have you further considered who would today build our subways, our highways, who would do manual labor in general if the Italian laborer were shut out; who would mine our coal and iron, work in our steel mills and industrial plants, if the Hungarian and Slavonic inflow were atopped; who would produce our clothing and underwear, would go into our textile mills and become the middlemen so important to the promotion of trade and commerce, if the Russo-Jewish immigrant were no longer permitted to come to our shores? . . . You would draw a cordon around this country, in order to preserve the comfort and self-indulgence of its people and shut your eyes to the woes of those who suffer either from persecution or oppression, or from unfortunate economic conditions.

In Schiff's eyes the right of Devine to air his opinions privately was absolute, but his indoctrination of students via the Schiff chair was intolerable. For a while, Schiff thought of demanding the professor's dismissal, but consultation with others and respect for academic freedom constrained him. Since Devine stood firm, all the banker could do was remove his name from the professorship.[11]

Endorsed by the report of the Immigration Commission, the literacy test found its way into a new congressional bill. Exemption was made for refugees of religious persecution, and because of Jewish agitation the requirement for certificates of character was dropped. Friends of liberal immigration now looked to the executive branch. They prevailed upon Taft to veto the measure shortly before he left office; and although Woodrow Wilson had pledged his opposition to restrictionism during the campaign of 1912, congressional adoption of a literacy test was only a matter of time. The outbreak of World War I reinforced the restrictionists. Nationalism and xenophobia were on the rise, and restrictionist legislation, embodying the literacy test, easily passed over Wilson's veto. Schiff, usually the optimist, gloomily but correctly predicted the passage of even harsher measures after the war. His long-held belief that America was the fail-safe haven for all immigrants was fast eroding.[12]

The American Solution: The Galveston Plan

An innovative plan of directing the immigrant flow away from the eastern cities, the Galveston movement was the last serious effort before World War I to achieve a widespread distribution of eastern European Jews. On the premise that the best refuge was America, it sought to demonstrate the ongoing viability of free immigration. By planting the newcomers in places other than the congested ghettos, it promised to allay American fears of the immigrants and thus stave off restrictionist legislation.

Most immigrants had effectively resisted the earlier plans of the established Jews on the issue of settlement, and the latter were forced to retreat step by step. When agricultural colonization failed, the stewards encouraged independent farmers. Since agriculture in any form proved unattractive, they established the Industrial Removal Office (IRO) and concentrated on removing immigrants to smaller *urban* areas. The IRO's meager results pointed up a major stumbling block to all attempts at removal: once they landed in New York, immigrants were loath to undertake a second voyage to unheard of destinations. To circumvent that obstacle the Galveston movement proposed to send the immigrants directly on an uninterrupted voyage from Europe to the Texas port for distribution in trans-Mississippi locations.

Schiff put forth the Galveston idea at the end of 1906, and like the Montefiore Home and the Harvard Semitics museum, it became his personal project. Although the AJC existed by then, it had no hand in the plan's management. At the banker's death, Israel Zangwill rather uncharitably called it "the only constructive idea my dear friend Schiff ever had."[13] In point of fact, as Schiff himself was quick to admit, the idea was not his. To be sure, he had thought of ports of entry besides New York as early as 1892, when he suggested that the Alliance Israélite Universelle send emigrants directly to San Francisco. In 1904 he briefly considered Baltimore, Boston, Charleston, and New Orleans as well as Galveston. But nothing came of those thoughts. A little over a year later, Schiff met the commissioner-general of immigration, Franklin P. Sargent, and the latter warned that New York and the other Atlantic ports, which were rapidly

becoming overcrowded, would soon be unable to "digest the foreign elements." When Schiff asked him to suggest a solution other than restriction, Sargent, a strong supporter of distribution, advised the diversion of
the immigrant stream to the Gulf ports.[14] Haunted by the prospect of restrictive legislation, the banker determined to act on Sargent's words.

Pressures heavier than before weighed on Schiff in 1906. While he
watched the Jewish situation in Russia steadily deteriorate, he asked himself daily in the Psalmist's words, "Me-ayin yavo ezri?" (whence will my
help come?). The Russian revolution of 1905 had brought no relief. When
mass violence flared into major pogroms during 1905–6, a frustrated and
despairing Schiff looked for new havens of refuge. The settlement of Russian Jews in Mesopotamia in conjunction with the projected Baghdad railway (1903) was never more than a glimmer of an idea; a return to Zion, distasteful in principle to Schiff, appeared more unlikely after Theodor
Herzl's death in 1904 left a weak Zionist movement even weaker.[15] The
United States remained the sole practical haven for large numbers, but
prospects for uninterrupted free immigration were growing slimmer. A re-
pugnance to the new immigrants, compounded by the rising popularity of
racist teachings, was stirring Congress to action. President Theodore
Roosevelt hinted darkly to Schiff that congestion in a few cities might
bring about in years of hard times "worse things than distress." As the designs of the restrictionists steadily mobilized support, the Galveston plan—
a "safety valve," Schiff termed it, to deflect immigrants and to disarm restrictionists—bought time for the Russian Jews. Since the president liked
the idea and since TR's new appointee to head the Department of Commerce and Labor (under whose jurisdiction immigration then lay) was
Schiff's close friend Oscar Straus, the opportunity had to be seized. Those
ghettos in existence could not be undone, but to give up on the benefits of
distribution would be tantamount to the abandonment of Russian Jewry.[16]

Schiff mulled over the idea, consulted with several friends, and within a
few months put up $500,000 to initiate the distribution of eastern Euro-
peans from the Gulf ports to western sites. He proposed finite but ambitious objectives: the settlement over a ten-year period of roughly twenty
thousand to twenty-five thousand immigrants who landed at Galveston.
(For a variety of reasons New Orleans was rejected early on.) The Galveston project sought neither to preempt Baron de Hirsch's earlier efforts for
settlement in Argentina nor to halt emigration to any other refuge.[17] Unlike many previous attempts at distribution, it had no blueprints for agricultural settlements.

Regarding his investment as seed money, Schiff reasoned that the first
settlers would attract a stream of followers. He enthusiastically envisioned
the distribution of Jews in America's hinterland, from the Mississippi to the
Pacific and from the Gulf to the Canadian frontier. Over time a settlement

of two million Russians seemed possible; and if a similar idea was adopted in England, another two million in Canada.[18] Although Schiff repeatedly stated that the Russian-Jewish question had to be settled in Russia, he remained skeptical of amelioration by an autocratic Russian government. Emigration was a necessity, and he strove to keep all options open for large numbers of the czar's Jewish subjects.

The objective was straightforward and seemingly simple, but each step required intricate machinery. In Russia, agents had to approach prospective emigrants, apprise them of the opportunities of western settlement, overcome their fears of an area bereft of familiar companionship, and finally, persuade them to book passage for Galveston rather than an eastern port. The agents also bore responsibility for encouraging "proper" emigrants or, as Schiff explained, "an element able to cope with new conditions: younger, sturdy people, ready to work of every kind and nature." (At first, Schiff stipulated that emigrants agree to work on the Sabbath. Under pressure he compromised; emigrants had to understand in advance that strict Sabbath observance was in most cases impossible.) The next step was to transport the emigrants to Bremen and see them aboard steamships of the North German-Lloyd Company, the one line that sailed directly to Galveston every three weeks. Meantime, on the American side, staff workers had to ferret out employment opportunities in various communities. Once the immigrants landed at Galveston after an arduous voyage of three weeks, they had to be received, moved through government inspection, and sheltered temporarily until dispatched to the available jobs. Where possible, jobs were matched to immigrant skills—carpenters were sent to furniture towns, butchers to stockyards.[19] In sum the Galveston plan was a formidable operation whose success depended on the efficiency of each link in a long chain.

Only a Schiff could have dared to undertake a project of such magnitude, and only a Schiff came so well armed. His reputation in non-Jewish as well as Jewish circles, both in Europe and the United States, was at a high, thanks to his business successes, his diplomatic pressure on behalf of eastern European Jewry, and his recent role as financial angel of Japan in its war against Russia. His wealth and position afforded him the means to underwrite the American side of the plan and the contacts for enlisting experienced and expert associates on two continents. Just because the plan was his, it was assured the attention of prominent Americans and full coverage in the general and Jewish press. When he advised that the idea be pushed at conventions of national organizations, the B'nai B'rith, the UAHC, and the National Conference of Jewish Charities complied. Not the least of Schiff's assets were his stubborn determination, his energy, and his concern for administrative details that he applied to the "uphill" work.[20]

Schiff paid little attention to the desires of the prospective emigrants. For them, as one administrator of the plan put it, the territory west of the Mississippi was a frightening land of mystery:

> The port of Galveston invited entry; but to take the plunge into the Hinter-land where Yiddish may be an unknown tongue, *kosher* food an unknown thing, and labor opportunities limited, was left only to the most daring. . . . [The Russian] could make his wants known in his own language in New York and other Eastern cities; and if his wants were dire, his friends and fellow-countrymen were ready to lend a helping hand. The West, on the other hand, loomed chill [*sic*]. No Yiddish news emanated from it that could . . . reach across the sea. The very names of these cities were almost as unknown in New York as in the Pale. As a result, the Russian immigrant regarded the Hinterland with the same feeling that a child might regard a dark room.[21]

To head the European side of the movement, Schiff decided on Israel Zangwill. The banker had met the British playwright at the turn of the century, and the two men and their wives became fast friends. Theirs was a curious relationship. Schiff genuinely respected Zangwill for his literary ability and his unselfish humanitarian activities; but like others, he found the writer almost impossible to deal with. Zangwill was brusque and out-spokenly critical, often to the point of rudeness. Nor did his views on Jews and Judaism jibe with Schiff's. Zangwill saw the Jewish future in the West-ern world in either/or terms—"total assimilation or territorial separa-tion"—and he defended the two seemingly contradictory positions. Mar-ried to a non-Jew, he preached the assimilation of Jews and their religion in a democratic society. His popular play, *The Melting Pot*, in which a young Kishinev survivor marries a Gentile whose father had served in the czar's anti-Semitic shock troops, was the classic example. At the same time, first as a Zionist and then as a territorialist, Zangwill loudly trumpeted the es-tablishment of a politically autonomous Jewish land. He had broken with the Zionist movement in 1905 after the Zionist Congress rejected Britain's offer of territory in East Africa. Opposed to the geographical limitations of classical Zionism, he became president of the newly formed Jewish Terri-torial Organization (ITO), which sought to "procure a territory upon an autonomous basis for those Jews who cannot or will not remain in the lands in which they at present live." No land if "reasonably good and ob-tainable" was beyond consideration. Palestine, or "Mount Zion," was un-available, but, Zangwill said, there were yet other mountains that could be climbed.[22]

Schiff rejected Zangwill's views on both assimilation and territorial sep-aratism. He found *The Melting Pot* a powerful play, but he strongly dis-agreed "that we must here give up our identity and that the God of our

Fathers and our God cannot be the God of our children." Nor was he attracted to territorial autonomy outside Palestine even though several of his close friends—Oscar Straus, Mayer Sulzberger, Cyrus Sulzberger—supported Zangwill and launched an American branch of ITO in 1906. Schiff shared their concern for something more "practical" than Zionism, and he too favored outlets for emigrants other than the Western Hemisphere, but he thought that territorialism, like Zionism, was merely a very expensive dream, "an utopia . . . which I fear will only block the way of something practical." Schiff could not be bothered by theoretical propositions or "isms" while the Russian problem "is becoming daily more burning." As a Reform Jew he also believed that the dispersion of the Jews was a salutary condition, that "the Jew must maintain his own identity—not *apart* in any autonomous body but *among* the nations where alone he can fulfill the mission, which is assigned to him, to promote the unity of God and the brotherhood of man among the people of the earth." In particular, Schiff opposed the goal of autonomy, "an altogether unnecessary stumbling-block" that would give rise to anti-Jewish prejudice and perhaps even foment Russian-like conditions for Jews in other lands. Yours is a "terrible scheme," he bluntly told Zangwill; Zionism at least had the justification of a past.[23] Fearful of ITO's attractiveness to men of substance and of the harm it might cause other emigration projects, Schiff used Galveston to co-opt Zangwill's organization and divert its attention to settlement in America. Along with his aim of countering immigration restrictionism, the hope of undermining Jewish nationalism, whether in the guise of Zionism or of territorialism, helps explain Schiff's focus on Galveston in 1906, a year after the birth of ITO.

Zangwill did not abandon ITO, but with mixed feelings he agreed to cooperate with Schiff. He believed that the dream of America "does more to counteract the efforts of the Jewish Territorial Organization than any other country" (in his words the country was "the euthanasia of the Jew and Judaism") but it still offered a better haven than other lands. He also understood the economic appeal of Galveston to Schiff; it was comparatively cheap, whereas mass settlement of immigrants in eastern cities "would reduce even Mr. Schiff to the poorhouse." Furthermore, ITO's exclusive management of the Galveston movement in Europe (as opposed to cooperation between ITO and the Jewish Colonization Association [ICA], which Schiff preferred but which both organizations rejected) stood to popularize Zangwill's movement and prevent its eclipse by other agencies. Participation in Galveston might even train ITO's leaders in lessons of emigration that could be applied another time on behalf of an ITO-sponsored land. Finally, no one turned down Schiff lightly, especially since cooperation might conceivably enhance one's influence with the banker. The potential for friction between the two remained high—as Schiff put it, both were obstinate men—but after initial differences were ironed out, Zangwill and Schiff joined forces.[24]

Schiff bolstered the European side further by securing the cooperation of the influential German relief society, the Hilfsverein der Deutschen Juden, particularly for overseeing the emigrants' journey through Bremen. Dr. Paul Nathan, executive secretary of the Hilfsverein, was a trusted confidant on Russian Jewish affairs, and he and the banker worked closely together. On the American side of the operation, Schiff put together a strong team by tapping Cyrus Sulzberger, David Bressler, and Morris Waldman, men seasoned in Jewish communal affairs and removal work. Under their direction the Galveston movement drew on a network of committees established by IRO in immigrant "receiving" communities across the country, as well as on local B'nai B'rith lodges. In the city of Galveston itself, where management lay in the hands of the newly created Jewish Immigrants' Information Bureau, Rabbi Henry Cohen was an active coworker. Schiff prodded his associates, who labored hard and well. Theirs was the primary responsibility of overall coordination with ITO—that is, matching pre-fixed jobs with the actual numbers recruited in Europe. At the hub of the operation sat Schiff, the policy maker and final arbiter.[25]

A shipload of sixty immigrants docked in Galveston in July 1907, and the first signs augured well. The local press sympathetically explained the workings of the bureau; the mayor warmly welcomed the newcomers. The immigrants themselves made a favorable impression. Rabbi Cohen, who found them an intelligent lot, recounted how they requested newspapers, Yiddish-English or Russian-English dictionaries, and even a chess set. Unfortunately, the initial momentum of the first year was lost when a serious economic depression throughout the United States brought the movement to a virtual standstill in 1908-9. Schiff, however, remained confident, and he spoke highly of an expanding settlement. The Russian, "of splendid stock," would strengthen the influence of American Jews. "He not only makes it possible through his work that we maintain and extend our commercial supremacy, but he also brings his ideals and a religious background, of which, with our materialistic tendencies, we stand in great need." He predicted to Zangwill that even if they two only looked into this Promised Land from the top of Mount Pisgah (another reference to Moses who was permitted to see but not enter Palestine), the Galveston movement would have proved a lasting victory.[26]

True to form, Schiff immersed himself fully in the details of the movement. He read a stream of reports that covered all steps from recruitment in Russia to settlement in America. He studied passenger lists as well as "before and after" photographs of the new arrivals; he knew of individual hardship cases and helped decide their disposition; he negotiated lower railroad rates for transportation from Galveston to final destinations. Tales of the inevitable difficulties and obstacles that beset the venture reached his desk: shabby treatment of passengers aboard ship, immigrants found to be ill-suited for labor, deportation actions by the government, complaints from receiving communities, and opposition on the part of the Yiddish press and the Zionists in the eastern ghettos. Although some immigrants desired to be sent elsewhere, the administrators disclaimed any obligation to finance or transport them. Problems were resolved by Schiff and his American associates or were brought to the attention of the Europeans. Continuing to campaign publicly on behalf of distribution, the banker was influenced neither by the obstacles nor by the criticism from the Jewish community. "I shall not let the fear that my popularity amongst our coreligionists here may suffer, as it possibly will, deter me from expressing my convictions."[27]

The banker's chief preoccupation was the maintenance of smooth relations between the Americans and the Europeans. Imperious though his manner was with subordinates and the immigrants, he handled the executives with care. A great deal of time was spent in running interference for Zangwill, whose manner alienated Paul Nathan as well as some of Schiff's American co-workers. For the sake of unity, Schiff explained away Zangwill's behavior while simultaneously lavishing much praise on the sensitive playwright. Zangwill in turn usually went along with Schiff. The Englishman confided to Mayer Sulzberger: "The difficulty with Schiff is that he is so charming that it is difficult to quarrel with him."[28] In one letter early in negotiations, Schiff wrote that he favored the settlement of small groups, which, if they succeeded, could lead to local self-government. It was his way of wooing Zangwill, but the latter understood it to mean that Schiff had finally succumbed to territorialism. In no fashion, however, did the banker ever endorse significant autonomous settlements in the United States. They were impossible to attain, and the very idea was a menace to Jews. He insisted rather that immigrants come as individuals and not as groups. As for local self-government, it doubtless meant no more to him than the status of the Woodbine agricultural colony, which was incorporated as an all-Jewish borough in 1903.[29]

Schiff tried to keep Zangwill focused on recruitment, admonishing him repeatedly to avoid the appearance of stimulated immigration and to uphold high standards for immigrant selection. Not only did immigrants have to pass the LPC test, but for pioneering in the West, Schiff preferred the manual laborer to the "merchant and clerk type."[30] For the sake of the Galveston movement and in the face of the mounting tide of restrictionist sentiment in Congress, he came out in favor of the type of immigrant least likely to arouse popular disfavor.

The solution of certain problems lay beyond the banker's abilities. For example, the incessant rivalry between ICA and ITO precluded a joint Eu-

ropean effort that Schiff considered necessary for assuring proper recruitment. And when Russia temporarily closed down most of ITO's stations in
1908, thus jeopardizing the entire operation, he could do little but ask Secretary of Commerce and Labor Straus to voice his approval of the Galveston movment and thereby shore up ITO's credibility with the czarist
government. When ITO ran out of funds (Zangwill relied heavily on
Rothschild money), Schiff was powerless to lend aid lest the entire plan appear to Americans as stimulated or assisted immigration.[31]

Another crucial blow to the Galveston movement was delivered by the
American government. As Bernard Marinbach has ably recounted, in 1910
the movement became a favorite target of restrictionist and anti-Jewish immigration officials in both Washington and the port city. Persuaded that the
operation violated the 1907 immigration law by actively soliciting immigration, the officials attempted a crackdown through the use of deportation orders. Assistant Secretary of Commerce and Labor Benjamin Cable said that
if he were to exclude those who fell under the LPC ban, he would exclude
them all. To be sure, a few deportations were on Galveston's record since
the very beginning, but now the numbers rose dramatically. Cases could be
appealed, and although some decisions were reversed, permanent damage
was done to the movement's popularity among prospective immigrants.[32]

This time, Schiff, who had always insisted on strict compliance with
American law, swung into action. He admitted privately that greater care in
the selection process might have avoided some deportations, but he was
firmly convinced that sheer malevolence on the part of American officials
accounted for the crisis. Although the deported "martyrs" captured his
sympathy, he couldn't reimburse them lest he validate thereby the charges
of assisted immigration. He warned that if the movement itself were
crushed by government policy, someone would be punished—"not the
man lower down, but the man higher up." To be sure, Schiff's relations
with the Taft administration were far less than cordial. Taft had reneged on
his promise to keep Oscar Straus in the cabinet, and he had dismissed
Schiff's recommendation of another friend, Louis Marshall, for Supreme
Court justice. Moreover, at that very moment, Schiff and Taft were at log-
gerheads over Russia's refusal to honor the passports of American Jews. But
the powerful banker, who was still a loyal Republican, enjoyed considerable leverage. Enlisting the help of Congressman William Bennet of New
York and a strong legal team of Galveston supporters, he orchestrated a defense of the movement that challenged the deportation orders and specifically Assistant Secretary Cable. In August 1910, Schiff wrote an indignant
letter to Cable (really meant for Taft) that accused his department of "wan-
tonly" destroying the movement. When Cable stood firm, Schiff called for
his resignation. He told Taft's secretary that "we cannot again enter upon
the legitimate—and I aver—desirable and public-spirited work we have

undertaken, *unless Mr. Cable retires.*" Politely but in no uncertain terms he threatened Taft and the Republican party with the loss of the Jewish vote in the 1910 elections.[33]

The threat apparently worked. On a visit to New York the president endorsed the diversion of immigration to other ports, which was interpreted by Galveston supporters as a change in policy. A few weeks after the elections, Schiff and three associates were granted a hearing before Attorney-General George Wickersham, Secretary of Commerce and Labor Charles Nagel, and Cable. Following an able legal presentation of the case for Galveston by attorney Max Kohler, an irate Schiff warned that continued hostility on the government's part, unwarranted in light of Taft's words, would end the movement. As Kohler later told the story, Schiff jumped up, shook his finger at Nagel, and said: "You act as if my organization and I were on trial. You, Mr. Secretary, and your department are on trial, and the country will rue it, if this undertaking—so conducive to promoting the best interests of our country, as well as humanity—is throttled, by your department's unreasonable obstacles!" The banker's aggressiveness irritated Nagel, but in the end he admitted to Schiff that he saw nothing illegal in the movement. (Less than two months later, however, Nagel spoke at the convention of the UAHC and defended in principle the policies of his department.) Throughout the fight against Cable's "harassment," which Schiff continued even after the conference, the banker disclaimed any pessimism. Indeed, his letters convey a sense of excitement, almost an enjoyment of confrontation and muscle flexing.[34]

Schiff won the skirmish, but the deportations permanently arrested the movement's development. Problems of recruitment and funding persisted, and only in 1913 did the number of arrivals to Galveston, 2,700, exceed the annual minimum of 2,500 that he had set in 1906. A new rash of deportations erupted during Wilson's administration, and for Schiff that was the last straw. Faulting the government's attitude, which he described as markedly rigid and repressive, the banker decided in the spring of 1914 to terminate the enterprise. He had seized on a constructive way of defusing restrictionist pressure, but largely for reasons beyond his control he failed to reach his goals.[35]

In retrospect one could even argue that the inability of European relief committees to direct the emigrant flow away from the Atlantic ports after the onset of the mass exodus had foredoomed the plan. The early immigrants who had settled largely on the eastern seaboard were a strong "pull" for later arrivals. Fewer than ten thousand immigrants made use of Galveston, and from 1907 to 1913 only Texas, Iowa, and Missouri absorbed over a thousand arrivals. The appeal of the eastern cities never lessened, and secondarily for Schiff, Zangwill's search for ITO-land continued as before. Indeed, it is legitimate to wonder whether Zangwill's preoccupation with possible settlements in Mesopotamia and Cyrenaica precluded the optimal administration of the Galveston plan in Europe. Nevertheless, the banker did not consider his work a failure. He still hoped that those who were brought in would attract others and that new efforts at western distribution would be made after the world war.[36]

The Galveston episode testified to Schiff's administrative skills and forceful character. He chose strong associates in the United States, and within the limits imposed by organizational rivalry he made good use of available European talent. Juggling the problems of recruitment and placement, as well as obstacles imposed by both America and Russia, he fearlessly pressured his business contacts and the Taft administration. From its inception in 1907 until 1914 he was the linchpin that kept the movement afloat.

When weighed on the scales of communal leadership, however, the Galveston movement marked a defeat for the banker with the Yiddish-speaking masses. His obsession with keeping America's doors open as long as possible was accompanied by a lack of concern about the desires of the eastern Europeans. In his grand design the prospective immigrants were pawns rather than partners. Ignoring the economic background and family situation of the Russians, Schiff defined the proper type of recruits for the plan, and he assumed the right to choose their destination. He, a man who abstained from work on the Sabbath, also advised that they be prepared to violate their day of rest. Nor did his usual concern for religious tradition and Jewish education extend to the Galveston arrivals. Since the movement could not lure prospective emigrants with plans for synagogues, schools, and other communal agencies that contributed to the drawing power of the large ghettos, it undercut both mass support as well as Galveston's chance of competing with the mid-Atlantic ports.[37] Schiff may have praised the ideals and cultural baggage that the newcomers brought with them, but his approach bespoke less a desire to comprehend the needs of the Russians than to refashion them, perhaps the last of freely admitted aliens, in an American mold.

The Territorialist Solution: Mexico and Mesopotamia

Although America was the primary focus of the eastern European emigrants, the possibility of directing them to lands outside Europe and the United States intrigued western Jewish leaders from the start of the mass exodus. In 1882, at an international conference that arranged for a division of labor with respect to the immigrant flow, the Paris committee was assigned the task of studying colonization in countries other than America and the British colonies. Barely ten years later, Baron Maurice de Hirsch, frustrated in attempts to improve Jewish life in Russia, underwrote the creation of the ICA, whose objectives included the colonization of Jews "in various parts of North and South America and other countries" and the purchase of lands for colonization "in any part of the world." The ICA proceeded to settle Jews in Argentina, and it also lent its aid to colonies in Palestine, Brazil, and Canada. Zionists and territorialists, bent on Jewish political autonomy, broadened the geographic horizons still further with plans for Jewish settlement in Palestine or other parts of Asia Minor or Africa. Shortly before his death, Theodor Herzl negotiated seriously, albeit unsuccessfully, on behalf of the Zionists for the northern half of the Sinai peninsula in Egypt.[38]

Schiff too acknowledged the importance of outlets other than the United States. He fought on two fronts, working to keep American doors open and searching for other safety zones, as if for purposes of insurance. The banker was a *territorialist* but not a *Territorialist*. Stoutly opposed to aspirations of both the Zionists and ITO for Jewish autonomy, he was, however, open to suggestions for settlement in countries that offered advantages to Jewish immigrants. If the areas in question coincided with his business interests and if they promised to reduce the skyrocketing philanthropic expenses of the American Jewish community, so much the better. Not philanthropy alone but philanthropy plus investments assuring a 4 percent or 5 percent return, he once said, would bring about land development, irrigation, and railways.[39]

The banker's direct involvement in the search for havens testified again to his wealth and influence. Although the magnitude of the tasks involved in developing any new land exceeded his private capacities, he could be counted on for substantial financial assistance. More important were his personal contacts with bankers on both sides of the Atlantic who looked for investment opportunities. Their cooperation would be essential for the fruition of any ambitious plan. The question of whether the stewards had the right to pressure eastern Europeans to some underdeveloped region in a backward country was never an issue. They, the self-appointed guardians of their unfortunate brethren, assumed that right, even as Schiff had in the Galveston movement.

Schiff watched the formative stages of Hirsch's Argentinian plans with keen interest. (He even suggested sending a rabbi to serve the Jewish settlers.) At the same time, respectful of the immense monetary and human sacrifices expended, he questioned the wisdom of building settlements in a country whose people and government were apt to regard the immigrants unfavorably. He warned the baron of the opposition of American Jews to an influx of discontented settlers from Argentina as well as of the instability of Latin American nations.[40] The latter objection, however, did not figure in his counterproposal to seek an outlet in Mexico.

Both Schiff and Ernest Cassel had substantial business interests in Mexico before 1900. The two men cooperated in financing various railway enterprises, and Schiff acted as Cassel's representative in the affairs of one line. In 1891, confiding his skepticism about the Argentinian scheme to his friend, Schiff suggested that Mexico was a better alternative. It offered fertile and cheap land, it appeared free of prejudice, and the government actively invited immigration. Since Mexico was closer than Argentina, colonies there could be more easily supervised. Schiff's case grew stronger when he learned that the Mexican government officially endorsed his project. In his mind the pieces began to come together: the needy eastern Europeans, a welcoming country, and an Alliance Israélite Universelle to flesh out the venture.[41]

At first, Schiff asked Cassel to recommend Mexico to the baron. The opinion of Cassel, who was chosen by Hirsch as a director of the ICA, would carry more weight. The baron in turn did not reject the scheme, but he wanted sure prospects of a fair return for the enormous capital investment. The goal of colonizing perhaps five million people required a serious investigation from a business, not a philanthropic, standpoint. He also stipulated that while Europeans handled the financial side and the transportation of emigrants, Americans had to assume the responsibility of management. At this point, Schiff took up negotiations directly with Hirsch. Drawing on the experience of American Mormons who had left Utah for Mexico, Schiff assured the baron that "certain parts of Mexico . . . offer the settlers every opportunity which can be expected anywhere from prudent and diligent work." He promised to pay for an investigation of suitable Mexican lands, but he insisted that the baron be prepared to follow through if the report was favorable. Agreeing in principle to a businesslike enterprise, he warned frankly that since American Jews were bearing the heavy costs of immigration, the scheme would find few investors in the United States. In this episode business habits tempered philanthropy.

For a few months things looked promising. The baron was prepared to listen, and Schiff, in contact with friends at home and abroad, sought out agents for the mission. Meanwhile, the president of the Mexican Central Railroad, Schiff's chief client in that country, approached the banker, asking that Russian emigrants be directed to lands owned by the railroad. Although he said that he and some friends were eager to help for humanitarian reasons, both he and Schiff understood that Jewish settlement augured profits for the Central line. Nevertheless, when Schiff learned that the immigrants would be faced with problems of low wages and severe competition, hope for financial gain and for the project itself died. The ill-fated plan resembled similar negotiations at the same time between Schiff and western railroad magnate James J. Hill. Failure in both cases, however, did not shake Schiff's conviction that immigrant distribution could defuse restrictionism.[42]

Longer-lived and far more intriguing to Schiff's circle was the thought of settling Russian Jews in Mesopotamia under Ottoman rule. The idea began with an 1892 pamphlet by a Semitics scholar at Johns Hopkins: Paul Haupt envisioned an international venture that would involve scientific and military personnel from the United States and other countries. Haupt carefully analyzed the resources of the area and its economic and defense needs, and he painted a rosy future for the ancient land of Babylonia. The professor was not Jewish, but he numbered Judge Mayer Sulzberger and several other prominent Jews among his friends. Sulzberger, Oscar Straus, and Haupt's student, Cyrus Adler, were particularly impressed by Haupt's views. Adler twice brought the pamphlet to the attention of Theodor Herzl; Straus sent a copy to the baron. Since Hirsch was then involved in Argentina and at odds with the Ottoman government, he turned it down. When Straus was minister to Constantinople, he broached the idea to Secretary Hay, and he raised it again during a private meeting with Herzl. Sulzberger later recalled that Herzl discussed the plan with the sultan, who was receptive, but that the Zionist leader was overridden by his Palestine-centered followers.[43]

Why Mesopotamia appeared more attractive than other sites that could equally have relieved the pressure on Jewish stewards in America suggests several explanations. Obviously, practical considerations loomed large. Turkey, the "weak man" of Europe, seemed amenable; the absorptive capacity of the area held great promise and it was cheaper to transport eastern Europeans to Asia Minor than to the Western Hemisphere. The stewards may also have been encouraged by the successful pioneering work of their French counterpart, Baron Edmond de Rothschild, in neighboring Palestine. But more was involved. Men like Straus and Adler opposed the Zionist movement, soon to be launched by Herzl, but they were pulled emotionally to the original land of the patriarch Abraham. In Straus's words, Mesopotamia was "the biblical Ur of the Chaldees," "the original habitation of the Hebrews, Abraham and his progenitors." Adler similarly spoke of a land that "has more than once been the home of the children of Israel" and was thus validated by both "religious sentiment and Biblical precedent."[44] If Mesopotamia filled their sentimental needs, it was on all scores a superior alternative to the Zionist answer. Since a Jewish state in Palestine disturbed the stewards for many reasons, they probably thought that a successful settlement in Mesopotamia might undercut the appeal of the potentially harmful Zionists. What sort of political status a

Jewish settlement in Mesopotamia would ultimately seek was too remote an issue to worry about.

Although Schiff did not express romantic notions about a Jewish return to Mesopotamia, he too understood the pull of sentiment on the eastern Europeans. He had assured Herzl that he was ready to assist "practical" proposals, but he thought that the Sinai plan would not work precisely because it flew in the face of Jewish sentiments. It would be ironic, he wrote, that, after thousands of years of celebrating the exodus from Egypt, Jews would settle there again. "I personally believe that the plan would arouse the antipathies of the [eastern European] Jews, from among whom the settlers after all would come and with whom sentiment plays such a great part." Mesopotamia, however, was a different matter. The plan seemed feasible when, in 1903, Turkey granted a German company the right to extend a railroad through Asia Minor. While the kaiser dreamed of a Berlin to Baghdad line, Germany invited the participation of English and French financiers. Kuhn, Loeb, largely through the Cassel-Schiff connection, had been involved in Turkish railroad investments since the 1890s, and although it sought a share in the new venture, American firms were excluded. Profit making was no longer a factor, but Schiff's interest persisted. He believed that with the help of Cassel, who had invested in the plan, the territory opened by the new line could be utilized for eastern European emigrants.[45]

Reviving Haupt's pamphlet, the banker immediately suggested to Cassel that the ICA seriously consider the Mesopotamian plan. "I know that you have shown great interest in our people and therefore do not hesitate to try to interest you," Schiff stated—words that incidentally contradict Cassel's reputation as one who was alienated from Jewish affairs. Meanwhile, using his nephew, Otto Schiff, as the intermediary, he alerted Lord Rothschild. As he had in the Mexican episode, he warned against counting on American Jews to supply the funds. (The rumor reported to Herzl that American financiers [read Schiff] planned heavy investments in the Baghdad line was unfounded.) A few months later, British opposition to the railroad forced Cassel to withdraw.[46] Nothing came of a Mesopotamian settlement in 1903, but the idea lived on in Zionist and non-Zionist circles.

A new burst of interest flared in 1909, and for the first time the Mesopotamian plan came to the attention of the Jewish public. In part it was due to the enthusiasm and magnetic appeal of Israel Zangwill. ITO's president had launched an American branch of the organization that attracted non-Zionist Jewish leaders like Sulzberger and Straus, and Mesopotamia ranked high on the list of far-flung regions that Zangwill was prepared to explore. Emboldened by the Young Turk revolt of 1908, which hinted at a shift of influence over Turkish affairs from Germany to England, he set out to mobilize support from ICA, the Alliance Israélite Universelle, and two prominent bankers, Cassel and Schiff. Doubtless his hopes were also raised by the appointment of Oscar Straus as American ambassador to Constantinople. Long a protagonist of the plan—Straus told Schiff in 1909 that "whoever will control the railroad to the Persian Gulf will be a mighty international power"—Straus was in a key position to push it along and to keep both ITO and American Jews better apprised of political and economic developments. Zionists too grew interested after hearing of Cassel's plan to establish a British-backed bank in Turkey. If Schiff, a friend of both Cassel and Zangwill, shared in the banking investment, then Mesopotamia might provide the means for cultivating Schiff on behalf of the Zionist Organization.[47]

Schiff never joined ITO; he reasoned that it would take decades before any ITO land offered relief for the eastern Europeans. Both he and Cassel were prepared, however, to consider the Mesopotamian plan, particularly since Schiff insisted that it be handled by the ICA, more representative of world Jewry than ITO and unencumbered by political demands. Without the support of Jews world-wide, he told Zangwill, the idea of a settlement would fail. In a public interview the banker repudiated any idea of linking the settlement with political or nationalist aims: "I have no sympathy with and will take no hand in any scheme involving political conditions such as the formation of an autonomy of any kind. I would have the Jews go to Mesopotamia as they do to America—to the former instead of to the latter because, with the Mesopotamian scheme of irrigation carried out their opportunities would be so much greater." He also denied, in an interchange with the president of the Zionist Organization, that Kuhn, Loeb was at that time involved in Cassel's banking venture or that he personally was ready to endorse Zangwill's schemes financially or otherwise. Although he needed Zangwill's cooperation on the Galveston plan, Schiff stubbornly dissociated himself from ITO. Forced to back down, Zangwill's organization became a participant in, rather than the exclusive engineer of, the Mesopotamian project.[48]

Schiff refused to commit himself to so large an undertaking without assurances of its practicability. As was his wont, he stressed the importance of a business-like approach: an investigation of the region, the formation of a Jewish corporation, and an appeal to Turkey for a charter. Toward those ends he suggested a cooperative international effort on the part of the ICA, ITO, Hilfsverein, Zionist Organization, Anglo-Jewish Association, and American Jewish leaders. Under ICA's leadership, the Jews should ask Turkey for a specific charter that granted the right to acquire and colonize the land and that guaranteed the capital for irrigation and communications. The entire plan, he insisted, depended on Turkey's active support, particularly by a guarantee of principal and interest. Estimating the costs at around $250 million, he warned against expectations that Jewish money without a Turkish subvention could cover the project.[49]

However ready he was with concrete advice, Schiff adamantly turned down Zangwill's proposition that he, Schiff, head the project. In a rare comment on the subject of leadership, he bemoaned the fact that while problems in America were ever increasing, "the number of *real* leaders does hardly appear to grow." Those like him were "over-burdened to the breaking-point." At the age of sixty-three and more concerned with the success of Galveston, it would be "sheer folly" for him to head the project. Ideally, he looked for "a younger man of great force, executive ability and personal magnetism . . . willing to devote himself entirely to this and give up everything else." His choice was Oscar Straus, only four years his junior, but the latter declined.[50]

Schiff's optimism slowly evaporated. In 1912 he opposed participation by the AJC in an investigation of Turkish lands for Jewish settlement, saying that it would lead the committee into Zionist and other "propaganda." The Mesopotamian project itself dragged on until dropped by ITO in 1914. A year later, Schiff concluded that "no attempt at mass settlement or colonization by Jews has ever been successful where it has been tried and, in my opinion, no such attempt ever will be successful." The failure of the Mesopotamian plan and the poor results of Galveston reinforced his conviction that more than five million Jews would always remain in Russia and that it was there that the Jewish question had to be solved.[51]

The Zionist Solution

The search for havens before World War I never drew Schiff to the support of mass Jewish settlement in Palestine. Whereas other possible solutions to the immigrant problem were judged mainly for their practicability, Palestine automatically raised the matter of Zionism. The subject had generated heated and ongoing debates ever since Theodor Herzl founded the Zionist movement (1897) that called for a Jewish "home" in Palestine "secured by public law." The lines were drawn between Herzl's Zionist followers and their opponents; and in the numerous clashes that ensued, a Jewish leader of Schiff's importance could not escape taking sides.

Appearing as a strong anti-Zionist during the first decade of the nationalist movement, Schiff was unafraid of feeding the public controversy. While he attacked political Zionism on ideological and pragmatic grounds, he purposely stayed away from a Palestinian solution for beleaguered Russian Jews. As an immediate refuge, Palestine was impractical; as a permanent solution to the problem of persecution, it was downright harmful. Furthermore, a focus on Palestine might erroneously link him with political Zionism. Worse, it was likely to step on sensitive toes, Christian as well as Jewish, and thereby overshadow the very objective of an apolitical refuge. In Schiff's calculations, Zionism, inherently wrong, undercut the chances of other refuges. Not only did it strengthen restrictionist sentiment against the immigration of Jews to America, but it weakened the appeal to Jews of any territorialist solution.

The banker's stand on Zionism underwent significant modification before the outbreak of World War I. Although he remained opposed to the idea of statehood or any form of Jewish political autonomy, a growing interest in Palestinian cultural and philanthropic institutions turned him into a non-Zionist. Slowly, he came to see a positive good in a Jewish Palestine. Meanwhile, his antipathy to political Zionism was fueled by an entirely different matter, that of leadership. Since American Zionists linked the aim of nationalism with democracy, they soon posed an increasingly serious challenge to his control of the Jewish community.

The idea of a Jewish return to Palestine was familiar to nineteenth-century Americans. Restoration figured in the theology of evangelicals and millenialists; some Christians suggested that world Jewry purchase Palestine from the Turks.[52] In 1891, William Blackstone, a religious Christian businessman of Chicago, circulated a mass petition that asked for the restoration of Palestine to the Jews by international agreement. Schiff refused to sign. Along with other Jewish and non-Jewish critics he called the idea impractical and undesirable.[53] Only after the founding of the Zionist Organization in 1897 did Schiff explain his opinions in greater detail.

Among the repeated arguments that Schiff mustered against Jewish political nationalism, religion was the most important. Calling himself a "faith Jew" rather than a "race Jew," he adhered to the classical Reform position adopted by the two major arms of that movement, the Central Conference of American Rabbis and the UAHC. The Reformers proclaimed that Judaism was only a religion and that Jews, the priest people, had been scattered among the nations by divine purpose to teach the unity of God and brotherhood of man. Ingathering into Palestine contradicted the very raison d'être of Jewish existence and, as Schiff thought, threatened the essence of Judaism. He decried the secular cast of the movement as well as its leaders—"phantasists" and adventurers, if not demagogues and agitators, who preached a pernicious "ism." But as a man who genuinely believed that "from Zion shall come forth the Law," Schiff was hard put to square that belief with Reform teachings. His image of Zion was murky, more a holy land of the past than a source of present or future Jewish creativity. In one early letter he interpreted the traditional verse to mean *the Jews came forth with the Law from Zion*. Exiled from Zion and dispersed among the nations, they set upon their divine mission to disseminate the land-free tenets of the Jewish faith: "Surely the inspired seer . . . would have added the

176   *Jacob H. Schiff*

words: 'to return to it,' if his inspiration had not told him that the law of
God went forth from Zion and its bearers became distributed among the
nations, to remain and to become part and parcel of them, so that they
might forever promulgate Israel's great mission."⁵⁴

Neither his grounding in Orthodox tradition, where a return to Palestine was central, nor his acceptance of Jewish colonization, whether in the
United States or Mexico or Mesopotamia, was sufficient to elicit his encouragement of Zionism. Yet the universalist argument trapped him in a
seeming contradiction. Logically, Reform's definition of Judaism as a religion put it on a par with American Catholicism and Protestantism, but the
banker's own behavior as the consistent champion of the Jewish *people*
rested on the basic premise that Jews were more than a religious group.
Schiff admitted as much. We are a people with its own culture, he wrote to
the president of the Federation of American Zionists (FAZ), "but we are
not a Nation."⁵⁵ Inconsistencies on issues like peoplehood and the meaning
of Zion reflected his own personal dilemma on how best to combine an
Orthodox background with Reformist principles.

Central to Schiff's antinationalist brief was the fear that Zionism would
spark accusations of dual allegiance against American Jews. Jewish nationalism was a myth, the banker told an audience of college students, and
American Jews never hoped for a future in another country. But the goal of
Zionism was not totally invalid. Inconsistent yet again, he admitted that
unemancipated Romanian and Russian Jews were perhaps justified in seeking a land of their own, but Jews who enjoyed political rights were not. "As
Americans, or where Jews are [equal] citizens of other nations . . . , we
should have no right to complain of attempts on the part of anti-Semites to
curtail such rights, if we ourselves proclaimed that we consider ourselves
only temporary dwellers in the land, and that our ultimate desire and purpose is to return to Palestine and to there re-establish a Jewish nation."
Zionists retorted that the patriotism of emancipated Jews had failed to prevent anti-Semitism in Germany or the Dreyfus affair in France. Nevertheless, while they mouthed Herzl's principles, the general consensus within
American Zionist ranks was that those axioms applied not to American
Jews but to their less fortunate European brethren.⁵⁶

Since Jewish and non-Jewish anti-Zionists frequently invoked the bogey
of dual allegiance, one of Schiff's own circle, Cyrus L. Sulzberger, was
prompted to counter the charge. Sulzberger wrote in 1904 that patriotism
was not exclusive and that just as Americans had fought for Cuban independence without besmirching their patriotism, so too could they justifiably sympathize with Zionism. Schiff disagreed; in his eyes political Zionism was at odds with loyalty to the United States and it reinforced the
anti-Semitic images of Jews as unwelcome aliens or as Orientals who
should return to the Orient. Not only would Zionism alienate Americans,

but it endangered Jews in the Turkish empire as well. True Judaism, a faith without nationalist trappings, mirrored the essence of Americanism. Both represented "*hope* and *courage* and a *conviction that better things are to come* to all mankind, while Zionism signifies despair and surrender."[57]

Convinced that Zionism was a flimsy, utopian scheme, the banker very much doubted that its aims would muster the support of the great powers or that, as he put it, "by the stroke of a pen . . . millions of people [would] migrate to a new country." Even as it splintered the ranks of American Jews, Zionism offered no immediate help for the persecuted eastern Europeans. Rather, it succeeded only in impeding sounder enterprises like the Galveston movement. A Jewish state in Palestine, were it to be established, was doomed to failure. "Even if half of the Jews of the world would and could settle there, would that be a nation which could secure the respect of other world powers and which could assure protection for those of the Jewish people who remain content to live among the other Nations of the earth? Would this Nation . . . not rather become a weakling, . . . the football of dissentions and passions from within and machinations from without, rather humiliating both to its own citizens and those of its race who have remained among the Nations of the world?" Zionism may have brought back a few Jews who were about to leave the fold, but the Zionist movement, "built upon the sands," had no practical value. Like other false messianic movements, Zionism's failure, Schiff predicted darkly, augured only mass despair.[58]

Another factor, usually overlooked, contributed to Schiff's hostility. Since Herzl had fashioned a democratic movement that defended leadership by the people, it became a weapon to be used by American Zionists against elitist control of the Jewish community. Upholding the right of the rank and file at least to be heard, they along with others had opposed the stewards on the direction of the National Committee for Relief of Sufferers by Russian Massacres (NCRSRM) and the formation of the AJC. While their appeal for democratic governance continued to gain ground, Schiff grew more restive. As one contemporary journalist noted, "His ancestors were *hof-juden* centuries ago. It is not to be expected that he should think outside the methods that have come down with that class through the ages." One who constantly preached Americanism to his fellow Jews, Schiff was nonetheless loath to see the application of American democratic precepts to Jewish communal affairs. To be sure, his rapport with the new immigrants was too solidly entrenched in prewar America to be breached seriously by his antinationalism. Zvi Hirsch Masliansky, the popular Yiddish lecturer and Zionist activist, acknowledged that Schiff was a great man even though he was not a Zionist. But the days of elitism and paternalism were numbered. Many of the newly acculturated immigrants who had been schooled in the multiethnic reality of eastern Europe were flocking to the nationalist and democratic banner. An apprehensive Schiff estimated that 75 percent to 90 percent of the masses were Zionists. If a democratic *golem* were to arise, what then of proper communal leadership and the vision of an American Jewry integrated in the larger society?[59]

At a time when, as one Jewish scholar put it, "no gentleman was a Zionist and no Zionist was a gentleman," Schiff's views were shared by most of the stewards. The banker's sentiments, however, never approximated the near hysterical anti-Zionist reaction of some leading Reform Jews. Nor did he reject any contact with Zionists. After Richard Gottheil, first president of the FAZ, complained that American Jews "of substance" refused their financial support, Herzl turned directly to Schiff. The banker had consistently distanced himself from Herzl, and of his close friends only Oscar Straus, while minister to Constantinople in 1899, had spoken personally with the Zionist leader. More sympathetic to Zionism than Schiff was, Straus doubtless reported his negative assessment of Herzl. In 1903 the latter secured Lord Rothschild's promise to involve Schiff in a scheme to colonize Jews in El Arish, the northern half of the Sinai peninsula, but the American opposed that short-lived idea.[60]

A year later, when Schiff was in Europe, Herzl proposed that the two men meet. Knowing that Schiff could not be recruited for political Zionism, he carefully phrased a vague appeal that could cover a variety of possibilities:

> You say that you are prepared "to the best of my ability" to give practical aid to our oppressed and unfortunate people. Coming from you, that is a big statement, and I am happy to have received it. Do not believe, however, that I intend to make some fatuous attempt to lure you onto all my paths. I would simply like to have your help, which I value very highly, on that stretch of the road which is common to both of us. Don't jump to the conclusion, for Heaven's sake, that I want to *schnorr* some money from you for our cause. . . . What I would like to obtain from you is your participation in each individual case which you are to examine first.

A meeting in London was arranged, but since Herzl was unable to attend, Dr. Nissan Katzenelsohn, a prominent Russian Zionist, served as his designated substitute. Katzenelsohn and Schiff discussed the banker's objections to political Zionism as well as his conditions for loans to Russia. According to Herzl's diary, Schiff also promised to present the Zionist leader's thoughts on Jewish colonization to England's Edward VII. The meeting failed to alter the banker's views. He praised Herzl's idealism, but he thought that the man's self-proclaimed accomplishments "amounted to naught." How far Schiff was prepared to go along with Herzl's plans is unclear, and the episode ended shortly thereafter with Herzl's death. Schiff predicted that Zionism would not survive without its leader, and he added hopefully that the sooner Herzl's followers realized that the movement lacked a "substantial foundation," the better it would be for all Jews. He optimistically believed that despite its aggressiveness Zionism would die out.[61]

The meeting with Katzenelsohn awakened Zionist hopes that perhaps Schiff might join the movement. Harry Friedenwald, a friend and fellow director of the Jewish Theological Seminary (JTS) who now stood at the helm of the FAZ, worked on the banker. Friedenwald may have thought that since the primary focus of the organization had shifted from political to cultural Zionism, there was a chance of finding common ground with moderate Reform Jews. To nip such pressure in the bud and to answer Zionist taunts that only the wealthy opposed the movement, Schiff began thinking, a few months after Herzl's death, about making public his views on Zionism. For a while he held back, hesitating to expose Jewish disunity at a time when the Russian question demanded closed ranks. Conceding that Zionism offered hope to eastern European Jews, he also believed that an anti-Zionist statement from him might add to their misery.[62]

Increasingly, however, Schiff came under conflicting pressures. On Friedenwald's side stood Solomon Schechter, president of the JTS and a man whom Schiff greatly admired. An inveterate foe of Reform and a defender of cultural Zionism, Schechter admitted privately in 1904 that "I was lately spending a good deal of time making [Zionist] propaganda . . . among the Jewish aristocracy [read Schiff and associates]." A year later, Schechter joined the FAZ. The banker reacted warmly to Schechter's exposition of cultural Zionism, but he refused to budge so long as nationalism remained the heart of the movement. He also wanted reassurance that the seminary was not indoctrinating the students with Zionism.[63] On the other side stood Schiff's old friend, Kaufmann Kohler, the president of Hebrew Union College (HUC) and archcritic of Schechter's position, whose purge of Zionists from his faculty in 1907 was condoned by Schiff. After a few days in Kohler's company, Schiff decided to enter the fray. Schechter's plea that he give the Zionists the benefit of his counsel instead of attacking them went unheeded. Apparently, the banker discussed the matter with Schechter, and the two men agreed to a public exchange of letters explaining the pros and cons of Zionism.[64] Doubtless the banker also believed that a statement from him, the acknowledged leader of American Jewry, was imperative at a time when immigration restriction and the concomitant discussion of immigrant loyalties were on the congressional agenda.

Aware that his action would shake the community, Schiff attempted, albeit unsuccessfully, to soften the blow by first introducing the subject in a well-publicized address to the Jewish Chautauqua Assembly in July 1907. Again stressing the necessity of immigrant distribution, he stated flatly that the promised land of the Jews was America, not Palestine. A few days later he fired a major salvo in a public letter to Schechter. To be sure, Schechter had the right to join the Zionist movement without incurring public abuse, and he, Schiff, shared Schechter's yearning for a return to Jewish ideals. But, he insisted categorically, Zionist calculations paid little or no attention to religion, and nationalist aspirations of whatever stripe flew in the face of the Jewish mission.

The core of the statement, however, was Schiff's charge that Zionism was at odds with patriotism:

> Speaking as an American, I cannot for a moment concede that one can be at the same time a true American and an honest adherent of the Zionist Movement. . . . The Jew should not for a moment feel that he has only found an "asylum" in this country; he must not feel that he is in exile and that his abode here is only a temporary or passing one. If those who come after us are to be freed from the prejudice from which this generation is, not unnaturally, suffering we need feel that politically no one has any claim upon us but the country of which, of our own free will, we have become citizens; that even if we are Jews in faith, there is no string to our citizenship.[65]

The Jewish and secular press pounced on Schiff's letter; friends praised the banker, and critics vilified him. Henrietta Szold, for one, called it "the greatest piece of Rishus [Hebrew for "evil" but used by German Jews as a synonym for anti-Semitism] ever perpetrated." At a mass meeting the Zionists, by formal resolution, repudiated Schiff's charges, affirmed their loyalty to the country, and called upon anti-Zionists to desist from such harmful accusations. Schechter too was enraged. As Schiff pointed out, Schechter would not have agreed to published letters if he had known in advance what Schiff intended to include. The president of JTS confided privately that he would continue to interpret Judaism in traditional fashion, under which he included Zionism. If those doctrines upset "Wall Street" and the seminary's Schiff-dominated board, he was prepared to resign.

Schiff felt impelled to retreat. In a second published letter his tone was more moderate. He had no quarrel, he stated, with Zionism insofar as it aroused a return to Jewish ideals, and he denied having said that Zionism was incompatible with patriotism. Using different words that conveyed the same meaning, he now wrote that political Zionism put a "lien" on citizenship, "the enforcement of which the Zionist, if he is honest, must seek to accomplish by every legitimate means." He added privately that Jews were obligated to keep faith with America.[66] The words were well suited to American hypernationalists, but from the leader of a minority group they were, at the very least, impolitic.

Throughout the episode, which reverberated over several months, Schiff was more keyed up than disturbed. He thought his letters proved how courageous he was in exposing the Zionist menace. Enjoying a good fight, he did not permit the differences in opinion to mar his friendship with Schechter. No doubt he was troubled more by the criticism of two close friends, Marshall and Oscar Straus. The former, Schiff's right-hand man and a non-Zionist, defended Zionist achievements and denied the charge of un-Americanism. The latter spoke warmly of Zionist idealism, which he likened to the idealism of the American founding fathers. Surely, they would not have found any incompatibility between Zionism and patriotism, Straus wrote. Although Schiff took the criticism of friends seriously, he never showed any concern that his views might weaken his power over the community. Again his approach reflected confidence in his personal leadership and his assumption of the superiority of the established Jews over the Zionists among the immigrant masses.[67]

Despite the fallout of the controversy with Schechter, Schiff continued his tirade against Zionism publicly and privately. Now he aimed his arguments specifically against those Zionists he respected. "We should rather seek to get *back to Judaism* than back to Judaea," he told the president of JTS. Unlike some non-Zionists, Schiff also disputed the value of a religious center in Palestine. Since biblical days, he wrote to Friedenwald, attempts to centralize religious authority had failed: "We do not want *a* Jewish centre, but Jewish *Centres* and the more of these we can establish, the less we shall be threatened with stagnation or anarchy of belief. . . . Be it only the prayer of the lone Jewish settler on the plains of Dakota, . . . there is there a more efficient Jewish Centre than you will ever be able to establish among a civilization, which represents the past and among surroundings, which are paralyzing to human ambition." Nor did he drop the charge that Zionism worked against Jewish integration into American society: "Go to the Public Library of this City, the dwelling place of so many thousands of those who in recent years have come among us, and the Librarian will tell you—as he has told me—that the Yiddish literature is devoured by throngs of young coreligionists, who frankly aver that a public school education is a secondary necessity, but that they must first prepare for the coming Jewish State." True, conditions were bad for European Jews, but a Jewish state was not the answer. Schiff's usual optimism and religious belief made him confident that the situation would improve without Palestine, "for lo, the guardian of Israel sleepeth not, nor doth he slumber."[68]

Several months later, Schiff visited Palestine. Surprising for one who was an avid traveler and who visited Europe and other continents countless times, it was his first and only visit. Shocked by the *halukkah* system (the allocation of monies raised abroad for Orthodox Jews who spent their days in study) and its abuses, he called for drastic reform. Instead of permitting Jews in Jerusalem to lead "lives of idleness" while they were supported by others, Zionists should depopulate Jerusalem of those "degraded" Jews and insist that they do "actual work" elsewhere. Only then could they hope to establish a "dignified" center in Palestine and restore "the honor of the Jewish name." Schiff made no mention of the Zionist pioneers or their work, and he concluded hastily that Palestine could not hold any more Jews.[69]

Although some Zionists still tried to convert him, the *American Israelite*, mouthpiece of Reform's anti-Zionism, correctly if sarcastically summed up Schiff's intransigence: "Poor Mr. Schiff has lost all possible chance of obtaining a front pew in the temple of Jerusalem even if he should back up such a request with his usual generosity."[70]

The Zionist Solution: Second Phase

Shortly after his trip and until World War I, Schiff was a non-Zionist rather than an anti-Zionist, a friend of the social, economic, and cultural development of Palestine but an opponent of a Jewish state. In large measure his position reflected the influence of Solomon Schechter. True, Schechter was an enrolled Zionist, but his emphasis on a Jewish homeland primarily to infuse Jews throughout the world with religious inspiration and cultural creativity impressed members of the seminary's board. Just as Schechter distinguished critically between Zionists and "Nationalists," or those who agitated solely for a secular state, so too did Schiff after 1907. His quarrel was now almost entirely with the rigid non- or antireligious statists rather than with the builders of a Palestinian Jewish center.[71] Very possibly, Schiff's change of heart was also prompted by a desire to undercut the nationalists' monopoly of Palestinian institutions and to augment thereby the power of the antinationalists.

Without any explanation as to why he modified his earlier opinions on the impracticality of Zionist work in Palestine, the banker grew increasingly involved in Palestinian matters after the public dispute with Schechter. In time, philanthropic contributions helped build a social infrastructure that would inevitably strengthen the call for and reality of Jewish political autonomy, but even if Schiff foresaw that eventuality, it did not deter him. By 1912 he described himself as sympathetic to cultural Zionism, indicating thereby that he no longer rejected Palestine as a Jewish center: "I have by no means become a Zionist, but I have learned to respect the effort to culturally build up Palestine, so that it shall cease to be a pauper refuge and that those who are drawn there by the longing for the land of our forefathers may be enabled to gradually turn it into a Jewish cultural— not into a National—center." He was "devoted to Palestine," he said, and he desired to see its physical revival.[72]

As a non-Zionist, Schiff contributed to a wide variety of charitable and educational enterprises in the *yishuv* (the Jewish settlement in Palestine before statehood). To respond to Jewish needs, in Palestine no less than in Europe or the United States, was an ingrained responsibility of the stewards. Schiff supported Jewish schools and charities in Palestine; later he helped subsidize Eliezer ben Yehudah's pioneering efforts in modern Hebrew lexicography. In 1911, for reasons of compassion, he contributed to Jews in Jerusalem despite his aversion to the *halukkah* system. During those years the banker admitted the special significance of Palestine. He keenly felt, he said, the pull to work for the "cultural elevation of the Jewish inhabitants of the land where the cradle of our people stood."[73]

In 1910, Schiff and another antinationalist, Julius Rosenwald of Chicago, enthusiastically shared the financing of an experimental grain station in Palestine under the direction of the renowned agronomist Aaron Aaronsohn. Similar to his support of agricultural pursuits for immigrants in the United States, he particularly liked the notion of training young Palestinians in American agricultural methods. Schiff's determination to shield such projects from nationalist control provoked sharp exchanges with Aaronsohn. The latter recounted how Schiff and his friends, fearing the Zionists, "expressed themselves in a manner particularly insulting to the Zionists. At which I informed them that I am not used to being insulted and that they could go to hell." He added a few days later: "Old Man Schiff said that he finds the Zionists unacceptable, and I retorted that I found that unacceptable. In the final analysis, someone had to back down—and it was he." Surprised by Aaronsohn's candor, Schiff, however, did not begrudge his support.[74]

The idea of a technical school in Haifa (Technikum and later Technion) especially appealed to Schiff in the prewar years. His interest was aroused in 1908 by Paul Nathan of the Hilfsverein, whose organization, like its French and English counterparts, maintained a network of schools in Palestine. Along with the wealthy Wissotzky family of Russia, Schiff contributed handsomely to the project. He immersed himself in the details of implementation, and he induced American Zionists and non-Zionists to lend their support. His purpose was twofold. First, he sought to train Palestinian Jews in crafts and industry and thereby end their dependence on *halukkah*—in his words, to teach the Jerusalem Jew "to know what self-respect and dignity mean." Second, he envisioned an undertaking joining Zionists and non-Zionists, Orthodox and Reform, on a nonpolitical platform—not to advance the progress of political Zionism but to foster Jewish unity. As he said, the school would be wedded to no "ism" but Judaism.[75] The banker appended an important condition to his donation. He stipulated that control would rest primarily with Nathan in Berlin, but he demanded, for the sake of Jewish unity, that the board of directors (curatorium) include members from other countries. He himself did not serve on the board, but the Americans he suggested, non-Zionists for the most part, were men who usually deferred to his wishes: Louis Marshall, Cyrus Adler, Julian Mack, Solomon Schechter, Julius Rosenwald, Mayer Sulzberger, Samuel Strauss, and Schiff's son Mortimer.[76]

With authority divided among various lands and parties and with the growth of imperialist pressures in the Near East, clashes over the Technikum were inevitable. During the "language war" of 1913–14 the American directors, who were usually consigned by the Europeans to a subordinate position in multinational deliberations, were very much involved. The issue—should Hebrew be the official language of the Technikum—was fought mainly in Europe and Palestine and pitted Zionists against non-Zionists. Germany, seeking to strengthen its foothold in the region, pressed the Hilfsverein to insist on German; France and England worried lest their influence decline. The World Zionist Organization divided, and the press throughout the Western world reverberated with charges and countercharges from prominent Jews. Within the *yishuv*, teachers boycotted schools; and when a decision was reached to recognize German instead of Hebrew, students and parents staged demonstrations.[77]

By the time the Americans took up the matter, the issue had become far more than the language of instruction. A bitter controversy now raged between the Zionists, who proudly looked upon the rebirth of modern Hebrew as their weapon against "senseless assimilation" and the so-called cringing ghetto spirit, and the non-Zionists, who were horrified by Zionist tactics in the dispute. Each side took its expected stand in letters to Schiff and in articles and speeches, many of which were reproduced in the secular press. Widely publicizing the rift, Paul Nathan printed a scathing attack on the Zionists in which, according to a report in the *New York Times*, he likened their tactics to pogroms.[78]

Caught between the European directors and the American curators, Schiff attempted to balance the multiple variables—the *yishuv*'s need for the protection of a great power, the lack of appropriate instructors and textbooks for instruction in Hebrew, the Technikum's reliance on funds from many groups, and the force of Jewish public opinion in Palestine and elsewhere. He sympathized with the Hebraists[79] although he saw the need of Arabic, Turkish, and Western languages, but the question of language was secondary to him. In close contact with Nathan and Judah Magnes, he was appalled primarily by the behavior of the Zionists (and he singled out in particular the prominent leader of the militants, Dr. Shmarya Levin) in Germany and in Palestine who resorted to extremist and "reprehensible" methods in attempting to seize communal control. He reported with satisfaction that even Schechter, an enrolled Zionist, agreed with him. Blaming the nationalist Zionist wing that shunned religion, Schiff continued to raise money for the Technikum, but he bemoaned the negative effect of the quarrel on international goodwill, on support for other cultural enter-. prises in Palestine, and especially on Jewish unity. "I only wish we still had a Sanhedrin," he wrote to Marshall, "which could condemn to death by stoning, anyone who tried to sow the seed of discord within our own ranks." Jews had enough to do, he said, defending themselves against attacks from non-Jews.[80]

Zionists around the world successfully raised money in defense of the use of Hebrew, and many in the United States looked to the American directors to come up with a settlement. Some cited the predominant share of funds contributed to the school from the United States, and others stated that the Americans, unlike the Europeans, were not blinded by chauvinism. The American directors finally suggested a compromise worked out by Schiff (who put pressure on Nathan) and Magnes, providing that as far as possible Hebrew was to be the dominant language of instruction. Julian Mack, a federal judge and new convert to Zionism, warmly congratulated Schiff for his peacemaking role. If the compromise held, "you will have done the finest of the many fine works of your life for the Jews of the world."[81]

The executive in Berlin accepted the compromise with some modifications, but peace in the *yishuv* was still elusive. The controversy between Zionists and non-Zionists continued as before. Even Schiff grew impatient with Nathan and told him that a language can't be forced on a people. Since leadership exacted sacrifices, he urged Nathan to keep on working despite Zionist attacks. Again he turned to the Bible, this time to Moses' plea, when he came down from Sinai, that God destroy him but spare the stiff-necked people.[82]

In the midst of the language war new obstacles arose. Formidable financial difficulties threatened the opening of the school, and all the American members of the curatorium, who were less sympathetic with the German trustees than Schiff was, resigned with Schiff's consent. Frustrated by the delay, Schiff told several Zionist friends that the situation might well cool his interest in "things Palestinian."[83] In July he himself stirred up a new round of communal infighting with a letter to the Anglo-Jewish press complaining about the tactics of the Jewish nationalists, who clamored for the cooperation of international Jewry for Palestinian work but "will not hesitate to stoop to employ the most reprehensible means in order to accomplish forcibly, if needed, their own purposes and designs." As Adler explained to Marshall, Schiff had resolved to attack the nationalists even though he felt very kindly toward the Hebraists. Most offensive to the Zionists was the banker's pointed warning: "International, and in particular American Jewry, had better carefully consider how far in such a state of affairs, it is advisable for the time being to increase its interest in and support of Palestinian projects and affairs."[84] Events would prove that by those words Schiff put his leadership on the line.

Louis Lipsky, chairman of the executive committee of the FAZ, was quick to reply, and so were other prominent Zionists like Shmarya Levin and Stephen Wise. Lipsky's defense of the Zionists cleverly used Schiff's own admission in an earlier address on the benefits of Zionism. The banker's letter was all the more unfair, Lipsky added, because the development of Palestine was the product of Zionist work, not of American Jewish contributions. Was it proper statesmanship for a leader like Schiff to advise American Jews to withhold their contributions? By terming the fight for Hebrew "a struggle for [Jewish] home rule in Palestine" and "for the right of an awakened Jewry to interpret its own life in its own terms," the Zionist leader implicitly argued the case of democracy over elitism. Shmarya Levin agreed that Schiff's warning was unstatesmanlike. The rabbis had taught that "wise men should be careful with their words," and since the Zionist movement had too great a meaning for Jews to be dismissed so cavalierly, he hinted that Schiff had shown his ineptitude as a leader. A more outspoken editorial in the *Jewish Daily News* (Yiddish) doubted that Schiff, an "ordinary philanthropist with a check book," could understand the spirit that infused Zionism. "Keep your check book, Mr. Schiff," it raged, because Jewish rebirth and liberation, for Schiff's benefit too, was destined to come from the people, not from philanthropists.[85]

Although Schiff retracted his warning to American Jews, Zionist rabbi Stephen Wise followed with yet another attack. He charged that wealthy Jews, shutting themselves out of the Zionist movement and ignoring the potential strengths of Zionist sentiment, failed as statesmen. Furthermore, they excluded Zionists from the councils of Jewry and refused to grant the movement a fair hearing. Like Lipsky, Levin, and the others, Wise attempted to prove how democratic Zionism exposed the weaknesses of elitist leadership. Along the lines of criticism that had greeted the NCRSRM and the organization of the AJC, Schiff's detractors harnessed Zionism to their case against communal stewardship. Anti-Zionist Simon Wolf, a prominent figure in B'nai B'rith, concluded that "unless [the Zionists] can rule they would rather ruin."[86] Schiff claimed that he was not disturbed by the attacks. Ironically, he said that as a non-Zionist he still hoped for greater cooperation with Zionists (but not nationalists) in Palestinian work. Toward that end he pleaded with the Zionists to dissociate themselves from the nationalists. In 1915 the Technikum, which Schiff had hoped would testify to Jewish unity, became the property of the Hilfsverein. The outbreak of the war precluded further progress, but so eager was Schiff to implement the project that in 1919 and 1920 he offered to purchase the school and turn it over to the Zionist Organization. As it turned out, the latter preferred to deal directly with the Hilfsverein. Meantime, in reaction to the language war, the Zionists determined not to yield on Hebrew. A plank in the 1918 platform of the newly created Zionist Organization of America (ZOA) read: "Hebrew, the national language of the Jewish people, shall be the medium of public instruction."[87]

Zionism, more than any other issue, set Schiff off from the masses. A man who often flouted critics, particularly from the immigrant ranks, he acknowledged the need to backtrack on Zionist issues in the dispute with Schechter, in the interchange with Aaronsohn, and again in the second round of the language war. Personal power and his passion for Jewish unity figured in his retractions, but he could disregard neither his own feelings about Palestine nor the attraction of Zionism for ethnic-minded American Jews. Just as Zionism had survived Herzl's death and was unlikely to disappear, so too was Schiff becoming more hard-pressed to maintain the line between non-Zionism and political Zionism.

The outbreak of World War I in 1914 hardened the banker's opposition to Jewish nationalism. Extreme nationalism in any form, and that included political Zionism, brought only harm. He explained sharply to a fellow philanthropist, Julius Rosenwald: "I consider *all* Nationalism, if carried to the extreme a curse and a danger. It is, for instance, the extreme nationalism of the different European peoples that has brought on the deplorable conflict now raging in Europe; and if we, as Jews, insist that we are a nation, we are steering into most dangerous waters." Jewish nationalist efforts could ensure neither the happiness of Jews nor of mankind. To offset the impact of articles in journals that favored Zionism, he arranged with the editors of the powerful *Outlook* to print an anti-Zionist piece by Rabbi Samuel Schulman. The latter planned to explain the "viciousness" of Zionism, and Schiff was prepared to underwrite the fees as well as the cost of distributing more than six thousand copies. "Whither are we drifting?" he asked despairingly. Were he but ten or fifteen years younger, he mused, he would fight more vigorously against the secular nationalists and the harm they were causing American Jews.[88]

Non-Zionism suited Schiff better than anti-Zionism. It flowed naturally from his sense of ethnicity, that is, his deep belief that he was bound to and responsible for his fellow Jews throughout the world. Louis Marshall, one who held similar convictions, commented privately about his friend: "A Jew of Mr. Schiff's calibre, who is born unto his people only once in a generation

. . . a man whose heart and soul are completely given to his people and whose only thought and concern is the fate of his suffering Brethren, cannot be opposed to the practical objects of Zionism."[89]

Schiff remained a non-Zionist in the years before America entered the war (1914–17), and he responded with alacrity to new relief needs of the *yishuv*. At the same time, criticism of his stand on Zionism as well as his undemocratic leadership was reaching a climax. Yet a discernible shift toward his acceptance of political Zionism was underway. By the end of the war, Schiff stood on the brink of affiliation with the ZOA.

6

The World at War

Questions of Loyalty

In January 1917, Schiff celebrated his seventieth birthday, an occasion that brought forth accolades from both friends and critics from all walks of American Jewish life. Although his nimble step and youthful vigor belied his age, increased loss of hearing, bouts of insomnia, and other physical ailments slowed him down.[1] He did little to reduce his business and communal workload, but he relied more heavily in the firm on his son and other partners and in matters of philanthropy and communal affairs on his son-in-law and Louis Marshall. Enjoying family life and his role as grandfather to the utmost, Schiff by no means retired from public life. The others bore new responsibilities, but he still passed on major policy and strategy.

The slight alterations in the banker's way of life were overshadowed by changes in his power as a leader. On Wall Street the war years tarnished Kuhn, Loeb's image. With respect to the Jewish community the change was more glaring.

The German Connection

Zionist leader Chaim Weizmann recorded an anecdote in his autobiography in the name of Shmarya Levin. The story goes that Levin heard Schiff announce at a public meeting: "I am divided into three parts; I am an American, I am a German, and I am a Jew." Levin's immediate question was whether Schiff divided himself vertically or horizontally. Whatever the answer, Schiff was not the first American Jew to see himself in three dimensions. Others before him had affirmed the legitimacy of multiple loyalties that they succeeded in harmonizing in their own behavior. Schiff certainly would never have questioned his passion for Americanism, Germanism, or Judaism. He was proud, he said, of the "trinity" of loyalties.[2] Nor would he have admitted that any of the three clashed with the others. The war years, however, particularly between 1914 and 1917, raised troubling questions. When foreign affairs touched Americans more closely than ever before, when hypernationalism engulfed the nation, and when Jews blatantly stood out as a hyphenated American group, it became more difficult for Schiff to reconcile all three loyalties in a comfortable fashion.

The banker's activities during the period of American neutrality illustrated the problems of melding disparate attachments into an indivisible pattern. Called upon to rethink priorities and readjust his behavior, he wrestled for the first time in his life with problems of self-identification. At times he spoke as the integrated American-German-Jew; at other times he was one or another. Now an elder statesman whose power was acknowledged by fellow Jews and by the American and foreign governments, his behavior was carefully scrutinized and analyzed by Jews and non-Jews alike.

At the onset of hostilities, Schiff cut short his summer vacation and returned to the city. The man who had confidently asserted during the Agadir crisis of 1911 that it was "inconceivable" that Germany and England would resort to war was taken by surprise. In the fall of 1914 the *New York Times* ran a full-page interview with Schiff that probed his views on the world conflict. More than questions and answers of a philanthropist or prominent businessman, it testified to the banker's renown within the larger community. Schiff openly admitted that his sympathies lay with Germany, who, he claimed, had not instigated the war. He also denied that he was anti-England, but for obvious reasons (the Jewish problem) he was anti-Russia. The heart of his message emphasized a speedy end to the war. He said that an unqualified victory for either side would bring only unnecessary slaughter and utter devastation. America could not live comfortably were either side to destroy the other, nor did the United States recognize the hardships and dangers ahead if it were forced to join the fighting. He suggested that properly mobilized American public opinion could bring about a conference able to mediate the conflict.[3]

The banker amplified his opinions a few weeks later in a lengthy published correspondence with Charles Eliot; but although the latter was strongly anti-German, the interchange was friendly. Far different were comments from London, where Schiff's interview with the *Times* was called a "brief for Germany" and a German stratagem to capture American sympathies from a man who was one of the "apostles of German Kultur." So cutting were the remarks that Israel Zangwill felt called upon to defend his friend as a noble philanthropist and a patriotic American who "speaks not as the mouthpiece of Berlin but with the voice of Jerusalem." Zangwill succeeded only in fanning the flames of resentment further and in evoking anti-Jewish threats against Jewish financiers from a group called the Vigilance Committee.[4] Similar criticism emanated from Paris, where Clemenceau maintained that Schiff's pro-German statement was aimed at depriving the Allies of their rightful victory. Since Germany attacked the peace message from a son of the fatherland even more bitterly, it was clear, first, that he had aroused the suspicions of both sides and, second, that neither side was prepared to end the conflict.[5]

Until 1917, Schiff continued to call for an end to "this holocaust." Repeatedly he suggested to the president and the secretary of state and to the public as well that the United States offer to mediate. Nevertheless, his support of the American Neutral Conference Committee, a small group of prominent persons who wanted mediation by Wilson, drew public criticism. Charged again with being pro-German, Schiff grew increasingly pessimistic. He predicted a long war that would end only in a draw, leaving both sides physically, materially, and morally bankrupt.[6]

More than sympathy with Germany made Schiff a champion of an early peace and of American neutrality. With relatives and friends serving in the opposing forces, he agonized over the horrors of the war. An early peace served his business interests as well. Like other businessmen, Schiff had been an outspoken supporter of international peace as far back as the Spanish-American War and as recently as the prewar arbitration treaties negotiated by Secretary William Jennings Bryan. A member of the Friends for Peace Society, he also served as an officer of the New York Peace Society and the League to Enforce Peace. The two latter organizations labored before and during the war for mediation of conflicts through the use of international law and, in the case of the league, for a postwar league of nations. At the same time, Schiff banked on a neutral Wilson to engineer a status quo peace. Objecting to the craze for military preparedness in America, he opposed the export of munitions and funds to the belligerents.[7] Where he could, as in the case of Japan, Schiff tried at the onset of hostilities to limit the scope of the war and simultaneously the number of Germany's enemies. Since Kuhn, Loeb held a major part of Japan's debt, he felt free to caution Japan against entering the war or interfering with the balance of power by closing the open door to Chinese markets. His attempt failed (and Japan joined the Allies), but his warm relationship with that country continued, proving that his pro-German sympathies were not absolute.[8]

The Schiff papers abound with letters testifying to the public renown that the banker and his activities had won. During the war private individuals sought his support of their schemes for peace. (Salmon Levinson, a key mover in what ultimately became the Kellogg-Briand peace pact of 1929, was one such correspondent.) Other Americans thought to draw on Schiff's past experience. The executive secretary of the League to Enforce Peace, for example, considered the idea of distributing democratic propaganda among German prisoners, just as Schiff and Kennan had done with Russian prisoners in the Russo-Japanese War. Still another letter suggested that Schiff, as the "foremost" American Jew, had a chance to end the war when he met in 1915 with Britain's outstanding Jew, Lord Reading, who was then in America to negotiate a loan for the Allies.[9] Clearly, respect for the banker on the part of Jews and non-Jews held firm in the early days of American neutrality.

German Americans divided sharply on their sympathy with the fatherland, and in Schiff's case pro-German sentiments appeared uppermost. Concern for German welfare, he said, is in "everyone in whose veins there flows German blood." Unlike Louis Marshall and Oscar Straus, who sympathized with the Allies, neither he nor his family had emigrated from Germany as a result of anti-Jewish experiences. He had memories of a comfortable childhood and a secure Jewish community. To be sure, he admitted that Jews had fared better in England, and he had for years been a member of the Pilgrims' Club, a London-based society that sought to promote Anglo-American friendship. But strong family ties and frequent visits to his homeland, climaxed by an audience with the kaiser in 1911, strengthened his pro-German sentiments. The banker had long supported numerous communal institutions in his beloved Frankfurt, and out of a desire to disseminate the culture of which he was so proud, he had funded projects of German studies at Cornell and Harvard. After all, he told Andrew D. White, his preoccupation with Jewish affairs did not preclude his interest in German culture.[10]

At the beginning of the war, Schiff's sentiments jibed with his belief in a German victory. "I have no fear that German civilization, German culture and German manhood can be downed," he wrote. Even then, however, he was a critic of German "militarismus" and an opponent of the country's expansionist designs. His sympathy with Germany, albeit thus modified, was compounded by a hatred of Russia. On balance, a German victory that would simultaneously end "wretched" czarism appeared by far the more desirable end.[11]

The Central Powers worked tirelessly to get Schiff and other sympathetic Jewish leaders to support their cause in the United States. While Germany concentrated on fund-raising and on swaying public opinion, particularly in the wake of atrocity stories and the German invasion of Belgium, it developed a cadre of American sympathizers abetted by special emissaries from Germany. One agent and propagandist, Dr. Isaac Straus, worked on the anti-Russian Jewish immigrant masses through a new periodical, the *American Jewish Chronicle*. Kuhn, Loeb, with its connections to the Warburg firm that heavily financed the German war effort, was also a natural target. German ambassador Johann von Bernstorff, along with Straus and another agent, Bernhard Dernburg, were in close contact with the banker even as they engaged in open propaganda work. (Von Bernstorff also asked that Kuhn, Loeb, with the cooperation of the American Red Cross, serve as treasurer for the German Red Cross in the United States.)[12] Although Louis Marshall thought that his friend's involvement on behalf of Germany was ill-advised, Schiff corresponded (before the sinking of the *Lusitania*) with the Austrian ambassador and with Arthur Zimmermann of the German foreign office.[13] Meanwhile, other active defenders of Germany who were well-known Americans—Harvard professor Hugo Muensterberg, Semitics scholar Morris Jastrow, and publicist George Sylvester Viereck (years later a leading propagandist for the Nazis in the United States)—turned to Schiff with ideas on how to arouse American sympathy.[14]

The Schiff papers do not reveal the extent of the banker's aid to his native land. He secretly guarded those activities even from his friends. He well knew the purpose of the German mission in America, but he claimed, with respect to Straus, that he broke off connections when he learned that the man was a German secret agent out to propagandize among the Jews. Overall, the tenor of Schiff's correspondence suggests that he was genuinely sympathetic toward those who appealed for his cooperation but that in most cases he offered no more than verbal encouragement. If requests of him demanded public demonstrations of loyalty to Germany or if the one who approached him was too aggressive publicly, acts that would have belied the banker's insistence on American neutrality, Schiff put an end to the association. It was one thing for him to say that he sympathized with Germany but quite another to have his name linked with what he considered to be extremist schemes. Besides, as he told Viereck, any time he uttered something meant for Germany's benefit he was attacked in the *German* press.[15]

In 1914, Schiff wrote a friend in Munich that American public opinion "is not as much in favor of Germany as we all would wish, but with a group of friends we are doing our best to spread the truth." Schiff's support of Germany, however, was not unconditional. He refused to contribute to the German-American Literary Defense Committee, explaining that he found some of its statements offensive. In addition, when advising Zimmerman and others on how they could best secure American Jewish sympathy, he was the Jew as well as the German. Calling Germany the birthplace of anti-Semitism, he asked first for an end to government prejudice that kept Jews out of civil and professional positions and ignored the ardent patriotism of German Jews.[16]

Although Germany wanted generous financial backing from Schiff more than his words of sympathy, the banker did not comply. Evidence that Schiff and Kuhn, Loeb were not significant financiers of the German war machine came from an American government panel. In 1918 a subcommittee of the Senate Committee on the Judiciary reported on the organized brewery interests, a suspected source of unpatriotic activities, and on the web of German propaganda in America in 1914. One Justice Department official, who had participated in a two-year government probe of German activities, disclosed that the scope of German propaganda in the United States was very wide. "It embraced the furnishing of news secretly to newspapers, the distribution of film, the sending of lecturers through the country, the sending of newspaper correspondents from Germany to this country to write favorable matter for the papers, the sending of American correspondents abroad to send back to this country propaganda favorable to Germany. . . . It embraced propaganda among the Irish, among the Jews, among the Catholics." To finance the operation and to secure American loans, the German agents came armed with $150 million in German treasury notes.

Among many others, Jewish individuals and the Yiddish press were investigated by the government, and so too was Kuhn, Loeb. Like other banks, Schiff's firm advanced a loan to Dernburg that was backed by German bonds, but the subcommittee could not prove that the firm knew of the purposes for which the funds would be used. To be sure, Kuhn, Loeb, again like other banks, also disposed of a small amount of German war bonds, but it failed nonetheless to live up to Germany's expectations. Schiff explained privately to Max Warburg that America's initial reluctance to deal in European securities, as well as Kuhn, Loeb's operational methods, forbade it from handling the financial arrangements that Germany desired. All told, Schiff and Kuhn, Loeb, in large measure because of the divided sympathies of the partners, disappointed the kaiser. A government witness told the subcommittee that the "vicious fire of gossip" about the firm notwithstanding, Kuhn, Loeb was proven neither pro-German nor other than neutral. "The sum total of the thing, is that, taking it by and large, you will find that the firm of Kuhn, Loeb & Co. imposed on the German Government such difficult conditions for financing that the German Government was compelled to turn elsewhere to do its financing." Unnoted by the subcommittee, albeit denied by Schiff in 1915, were his two private monetary contributions to the German cause.[17]

Kuhn, Loeb's minimal financial help to Germany on top of Schiff's first peace message and, more important, the report (soon discredited) that his firm was participating in the large Allied loan in 1915, gave Schiff a bad name in the German press. Max Warburg, who functioned as a conduit between Schiff and the German government, reported that one Berlin newspaper warned Germany to keep a safe distance from the American. Harsh criticism also came from the *American Jewish Chronicle*, the periodical funded by the German government.[18]

Answers from a hurt and indignant Schiff revealed the personal dilemma of a man who desired to blend his Germanism with his Americanism. World peace was his priority. He opposed German militarism, but
hadn't he also criticized England's expansionist aims in the piece for the
New York Times? Furthermore, as he explained to Max Warburg, he was
caught in a clash of beliefs. On the one hand was his "reverence" for Germany and on the other his aversion to German political authoritarianism,
which Americans, steeped in Anglo-Saxon institutions, could never condone. He added bitterly to Paul Nathan that the Germans completely forgot that he, Schiff, was an American citizen even before there was a German Reich.[19] Denounced by his former countrymen, Schiff was another on
the long list of American immigrants who sought to square their ties to the
land of their birth with their loyalty to America.

The banker spoke out frequently against Russia, but never did he actively propagandize for Germany within the Jewish community. Nor was it
necessary; the Jewish rank and file and the Yiddish press took a similar pro-
German stand. There were some whose genunine love of Germany was the
prime consideration and others, like the Socialists, who repudiated war in
principle. To most, however, the Allies meant Russia. The Jews held no
specific brief against England, but they could not imagine any self-
respecting Jew on the side of the detested czarist government. The fact
that the eastern European Jews clung to those views despite Gentile pressures and the strong pro-Ally sentiment of most Americans indicated the
depth of their feelings.[20]

In March 1917, Schiff announced that he had reversed his stand. He
told Charles Eliot that his love for Germany had not abated but that there
had been a "thorough change" in his attitude ever since Germany embarked on a course of submarine warfare.[21] Written at the same time that
revolutionary events heralded the czar's imminent abdication, Schiff, now a
a disillusioned German American, could support America's imminent
entry into the war without reservation.

Loans for the Allies

The fortunes of Kuhn, Loeb suffered during the war. Not only was its ac-
tivity curtailed, but in the eyes of the Anglophile banking houses domi-
nated by the House of Morgan it became an object of suspicion and anti-
Semitic attacks. While charges against the allegedly disloyal pro-German
Jewish banking firms reverberated, Schiff called at 23 Wall Street after the
sinking of the *Lusitania* (1915). Tendering his personal apology to Jack
Morgan (J.P.'s son, who now headed the firm), he was rudely rebuffed.
Schiff sullied his own reputation again in 1916 when he addressed the

League to Enforce Peace. His message, which the organization quickly disavowed and which ran afoul of Allied sentiments, urged an immediate end to the war and just treatment of all nations. That, like his participation in the Neutral Conference Committee, which also stood for immediate mediation, fed the accusation that he sought a peace that would be in Germany's best interest. It made little difference to his critics that before America entered the war he had contributed generously to relief drives on behalf of Belgium and the Entente.[22]

Just as the Germans inflated their expectations of Schiff, so did the English exaggerate his importance in their own struggle for American loans and goodwill. The myth of Jewish control of finance and of the press pervaded the British foreign office, and Schiff was regarded as a prime example of Jewish power. Sir Cecil Spring-Rice, ambassador to Washington, readily abetted anti-Jewish attacks and fed the myth by ranting against Jewish bankers in general and against Schiff's inordinate influence in particular. Not only were the American Jews "far better organized than the Irish and far more formidable," Spring-Rice wrote, but "the German Jewish Bankers are toiling in a solid phalanx to compass our destruction. . . . The principal Jew is now Schiff." Although Schiff held no grievance against England itself, he thought that the recent situation of British Jewry had worsened. "I am afraid that England," he said, "has been contaminated by her alliance with Russia."[23]

London knew that American Jews, even if it had their sympathies, regarded Russia's presence in the Triple Entente as the primary obstacle to help for England and France. "Russia is of course a bone in the throat of every Jewish sympathizer with the Allies," a Jewish writer stated. In a similar vein, Oscar Straus argued with the Russian ambassador that the Jewish situation weakened the Allied cause and alienated public opinion. Louis Marshall too chided American banks for lending money to Russia as long as Jews there suffered disabilities. He argued that such bankers flouted the principles that underlay abrogation and thereby made a mockery of American honor and the integrity of American citizenship. Marshall relayed the American Jewish Committee's (AJC's) terms for financial aid to a Russian agent in 1915. They had not changed since originally spelled out by Schiff: Were Russian Jews granted civil and religious rights, Marshall said, "the leading Jews of the United States, including Mr. Schiff, have no hesitation in giving the assurance that arrangements can be made to secure for Russia a loan of one, or even two, hundred million dollars."[24] The Jewish leaders, however, labored in vain. In response to demands of business, the Wilson administration in 1915 lifted its ban on loans to the belligerents. The AJC realized that the ensuing business with Russia militated against their efforts on behalf of Russian Jewish emancipation.[25]

Schiff's stand became front-page news in 1915 when Lord Reading led an Allied mission to the United States to secure a major loan for the Allies. In this instance, the banker again sought to balance his loyalties. A German sympathizer with a deep Jewish aversion to Russia, he and his firm were nonetheless American and, aside from the profits involved, obligated to promote the nation's commerce and industry. The partners of Kuhn, Loeb divided on how to proceed—Otto Kahn and Schiff's own son favored participation in the loan—and a conference was called. Schiff was prepared, he said, not to oppose the loan as long as its advantages in no way accrued to Russia, but they all understood that the idea of separating Russia from England and France would be rejected. The drama of the conference as told by Cyrus Adler lay in Schiff's opening remarks:

> I have thought about this situation all night. Before asking your opinions, I want to tell you that my mind is made up, unalterably. I realize fully what is at stake for the firm . . . in the decision we are going to make. But come what may, I cannot run counter to my conscience, I cannot sacrifice my profoundest convictions for the sake of whatever business advantage, I cannot stultify myself by aiding those who, in bitter enmity have tortured my people and will continue to do so, whatever fine professions they may make in their hour of need. I ought not to be asked to do so. It is not fair to put me in this dilemma. . . . I know your objections and counter-arguments and criticisms. They do not and cannot affect my conclusion. This is a matter between me and my conscience, and no one but I myself can solve it for me. You are younger men. Some of you do not feel as I do on what I consider the morally controlling element of the question. The future of the firm is yours.

Schiff offered to resign if the partners did not agree with him, and at that dissent collapsed. Several partners subscribed privately to the loan, but Schiff's law still ruled the rarely divided firm. The banker continued his efforts to block loans to Russia, arguing eloquently but futilely that such aid was "truly a reason for the American people to bow their heads in shame and mortification." Ironically, in the face of wartime needs, London discreetly pressured the czarist regime to make concessions to the Jews.[26]

Kuhn, Loeb not only lost out to the pro-England Wall Street houses, but the matter reinforced the image held by the Allies and the general American press of Schiff as a German partisan. Among Jewish leaders who sided with the Allies, Rabbi Stephen Wise called him more pro-German than pro-Jewish. The banker wryly noted to Israel Zangwill that, because of his primary desire for an honorable peace, Germany found him inadequately pro-German, while at the same time England and France regarded him as an agent of the kaiser. In some Yiddish circles, however, his stand was acclaimed. The loyal *Day* congratulated the banker in an editorial emphasizing his Jewish loyalties. "A man who occupies such an important place in the public life of the country must have great courage to come out publicly and to say that he cannot take part in this loan because he does not want to help Russia. Regarding Jacob Schiff we can say with truth: . . . Few are the Jewish millionaires who behave like Jews and with whom the honor of the Jewish people stands higher than does the dollar."[27]

Acting on its own, Russia also approached Schiff for financial help. A friendly and flattering Gregory Wilenkin, now openly admitting his Jewish origins and vaguely promising assistance on the Jewish situation, surfaced again in 1914. Schiff, equally friendly, remained adamant. He had no faith in czarist promises, and he wanted concrete evidence of a change of heart. If now, despite the patriotism of the Russian Jews, rumors of civil rights proved false, Russia would forfeit any chance of cooperation.[28]

Not surprised that the desired action failed to materialize, Schiff, along with Marshall and Straus, worked determinedly to vitiate Russian efforts for private American loans and for credits from banks within the Federal Reserve system. For a while they even toyed with the idea of using the issue of Jewish rights as a point of leverage with the Reading loan commission. Unsuccessful in that attempt, they resorted to publicity for influencing popular opinion and undercutting Russian machinations. Schiff, for example, gave an emotional as well as a business reason in talks that explained his opposition: Russian banks were only tools of the "detestable and inhuman" government and unable to cover payments on loans. He also lobbied actively with the White House and with ranking senators against America's extension of financial credit to the czarist government, but a similar plea to the Morgan firm against credits to Russia was summarily dismissed.[29]

On the subject of Jewish rights in Russia, Schiff trod a familiar path. He feared neither a backlash from the Jewish or larger communities nor any adverse effects on his image. In addition to loans, he and his circle worked on several other Russia-related matters, such as atrocities by czarist troops against Jews in Poland and Galicia, inhumane treatment of prisoners of war in Siberia, and the possibility of a new commercial treaty between the Russian and American governments. Determined that a treaty not repeat the inequities of the 1832 accord, the AJC called the attention of the president, the ambassador to Russia, and the influential Chamber of Commerce to assurances of Jewish equality in the party platforms of 1912. Schiff reminded Wilson of his indignation at Russian discrimination and the support he had lent to abrogation in 1911. How would it look, therefore, for the administration to disregard the passport question in negotiations for a new treaty?[30] Unlike the abrogation campaign, a quiet approach rather than mass appeal was employed for the perceived threat. Since the expected treaty was not drawn up, the efficacy of elitist control was again proved to the stewards.

America at War

Schiff's pro-German sentiments never compromised his loyalty to America. He was an American first: "I believe I may say that my sympathies for the land of my birth are as warm as anyone's, but I have been an American for fifty years, and mean to remain so first and for the remainder of my life." A preacher against hyphenated Americanism—"God forbid that we permit a hyphen to be placed between Jew and American"—he rejected anything that smacked of dual political allegiance. Although he retained his Jewish and German *cultural* interests, he believed that all immigrants, not only Jews, were morally bound to become naturalized rapidly and divest themselves of other than American *national* attachments.[31] Indeed, the last was an issue on which he and Germany clashed.

The banker's feelings for the United States were predicated on an abiding respect for the land, its institutions, and its heroes. In 1913, the year in which Charles Beard published *An Economic Interpretation of the Constitution*, he deplored the growing popularity of Constitution debunking. From the onset of his career and like proper upper-middle-class businessmen, Schiff joined many civic causes and organizations, donating handsomely to museums, schools, and libraries and fighting Tammany for good government in New York City. Like his philanthropic and defense activities, his affiliations meant time and service in addition to financial aid.[32] Out of a sense of civic duty as well as business and Jewish interests, he also became marginally involved in politics. A loyal Republican, except for his support of Wilson in 1912 and 1916, his name was familiar to local and national leaders of both major parties. Schiff may not have been close to many, but when he wanted to discuss public policy or to suggest candidates for government office, there was little doubt that the politicians would hear him out. Preferring to work behind the scenes, he showed no ambitions for public office. He served from 1882 to 1884 on New York City's Board of Education, and in 1904–5, without any encouragement on his part, a short-lived movement sprang up among Republicans to draft him to be their candidate in the city's mayoralty race.[33]

A donor and active campaigner for Wilson's reelection in 1916, the banker not only left the Republicans but abandoned his erstwhile idol, the Progressive candidate Theodore Roosevelt. Foreign affairs was his paramount concern, and he supported the administration's policies before and after the election. In 1917 he heaped lavish praise on Wilson's "peace without victory" speech. Neither utopian nor visionary, the address was, in his opinion, "one of the greatest state papers in the history of nations," and it heralded a new era in international relations.[34] When the United States declared war, Schiff enthusiastically followed the administration in its "moral" crusade. Now convinced that a war against Germany served the cause of justice, he said it was Germany's responsibility to admit its "outrageous" behavior. A private confession of faith explained his about-face:

> I am a man of peace . . . and I know that there is no blessing like peace, and I would rather see our country bring the great material sacrifices it is now called upon to offer for peaceful purposes than for war. But I know that unless we succeed in making an end to what is generally understood by "militarism," which means permitting one single nation to acquire such physical might and power that it can defy almost the entire world and hold it at bay, as Germany has been able to do these past three years, there can be no return to lasting happiness and prosperity amongst the nations. . . . I have not always felt thus since the conflict broke loose, three years ago, but the progress of the war, the mode of its conduct by Germany, and the [antidemocratic] attitude of Germany's ruling class . . . towards its own people . . . forced me into the position toward the country of my birth.[35]

Unsaid but doubtless of major significance in his renunciation of the Central Powers was the simultaneous fall of the czarist regime.

Despite his full support of the Americanization crusade in 1915–17, Schiff was tagged as pro-Germany since 1914. Sensitive to public opinion, he had offered at the beginning of the war to relinquish responsibilities in the Red Cross should his presence prove embarrassing. In 1914 he deplored the fact that "foreigner" (as well as "Jew") greeted the nomination of his partner and brother-in-law, Paul Warburg, to head the newly created Federal Reserve Board. (Schiff was also mentioned as a possible candidate for the post, but he neither thought it likely nor was prepared to accept.) [36] Once America joined the Allies, the banker stopped speaking German publicly, and he changed the name of the Schiff endowment at Cornell—from the Promotion of Studies in German Culture to the Schiff Foundation for Human Civilization. To avoid further criticism, he opted for a low profile, even relinquishing his box at the opera for less conspicuous seats. But negative imagery was difficult to erase. After the war, James Cox, the Democratic candidate for the presidency in 1920, allegedly called Schiff a "Hun."[37]

On April 6, 1917, Schiff volunteered his services to Wilson, but he was not tapped for any significant post. Never wielding the influence of Louis Brandeis or Bernard Baruch, he was, however, consulted frequently from 1914 to 1919 by Secretary of the Treasury William McAdoo and other officials on numerous aspects of wartime finance—liberty loans, currency and banking, foreign exchange, taxes, the cooperation of business with government, and the government takeover of railroads. The banker spoke at liberty loan rallies and served on various municipal and federal committees for honoring dignitaries. He also cooperated with the Committee on Public Information and with the National Security League in propaganda work directed at the foreign-born. As personal contributions to the war effort, he put part of Montefiore's medical complex at the disposal of the army, he turned over his summer house to the War Department for use as a rest home for army nurses, and he donated his automobile to Lillian Wald and her nurses during the influenza epidemic. Caught up in the popular frenzy of wartime hypernationalism, he gladly lent his name to patriotic and Americanization organizations. Not surprisingly, one of the latter was the American Friends of German Democracy, which aimed at educating Germans in the United States in the principles of democracy.[38]

Yet Schiff the American patriot was also Schiff the Jew, or as he was known by then, "the greatest Jew in America."[39] Again there was a potential clash of loyalties. Since anti-Jewish prejudice intensified during the war, the stewards were saddled with two seemingly contradictory responsibilities. On the one hand they insisted on unconditional patriotism and conformity from their fellow Jews, and on the other they defended Jews against prejudice that was cloaked in the name of Americanism.

America's entry into World War I, John Higham has written, "called forth the most strenuous nationalism . . . that the United States had ever known." The pervasive spirit of 100 percent Americanism, almost evangelical in fervor, dictated single-minded loyalty along with service to the nation. A national crisis of major proportions often served as a unifying factor, but in 1917 American wartime nationalism unleashed ugly forces of nativism as well. Age-old stereotypes of the alien and unassimilable Jew, the international and clannish Jew tied only to other Jews and incapable of rooting himself in non-Jewish society, or the physically stunted Jew unwilling or unable to engage in armed combat still colored Christian perceptions. Whether or not Jews ran afoul of patriotic expectations, they became objects of suspicion. Doubtless because of Schiff's dominance, the neutral AJC, for example, was charged with being pro-Germany. One Yiddish pacifist complained of the double standard that made Jews no better than second-class citizens. Whereas "genuine Americans can afford to be for war or against war," Jews had to line up unanimously in favor of the war effort.[40] With regard to Jewish behavior, Schiff took his cue from the general American mood. Ever fearful of anti-Semitic repercussions, he and his associates focused principally on Jewish loyalty. Anti-Jewish discrimination could not be ignored, but proper Jewish conduct was the first priority.

It was difficult to effect a rapid and dramatic change in the attitude of American Jews toward the belligerents, but the stewards tried. Although accounts have stressed the "revolutionary" shift to a pro-Ally stance in the wake of events in Russia (March 1917), the concerns of Schiff and his friends suggest that the goal of 100 percent Americanism had not been reached, at least not to the public's satisfaction. True, most spokesmen for the Russian immigrants quickly fell into line, and the nonradical Yiddish and Anglo-Jewish press created the Jewish League of American Patriots, an organization established to stimulate patriotism and to propagate anti-German sentiments. But on one issue, the immediate Jewish response to conscription, Jewish leaders had their own misgivings. Marshall candidly reported shortly after America declared war: "I have made many inquiries during the past two weeks on the precise attitude of the Jewish people going into the service of the country. I find a strong undercurrent of indifference, as well as decided and affirmative opposition in some quarters." Schiff, who had always trumpeted the patriotism of the Russian Jews, agreed privately that many recent immigrants were "slackers" at the start of the war. Worried no doubt about the consequences of such behavior on the community as a whole, he went so far as to urge Jewish soldiers to seek service in the front ranks. The banker blamed the eastern European Zionists in particular. The great majority of them, he charged, resisted conscription, and the only way to reach "those people" was through the less than respectable Yiddish press. Pointing a finger at the Zionists, he called it their responsibility to prove the compatibility of Jewish nationalism with true Americanism.[41] Despite his growing sympathy with Zionist principles, he appeared as the uncompromising defender of a monolithic America.

At the same time, Jewish organizations honed defense strategy. Prevention of negative images, like that of the draft-dodging Jew, took on a dual function: to prevent dissemination of the ugly stereotypes and to counter those that had already entered the marketplace. A resolution of loyalty passed by the AJC pledged the lives and possessions of the members to the perpetuation of American ideals and institutions. The committee also resolved to plan for "the education of the [Jewish] public on the questions now before the people of the United States in connection with the war." While members spoke to Jewish audiences urging registration and compliance with the draft, the AJC published accounts of Jewish loyalty and, under Louis Marshall's leadership, kept close count of Jews, replete with biographies and lists of decorations, who served in the armed forces. Marshall optimistically believed that a statistical follow-up on Jewish servicemen, whose 5 percent in proportion to Jewish numbers contrasted favorably with the 3 percent of the nation at large, would "enable us to laugh . . . [at] any question as to the patriotism of the American Jew." For its part the Anti-Defamation League formed a special committee to deal with popular stories, articles, and cartoons depicting Jews as slackers and poor soldiers. Protection of the Jewish name both before and after it was besmirched became a top priority of the established Jews.[42]

Integration and Americanization were the twin components of the message sent by the Jewish leaders to the community. Schiff, who always opposed Jewish separatism except on religious grounds, dismissed ideas of separate Jewish combat units or Jewish liberty loan drives. Wartime conditions also led him to suggest that the Hebrew Technical Institute be opened to non-Jews. But convincing Jews of the blessings of integrating with non-Jews was but half the problem. It took two to integrate, and acceptance of Jews by the larger society was often less than cordial. Discrimination in the form of slurs against Jews and exclusion appeared in the armed forces, in other government agencies, and in private institutions. (One businessman reported that government representatives asked him in all innocence, "Is it not true that the Jews are all internationalists and have no national patriotism?")[43] Although discrimination was more the product of traditional anti-Semitism than a response to Jewish wartime conduct, defenders like Schiff and Marshall refused to admit that Jewish behavior made little difference. They assumed that Jews could break down prejudice by a show of patriotism and efforts at integration, and they ignored the fact that American hyperpatriotism was itself to blame for discrimination. In practice, Schiff labored on two separate fronts. He urged the Jewish community to keep to a strict American course at the same time that he fought against anti-Semitism and for Jewish equality.

For years the banker had been a loyal worker and generous donor to the numerous relief drives of the Red Cross. He served as treasurer of the New York County chapter, trustee of the endowment fund, and member of the International Relief Board. Acting on a suggestion from Lillian Wald, he donated $100,000 to found the Town and Country Nursing Service for the benefit of rural communities. His wartime contributions, exclusive of the purchase of five ambulances and the loan of his summer home to convalescent nurses, came to several hundred thousand dollars. That record easily permitted him to test his influence within the organization.[44]

In 1917, Schiff became aware that the Red Cross was excluding Jews from high office. America's entry into the war had magnified the gravity of the issue. Now the Red Cross, no longer neutral, was virtually an auxiliary of the armed forces. Since the stewards were striving at the same time to prove unalloyed Jewish patriotism, discrimination by the organization was tantamount to government mistrust. In a quiet attempt to dispel the prejudice, Schiff determined, as he put it, to show how valuable the Jews were to the Red Cross. Chosen to head one of thirty fund-raising teams in a mammoth relief campaign, he picked only Jews for his team. Much to his satisfaction, they raised over $11,000 in one week and went on to rank among the top four teams.[45]

Although Schiff believed he had proved his point, the Lee Frankel episode, which followed shortly thereafter, compounded his uneasiness. Frankel, an expert on social welfare, had been named by the Red Cross to a relief commission designed to aid the new Kerensky government. Almost immediately, however, doubts on the part of the organization (and/or the State Department) about the wisdom of a Jewish appointee to Russia forced him to withdraw. Since the Russian envoy to the United States denied that his country would disapprove of a Jew, Schiff concluded: "I am getting more and more the impression that somewhere, be it in the Administration or in the Red Cross, the love for our people is not as great as we are ... led to believe."

The banker turned directly to Henry Davison, a member of the Morgan firm who now served as chairman of the Red Cross War Council, charging that the Frankel affair had confirmed Jewish suspicions of discrimination. He spoke bluntly: since Davison didn't want Jews to believe that their cooperation was unwelcome, he had to decide whether amends were in order. Davison understood the message, and several Jews were appointed to executive posts. Schiff commended him for his stand against prejudice, but ever careful not to publicize matters that could boomerang against the Jews, arousing perhaps the notion that they had "bought" their way in, he denied that his intervention accounted for the change. His faith in the Red Cross at least temporarily restored,[46] the banker kept up an active involvement in its affairs. While he urged support from his fellow Jews, he cautioned against separate Jewish relief drives under the organization's auspices. If, as Schiff now said, the Red Cross was the "greatest *American* society" that bound together all groups in the United States, separate campaigns could well arouse charges of Jewish self-segregation or nonconformity.[47]

When, also in 1917, a ruling of the State Department announced that no naturalized Germans and Austrians nor their children would be sent to Europe to work in Red Cross hospitals, both Schiff and Marshall worked determinedly for its rescission. The order was taken as a personal insult. Not only did it come at the same time that the Red Cross discriminated against Jewish appointments, but it hit the established Jews as well as the immigrant community. One of Schiff's friends argued that logically the same people mentioned in the order should be excused from the armed services. Although the word *Jew* was not used, other associates suspected deep-seated discrimination; as usual, "Der Jude wird verbrennt." According to Schiff, the order, a manifestation of "chauvinism," violated the fundamental principles of the nation. He protested to Secretary Robert Lansing that his loyalty to the United States and that of his children was well proved by his life of over fifty years in the country. It was "mortifying" (one of Schiff's favorite words) that the government thus distinguished among its citizens. In an unsigned letter to the *New York Times*, Marshall, who thought it more prudent not to make it a Jewish issue, lashed out at the discriminatory ruling. Theodore Roosevelt was also alerted, and the ex-president's spirited response was highlighted in a newspaper article entitled "All Loyal Citizens Alike To Roosevelt." As a result of the publicity and pressure, the War Work Council of the Red Cross rescinded the order.[48]

The Jewish community in general found little reason to dispute the banker's activities with respect to integration or discrimination. Certainly, they had no cause to take issue with the ongoing pressure applied by him and the AJC against the immigration bills of 1915 and 1917 that included the objectionable literacy test. Despite Schiff's personal pleas to Congress and Wilson—"Woe to the land where cities grow and men degenerate," he intoned—the 1917 bill passed over the president's veto. In those matters, American Jews recognized the familiar Schiff, the protagonist of Americanization and the defender of free immigration.[49]

For a small segment of the community a new element of disaffection with elitist leadership did emerge. During the war years the militant pacifists among the Jewish Socialists saw the banker not only as the undemocratic steward but as the symbol of a capitalistic and imperialistic war. Schiff in turn was shocked by the thought of "bellicose pacifism" on the part of any American Jews. He had scant patience with the radicals; socialism was un-American by definition, and when joined with pacifism during a war, it spelled virtual treason. Nor could the dissenters seek refuge behind constitutional liberties. Addressing a Jewish audience, he said in the spirit of the newly passed Espionage Act: "Free speech, and those who demand free speech that has as its purpose to hinder the President or retard prosecution of the war have no rightful place in the country today." Jews were hardly the only pacifists, but since such Jews, irrespective of numbers, menaced the security of the entire group, he assumed the responsibility of damage control.[50]

Jewish workers on New York's Lower East Side constituted a dominant force within Socialist ranks. Despite divided loyalties with respect to the belligerents, their vote for the party mounted noticeably between 1914 and 1917. They stood for pacifism (until 1918) and, in some circles, against American hypernationalism, which was seen as "coercive" conformity without regard for the values of the ghetto. Socialist opposition to the war translated in 1917 into resistance to the draft, or what Meyer London, the first Socialist to sit in Congress, called "the democracy of the cemetery and the equality of the slaughterhouse." Not even the March 1917 revolution in Russia changed the mind of the pacifists, who attempted to turn a public celebration of the revolutionary change into an unruly demonstration for peace.[51]

Opposition to the militant pacifists came to a head in the mayoral election of 1917, which pitted a Socialist and Jew, Morris Hillquit, against John P. Mitchel. By then, differences within the pacifist wing had intensified, and animosity generated by Socialist "un-Americanism" engaged Jews and non-Jews, pacifists who sided with the war, and even the government in an anti-Hillquit smear campaign. The campaign joined uptown and downtown. Spokesmen for the anti-Hillquit Jews interpreted support of the Socialist primarily as a Jewish issue that could only harm the community. A former Jewish member of Congress put it this way: "The Socialist party is regarded by the people of the country . . . as un-American . . . and as voicing sentiments that are pro-German, and as antagonistic to American institutions and ideals. The East Side, because of the . . . Socialist party there . . . has been charged with being unpatriotic, and serious misgivings have been indulged in because of the un-Americanism that has prevailed."

Representing the stewards and urging a "house-cleaning of our own," Louis Marshall wrote a strong letter to the Yiddish *Forward*. He denied that he opposed Hillquit because he was a Socialist, but he indicted the candidate for urging "a premature peace, a peace which would be a German peace, . . . and a large vote in his favor would be hailed with delight by the enemies of America." "I am alarmed at the thought that the Jews of New York," Marshall continued, "shall be charged by the American people . . . with virtual treason and sedition, and with the purpose of creating for themselves in the United States a ghetto of separatism, of taking them out of American life, and of nullifying all that has been done through these many years to prove that the Jew is a loyal, faithful, patriotic American citizen." Like Marshall, who feared anti-Jewish charges of disloyalty and bloc voting, Schiff and other prominent Jews endorsed Mitchel. Calling for Jewish repudiation of Hillquit, the banker contributed to Mitchel's campaign.[52]

Schiff's anger at the militant Socialist pacifists cooled in the case of Judah Magnes. Magnes was not the typical wild-eyed, atheistic radical. A rabbi and spokesman for religion, a man of great charm who selflessly devoted his marked talents to Jewish causes, and Marshall's brother-in-law, he had long bridged uptown and downtown. A member of the AJC and the driving power behind the *kehillah*, he earned Schiff's respect for his tireless communal work and for his sincere if misplaced principles. Magnes was a maverick and a critic in the circle of the stewards but, basically loyal, he was their beloved bad boy. Schiff disapproved of Magnes's Zionism, and he admitted that Magnes's pacifism endangered the Jews (one Jew told Schiff that he refused to donate to Jewish war relief because of Magnes), but Schiff's affection for his young associate lasted. The rupture came only at a publicized AJC executive meeting in 1918 where Schiff attacked the Bolsheviks in Russia and on the Lower East Side who harmed their fellow

Jews. When Magnes retorted that his own sympathies lay with the Bolsheviks, his barefaced contradiction of Schiff, the man who was "Mr. Committee," could not be tolerated. The rabbi had no choice but immediate resignation. Militant pacifism on the Lower East Side gradually faded in 1918,
but it left scars on the community and on the elitist circle.[53]

Jewish pacifism took on an international dimension after the overthrow of
the czar in March 1917. The issue concerned the Allied war effort: Would
Russia end its fighting and negotiate a separate peace with Germany? The
question troubled all friends of the Allies, including the United States, but
it assumed a different meaning with respect to the Jews. Schiff expected the
Jews in Russia to be blamed for the peace campaign, and indeed the English and French so charged (on the theory that Germany had engineered
the Russian Revolution and that the Jews sympathized with Germany).
The implications were grave: first, that Jewish wartime loyalty in any country was questionable and, second, that the bulk of Russian Jews had cast
their lot with the militant peace party, the Bolsheviks. The image of the
Jew as revolutionary Bolshevik rapidly gained worldwide credence and
added grist to anti-Semitic mills.[54]

    Fearing dire consequences, the AJC expressed its alarm to Russian Jews
over a "disastrous" separate peace that could lead to the return of autocracy
and the further degradation of Jews. The organization promised Paul Miliukov, foreign minister of the Provisional Government, that it would
cooperate with its fellow Jews in support of the new government's continued role in the war. Although some Jews on New York's Lower East Side
sympathized with the idea of an immediate peace, Schiff and Marshall insisted publicly that American Jews were unanimously opposed. Other
prominent American Jews pleaded directly with friends in Russia for Jewish support of the new government. Miliukov in turn vigorously denied
that Russian Jews favored a separate peace; so did Baron Adolphe de
Guenzberg, as well as an investigative report commissioned by Louis Marshall. But so serious was the charge that the Alliance Israélite Universelle
suggested that an international Jewish delegation visit Russia and influence
Russian Jews to stand with the government.[55]

    The peace issue doubtless contributed to the AJC's efforts to secure a
Jewish appointment to the government's goodwill mission to Russia. Led
by Elihu Root, the delegation aimed at keeping the Provisional Government firmly on the Allied side. The AJC believed that a Jewish presence
would lift the morale of Russian Jewry and improve its image. Nevertheless, despite pressure by Schiff and his associates, no Jew was included.
Root himself was considered unsympathetic to Jews, and the administration was afraid to "overplay" the Jewish element.[56]

Jubilant New Yorkers staged mass meetings to celebrate the overthrow of the czar. Jews were especially elated; their archpersecutor had fallen, and since Russia's significance as a major belligerent was rapidly waning, the plight of Jews in war-ravaged countries became less acute. "We are singing a paean of victory; we are rejoicing at the answer to our prayers," Louis Marshall said. Schiff, whose congratulations to Russia and exchange of wires with Paul Miliukov were widely circulated in Russia and America, spoke of "a miracle" that ended Romanov rule. Passover in 1917, he predicted, would be celebrated with greater fervor, for like the ancient Hebrews in Egypt, the Jews had been delivered from oppression. Identifying himself to Miliukov as "a persistent foe of the tyrannical autocracy, the merciless persecutors of my co-religionists," he added exuberantly, "Just as before I hated most intensely the Russian government, so now I love deeply the new Russia."[57]

When Russian officials assured Schiff and his friends of Jewish emancipation and equality, the revolution more than ever became a Jewish victory. Ex-President Taft, Schiff's adversary in the fight for abrogation, also singled out the special Jewish interest, praising the Jews "for having retained their racial identity in the face of centuries of persecution." For Schiff and his associates the moment cried for support of the new government that would prevent the revival of autocracy and Jewish disabilities. Now urging financial aid to Russia, Schiff called for Jewish subscriptions to the Russian liberty loan, to which he personally subscribed 1 million rubles.[58] Unconcerned lest Russians oppose a government that dealt closely with Jews, Schiff's euphoria prompted him to find additional ways for demonstrating his support—service on committees for the encouragement of democratic government in Russia, treasurer of a fund through which American Jews planned to present Russia with a replica of the Statue of Liberty, and host to a Russian delegation at a reception in the house on Henry Street.[59] Schiff obviously did not bring about the Russian Revolution, but he liked to think that his efforts to weaken the czarist regime through financial pressure, aid to Japan, diplomatic lobbying with American presidents, and propaganda to Russian prisoners of war in 1905 had helped. His efforts for Russian Jewish emancipation, even if unsuccessful in their immediate results, had earned him the gratitude of both Russian and American Jews and shored up his claims to communal leadership.

Outwardly delighted about the emancipation of Russian Jewry, the stewards did not let down their guard. In the face of the political turmoil that enveloped Russia, the rescission of rights was a distinct possibility. The AJC established contact with the ambassador of the Provisional Government, a contact that could prove significant. At the same time the committee prepared a five-hundred-page memorandum on anti-Jewish legislation in Russia. Thus, even if the Provisional Government was overhauled, the rights might be saved: "Publication of this work will serve to show the world the enormous stride towards civilization which is certain to result from the abolition of the special laws against the Jews."[60]

The March revolution and the emancipation of Russian Jewry did not end American Jewish concern for their brethren. Looming on the horizon as the Bolshevik revolution in November drew closer were the problems of continued anti-Semitism and the charge heard round the world that Jew meant Bolshevik. For Schiff personally, Jewish rights in Russia contributed to a dramatic change in his attitude on an unrelated issue. The man who had always believed that legal equality promised the most security for diaspora Jewry now drew closer, in part because of legal equality in Russia, to the Zionist cause.

Questions of Leadership

While Schiff was coping with the problem of multiple loyalties, his power as a Jewish leader was increasingly challenged. He now confronted a rapidly maturing American Jewry, far different from that before the turn of the century. The once submissive and cowed immigrants had gained remarkable strength through numbers and economic mobility that enabled them, despite countless differences in beliefs and customs, to resist authoritarian tutelage from the established Germans. To be sure, they were ever sensitive to discrimination abroad and at home. Echoes of the notorious Beilis affair in Russia (1913) still reverberated, and the Leo Frank case in Georgia (1913–15) dramatically testified to ongoing Jewish vulnerability. Nevertheless, although they may have depended on the philanthropic and defense networks of the stewards, their first recourse was to the ever proliferating institutions of their own. Similarly, their primary fealty went to men from within their ranks, like labor leaders, Yiddish journalists, and Zionist activists. Not that Schiff lost his influence, but the power that he had long wielded in areas of philanthropy, immigrant adjustment, and aid for Jews in Russia did not extend automatically to war-generated communal concerns. At a time when new problems faced American Jewry, he, its foremost leader, failed to win unquestioned allegiance on the major issues of Jewish wartime relief and the American Jewish Congress. Between 1914 and 1918, as tests of his leadership multiplied, his long-sought goal of American Jewish unity under elitist domination grew ever more elusive.

Schiff neither abdicated his leadership of the community nor was it called for, but more than ever before he was forced to learn that an effective leader was one who moved with the times and who did not resist change or avoid compromise for the sake of rigid principle. Less concerned with the aggrandizement of personal power, he spent the latter years of his life in efforts to adjust himself and his fellow Jews to changed world realities. In some instances prior roles were reversed; the directives came from the community, and Schiff followed suit.

The Zionist effort for an American Jewish Congress was the most blatant test of elitist leadership. Prior struggles with the Jewish nationalists looked insignificant when measured against the popular call for a representative body under Zionist leadership to present the case for European Jewish rights at the postwar peace conference. The growing assertiveness of the ethnic-minded immigrants had received an unexpected boost when Louis D. Brandeis assumed the chairmanship of the Provisional Executive Committee for General Zionist Affairs (1914). The "people's attorney" and adviser to President Wilson and a man who moved comfortably in the upper echelons of WASP society, Brandeis put a seal of respectability and attractiveness on the American Zionist movement. Infused with determination, the Zionists pressed for a congress. The issue was not Zionism versus anti- or non-Zionism but rather the nature of communal governance. Representatives of the far-flung Zionist network of lodges and local societies advocated a democratic structure, a goal impossible to achieve independently as long as the stewards controlled the American Jewish purse. In the inevitable clash that ensued, Schiff and his circle were forced to yield. They preferred a compromise on power to total abdication.

Jewish Wartime Relief

The clash over leadership was presaged in the more immediate problem of wartime relief for Jews in Palestine and the European war zones. Seventy-eight thousand Jews then lived in Palestine under the Turks, and three and one-half million resided in divided Poland, the scene of the bloodiest fighting. In Palestine the economy of the *yishuv*, dependent largely on the export of its crops and on donations from abroad, was stopped by the Anglo-French blockade of the eastern Mediterranean. A Palestine Oranges Committee informed Schiff that Jaffa oranges merely rotted while waiting for shipment. In central and eastern Europe, directly in the path of the contending belligerent armies, Jews suffered atrocities at the hands of both sides. Horrified by reports, Schiff gloomily concluded that in such conditions the dead were better off than the living. The banker protested to Max Warburg and to the Austrian ambassador to the United States. Protests proved futile, however, and since the war made emigration an unrealistic option, the trapped victims depended solely on relief from abroad.[61]

At an emergency meeting immediately after the eruption of hostilities, the AJC turned to the problem of relief. All recognized that unity among American Jews was essential to meeting the staggering needs, and they agreed with Schiff that Jews could not look elsewhere for assistance. An appeal to non-Jews, the banker said, would mean a loss of Jewish dignity and self-respect. The committee also considered a message from Brandeis. Asking for the AJC's cooperation in raising $100,000 for the support of international Zionist institutions, the message took the stewards by surprise. They had automatically assumed that the committee would handle foreign relief, a familiar issue that had proved their expertise, for both Europe and Palestine. Besides, they could never agree that relief be limited to support of Zionist work. Although suspecting, as did Marshall, that the Zionists— "self-advertisers," "fanatics" who considered themselves above the ordinary rules of decency—desired outright control of relief in order to concentrate on Palestine, Schiff immediately spoke up for cooperation but on the committee's terms. He made it manifestly clear who was to lead the community and who was to be led. "Mr. Schiff stated," the minutes read, "that . . . the American Jewish Committee, the Zionists and any other organizations which are willing to do so, were to join hands. . . . He thought that the American Jewish Committee, being the representative Jewish body in America, ought to lead this movement for the amelioration of the condition of the Jews throughout the world, and not the Zionists. . . . [He] declared that the Committee should guard and maintain its identity and leadership, because it represents all Jews—Zionists as well as non-Zionists."[62]

The committee won the first battle with the Zionists when at subsequent community-wide meetings it established the American Jewish Relief Committee (AJRC) under its domination. Overall unity was undercut, however, by ongoing Zionist–non-Zionist divisiveness and by competing relief groups, notably the Central Relief Committee (Orthodox) and the People's Relief Committee (labor). By the end of the war the Joint Distribution Committee (JDC), a loose union of the different groups under the chairmanship of Felix Warburg, had collected some $15 million. But along the lines set a decade earlier, when relief for the victims of Russian pogroms forced the stewards to raise funds from the rank and file, the very establishment of the JDC proved that exclusive elitist control had slipped another notch.[63]

In a front-page story the *New York Times* described a dramatic mass meeting for Jewish relief at Carnegie Hall in December 1915. Judah Magnes, the major speaker and a man dubbed "Billy Saturday," had raised the crowd to a feverish pitch, and gifts literally poured in—checks, pledges, cash, and jewelry. "The very first person to make a gift . . . strode down a long aisle to the stage, turned his trouser's pocket inside out and deposited several bills and some silver at the speaker's feet. He turned away, but in doing so put a hand into another pocket, and, finding money in it, turned back and emptied its contents upon the stage also. . . . One man sent a dollar bill, with a note saying that he had with him only $1.05, and needed the 5 cents for carfare home." "Never," the newspaper concluded, "was such a scene witnessed in Carnegie Hall."[64]

Aside from intergroup rivalries and duplicatory efforts, a host of problems surfaced that were endemic to the very nature of wartime relief. To begin with, did Jews as well as non-Jews know the facts of the situation? While misrepresentation and exaggeration colored the charges of atrocities by the opposing belligerents, Schiff grumbled that the public knew all about atrocities in Belgium but nothing about the worse misery in Poland. Contacts with foreign officials and with European Jewish organizations and individuals supplied the AJC with facts, but the Jewish public, privy only to scanty information, needed additional data to feel a sense of urgency. Furthermore, what kind of relief was needed, money alone or foodstuffs and medical supplies as well? How could contributions be most safely transmitted and distributed in order to reach the intended beneficiaries? Would relief be tainted by partisan or Zionist considerations and thereby increase atrocities by either side? Were American Jews able to support domestic causes like charities and the Baron de Hirsch Fund, as well as general American relief drives, if they assumed additional burdens? For the first time even Schiff claimed that he personally was strapped for funds, the result, he explained, of higher taxes, lower income, and additional wartime demands.[65]

The difficulties notwithstanding, the stewards launched mammoth relief drives, climaxed by campaigns of $5 million in 1916 and $10 million in 1917. An outstanding success, the 1917 campaign was pitched primarily to the wealthy. The Guggenheims refused Schiff's personal pleas for a large contribution, but Julius Rosenwald of Sears, Roebuck promised to match every $1 million gift with $100,000. Communities were tapped, too. A tactic put forth by Schiff and adopted by the campaign called for asking each community to contribute twice as much as it could afford.[66]

Schiff's active participation, primarily through the AJRC, testified once again to his sense of responsibility and personal drive. At a vigorous pace that belied his age, he spent countless hours on all facets of the relief problem. In personal letters and at meetings in various cities he cajoled and badgered his affluent fellow Jews to contribute generously. "We are justified in expecting from all whom God has so richly blessed, to give again and again—*and not sparingly!*" he wrote to one acquaintance. No man, he asserted, could justifiably seek to increase his personal fortune during the war. Indeed, he saw no reason why three million American Jews, especially the wealthy ones, could not raise $30 million. Although he complained of Jewish apathy—lashing out in particular at the Jews on the Pacific Coast— and of the inadequacy of the funds raised, he simultaneously warned donors not to forget the needy at home.

Schiff left the mechanics of administration principally to his son-in-law, Felix Warburg, but his own hands-on style was apparent throughout. His numerous papers relating to the relief drives illustrate his role as a fund-raiser and major donor (his personal contributions by July 1917 amounted to over half a million dollars), a judge of relief priorities, and an overseer and conciliator of a wide distribution network. He hosted countless meetings at his home, he organized canvassing teams, and he was in constant communication with Jacob Billikopf, a communal worker who administered the relief campaigns. During the war the campaigns were joined with those of the Jewish Welfare Board, a body serving Jews in the armed services. In the case of the Jewish Welfare Board, Schiff defended Jewish separatism, arguing that inaction would draw the contempt of both Gentiles and the Jewish servicemen.[67]

While Schiff enlisted the interest of the Rockefeller Foundation in the matter of Polish relief, the AJC prepared and widely circulated detailed reports of the war sufferers in a book entitled *Jews in the Eastern War Zone*. In a more unusual move, the organization received the State Department's clearance to petition the pope, Benedict XV. The AJC begged the pontiff to use his influence with the Catholic clergy in Poland to help end persecution, particularly the Polish economic boycott of the Jews. The pope declined to address the matter, but he wrote a strong consoling answer, subsequently published, avowing his personal aversion to anti-Semitism.[68]

The stewards alone were unable to meet the relief needs. Since wealthy Jews failed to respond adequately, the established leaders were forced to turn fund-raising into mass appeals. Meetings in the larger cities, reinforced by Wilson's designation of a day for relief contributions and popularized in the press, augmented donations. So did the gift of one day's pay from the rank and file of the major Jewish labor unions. But turning to the masses provided critics like the Zionists with another entering wedge for demanding a share in communal governance. Just as the campaign of the National Committee for Relief of Sufferers by Russian Massacres (NCRSRM) in 1905 had given rise to ideas of a democratic defense organization, so did wartime relief feed the opposition to elitist leadership.[69]

The Zionists proved unequal competitors on matters of relief. They had neither the stewards' experience in lobbying with officials nor, more significant, equal access to sizable funds. To be sure, they cooperated with the stewards on sending a relief ship to Palestine (a scheme whose practicality Schiff doubted), but in that episode both parties worked separately to obtain necessary aid from the State Department. Recognizing the inadequacy of their independent attempts at fund-raising, the Zionists joined the stewards in 1915 in the JDC, but mutual suspicion and hostility persisted. Since the Zionists particularly disliked the stewards' reliance on the Hilfsverein, an organization that seemed to them more German and anti-Zionist than neutral, they sought a greater say in the allocation and distribution of funds. To avoid a rupture over relief, Schiff therefore proposed a small commission headed by Judah Magnes, a man palatable to both sides, to survey distribution in Europe.[70]

His criticism of Zionist relief efforts notwithstanding, Schiff plunged readily into work for Palestine. Again personal contacts served him well. From his friend and ambassador to Constantinople, Henry Morgenthau (who as a Jew was a target of German intimidation) and from Morgenthau's successor, Abram Elkus, as well as from a few other witnesses, Schiff and his circle were alerted to the deplorable conditions in the *yishuv*. They also learned of Turkish suspicions of foreign Jews, Zionists in particular, and of Turkey's idea of a mass expulsion of Jews. Not only was Schiff in a position to turn directly to Red Cross officials, asking for medical supplies on behalf of Jerusalem's hospitals, but he freely requested permission from Secretary of State Lansing for certain families in Palestine to enter the United States. In line with Morgenthau's suggestion, he spearheaded the establishment of a free loan society for Palestinian Jews and a special fund for orange growers. To ensure that the monies for Palestine reached their proper destination, Schiff arranged with business contacts at Standard Oil for the safe transfer of funds. He and the committee also investigated and disproved a curious story, circulated in Morgenthau's name, that Turkey was prepared to sell Palestine.[71]

His eyes on Turkish ill-will, the banker resented the Zionists and their "dangerous" nationalistic ideals all the more. He was willing to work together, he said, provided the Zionists recognized the right of Jews to hold different views, but he was at best grudgingly cooperative. He charged that, in their constant attempts to bypass the stewards, the Zionists earmarked the greater portion of their separate relief fund for the *yishuv*— help that would have proved hopelessly inadequate had non-Zionists not come to the rescue—at the expense of European Jews. More worrisome, he agreed with Morgenthau's private assessments that the nationalists incited anti-Jewish feeling in Turkey. His fears were borne out in 1917 when German philologist A. S. Yahuda and Zionist leader Max Nordau reported a massacre in Palestine. Once again the diplomatic network of the AJC was called into service, but a bitter Schiff became increasingly convinced as the war ground on that the irresponsible Zionists were working solely for their own political agenda.[72]

A Jewish Congress

Quarrels over wartime relief were eclipsed by a stormy debate within the community on an American Jewish Congress. None denied the need to press for Jewish rights in postwar Europe, but sharp differences flared over who would formulate and present those demands to the peacemakers. The well-known story, whose genesis lay in the movement for a congress in 1905–6, renewed the debate on matters that had always separated Zionists from anti- or non-Zionists: Jewish peoplehood and Jewish loyalties. Louis Marshall added still another point. He told Lord Reading that the congress movement was supported, except for Schiff, by Jews who were sympathetic to Germany.[73]

At bottom, however, the issue was a struggle for power between the stewards and the Zionist-led congress partisans. The former, represented by the AJC, favored control by the committee, which would conduct private and discreet diplomatic negotiations; they shuddered at the thought of "agitators" and "hotheads" engaged in open diplomacy that might well boomerang at the same time that it conjured up the image of the separatist and nationalist (and hence patently un-American) Jew. Schiff and his circle insisted on a democratic America, but they refused to condone democratic governance within the Jewish community. Their opponents, on the other hand, stood for a democratically elected body of representatives to draw up and submit the Jewish demands at the peace conference. They boldly challenged the rule of the "autocrats," specifically the AJC, which, as on the relief question, had assumed that it would direct Jewish postwar planning. The congress partisans were not out to eliminate the stewards from communal affairs; indeed, they would in all likelihood choose the stewards to represent them. Rather, they sought to share power within a democratic framework. A downtown circular, for example, supported the AJC—a reformed committee, to be sure, and one that heeded the voice of the people but the AJC nonetheless.[74]

Privately and publicly, the two sides traded harsh insults, and attempts to achieve Jewish unity in the fight that raged from 1914 to 1917 repeatedly broke down. Judah Magnes, for one, concluded unhappily that the Jews were a sick, individualistic people. As the clamor for a congress grew louder, the committee was forced to plot a counterstrategy. It still had the advantages of expertise and money, but its rivals were in a far better position than in 1906. They commanded the numbers, the popular Yiddish press, and the prestigious leadership of Louis Brandeis and his associates, men like Stephen Wise, Felix Frankfurter, and Horace Kallen. Forced to compromise, the AJC suggested a conference of national organizations. A conference would be more broadly based than the AJC itself, but under the committee's direction it promised to avoid the populistic dangers of a congress.

The committee's scheme ultimately failed, in large measure because it was unable to counter the ideological appeal of a congress. Not only was the congress idea a confident assertion of Jewish peoplehood within the larger society, but during the Progressive era, when Americans were adopting new devices to augment the political power of the common man, the push for a *democratic* congress had become, as Brandeis asserted, a moral issue and one that Zionists said could not be stayed. Frankfurter, one of several prominent figures who resigned from the AJC on the congress issue, explained the democratic imperative: "Democracy is not a political fetish, but a ruling faith that the Jews in America must think their own thoughts, . . . express their own will, choose their own leaders, if Jews in America are ever to reach self-respect that entitles them to be heard and the weight that will give them a hearing, here and abroad."[75] Put simply, elitism was no longer politically correct.

Marshall, now president of the AJC, and Adler handled the day-to-day maneuvers of the committee, but they deferred to Schiff on strategy. The latter blamed the sensationalist Yiddish press and the Zionists for the serious communal rift and for allowing the formation of a distinct "Hebraic" element versus "those of us" whose primary attachments were American. Since Palestine under Turkish control was now closed to Jews, the Zionists, Schiff claimed, fixed on a congress for other objectives—to spread nationalist propaganda and to put control of the Jewish masses and Jewish affairs in the hands of Zionist leaders and their self-seeking followers. Not only did they divert attention from the primary goal (i.e., rights for European Jews), but they compounded Turkish suspicions of Jews. By raising the specter of dual loyalties, Schiff added, the proposed congress also threatened to exacerbate anti-Semitism worldwide and thereby drive future generations of Jews to abandon Judaism. The only legitimate congress for Jews in the United States was the American Congress; any other would be intolerable to Americans and was bound to weaken the well-being and security of their fellow Jews.[76]

At a meeting of the AJC's executive committee, Schiff spelled out his ever-present fear:

> The question is now to be decided, and I am afraid decided in the affirmative as to whether the Jews are a nation within a nation. The holding of a Jewish Congress means nothing less than a decision in the affirmative, that we are Jews first, and Americans second. If we are not Jews first, if we are Americans of the Jewish faith or Jewish people only, we have absolutely no right to hold such a Congress. The Congress means the establishment of a new government, a government for the Jews by which the Jews are to be bound. . . . It will be the darkest day for Jewry. We will become a people by ourselves. We will become a compact mass of Jewish Americans, and not of American Jews.[77]

He said that only as representatives of a religious group, not as a national entity, would Jews command a hearing at the peace conference. Doubtless, the banker was also personally offended. He had talked of the need of post-war planning as soon as the war broke out, and although some, like a writer for the Yiddish *Wahrheit*, agreed that he, Schiff, was the logical choice to start the planning process, the congress upstarts were bent on repudiating him.[78]

The congress people also fully recognized that communal leadership was at stake. Schiff, who theoretically favored aristocratic assimilation, or the empowerment of acculturated new immigrants under the direction of the stewards, angrily deplored the distrust of old leaders and the substitution of new, democratically chosen ones. Claiming that "leaders need to develop and come forward by their own deservedness," he warned that democratic selection of leaders often brought forth demagogues. Proper leadership was based on responsibility, and again he found a biblical precedent that hinted at his identification with Moses. If the committee ignored its responsibility to European Jews, its foes who danced around the "golden calf" (the congress) could rightly proclaim that "this man Moses [the Schiff-dominated AJC] is dead, these are your gods, O Israel." The banker admitted that the AJC was not sufficiently representative, but he thought that a small conference of national organizations would resolve the problem.[79]

Congress supporters took an antithetical stand. In the words of Rabbi Stephen Wise: "The time is come for a leadership by us to be chosen. . . . Are we forever to suffer men to think and act for us, not because we have chosen and named them, but because they have decreed that we are not fit to be trusted with the power of shaping our own destiny?" Privately Wise added: "Our 'leaders' I loathe—self-seeking insincere toads and vermin many of them." Despite the wide chasm that separated them, both sides drew on American principles; the congress people called for democratic control, while their opponents objected to "un-American" ethnic separation.[80]

In the middle stood Judah Magnes, often the liaison between Zionists and non-Zionists. He listed the faults of both sides in frank letters to Schiff—uptown's "ignorance and apathy," downtown's "politics and talk, talk, talk":

It must be said of [the Zionists] that they have zeal, and that Jewish affairs are to them of primary importance. They have an organization, built up after much sacrifice. They have a devoted following. What is of greatest importance, they look at the Jewish question as a whole and . . . as affecting the Jews as a minority People. What do we find on the other side? A handful of serious, large-minded, exceedingly busy men of affairs, for whom, to be sure, Judaism is a primary concern. But as for their followers, almost complete indifference to Jewish affairs, except perhaps to Jewish physical charities. But even among this handful of men, how hard it is to get them to understand the real state of Jewish affairs, and to think and act opportunely and comprehensively.[81]

For their stand on a congress, Schiff, his cohorts, and the AJC were subjected to constant abuse. The Yiddish press led the attacks, calling the stewards who mistrusted the people unfit to manage Jewish affairs. Patience wore thin, tempers flared, and friends clashed as the opposing camps dug in their heels. Adler, who threatened to resign the chairmanship of the committee's executive, bitterly affirmed that the Zionist critics, allied with the labor unions, socialists, and anarchists, were following an organized plan for the total destruction of the committee. Schiff wondered why the masses supported such dangerous agitation instead of focusing on important Jewish issues. Regretting his subsidies to certain errant newspapers, he tried for a while to offset their influence by building up the new Yiddish *Day*. (Magnes counseled Schiff to make an outright purchase in order to reach downtown, but the banker replied that such action would increase attacks by other Yiddish journals.) Prominent individuals joined the chorus, sometimes at the cost of friendship. A case in point was Dr. Harry Friedenwald, a founder of the AJC and an officer of the Federation of American Zionists (FAZ). In a forceful defense of the masses—their right to participate in the solution of their own problems and their lack of confidence in the committee—Friedenwald resigned from the AJC, indicting it for ignoring the people and for causing the schism that tore the community apart. He predicted that "the new generation will not follow blindly in the footsteps of Marshall and Schiff any longer." Friedenwald's resignation and the sharp rebuttal from the committee estranged him forever from an old friend, Cyrus Adler.[82]

Non-Jews watched the controversy too. In London, David Lloyd George dismissed the congress idea with contempt: "A war cannot be run by a Sanhedrin." In America, Charles Eliot asked Schiff for an explanation after he read Brandeis's charges that the AJC operated secretly and was self-perpetuating. Recalling Schiff's pressure on Witte at the end of the Russo-Japanese War, Eliot suggested that an agent for the international Jewish bankers submit the Jewish case at Versailles. After all, they had the experience of international dealings, and they enjoyed confidential relations with each other.[83]

Put on the defensive, Schiff doubted whether mass support for a congress could be stopped and whether "we shall be able to counteract these influences and succeed in leading the Jewish masses aright." Despite his pessimism, he counseled prudent but positive action that could enhance the committee's bargaining power even if the congress supporters were to win. Since an active minority was more likely than a passive one to curb the majority and salvage some concessions, he insisted that the AJC, the best agent for American Jewish unity, keep to its plans for an orderly conference. American Jews rightly expected activity on behalf of Jewish rights in Europe, and if the committee abstained, others less qualified would take an undesirable path. Nor did Schiff rule out compromise by the committee to save the community from those he called "undesirable leaders."[84]

Meanwhile, reasoning that Brandeis was the only one who could call a halt to the agitation, Schiff cultivated the new Zionist hero. At first he and his friends had scant regard for Brandeis's Jewish credentials and his meteoric rise to national Jewish leadership. "It appears to me," Schiff once said, that "he should have become a follower for a while instead of an immediate leader." Now, however, he spoke highly of Brandeis, entertained him at dinner, and denied having opposed Brandeis's appointment to Wilson's cabinet in 1913. In warm support of the attorney's nomination to the Supreme Court, he let President Wilson know that Jews would be highly gratified to see one of their own tapped for the high court.[85]

It is very possible that Schiff also saw the appointment as a way of removing Brandeis from Jewish affairs, thereby undercutting the Zionist movement and shoring up leadership by the stewards. In a long letter to Brandeis the banker wrote: "It will likely not be long before you will be called upon to assume the high position for which the President has recently nominated you, and as I take it, you will then no longer be able to continue as leader of the Zionist and Nationalist movement in this country." For the sake of communal unity, the letter also urged Brandeis to end the clamor for a congress. Brandeis's reply was noncommittal; he mentioned neither the congress nor his retirement from Zionist activities.[86]

As the movement for a congress rapidly gained momentum, Schiff continued to air his opposition publicly. Two themes resounded in his talks: the un-American character of the congress and the need of communal unity. On one occasion, however, the applause that greeted his pleas for unity between the "yahudim" (German Jews) and the "yidden" (the eastern Europeans) was offset by comments like that of the Yiddish *Tageblatt*, which called the committee's way of ignoring the masses the "unity of silence" but the workings of a democratic congress the "unity of action." In March 1916, before the Hebrew Sheltering and Immigrant Aid Society, Schiff stressed the importance of seasoned leadership, and yet again in the role of Moses, he likened the congress challenge and its dire consequences to the biblical story of Korach's rebellion against Moses.[87]

A few days later the banker fired a stronger salvo. In an interview with the *Wahrheit*, he focused on the evils of Jewish separatism. Instead of taking on tasks for the benefit of America, advocates of a congress worked for self-segregation, an attitude that he defined as "almost treason" to the principle of American citizenship and loyalty to the country. By resurrecting the charge of Zionism's incompatibility with Americanism, reminiscent of his letters to Schechter in 1907, Schiff infuriated the Zionists. Rabbi Gustav Gottheil of Temple Emanu-El charged that Schiff's statement was "worse than anything said by an anti-Semite of the purest dye"; Brandeis called Schiff an "unworthy" son of American Jewry.[88] Schiff never acknowledged that his attacks compounded the divisiveness that he so deplored. Nor was he deterred by the likelihood that his remarks could well undermine his own popularity within the community.

His denunciations of a congress made Schiff the chief target of the congress supporters. In April 1916, the *Zukunft*, a left-wing Yiddish journal, ran a character sketch of the banker by Yiddish writer Sholom Asch. Asch's scathing attack had been prompted by the congress issue, but the sketch included more. Asch said that Schiff's importance, predicated on American standards, lay only in his wealth. A dictator rather than a leader, the banker neither understood nor loved his fellow Jews. His philanthropy, which aided non-Jewish causes at the expense of Jewish needs, ignored the real interests of the recipients. Just because Schiff thought of himself as Moses, Asch sneered, did not mean that he ranked alongside true Jewish leaders like Sir Moses Montefiore and Baron Edmond de Rothschild.

Since the sketch was distributed by the thousands in leaflet form, Schiff deliberately set out to mend his fences. His first public response came in an address to the Jewish Publication Society in May, where again he attacked the Zionist power-hungry "agitators" who were Jews "only for questionable nationalistic machinations." Alluding more directly to Asch, albeit not by name, he also took issue with the eastern European immigrants for clinging to Yiddish, "not a modern language, if a real language at all." "Enslaved" by the Yiddish press, the new arrivals were saddled with obstacles to their Americanization. Schiff drew criticism from Yiddishists, and even Cyrus Adler, who dismissed the importance of the *Zukunft* piece, pointed out that Schiff had erred in attributing Asch's views to the eastern Europeans as a whole.[89]

Shortly thereafter, Schiff invited Asch to a private meeting. Explaining that Asch had undermined Jewish confidence in his, Schiff's, leadership, he succeeded in securing an admission that the writer had done him an injustice. In a total about-face, Asch now praised Schiff's leadership, charity, and "good heart." Mollified only in part, the banker answered that he would indeed be a poor leader if he didn't publicly condemn the fatal mistake of a congress. He promised to continue serving his people no matter the criticisms and attacks and—as a parting shot at Asch, who had been in the United States for less than two years "by those who have not yet reached an understanding of what it means to be an American Jew."[90]

Asch's article continued to rankle, and Schiff's determination to counterattack exacerbated the differences between the stewards and the masses.

Still seeking public vindication, the banker recounted the Asch episode in full at the dedication of the Central Jewish Institute in May. There he lashed out against Jewish separatism, which all understood to be directed against a congress. Pressing for Americanization, he warned of anti-Semitism should American Jews, like the Jews of eastern Europe, hold fast to Yiddish and act as a separate people. In the course of his extemporaneous remarks he said: "I feel, my friends, that unless we live our Judaism as a religion, our posterity may become subjected to great prejudice." Another sentence drew the most criticism: "It has occurred to me . . . that if the Jews of Russia and the Jews of Poland would not have been kept as a separate people by discriminatory laws, the prejudice and persecution to which they have been subject would not have reached the stage to which we all regret."[91]

Unfortunately for Schiff, the attempt at rebutting the Yiddish yellow press boomeranged. When the *New York Times* reported him as having said that the eastern European Jews had in large measure brought persecution on themselves, a storm of protest broke out against Schiff the "traitor" who delivered "the deadliest blow" ever dealt the Jews. The banker thereupon produced a stenographic record of his address proving that he had been misquoted, but the damage could not be undone. Important Yiddish newspapers stuck by the *Times* version, while Brandeis and the Zionist journal *Maccabaean* hinted at the inauthenticity of the stenographic report. Some periodicals delighted in maligning or threatening Schiff. One asked the masses to "excommunicate" him; another discredited him by way of cartoons. Among the harshest critics was the *American Jewish Chronicle*, a paper funded by the German government. The *Chronicle* wrote that Schiff sweetened his attacks on popular Jewish values with large donations. It estimated that he had paid a few hundred thousand dollars for his campaign against Zionism and twenty-five thousand for the defeat of the congress movement. In Schiff's mind it all added up to what he termed "terrorism."[92]

Commendation for the banker also came from both Jewish and non-Jewish friends. While Cyrus Adler suggested that Schiff write out his addresses, Paul Warburg counseled his partner to treat downtown like children who were feeling their strength for the first time. Simon Wolf added that if God and Moses couldn't satisfy the children of Israel, Schiff could hardly expect to do so.[93]

Despite his denial to the contrary, the banker was deeply wounded by what he considered rank ingratitude. A final attempt at "spiking the guns" (his words) of those who attacked him and the AJC came at a dramatic session of the *kehillah* convention two weeks later. Schiff's voice trembled, and there were tears in his eyes as he answered the charges of his critics. Those charges, he said, would delight the czarist regime, "because you are battering down the man who has stood between persecution, between anti-Semitism, as far as his power goes, and the Russian Government." He interpreted the vilification he endured as part of a "well-conceived" plan. Repeatedly, he had been told that "if I did not stop my opposition to the Congress movement I would be first attacked, as perhaps the most conspicuous member of the American Jewish Committee; that the confidence of the Jewish people in me would be undermined, and I would be broken down." His concluding remarks startled the audience: "I may say this by way of valedictory: I have been hurt to the core, and hereafter Zionism, Nationalism, the Congress movement, and Jewish politics, in whatever form they may come up, will be a sealed book to me." He promised to continue to work for "the uplift of my people" and to cooperate in the task of securing rights for Jews in eastern Europe and Palestine, "for they are all flesh of my flesh and bone of my bone. But beyond this, my friends, my duty ends." The *American Hebrew* took up the story: "The unexpected announcement threw a spell over the hall and for several seconds, as Mr. Schiff was leaving the platform, a solemn silence reigned; then, as if a thunderbolt had struck the audience, there came forth a peal of applause that shook the auditorium. The ovation lasted until Mr. Schiff had left the hall."[94]

Never before had Schiff been reduced to that position, and never before had he threatened to remove himself from major Jewish issues. For the moment, however, he won. The *kehillah* overwhelmingly passed a vote of confidence in him; the only dissenting voice was that of a representative from the *Tageblatt*. Support of the banker also came from Jewish communities and institutions across the country, as well as from some secular journals. The *Hebrew Standard* of New York, which had often criticized Schiff, now said: "Frankly do we admit that we, as a community, are much more in need of Jacob H. Schiff than he is in need of us." Even the Socialist *Forward* defended him as a humanitarian who was far nobler than his attackers. To be sure, Schiff's "valedictory," if interpreted broadly, left him free range to delineate the parameters of his involvement in Jewish affairs and to continue even as he had before. But the event hastened the demise of undisputed elitist leadership.[95]

Before Schiff's outbursts rocked the community, the AJC had formally agreed, albeit conditionally, to join a democratic congress. Its strategy, like that in the formation of the *kehillah*, was to bow to public pressure and by its participation temper the more radical elements in the congress. Realistically, it reasoned that the only other options—an unyielding repudiation of the congress or an unqualified acceptance of a congress on Zionist terms—would invalidate its claim to communal leadership. Proving that the elitists too were responsive to public opinion and no doubt influenced by the congress movement, the committee was simultaneously deliberating a broader representative base for its own membership.[96]

Schiff and Marshall worked out the committee's strategy, leaving Adler, who bitterly criticized them for succumbing to "mob rule," in the opposition. The banker was unhappy at the prospect, but, as in business, the situation demanded that the stewards cut their losses. Communal unity was the desired end, and if participation in a congress achieved that unity, checked the so-called mischief makers, and assured the continued viability of the committee, so be it. Flexibility allowed the AJC to reach a settlement with the congress partisans in the summer of 1916. Although it had yielded to the majority on the basic issue, it won significant concessions: first, agreement that the American Jewish Congress was only a temporary organization and, second, changes in the wording of the congress platform in order to make it more palatable to non-Zionists. At President Wilson's suggestion and to Schiff's satisfaction, it was also agreed to postpone the congress until after the war. When the congress proceeded to elect Schiff as its treasurer and to its committee on foreign correspondence, and committee members Marshall and Harry Cutler as two of its vice presidents, it proved that the supporters of democratic governance had never intended to dispense with the stewards.[97]

The AJC quickly regained the initiative. At the peace conference it was Marshall who, for all intents and purposes, led the international Committee of Jewish Delegations in the fight for minority rights. He and Adler (as the special representative of the AJC) were better prepared on the European Jewish condition and more skilled than their erstwhile opponents in the ways of diplomatic lobbying. Not only were they pivotal in bridging the differences among delegations, but they presented the face of a united American Jewry when they argued the case of minority rights for Jews in eastern Europe. The strategy of joining the congress if it proved unbeatable appeared amply justified, and success at Versailles bolstered in turn the image of the AJC in America. While Marshall and Adler were at Versailles, Schiff watched the peacemaking process from America. Now reconciled to the congress, he helped to defray its costs and, in a typical Schiff-like gesture, offered to cover 10 percent of expenses incurred by needy delegates.[98]

Much is revealed about Schiff in the congress episode—his energy and persistence, his readiness to take on opponents publicly, and a pride in his record of communal service. The dispute also showed a sensitivity to criticism and a need of appreciation. Just as he called Asch for a meeting, so did he keep careful tabs on other well-known Jews. Answering their arguments or acknowledging their praise, he expected public support from his close associates. Throughout the public wrangling, Schiff preferred to operate independently. In his addresses and his dealings with Brandeis he spoke for himself and never as the agent of the AJC. Ignoring any restraints imposed by organizational affiliation, he capitalized on the personal loyalty he had won from the community by his philanthropy and his war against Russia. His vindication by the *kehillah* stemmed precisely from that loyalty. At the same time, however, he was taught that popular support could not be taken for granted. He may have acknowledged the rapid maturation of the eastern European immigrants,[99] but he interpreted the call for democracy, at least in part, as a personal insult. Preferring the role of benevolent despot who could sway an obedient community to his way of thinking, he was wounded by the popular revolt, especially since it was directed by the Zionists. Nevertheless, his threat to retire from Jewish politics proved empty, and until his death in 1920 he remained a dominant force in American Jewish affairs.

Questions of Zionism and Unity

A Shift toward Zionism

The war years witnessed major changes in the American Zionist movement. Under the leadership of Louis Brandeis, membership increased almost twentyfold. An expanded budget and structural reform tightened the administration of the FAZ, which in 1918 became the Zionist Organization of America (ZOA). By the end of the war, the organized Zionists, still basking in Brandeis's fame and in the Balfour Declaration (England's promise in November 1917 to aid in the establishment of a Jewish national home in Palestine), had emerged as a weighty force in communal affairs and a more serious threat to the Jewish establishment.[100]

Ironically, at the same time that Schiff was attacking the Zionists on the issues of the Technikum, wartime relief, and an American Jewish Congress, he was inching toward affiliation with the Zionist organization. The man who had lashed out against Zionism in letters to Schechter (1907), who had said that Palestine could hold no more Jews (1908), and who lost no opportunity to vilify the Jewish nationalists became receptive in 1917 to the idea of a Jewish homeland in Palestine. To be sure, officially he remained an antistatist, but the differences that separated him from Zionist ideology were noticeably fewer. Turning away from the teachings of classical Reform, he openly supported the need of a Jewish cultural and religious center in Palestine. Jews were a people as well as a religious group, and dispersion and exile could not guarantee that people's survival. Why Schiff adopted a new posture and how far he went in patching up differences with the Zionists also reveal his ongoing preoccupations with American Jewish unity and communal leadership. Had he affiliated with the Zionists, it would have been the first time that he joined a major communal enterprise in whose establishment or direction he had played no part.

Schiff's change of heart has been analyzed by historians. Evyatar Friesel notes several important reasons for it: the growing respectability of Zionism after the Schiff–Schechter dispute, the emphasis on cultural Zionism by the FAZ during the tenure of Harry Friedenwald, the common social background of the Schiff and Brandeis groups, and concern, triggered by the emancipation of Russian Jewry, over the disintegration of Judaism under the forces of assimilation. Yonathan Shapiro emphasizes yet another factor, the desire of both the Brandeis circle and the non-Zionists to lead their fellow Jews away from the "misguided" or extreme nationalistic ideas of the eastern European immigrants. Schiff himself explained publicly that his conversion to Zionism stemmed from his worry about the evaporation of Jewish culture after the March 1917 revolution in Russia. Calling Russia the "reservoir of Jewish culture," he tacitly admitted, sooner than his contemporaries did, that Jewish culture even in the United States had depended largely on eastern European Jewish creativity[101]

The validity of those explanations notwithstanding, a deeper study of Schiff points to other influences as well. First of all, kindlier sentiments on his part toward Zionism had surfaced well before the Russian Revolution. In 1912 he described himself as sympathetic to the idea of a Jewish cultural center in Palestine. Two years later he discussed the subject in an address to the Menorah Society of City College. Although he again raised the issue of the incompatibility of Jewish nationalism with Americanism, he evaluated Zionism more positively than ever before. After a sympathetic account of Herzl's response to anti-Semitism, he explained the spread of the movement and his own position:

> We know how [Zionism] has spread like wildfire—how it took hold of the Jews of every shade of belief and unbelief, how it brought under its banner old and young, and we may concede, how it awoke a new Jewish consciousness and self-respect. I am not a Zionist, if the term is used to designate the Jew as a national separatist . . . but I do not wish for a moment to belittle the unifying force Zionism has proven to possess. . . . It has proven to the Gentile world that the Jew has not lost his self-respect, [and] . . . it has more than possibly anything else . . . shown the [Jew] the value of his own heritage. It has quickened the efforts to rehabilitate Palestine and even if it cannot . . . reestablish there a Jewish State, it is at least effectively leading in the reclamation of the land of our birth from the slough and degradation into which it . . . has fallen. . . . In this sense we can, wherever our own homes may be, become supporters of Zionism.

A Zionist of whatever variety would hardly have quarreled with those sentiments.[102]

Early in 1916 the banker was attracted to a program (discussed below) put forth by Lucien Wolf of the Board of Deputies and the Anglo-Jewish Association in London that suggested a way of uniting Zionists and non-Zionists under a pro-Palestine banner. The evidence reveals, therefore, that Schiff's growing closeness to the Zionist tenets and his positive thinking about ways to cooperate with Zionism had roots that antedated 1917.

The influence of friends on the banker is also apparent. His words, the words of a cultural Zionist, echoed the teachings of Solomon Schechter. In 1917, Louis Marshall, now publicly sympathetic to cultural Zionism, credited Schechter's influence on him, Marshall. Since Schechter and Schiff had remained good friends despite the 1907 controversy, Schechter may have reached Schiff also, directly or through Marshall. Still another friend, Horace Kallen, was the source for the principle of group survival, an elemental component of Zionism, that Schiff defended in 1915. "Group individuality" according to Kallen, the exponent of cultural pluralism, included historical and cultural traditions as well as a shared national experience. To be sure, Schiff's hyper-Americanism during the war, his constant harping on Jewish integration and his repudiation of group separatism, indicated that he still was unsure where to draw the line between American nationalism and Jewish ethnicity. But he had moved well beyond the "faith" Jew that he once said he was.[103]

More important, it can be argued that a readiness on Schiff's part to work with the Zionists owed much to the fight over the American Jewish Congress. His position in that affair had badly shaken his unquestioned control of American Jewish affairs, and now he was propelled to recoup his losses. The episode had taught that support of Zionism by the masses was virtually ineradicable, particularly when the movement was headed by the glamorous Brandeis. Unrelieved and ongoing opposition to Zionism by Schiff, coming on the heels of his addresses in 1916, could significantly weaken his power. Therefore, in the interest of leadership, he needed to modify his approach. That line of reasoning was endorsed by Kallen, a Brandeis follower and a man whom Schiff respected. Leadership had a price, Kallen once told him: it required public obligations, noblesse oblige, and the duty to follow popular sentiment even if it clashed with the leader's personal opinion. Hence, becoming a shekel-payer, or a dues-paying Zionist, was qualitatively no different from Schiff's capitulation on the issue of a congress.[104]

Influential Zionists, who eagerly sought an alliance with Schiff in order to boost their own prestige, appeared more than ready to acknowledge his importance. Julian Mack's first act in 1918 as president of the ZOA was to invite Schiff, along with Marshall and Adler, to pay the shekel. In Palestine, Zionist lexicographer Eliezer Ben Yehudah called it a misfortune that Schiff, "one of the noblest sons of Israel," stood outside the Zionist camp.

Schiff may have expected that his affiliation with the movement would aug-ment his influence with both Zionist leaders and the community at large. He was not about to stump for a Jewish state—"I . . . doubt that I can bring myself to bodily come into Zionism"—but he was prepared to gamble that the Zionists might tailor their priorities as payment for his affiliation. What more effective way to wean the community away from the extremist ideas of statehood and political group rights than to join forces with the Brandeis camp and bore from within? If, as Schiff hoped, Brandeis would remove himself from Zionist affairs upon his appointment to the Supreme Court, so much the better. The jurist's less charismatic successors would be hard put to control the rank and file as successfully.[105]

The banker's often-repeated plea for communal unity, both to strengthen communal resources and to gain Gentile respect, clearly played a signifi-cant part in his calculations. He was convinced that "it is most important for our people to get together if we are to emerge from the convulsion of the [World War] stronger and better situated than has been the case in the decades through which our generation and that which preceded it has been passing." In the congress dispute he had sought a common platform on which the opposing factions could unite. When he recognized that he and the AJC were in the minority, he advised the committee to yield to the Zionists and by so doing project the image of a united Jewry. Caught up in the heated congress debate, he backtracked on what he had said to the Me-norah Society in 1914. Now he claimed that Zionism bred only divisive-ness. "Instead of being a unifying force [Zionism] is rapidly becoming a se-rious disintegrant, its leaders consisting either of idealists or self-seeking schemers who in reality have little use for Palestine, except as a phantom with which to lead the masses." Thus, just as the AJC had accepted a con-gress, so would it be in the best interests of the Zionists to seek a compro-mise with non-Zionists on Palestinian matters. Before the war, Schiff had supported Jewish institutions in Palestine independently of the Zionists, but for the sake of communal unity he was prepared both to negotiate a set-tlement with the Zionists and to work with them in practical endeavors.[106]

Schiff found what he considered neutral ground for allying Zionists with non-Zionists in the platform adopted by Lucien Wolf's National Union for Jewish Rights in London. The union had resolved to steer clear of Jewish nationalism, and it limited its approval of minority rights to "communal" and "educational" autonomy. With respect to Palestine, it substituted Palestinianism for Zionism, asking for "adequate facilities for immigration . . . and for the establishment of Jewish colonies in that coun-try together with full political rights and such municipal privileges as may be necessary." In February 1916, along with a pointed criticism of Jewish statehood, Schiff called the program to Brandeis's attention. No matter who controlled Palestine after the war, he said, a Jewish state would not be tolerated. Furthermore, demands like the union's promised "close cooperation between all elements in Jewry, a desideratum which . . . appears particularly in present conditions so very important and necessary." Accordingly, by taking statism out of Zionism, the union provided for a "sane" Zionism that united different Jewish factions, one with which Schiff could feel comfortable. True, the program made no mention of religion, but if Brandeis endorsed a modified Zionism in return for unity and for Schiff's promise to affiliate, the chances of securing Zionist acceptance of Palestine as a religious center were improved. To Schiff's disappointment, Brandeis showed no interest in the program. Nevertheless, the banker continued to support the stand of the National Union, adding a proviso that emphasized Jewish loyalty to the countries in which they lived.[107]

Schiff now toned down his rhetoric considerably when he spoke about or to Zionists, even though his earlier views on the evils of nationalism, especially on secular nationalism and on the incompatibility of political Zionism with patriotism, were for the moment fixed. What had changed was a willingness to join forces in securing free Jewish immigration into Palestine and the establishment there of a Jewish center. Open to various interpretations, a "center" left room for further discussion and compromise.

The banker shared his thoughts with various associates. Zionist Judah Magnes also saw in a pro-Palestine program the possibility of strengthening the Zionists by uniting them with their critics. In letters to Schiff, Marshall, Adler, and Mack he urged that the AJC commit itself "to the general Palestine program." Magnes agreed with his colleagues on the committee that Zionist goals should include specific mention of religion, but he deemed it wiser to establish first a united front of Zionists and non-Zionists and only then to work out precise formulas. In response to the ideas of both Magnes amd Schiff, the AJC planned months before the Balfour Declaration to formulate a policy statement on Jewish settlement in Palestine.[108]

Schiff publicly endorsed a Jewish homeland and a religious center in Palestine when he addressed the League of Jewish Youth on April 22, 1917. Reminded of the abandonment of Judaism by the post-Mendelssohn generation in Berlin, he feared that the emancipation of Russian Jewry might breed indifference to Judaism and Jewish culture:

> It has come to me, while thinking over events of recent weeks . . . that the Jewish people should at last have a home land of their own. I do not mean by that that there should be a Jewish nation. I am not a believer in a Jewish nation built on all kinds of isms, with egotism as the first, and agnosticism and atheism among the others. But I am a believer in the Jewish people and in the

mission of the Jew, and I believe that somewhere there should be a great reservoir of Jewish learning in which Jewish culture might be furthered and developed, unhampered by the materialism of the world, and might spread its beautiful ideals over the world. And naturally that land would be Palestine.

Having thus squared, at least to his satisfaction, a Jewish homeland with Reform's interpretation of a dispersed priest people, he developed the theme in numerous letters. To Israel Zangwill he insisted that he wanted Zion without any "ism." To another friend he added his hope that "once more 'Jewish law and Jewish culture go out from Zion and the word of God from Jerusalem.'"[109]

A most revealing letter was written by Schiff to a rabid anti-Zionist rabbi, David Philipson, of Cincinnati. The latter had warned that Schiff's April address would be interpreted to mean that Judaism was only a ghetto religion unable to survive in free surroundings. Schiff's answer again emphasized the disintegration of Jewry after their emancipation, not only in Russia but also in France, Germany, and the United States. The Jews needed a center in Palestine, he maintained, where a large Jewish population would stimulate Jewish thought and learning throughout the world. Doubtful now about the desirability of total integration, even in America, he wrote:

Look at our Synagogues and Temples; they are becoming empty more and more! My children and your children and almost everybody else's children may have some interest yet in our religion, because of the example of their parents, but look at the third generation, with how little attachment for our religion they grow up, because their parents are even more indifferent than their parents' parents may have been in the religious education of their children.

The banker could well have been describing his own family—the sketchy Jewish education of his two children and their and their children's progressive alienation from things Jewish. Having reached the age of seventy in 1917, Schiff had grown more introspective, perhaps taking at least partial responsibility for the drift of his descendants from Judaism. Not surprisingly, he admitted later that his son did not understand his father's "conversion" to Zionism.[110]

A slightly fuller version of the letter to Philipson appeared in the press. There Schiff explained that religious motives underlay his support of a Palestinian center rather than a state. Since 50 percent to 75 percent of the nationalists had no interest whatsoever in religion, he doubted whether a Jewish state established by them would advance the cause of Judaism. Whichever version of the letter is accepted, Schiff's focus on the continuity of a vibrant religion and culture rooted in a Palestinian matrix not only clashed with Philipson's Reform views on the blessing of dispersion, but it flew in the face of the typical Jewish response to political emancipation ever since the French Revolution.[111]

Assuming that he had joined their ranks, the Zionists pounced on Schiff's April address and congratulated him "upon having seen the light at last." But Schiff assured Philipson and other Reform critics that the response was premature. He wrote that he would not become a Zionist so long as nationalism, or the movement for a state, was synonomous with Zionism. Calling himself a non-Zionist, Schiff continued to distinguish between Zionists and nationalists. The latter were the dangerous agitators who rejected the Jewish religion and whose call for a Jewish state or Jewish national rights compromised Jewish loyalty to the lands in which they lived. The former were the cultural Zionists who, very much like Solomon Schechter, wanted to see Palestine as the center of *Judaism*. To be sure, Schiff's statement and his involvement in Palestinian affairs, predicated on a definition of Jews as an ethnic rather than solely religious group, moved him closer to cultural Zionism than ever before. But his long-standing criticism of religion-less Zionism endured. In the end it proved to be the stumbling block that prevented his formal affiliation with the ZOA.[112]

Elisha Friedman, a young Zionist and economist stationed in Washington during the war, followed up Schiff's April speech. His initial letter to the banker began a seven-month period during which the latter's affiliation with the Zionist movement was debated by leaders of the ZOA. At first, in a seemingly endless stream of letters and meetings, Friedman, the intermediary between the banker and the Brandeis group, attempted to win Schiff over. He played down statehood and national rights and, encouraged by Schiff's printed letter to Philipson, emphasized the similarities between the banker's position and Zionism. Arguing that Jewish homelessness caused religious decay, he defined Jewish nationalism as a spiritual force. Non-Zionism, he added, was an empty concept that connoted only staying put. For his part, Schiff insisted that his quarrel had never been with Zionism but with Jewish nationalism, and he stuck by points he had raised previously. A state was an "absurdity," and citing resistance to conscription on the part of the Zionist eastern Europeans, he still maintained that Jewish nationalism clashed with patriotism. His criticism of the antireligious character of the movement persisted too. In an address at the end of 1917 he called for a "Jewish revival," saying that just as disregard of the true faith had led to the destruction of the biblical commonwealth, so too would a new Jewish nation fail unless Jews first returned to their God.[113]

At the same time, Schiff began speaking, albeit vaguely, of the reestablishment of an "autonomous commonwealth,"[114] a term that linked him still closer to Zionism. Thus, his stand was riddled with contradictions and conditions—a commonwealth but no state, political autonomy but only for the purpose of strengthening religion, a Jewish center in Palestine to halt the disintegration of Judaism but the incompatibility of nationalist goals with patriotism.

By the fall of 1917, the dialogue between Friedman and Schiff was broadened to include meetings of the principals with Brandeis and his lieutenants on one side and Marshall and others of the AJC on the other. With his eye on leadership, Schiff desired the support of his associates, explaining to Marshall that a consensus of committee members would carry greater weight "with those of our people whom we honestly seek to guide" than would the opinion of an individual. The conversations and meetings continued, but despite Marshall's assurance that "very little difference" separated the Zionist and "our" views—indeed American Zionist leaders were then adopting a pragmatic economic rather than a political approach to Palestine—Schiff's enrollment in the movement with or without his friends was as yet elusive.[115]

At the banker's urging the American Zionists drafted a statement to be sent to leaders of the World Zionist Organization, clarifying the aims of the Basel program, the national platform adopted by the first Zionist congress. Schiff's terms included a homeland in Palestine as a protectorate of a great power (probably England), Hebrew as its official language, free Jewish immigration controlled by a chartered Jewish company, and full civil and religious rights for the Jewish and non-Jewish communities in Palestine. He also advised that Zionist leaders like Brandeis and Mack admit publicly that Zionism clashed with the patriotism of Western Jewry. Letters flew back and forth as Schiff and the Zionists debated phrases and wording.

The statement finally presented failed to meet Schiff's approval. Verbal promises about nationalism and a state notwithstanding, the Zionists feared that since the the masses were apprehensive about negotiations with the "yahudim," they were bound to feel betrayed by an official endorsement of a center as opposed to a state. At the very least, the Zionists could not permit Schiff's objectives to be confused with theirs. The banker too grew less tractable. He came down more forcefully on the need to emphasize religion, and he demanded permission to air that view (i.e., his interpretation in religious terms of Zionism's raison d'être) simultaneously with his formal affiliation.[116]

Meanwhile, the Zionists grew more disenchanted about the price they would have to pay for enrolling Schiff. Stephen Wise, for example, asked, "Have we won Schiff to Zionism, or has Zionism been won over to the Schiff point of view?" Concerned about communal leadership as much as Schiff was, they knew that were they to knuckle under to his dictates and bring their archcompetitor into the movement, their own power would be undermined. Brandeis finally advised that the entire matter be dropped, and no official response to Schiff was sent. Complaining of Zionist discourtesy, the banker wrote Mack, who in fact had agreed to Schiff's conditions, that the more he saw of Zionist leaders, except for Brandeis, the less he respected them. Nevertheless, he determined to continue his cooperation from the outside.[117]

Some prominent Zionists, like Mack, attempted in 1918 to revive the overtures to Schiff. While Professor Israel Friedlaender of the Jewish Theological Seminary told the banker that the best way to put religion into Zionism was to fight for it from within the ranks, Horace Kallen appealed on behalf of the Jewish people: "I know at this moment of no act that would be more genuinely helpful to the future of Israel and the realization of your hopes for our people . . . than your regularly joining the [Zionist] organization." However, such efforts that argued the right of different opinions under the umbrella of the Basel program proved futile. Schiff, who blamed the Zionists for the breakdown of negotiations, told Mack in April 1918: "I wish I could . . . see my way . . . to join the Zionist organization. You know I was very ready to do so four months ago, but my expressed consent was received with little courtesy, and not acted upon."[118]

Nevertheless, true to his word, Schiff contributed generously for the physical restoration of Palestine. Since Brandeis aimed for a rapprochement with Schiff and Marshall toward that same goal, Schiff's nonaffiliation did not stop Mack from frequently consulting the banker on Palestine matters. When Mack and Brandeis discussed the financial needs of postwar Palestine with a sympathetic Schiff in 1919, the latter responded by calling a conference at Temple Emanu-El for the purpose of launching a fund-raising campaign for Palestine together with that of the JDC. His remarks at the conference underscored both the centrality of Palestine in the "larger Jewish question" of Jews in eastern Europe and the ongoing need for unity among Jews. "It is high time," he said, "that American Jewry forget its differences . . . and join hands with those who have heretofore made the Zionist Problem their specialty, in order that, united, they may find a solution for the Jewish question . . . which shall prove satisfactory to all, and of which I verily believe Palestine has become the corner-stone." Schiff's idea of joint fund-raising was rejected, testifying yet again to the difficulties of achieving communal unity. Schiff never joined the ZOA, but until his death in 1920 he continued to preach unity for the rehabilitation of Palestine. "It is not the duty of every Jew to be a Zionist, but it is the duty of every Jew to help restore Palestine." A self-appointed peacemaker, he juggled the interests of both sides in an attempt to assure each faction of his genuine sympathy.[119]

In the interests of the non- or anti-Zionists, Schiff urged the Zionists to ignore nationalism and concentrate on the physical "redemption" of Palestine. His opposition to national rights and his assertion that "I am as little as ever interested in political Zionism and the establishment of a

Jewish nation" helped as well to placate the critics of Zionism. Moreover, in a letter to millionaire Julius Rosenwald, Schiff played up the financial benefits of a reconstructed Palestine, one that would help solve the Jewish problem in Europe and thereby lessen the economic burden on American Jews. The specter of a Jewish state that haunted the anti-Zionists was neutralized by the banker's very choice of words. "Center" or "homeland" or even "commonwealth" ignored statehood and hinted rather at an essentially benign and acceptable refugeeism largely for the benefit of eastern European Jewry.[120]

More farsighted than others, Schiff may have well understood that non-Zionist contributions to the development of the *yishuv* were qualitatively different from other philanthropic gifts. Whether or not earmarked for economic and cultural purposes, they helped to build the infrastructure of a Jewish center, if not a state. Nevertheless, he assured the anti- and non-Zionists that British sovereignty over Palestine had made Jewish statism a dead issue. Those nationalist leaders who continued to delude their followers into believing that the "chimera" of a Jewish state "is on the eve of realization" were out only—and here again Schiff was sensitive to the issue of leadership—to maintain their power.[121]

Speaking to the Zionists at the same time, Schiff denied that Palestine would be merely an asylum for the refugee emigrants from eastern Europe. He continued to depict a center of spiritual creativity and an opportunity for a Jew "to live under conditions which, freed from the materialistic influences of the western world, will make it possible for him to develop to the full those qualities which have enabled the Jew to make such valuable contributions to the highest assets of mankind." Nor did he completely rule out the possibility of a Jewish state in the future. Rather, he adopted a wait-and-see attitude. Writing for the *Nation*, he stated that "after the population of Palestine shall have become overwhelmingly Jewish, the Jews actually there can determine for themselves what kind of government to choose."[122]

Not fully acceptable to either side, Schiff's compromise boiled down to a give-and-take by both groups. If the Zionists suspended their political goals, they could secure the financial help of the non-Zionists for the rehabilitation of Palestine and thereby more easily construct the base of a state. If the anti- or non-Zionists contributed to the physical restoration of the land and thereby to a haven for prospective European emigrants, they saved money and, more important, they had the Zionists' assurance that the prospect of a state "cannot be realized for many a decade." As Marshall put it to one AJC member, "Neither you nor your children nor your children's children will live to see the formation of a Jewish sovereign State in Palestine. I do not, therefore, see any occasion for excitement." Were the two groups to unite, Schiff optimistically predicted that the inhabitants of Palestine under British control would benefit from improved administrative methods, that peace would reign between Arabs and Jews, and that a Jewish homeland would develop more quickly.[123] Events in the 1920s and 1930s proved at least some of his predictions inaccurate, but for the time being his views contributed to easing the tension between Zionists and non-Zionists and the transformation of American Zionism into Palestinianism.

The Balfour Declaration

In November 1917, when a climax was approaching in negotiations between Schiff and the Zionists, the latter joyfully celebrated the Balfour Declaration. Transmitted in a letter from British foreign minister Arthur Balfour to Lord Lionel Rothschild, honorary president of the Zionist Federation of Great Britain, a month before the British captured Jerusalem, the declaration stated: "His Majesty's Government view with favor the establishment in Palestine of a national home for the Jewish people, and will use their best endeavors to facilitate the achievement of this object, it being clearly understood that nothing shall be done which may prejudice the civil and religious rights of existing non-Jewish communities in Palestine, or the rights and political status enjoyed by Jews in any other country." A keen desire to win the sympathy of American Jews for the Allied cause had prompted England's action, and although the British ambassador to the United States, Sir Cecil Spring-Rice, remained skeptical of its success, Zionists the world over rejoiced. The declaration went further than the Basel program, talking of a "national home" instead of merely a "home" in Palestine. "Zionism is no longer a dream," Judge Julian Mack said. "It has passed into the realm of practical possibility." Subsequently endorsed by Wilson, a majority in Congress, and American public opinion, the declaration transformed the idea of a national homeland, which many understood to mean a state, into an Allied war aim.[124] Thus, while it confirmed the rights of Jews in the diaspora, it also promised American Zionists relief from the charge of dual allegiance.

By stamping Zionism with the seal of international respectability, the declaration strengthened Zionist resistance to Schiff's conditions for affiliating with the movement. For the banker, however, the declaration was primarily another issue that testified to the needs of proper American Jewish leadership and especially American Jewish unity. Although he questioned the depth of England's commitment to Zionism, he publicly lined up with the Zionists in praise of the statement. He hoped, he said, that the declaration would unite Jews in preparation for reassuming "their glorious inheritance." Jews held different views on how to achieve a secure foothold in Palestine, but at bottom the imagination of *all* was fired by the "hope for the restoration of the Land of the Fathers to the children of Israel."[125]

The goal of unity was uppermost in Schiff's mind when the AJC discussed whether and how it should respond to the declaration. The committee itself included Zionists, non-Zionists, and anti-Zionists, and until 1917 its public stance on Zionism had been one of neutrality. President Louis Marshall, who was loath to consign Palestine to the exclusive jurisdiction of the Zionists, listed three options: the committee could ignore the question, it could fully support the Zionist position, or it could take a middle-of-the-road course. Since Marshall believed that as a war aim the declaration could not be resisted, he summarily dismissed the idea of an anti-Zionist resolution. In a heated debate that followed, Schiff at first suggested that the committee not address the issue. "You know how much nearer I have myself come to Zionism," he admitted, but the matter appeared so volatile that in all likelihood it would tear the committee apart. Toward the larger goal of communal unity, he preferred to see the AJC deal with international questions rather than with controversial matters. Furthermore, if the Zionists agreed to a division of labor (i.e., that they handle the question of Palestine and the committee handle the interests of American and other Jewries) and if they agreed to cooperate with the committee should the two areas of jursdiction overlap, "we can give to the world the spectacle of a united Jewry whereas otherwise we will have conflict." Schiff changed his mind, however, when Mack argued that ignoring the declaration was tantamount to an abdication of leadership. Now seeking a response that would neither split the committee nor compromise its leadership, Schiff suggested a statement in sympathy with the Balfour Declaration "which shall not however commit the Committee to a definite policy." Cyrus Adler and Mayer Sulzberger, doubtless recalling how committee leaders had been burned by the Zionists in the congress episode, initially opposed any expression of approval, but Schiff's weak resolution was adopted unanimously.[126]

The banker contributed to the drafting of the statement, which was then cleared with Secretary of State Lansing. At best a bland compromise, it disappointed Zionists like Mack. Schiff himself heartily but privately endorsed Mack's call for a national homeland rather than a center in Palestine, but in the interest of unity he did not attempt to foist his new feelings about Zionism on his non- or anti-Zionist colleagues. In its statement the AJC said that it appreciated the Balfour Declaration and that it would cooperate with those who sought "a center for Judaism" in Palestine. But it talked of "a" center, not "the" center; a center for *Judaism*, not a political state; and it underscored the loyalty of Jews to the lands in which they lived. Schiff and Marshall steered the AJC thereby on a path of non-Zionism, one that preserved unity within the organization while it permitted greatest latitude on Palestinian affairs.[127]

In line with the committee's stand, Schiff and Marshall refused in September 1918 to join David Philipson in a conference for combating Zionism. Schiff reaffirmed his new attitude toward Zionism, one that was "in the best interests of our People. Greatly more than I did when I first ceased my opposition to the Zionist Movement, do I feel now that the creation of a Jewish Home Land is most desirable." Opposition from the "Grand Old Man of American Jewry," as Philipson called him, allied with other non-Zionists on the committee, put an end to the anti-Zionist scheme.[128] In 1920, Schiff approved of the decision at San Remo to award the mandate over Palestine to England. Henceforth, he said, it would be easier to prepare Palestine as a Jewish homeland in conformity with the Balfour Declaration.[129]

The entire episode of Schiff's flirtation with the Zionist organization until his death is clouded by an element of make-believe. Not only were his contributions as a non-Zionist just as important for the development of a state as Zionist contributions, but the ideological differences that separated him from the Zionists, especially the cultural Zionists, had little substance. Only the payment of a shekel distinguished his stand from Schechter's. Even the political Zionists, the leaders from the Brandeis circle as well as rank-and-file members, had long bent the tenets of Zionism in keeping with an American setting. In theory they subscribed to the teachings of Herzl and to the movement for a state, but most would have agreed that Herzlian laws on how anti-Semitism mandated Jewish national separatism did not apply to the United States. They welcomed the Balfour Declaration for its approval of a national homeland in Palestine, but, as he wrote to Mack, so did Schiff. Since hardly any Zionist would have denied the security of American Jewry or posited the primacy of Jewish over American loyalty or requested national rights for America's Jews, American Zionism from its inception developed largely into a movement for the benefit of Jews not fortunate enough to live in the United States.

Non- and anti-Zionists balked at both the theory of diaspora nationalism and the definition of *ethnic* in broad political terms, but American Zionists too invoked those ideas almost exclusively for eastern European Jewry. Whereas the latter may have embraced Zionism as a personal commitment, American Zionists scarcely thought of emigration to Palestine as a serious option for themselves. True, among Zionists whose roots lay in eastern Europe, where distinctions among ethnic groups were common, a keener sense of peoplehood prevailed than in the case of Jews like Schiff who stemmed from western Europe. But even the Zionists were spectators rather than active participants. In the calculations of the World Zionist Organization as well, American Jews were primarily the ones who would supply the funds rather than the bodies for rebuilding a Jewish Palestine. After the war, when emphasis on the economic development of the *yishuv* displaced statehood as the first priority of Zionism, the differences between Zionists and non-Zionists paled further. In sum, aside from the factor of religion, Zionist policy was less important in the Schiff–Zionist negotiations than clashes of personalities (e.g., the anti-Schiff animus on the part of Stephen Wise), competing claims to leadership, and, above all, Schiff's unending search for communal unity.

On the scale of leadership, Schiff's change of heart on Zionism scored high. The banker's genuine commitment to a Jewish Palestine, more in keeping with his traditionalist background, sat well with the majority of the community and regained ground for him that he had lost during the congress fight. In his peacemaking role, which raised him above the contending sides, he steered clear of confrontation or abrasive tactics. The Jewish press applauded Schiff's determined efforts[130] and the new immigrant masses, who saw a generous and mellow elder statesman, had no cause to challenge his authority.

7

The End of an Era

A New Europe

Until his death barely two years after the armistice, Schiff remained very much involved in Jewish affairs. Failing health prevented him from undertaking new assignments or maintaining a hands-on direction of institutional policies. But although he delegated more control to others, he still played a significant role in guiding his favorite charities and organizations: Montefiore, the Jewish Theological Seminary, the Henry Street Settlement House, the Baron de Hirsch Fund, and the American Jewish Committee (AJC).

Schiff's commitment to causes generated by the war, like relief for European Jewish war sufferers and the building up of Palestine, also continued. On the matter of relief he had correctly predicted that postwar needs would require greater sums than those of wartime. Nor did he close the books on older and familiar subjects that were revived with new intensity after the war by nativist Americans. First, he still intervened where possible in cases of discrimination against the employment of Jews. His earlier efforts notwithstanding, the banker admitted at the end of 1918 that the policies of the National Employment Exchange had not changed a bit. Second, in anticipation of a large influx of immigrants after the war, he reiterated his opposition to restrictionism. As before, he emphasized the advisability of distribution and of training the immigrants in agriculture.[1] At a time when the country hardened barriers against immigrants and minority groups, his views on those subjects clashed with public opinion.

Since Americans turned their backs on international involvement in the aftermath of the war, Schiff again was out of step with the mood of the majority. A supporter of the Democrats in the by-elections of 1918, he endorsed President Wilson's peace plans. Calling for Senate ratification of the Versailles treaty and the establishment of a League of Nations, he looked forward to the resumption of commercial and financial relations with Germany and to the resurrection of "civilization" in that country. Senator William Borah of the Senate Foreign Relations Committee, the leader of the anti-Wilson irreconcilables, hinted darkly that Schiff and five other financiers supported the treaty for private economic reasons, but there is no evidence in the Schiff papers to substantiate that charge. In 1920, Schiff favored the nomination of Herbert Hoover on the Republican ticket, doubtless because of Hoover's reputation as an internationalist, but his countrymen preferred the normalcy of Warren Harding.[2]

From 1916 on, Schiff gave much thought to the postwar economic restoration of Europe. In a grand gesture reminiscent of the old Schiff, the banker talked immediately after the armistice of a multimillion-dollar fund for that purpose. He discussed the matter with an enthusiastic Julius Rosenwald, who agreed that he and Schiff would contribute $5 million each. (Initially, they had talked of $1 million each.) Schiff also planned to invite the participation of other wealthy men, like J. P. Morgan and Henry Ford. Since Schiff and Rosenwald wanted American initiative to guide the project, they thought of approaching Wilson and asking him to name an American commission for restoration in Europe. The Schiff papers yield little more on the nature of the plan—how it would be structured and the respective roles of the private sector and the government. The president, however, left for Paris before an interview was possible, and the scheme collapsed.[3]

Of all the issues that concerned Schiff after the war hardly any was more nagging than the condition of the Jews in central and eastern Europe. Indeed, his focus on Jewry in the new states about to be created in central and eastern Europe antedated the armistice. He hinted broadly to Thomas Masaryk, who would become the first president of Czechoslovakia, that he, Schiff, agreed with Wilson's ideal of national self-determination but that he had no sympathy with the anti-Semitism of the Poles and Romanians and, by implication, the Czechoslovakians. Invited to serve as a vice president of the League of Small and Subject Nationalities, he refused, saying that he first needed the assurance that Poland and Romania, who wanted their own rights so badly, would grant rights to their Jews. He told his friend Charles Eliot, however, that he expected nothing from Poland. "My sainted mother often used to say that when servants became masters, they generally became intolerant and despotic masters against their own servants."[4]

Jews in the United States watched events in Poland with grave concern. Since Americans generally favored an independent Poland, and indeed that was one of Wilson's Fourteen Points, efforts to relieve the Jewish situation were made more difficult. Jewish leaders, for example, found reports by

American officials in Poland to be inaccurate and biased. While Marshall accused the Red Cross of discrimination against Jews, Schiff charged that newspapers suppressed information on the persecutions. Complicating the issue still further was the carryover of Polish–Jewish animosity in the United States. In several cities, Polish priests advocated a boycott of Jewish businessmen, while in New York there were reports of Jewish attacks on Polish organizations. In the spring of 1918, Marshall arranged for representatives of the AJC to begin negotiations with Polish leaders. The latter had requested a meeting to secure Jewish endorsement of and capital investment in an independent Poland. Nevertheless, the Poles took no pains to mask their anti-Semitism, and deliberations made no headway. Schiff participated in the first round of talks, but it was Marshall who orchestrated the overall direction of Jewish moves.[5]

Schiff contributed where he could to relieve the Polish situation. He helped to formulate appeals to Wilson and Senator Henry Cabot Lodge that asked for government remonstrances, and in December 1918 he joined Jewish workers and Socialists at a rally to protest Polish treatment of Jews. So different from his earlier position of ignoring the masses in matters of Jewish diplomacy, the sight of Schiff amid eight thousand Yiddish-speaking workers at a Socialist meeting begged for an explanation. The banker supplied one: He disagreed with the "serious doctrines" of socialism, but he very much supported the purpose of the meeting. "Because we have Jewish hearts, and because the Jewish heart rebels wherever injustice is done against men of whatever station, I am here." He bitterly denounced Polish leader Roman Dmowski, and he called upon the president, the public, and the peace conference to stop Polish oppression. Making sure to send a copy of his speech to Wilson, he said that the latter needed to understand the sentiments of American Jews.[6]

Anti-Semitism flourished in other lands too. While the peacemakers were redrawing the map of Europe, adjusting boundaries, and carving out new states from the former empires on the continent, seemingly endless stories were reported of Jewish suffering in the Ukraine, Romania, Czechoslovakia, and Galicia, as well as Poland. Not only did Jews in those lands endure abject poverty and economic ruin, they also were subjected to boycotts, legal disabilities, anti-Semitic agitation by the press, mass rioting, and bloody pogroms. The number of those killed between 1918 and 1921 was counted in the tens of thousands.

As the situation worsened, voices were raised in efforts at amelioration. At Versailles individual American Jews privately discussed specific conditions in Czechoslovakia, Poland, and Russia with Wilson; his aide, Colonel Edward House; Herbert Hoover (then in charge of food relief for Europe); and one of the American peacemakers, General Tasker Bliss. To undercut

Polish animosity the Jewish leaders also urged Polish Jewry to cooperate in good faith with the new government. Meanwhile, in the United States resolutions of sympathy and protest were passed by non-Jewish organizations and by state legislatures and Congress. Jews staged mass meetings and wrote memorials; the AJC and the American Jewish Congress sent delegates to Washington to confer with Wilson, Secretary of State Robert Lansing, and Senator Lodge, chairman of the Senate Foreign Relations Committee. Although the senator was patronizing, Wilson was sympathetic. When he asked for practical suggestions, the AJC advised a public announcement warning nationalities that persecution jeopardized their claim to independence. Nevertheless, the president, whose primary concern was to gain American acceptance of a treaty with a League of Nations, offered no substantive help.[7] In the end the goal of the Jewish delegates was reached. Minority rights under the protection of the League and approved by Wilson were incorporated into treaties with Poland, Romania, Yugoslavia, and Czechoslovakia. But regardless of the strength of the League, Schiff calculated that it would take many years to iron out all the trouble spots for European Jewry. Cyrus Adler grimly predicted that the question of minority rights would occupy the AJC for the next twenty-five years, and as history soon proved, Wilson's faith in the minority rights treaties was sadly misplaced.[8]

For the first time in over thirty years, Schiff was not center stage in American Jewish lobbying for eastern European Jews. Forced by physical problems to be a spectator rather than a player and never enjoying the same relationship with Wilson that he had had with Roosevelt and Taft—he once said that the president did not like him—he depended on Louis Marshall and a few others at the peace conference to keep him informed. For a while, Marshall, representing the American Jewish Congress, led the multinational Committee of Jewish Delegations that spoke at Versailles for minority rights; and Cyrus Adler, the official representative of the AJC, also cooperated. The attorney was the closest to a substitute for Schiff. Called a "big force" in Jewry by the banker, Marshall also plotted Jewish strategy in the United States. He loyally told Schiff of all moves, and the latter in turn took care not to compromise his friend's authority. When he was personally contacted (e.g., a letter from Ignace Paderewski asserting Poland's democratic aims or a cable from European rabbis on Jewish suffering in Poland), Schiff referred the matter to Marshall. Doubtless frustrated at being confined to the sidelines, especially during the peace conference, he served as liaison between the American delegation to Paris and individual European Jewish leaders. It was a necessary task but an unexciting one for a man like Schiff.[9]

Bolsheviks and Jews

The jubilation with which Jews had greeted the overthrow of the czar was short-lived. The Bolshevik revolution in November 1917 swept away the Provisional Government and marked the onset of a civil war between the "Reds" (the Bolsheviks) and the "Whites" (supporters of the czarist regime who were helped by the Allies). Russian Jews were caught in the middle; accused of Bolshevist sympathies by the Whites and attacked as members of the hated bourgeoisie by the Reds, they suffered economic and cultural deprivation if not torture and mass executions. Jews reported that some pogroms were incited by the Germans, and Schiff too called for an end to the "Bolshevik German terror." But no matter who the instigators were, the atrocities proved that the end of czarist rule had not eradicated Russian anti-Semitism.[10]

The complexities of the situation put American Jewish leaders in a no-win position. To side with the Reds, the enemies of private property and religion, particularly when the United States sent a military expedition into Russia to curb the Bolshevik troops, was thoroughly unpalatable. To side with the Whites, the representatives of an anti-Semitic old regime that was anathema to the eastern European immigrants, was equally unthinkable. Moreover, any stand by American Jews threatened to fuel the wrath of the other side and cause additional suffering for the victims. Appeals to the president and State Department to warn the perpetrators that they would be held accountable also failed. Lansing explained, in the wake of Jewish massacres in the Ukraine, that intervention was impossible, since the United States had no diplomatic relations with any of the groups struggling for power.[11]

The AJC gathered pertinent information on the Russian situation from published articles and from knowledgeable Russians in America. Although Schiff left most decision making to Marshall and the AJC during the last years of his life, he still cultivated his own sources on the Russian problem. A Mr. Kurbatov, introduced by Lord Swaythling (Samuel Montagu) and identified by Schiff as a Cossack, discussed the persecutions with him. So did A. J. Sack, director of the Russian Information Bureau in New York, whose primary purpose was to propagandize on behalf of Admiral Alexander Kolchak and the Whites. Without the cooperation of the American government, however, there was little that the committee or Schiff could do. Even relief drives were stymied as long as the money could fall into the wrong hands. Meanwhile, Schiff withdrew his offer of a medical unit for Russian Jews that he had made in April 1917, and he wrote off his loan of 1 million rubles to the pre-Bolshevist regime as a total loss.[12]

Most worrisome to the Jewish stewards was the linkage of Jew with

Bolshevik. The charge that Jews had engineered the November revolution in an international conspiracy for world domination was not confined to Russian Whites. Gaining credence from the fact that some Jews were prominent in Bolshevik councils, it was picked up in western Europe and the United States. The Jew=Bolshevik charge quickly became a common theme in popular parlance and a major weapon in the hands of anti-Semites. The more it was repeated, the broader it became; limited at first to the Russian Revolution, it easily grew into claims, heard on both sides of the Atlantic, that Jews worldwide were Bolsheviks who plotted the over-throw of Western countries. It mattered not that the older stereotype of the Jew as unscrupulous capitalist logically conflicted with the new image. In fact, the two images were harnessed for the same purpose. Whether in the guise of capitalist or Bolshevik, the Jew was bent primarily on destroy-ing Christian civilization. An article in the staid London *Times*, for exam-ple, combined the two images when it linked Leon Trotsky with Jewish fi-nanciers of New York.

In the United States similar statements abounded. Following the visits of Trotsky and Nikolai Bukharin to New York during the war and the flood of new members into the foreign-language Socialist federations after the Bolshevik revolution, the Jews (non-Socialists as well as Socialists) became favorite targets of American nativists. An anti-Semitic journal in Brooklyn, the *Anti-Bolshevist*, called itself "A Monthly Magazine Devoted to the De-fense of American Institutions against the Jewish Bolshevist Doctrines of Morris Hillquit and Leon Trotsky." More respectable sources followed suit: An official of the American Red Cross, Robert Davis, wrote in *McClure's* that the Russian problem was essentially a Jewish problem and that Bolshevism paved the way for Jewish control of economic life; com-munal leaders in Philadelphia warned that Jewish identification with the Bolsheviks would cause an anti-Semitic backlash in the United States; a businessmen's organization in Iowa spread the image of the "Jewish Bolshevik" among Rotary Clubs. The alacrity with which average Ameri-cans latched onto the Bolshevik image and refused to question its accuracy suggests that it was more anti-Semitic—"an innate prejudice," as Louis Marshall put it—than anti-Bolshevist. Directed against the "international" Jew, the Jew=Bolshevik equation generally ignored class distinctions within the Jewish community. The established German Jew no less than the im-migrant Russian Jew was fair game for attacks.[13]

Desperately searching for an effective defense, the AJC appointed a committee on Jews and Bolsheviks in the fall of 1918 to consider the mat-ter. The best it could come up with was a statement, to be drafted by the AJC but issued by the State Department, dissociating Jews from Bolshe-vism. No action was taken, suggesting that the committee was afraid of a public stand that might boomerang against the Jews. The organization gathered testimony from sympathetic Russians, like the former Russian envoy, Boris Bakhmetev, contradicting the charge, but such denials were useless in the face of the big lie. Equally ineffective in the larger picture was Marshall's time-consuming practice of handling slanderers individually.[14] Bereft of viable options, the AJC somewhat reluctantly considered using Sack, the agent of the Whites, and the Russian Information Bureau.

Fully aware of the atrocities perpetrated by Kolchak's army, the Jewish stewards nonetheless gave Sack a hearing. Since it was in the latter's interest to incite opposition to the Reds, he enthusiastically urged the committee to bold action contradicting the Bolshevik image. He even suggested, albeit unrealistically, that American Jews intervene in Russia for the restoration of order. He reasoned too that if they aided non-Jewish Russians in the American army or sent relief to non-Jews in Russia, the latter would become more friendly to Jews and thereby weaken the identification of Jews with Bolshevism. Schiff, who corresponded regularly with Sack until a few months before his death, made several financial contributions to the Russian Information Bureau and was given the title of "honorary adviser." Doubtless the purpose of his contributions was to ensure that the articles disseminated by Sack, if not by his sponsors, were favorably disposed toward Russian Jews. To be sure, cooperation with Kolchak's agent could further infuriate the Reds, but it might perhaps protect Jews from the Whites and undermine the charge of Jew=Bolshevik.[15]

American Jews were thrust into the anti-Bolshevik spotlight in 1919, when Methodist minister George Simons testified before a Senate subcommittee on Bolshevik propaganda. Simons, who had served in Russia, talked seriously about a connection between Russian Jewish Bolshevik leaders and American Jews of New York's Lower East Side. He also charged that nineteen out of twenty Bolshevik propagandists in the United States were Jews. "I have no doubt in my mind," he added, "that the predominant element of the Bolsheviki movement in America is . . . the Yiddish [*sic*] of the East Side." Although in this case Simons exempted the "better class" of Jews, the stewards were infuriated, particularly since the subcommittee was favorably impressed by him. Schiff termed the "so-called testimony" outrageous and libelous, and Marshall offered a detailed rebuttal, along with a statement showing the incompatibility of Judaism and Bolshevism. Neither man denied that some Jews, but only a small number—Schiff called them "black sheep" that could be found among any people—favored the Communist experiment.[16]

The Red Scare of 1919–20, to which the Simons episode belonged, faded rapidly. Its anti-Semitic component, however, lived on and gained widespread public acceptance, largely through the publication and popularity of the *Protocols of the Elders of Zion* and the rantings of Henry Ford's *Dearborn Independent*. The auto king hammered away at the "international

Jew" for several years. Although Marshall pressed for an immediate campaign against Ford, the AJC deferred to Schiff. In one of the last letters of
his life, the banker counseled caution. "If we get into a controversy we shall
light a fire, which no one can foretell how it will become extinguished, and
I would strongly advise therefore that no notice be taken of [the *Dearborn
Independent*] and the attack will soon be forgotten." The attack was not
soon forgotten, but only after Schiff's death did the committee reverse its
stand and undertake to fight Ford publicly.[17]

The names of Kuhn, Loeb and Schiff figured prominently in anti-Semitic
attacks. After the war the myth of the powerful and rapacious international
Jewish banker as propagated by the *Protocols* was joined to the new charge
that Schiff had financed the Bolshevik revolution. In the *Dearborn Independent*, Schiff, along with the Warburgs, Bernard Baruch, and the Rothschilds, was accused of international machinations to control the world's
economy. Describing one of the subplots of the larger Jewish design, the
paper also blasted him for his alleged connection with the Bolsheviks.[18]
While Ford ran an American crusade, French sources in the 1920s spread
similar accusations. On Schiff in particular they picked up the Bolshevik
connection, claiming that Schiff had bankrolled the Communists to the
tune of $12 million. The same charges were regurgitated in the 1930s in a
vast array of anti-Semitic tracts, some of which confused Schiff's participation in the dissemination of revolutionary propaganda among Russian prisoners (1905) with the November revolution of 1917. Decades after World
War II the two themes still resonated. Pat Robertson rehashed them in *The
New World Order* (1991), but this time the sum allegedly given by Schiff to
the Bolsheviks was set at $20 million in gold![19]

In Conclusion

Once Schiff passed his seventy-second birthday, his health steadily worsened. Nevertheless, he did not permit his ailments to overshadow his business and commercial interests or even his recreation. Always an avid
walker, he still hiked for several hours at a time in Bar Harbor during August 1919, his last summer in Maine. The next thirteen months saw a rapid
physical deterioration. The doctors said that the hikes had overtaxed him,
but he attributed his cardiovascular problems at least in part to the depress-
ing state of world affairs. Despite his frailty he tried to keep to a normal
routine as long as possible. Even friends and associates were unaware of
how serious his ailments were. On Yom Kippur, September 22, 1920, he
was too weak to attend services, but he fasted the entire day. Three days
later he died at home.[20]

New York City paid its final tribute to Schiff, the first to die of the inner circle that included Marshall, Adler, Straus, and Sulzberger, on September 28, the day of the funeral.[21] The hearse, accompanied by the family, traveled thirty blocks down Fifth Avenue from the Schiff home to Temple Emanu-El on Forty-third Street. In keeping with Schiff's instructions, no eulogies were made at the Orthodox service conducted by Rabbis Joseph Silverman, H. G. Enelow, and Samuel Schulman. Newspaper editor Arthur Brisbane was impressed: "Happy is the man who like Mr. Schiff can forbid any praise at his funeral. He needs none."

Two thousand people filled the temple to capacity, with the governor and the mayor of New York leading a galaxy of non-Jewish as well as Jewish notables from the fields of business, politics, and philanthropy. Thousands more lined the streets, where they stood silently before and during the service. Since the funeral fell on the Jewish holiday of Sukkoth, many observant Jews had walked from the Lower East Side. Three hundred fifty policemen kept Fifth Avenue clear for the cortege; the block from Forty-third Street to Forty-second Street was closed entirely to traffic. After the forty-minute temple service, twelve motorcycle policemen led the procession to the Queensboro Bridge and then on to its final stop at a Brooklyn cemetery. Along the way representatives from various Jewish institutions fell into line and marched with the cortege.

The banker's death was reported in newspapers throughout America and in the foreign press. The *New York Times* ran the story in its lead article on page 1. Most accounts mentioned his background and family, some personal characteristics, and his rise to riches. His fortune was estimated at $50 million to $100 million, but careful not to feed the myth of the international Jewish banker, Brisbane speculated that Henry Ford made twice the amount in one year. Reporters retold Schiff's part in the Union Pacific affair and the Russo-Japanese War. Many commented too on his ardent Americanism and his philanthropic activities. The loyal *Times* implied that Schiff was more worthy a philanthropist than Carnegie or Rockefeller, for those men, unlike Schiff, became philanthropists only *after* they had built up their fortunes. He was, as one columnist wrote, the "model multimillionaire."

Newspaper stories as well as editorials eulogized the banker, and so did minutes and resolutions of numerous organizations. The family received countless messages of condolence, including one from President Wilson and one from ex-President Taft. Among the most poignant was that of Sir Ernest Cassel to Therese Schiff: "My warm sympathy goes out to you who have lost the best of husbands as I have lost the best of friends."[22]

Some newspapers commented on the contrast between a man who had lived in one of the richest sections of the city and the throngs of sincere mourners, Christians as well as Jews, from poorer neighborhoods. They were struck too by the responses of Jews on the Lower East Side—institutions that flew flags at half staff, merchants and pushcart peddlers who closed their shops or packed up their wares, those who flocked to synagogues to say *Kaddish* (the prayer for the dead), Orthodox women with bright brown wigs who walked to Fifth Avenue the day before the funeral to maintain a silent vigil in front of his house, those who displayed placards reading in English and Hebrew: "The East Side Mourns the Loss of Jacob Henry Schiff," and those who simply wept. Like the rabbis who dedicated their Sukkoth sermons to Schiff, they all paid tribute to the man who was recognized as the "greatest Jewish leader of the age."

If confirmation was ever needed of the strong rapport between Schiff and the eastern European masses, it was more than amply supplied at his death. He himself would have been touched by the genuine outpouring of respect and affection that his forty years of communal service had earned.

"The world will never be the same again," Schiff had gloomily observed at the onset of the war. Although his focus then was on the international scene, his words well suited the postwar condition of American Jews. Not only did his death mark the end of the "Schiff era" (1880–1920), a phrase coined by his successor at Montefiore,[23] but never again could a Schiff era, in the generic sense, be replicated. To be sure, some echoes of Schiff's leadership resonated in the activities of Louis Marshall and Felix Warburg, but neither wielded the same influence on both American and European Jewish issues. Marshall's immersion in Jewish affairs approximated Schiff's, and the quip that in the 1920s Jews lived under "Marshall law" was eminently appropriate; but the attorney lacked the power of wealth and the network attendant upon international banking. Warburg had the wealth but not the all-encompassing understanding of or sympathy with Judaism or Jews. Neither one displayed the combination of personality traits that underlay Schiff's leadership—aristocratic but businesslike, forceful but sympathetic, aggressive but kindhearted, arrogant but hurt by harsh criticism, boldly innovative but respectful of expert advice. Nor did either man share Schiff's almost religious belief that his leadership was ordained by a higher power.

The totality of Schiff's activities—a seamless web of Jewish defense, philanthropy, and diplomatic lobbying—brought the age of individualism in American Jewish communal affairs to a dramatic climax. His pioneering efforts on behalf of a minority group, newly exposed to freedom and modernity and buffeted by the forces of assimilation, aimed at ensuring Jewish security and survival in a democratic nation. Schiff had few precedents on which to draw, for the American experience differed greatly from that in western Europe. Yet the essence of his overall plan—defense, integration, and unity—and the tactics he used were not unheard of in Jewish history.

One medieval historian's description of the power and communal vision of Jewish notables in the golden age of Spanish Jewry fits, with but minor emendations, Schiff's views on leadership. The description reads:

> Much of their [the notables'] power was owing . . . to the ability of the Jewish leadership to mobilize the Jewish community in support of the causes which their Gentile masters espoused. This meant that they could "deliver" the Jewish community, which in turn depended on their ability to keep the Jewish community loyal to themselves. The leadership depended on a Jewish community that could look to them with admiration and gratitude for ensuring their community a security and sense of distinction . . . a sense of greatness and a sense of collective vision. By endowing institutions and creating agencies through which people of ability could find the means to give expression to their talents, they created a communal fabric where people of the most diverse pursuits felt related one to the other, to the community at large, and to the Jewish people as a whole.[24]

The way in which Schiff usually pursued the "collective vision" did not, however, fit post–World War I realities. As in the prewar economic scene, where bankers had flourished in a largely laissez-faire society, so too in Jewish matters, whether charities or problems of discrimination, initiative and control rested primarily with wealthy individual volunteers who were accountable only to themselves. And just as the early captains of industry steadily lost ground to government control during the Progressive era and the war, so too were the "captains" of national communal institutions increasingly eclipsed by faceless, centralized organizations and federations. The managerial revolution that accompanied economic concentration was experienced in communal affairs, too. In both areas the power to shape policy was shifting from the owners of corporations or, in the case of the community, from individual and charismatic stewards to executive managers and paid professionals. More and more, the Jewish agencies they serviced abandoned the Schiff-era practice of organization from the top down. The American Jewish Congress, for example, which became a permanent organization in 1922, boasted a democratic base and a commitment to antielitism. Four years later, the president of the Philadelphia Federation stated unequivocally that "there must be . . . a democratization of the Federation as to make it wholly representative of the people who supported it." Simultaneously, the banker, who in Schiff's day stood at the top of the economic ladder, lost much of his prestige, first in the Pujo investigation of the money trust in 1912–13 and later in the wake of the market crash in 1929.[25]

The new style of leadership kept pace with the radically changed face of American Jewry. In 1920 the Jewish population was 3.6 million or more than three times what it had been in 1900. Jews now constituted 3.4 percent of the American population, compared to 1.4 percent twenty years earlier. The number of new immigrants who arrived in 1921 totaled over 119,000 (it had peaked in 1914 with 138,000) but dropped dramatically under the quota system introduced by Congress during that decade. While large numbers of prewar immigrants were moving horizontally and branching out from the urban ghettos into the second and third areas of settlement, so too were they moving vertically up the economic ladder. Aspiring to middle-class status, many of them—and more of their children—proceeded to exchange factory labor and the proletariat class for a higher education and for white-collar jobs and the professions. Rapidly acculturating, they ceased to be the wards of the establishment to be led "for their own good." The despotism of 52 William Street, no matter how benevolent or well intentioned, became a vestigial reminder of the past.[26]

Schiff himself had yielded more than once to the forces of rational organization and democratization. His experience with the federation movement and with the *kehillah* and American Jewish Congress convinced him of the need to adapt to changes within a rapidly maturing community. Moreover, his support of elitist rule, by definition undemocratic and therefore un-American, logically contradicted his demands for total Americanization on the part of his fellow Jews. To be sure, he foresaw the shift in communal leadership from the Germans to the new immigrants years before World War I. But his predictions on the coming of age of the eastern Europeans were borne out in the 1920s, perhaps even sooner than he had expected.

Economic progress, larger numbers, and acculturation also made for greater fragmentation. Despite the abundance of national organizations alongside the local, self-directed religious, fraternal, and cultural institutions that defied centralization, no single individual or agency could claim to speak for the entire group. Marshall, the president of the AJC, who, after Schiff's death, came closest to being a Jewish *national* leader, died in 1929. In a divided community no successor was found or even sought, and Schiff's goal of a united Jewry, which often was effected through his persona alone, steadily dimmed. Nor did the 1920s prove a time for social experimentation and Schiff-like designs of the magnitude of the Galveston project, immigrant charities, or theological seminaries. For one thing, the mood of bitterness and cynicism that followed the war successfully quenched the optimism of a Schiff and faith in the powers of rational enlightenment. Moreover, although the war raised American Jewish power in international Jewish affairs just as it set America center stage in world diplomacy, the government no longer considered appeals based on humanitarian diplomacy. When anti-Semitism swelled during the "Anglo-Saxon decade"[27]—in the attacks of Henry Ford and the Ku Klux Klan, the debates on immigration restriction, and the hardened patterns of social exclusion—American Jews recoiled. Like the United States itself, they looked inward, more fearful of public opinion and less concerned with fellow Jews in Europe or Palestine.

In the summer of 1919, Schiff called Warburg, Marshall, and Adler to a meeting at his home. According to Adler, the purpose was to consider the general situation of Jews abroad. Adler offered few details about the long discussion that took place, but it is very likely that the men talked about the Versailles treaties (Marshall and Adler had returned from Paris only a few weeks before) and the persecutions in eastern Europe. Any defense strategy they agreed upon doubtless concerned the AJC; both Schiff and Marshall wanted a stronger committee and opposed the perpetuation of an American Jewish Congress. The men also discussed the "chaotic" situation of American Jewry and the question of leadership. Adler suggested a division of labor: Warburg to lead the Joint Distribution Committee, Marshall to run the AJC, and Adler to oversee Jewish education in the United States. Although rejected, the plan, which was tantamount to the carving up of Schiff's empire, testified to the expanded needs of the community. It was a tacit acknowledgment as well that no single individual could replace Schiff in the overall direction of American Jewry.[28]

Notes

Most of the material for this study comes from the Schiff Papers in the American Jewish Archives in Cincinnati. Microfilm reels 676–97 contain drafts of Cyrus Adler's biography of Schiff and countless letters written by Schiff that were chosen from the 80,000 amassed by Adler and Schiff's son. Before 1914, Schiff saved hardly any of the letters to him, but fuller records were kept for 1914–1920. Those are found in reels 1976–86 of the archives. Other files of Schiff papers exist in the archives of the Jewish Theological Seminary in New York and Jerusalem, the American Jewish Committee, and the American Jewish Historical Society. The collected papers of a few of Schiff's associates also contain useful material.

Except for the microfilm reels at the American Jewish Archives, the location of manuscript files is indicated in the notes for each chapter. Relevant material in Adler's first drafts of the biography which appear in reels 676–97, is cited as CA MSS, with Adler's pagination where available.

The following abbreviations have been used in the Notes:

AH	*American Hebrew*
AJC	American Jewish Committee
AJHS	American Jewish Historical Society
AJRC	American Jewish Relief Committee
IRO	Industrial Removal Office
JTS	Jewish Theological Seminary
NCRSRM	National Committee for Relief of Sufferers by Russian Massacres
NYT	*New York Times*
PAJHS	*Publications of the American Jewish Historical Society*

Preface (Notes to Page xi)

1. "The Greatest American Jewish Leaders," *American Jewish History* 78 (Dec. 1988): 169–200.
2. The problem is presented in John Higham, ed., *Ethnic Leadership in America* (Baltimore, 1978), introduction; Benny Kraut, "American Jewish Leaders," *American Jewish History* 78 (Dec. 1988): 201–36.

1. The Making of a Leader (Notes to Pages 1–40)

1. Reel 685, memo by Cyrus Adler, 29 July 1926; reel 678, CA MSS, chap. 13; reel 694, Schiff to J. Rosenwald, 18 Apr. 1918; Ira Robinson, ed., *Cyrus Adler:*

Selected Letters, 2 vols. (Philadelphia, 1985), 2:39–40; Frieda S. Warburg, *Reminiscences of a Long Life* (New York, 1956), pp. 4, 8, 10. A letter from Clara Schiff to her son, 23 Apr. 1875, in Warburg, p. 10.

2. Warburg, *Reminiscences*, p. 4; reel 680, CA MSS, pp. 1204–5, 1231; reel 682, CA MSS, p. 1239; reel 693, CA MSS. Schiff's donations in memory of parents were made as early as 1881 and were also included in his will. *AH*, 13 Jan. 1881; reel 694, Schiff's will.

3. Cyrus Adler, *Jacob H. Schiff*, 2 vols. (Garden City, N.Y., 1929), 1:2–3; Paul Arnsberg, *Jakob H. Schiff* (Frankfurt, 1969), pp. 9–10; Gertrude Hirschler, ed., *Ashkenaz* (New York, 1980), pp. 284–85; Gotthard Deutsch, *American Israelite*, 4 Jan. 1917; reel 685, L. Jung to C. Adler, 11 Apr. 1927.

4. Robert Liberles, *Religious Conflict in Social Context* (Westport, Conn., 1985), chap. 3; reel 696, CA MSS, pp. 1–3.

5. Max Heller, "Samson Raphael Hirsch," Central Conference of American Rabbis, *Yearbook* 18 (1908): 197; Arnsberg, *Schiff*, pp. 10–11; Adler, *Schiff*, 1:4; reel 694, Schiff to H. Spaulding, 11 June 1920; Cyrus Adler, "Jacob Henry Schiff," *American Jewish Year Book* 23 (1921–22): 23, 40; reel 23 (JTS archives), CA MSS; *Magazine of Wall Street*, 16 Oct. 1920.

6. Deutsch, *American Israelite*, 4 Jan. 1917; Arnsberg (*Schiff*, p. 23) posits that the spirit of Frankfurt underlay all of Schiff's activities; reel 685, S. Ehrmann to C. Adler, 3 Aug. 1928; reel 680, CA MSS, p. 1210; reel 693, Schiff to M. Hirsch [10 Feb. 1893].

7. Adler, *Schiff*, 1:4–5, 7; Warburg, *Reminiscences*, p. 4, 8; reel 685, memo by Cyrus Adler, 29 July 1926; reel 693, Schiff to E. Cassel, 13 Oct. 1896. Many years later, when his own son departed for an extended stay in Europe, Jacob first understood how difficult the parting had been for his parents.

8. Avraham Barkai, *Branching Out* (New York, 1994), esp. chap. 6.

9. Reel 680, memo by Paul Warburg, p. 1234.

10. Adler, *Schiff*, 1:6–7; reel 688, memo by Max Bonn, 29 June 1926.

11. *NYT*, 16 Feb. 1914; Adler, *Schiff*, 1:7; Arnsberg, *Schiff*, pp. 11–12; reel 684, memo by Henry Budge, 10 Oct. 1926; Fritz Redlich, *The Molding of American Banking*, 2 vols. (New York, 1951), 2:386.

12. Warburg, *Reminiscences*, p. 8; reel 23, Schiff to A. Schulman, 30 Mar. 1910; Jeffrey Potter, *Men, Money and Magic* (New York, 1926), pp. 22–23; reel 685, Schiff to E. Cassel, 2 May 1892.

13. Reel 694, CA MSS on family; reel 693, CA MSS; Moses Rischin, *The Promised City* (New York, 1964), chap.1.

14. Jacob R. Marcus, *To Count a People* (Lanham, Md., 1990), pp. 149–50; *AH*, 1 June 1900; Warburg, *Reminiscences*, p. 121. Schiff served on the board of the YMHA; Adler, *Schiff*, 2:59–60. Another young man of a prominent Jewish family, Myer S. Isaacs, also alluded in his unpublished diary, 1868 (American Jewish Archives), to unfulfilled Jewish cultural needs.

15. Adler, *Schiff*, 1:8–9; Warburg, *Reminiscences*, pp. 9–10, 45.

16. "Many-Sided Jacob H. Schiff," *New York World Magazine*, 16 Apr. 1905; reel 685, memo of Cyrus Adler's coversation with Mortimer Schiff and Felix Warburg, 8 July 1927; *Solomom Loeb: A Memorial* (privately printed, n.d., courtesy of David T. Schiff), pp. 3–13; Vincent P. Carosso, "A Financial Elite," *American*

Jewish Historical Quarterly 66 (Sept. 1976): 76; Adler, *Schiff,* 1:11–16; Warburg, *Reminiscences,* pp. 11–14, 45, 56–57; James P. Warburg, *The Long Road Home* (Garden City, N.Y., 1964), pp. 9–10; Leon Harris, *Merchant Princes* (New York, 1979), p. 44.

17. Barry E. Supple, "A Business Elite," *Business History Review* 31 (summer 1957): 143–78; Adler, *Schiff,* 1:155–58; Edwin P. Hoyt, *The Guggenheims and the American Dream* (New York, 1957), pp. 145, 194. William Miller, who discusses the social background of 190 outstanding business leaders at the turn of the century, lists three Jewish firms: American Smelting and Refining (Guggenheim), Kuhn, Loeb (Schiff), and Speyer & Co (James Speyer). William Miller, ed., *Men in Business* (New York, 1962), pp. 313–19.

18. John Kobler, *Otto the Magnificent* (New York, 1988), p. 21; Adler, *Schiff,* 1:16; both Kobler (p. 21) and Ron Chernow (*The Warburgs* [New York, 1993], p. 49) point up the striking differences between Schiff and both Warburg and Kahn; Adler, *Schiff,* 1:16.

19. Adler, *Schiff,* 1:16–21; reel 685, Schiff to E. Cassel, 26 Apr. 1896; reel 676, Schiff to E. Cassel, 18 Jan. 1897; Supple, "Business Elite," p. 164; Priscilla M. Roberts, "A Conflict of Loyalties," *Studies in the American Jewish Experience,* vol. 2 (Lanham, Md., 1984), pp. 3–4; Carosso, "Financial Elite," p. 87; "Mr. Kuhn and Mr. Loeb," *Fortune* 2 (1930): 89ff.

20. Carosso, "Financial Elite," pp. 77–79.

21. Philip Cowen, *Prejudice against the Jew* (New York, 1928); Todd M. Endelman, *Radical Assimilation in English Jewish History* (Bloomington, Ind., 1990); W. E. Mosse, *The German-Jewish Economic Elite* (Oxford, 1989); Naomi W. Cohen, *Encounter with Emancipation* (Philadelphia, 1984), p. 260.

22. When not abroad, the Schiffs usually divided the summer between a house that they owned in New Jersey and one that they rented in Maine. Warburg, *Reminiscences,* p. 58; on the Schiffs in Maine, see Judith S. Goldstein, *Crossing Lines* (New York, 1992).

23. "Many-Sided Jacob H. Schiff," *New York World Magazine,* 16 Apr. 1905; Warburg, *Reminiscences,* pp. 46, 51–52; Adler, *Schiff,* 2:330–1; *AH,* 8 Oct. 1920; reel 684, notes by Robert De Forest.

24. Frederick Lewis Allen, *The Lords of Creation* (New York, 1966), pp. 82–97; Priscilla M. Roberts, "The American 'Eastern Establishment' and World War I" (Ph.D. diss., University of Cambridge, 1981), introduction and chap. 1.

25. Kobler, *Otto the Magnificent,* p. 19; Carosso, "Financial Elite," p. 81; Ron Chernow, *The House of Morgan* (New York, 1990), p. 89.

26. *Solomon Loeb,* p. 12; Warburg, *Reminiscences,* pp. 13, 56–57; reel 696, Schiff to T. Coolidge, 1 Sept. 1899; reel 687, Schiff to M. Bonn, 6 Jan. 1904; Adler, *Schiff,* 1:14.

27. Reel 679, CA MSS, p. 22; reel 676, Schiff to J. Hanauer, 18 Aug. 1919; Barnard Powers, "Jacob H. Schiff: Wall Street's Grand Old Man," *Magazine of Wall Street,* 28 Sept. 1918; Carosso, "Financial Elite," p. 79.

28. Carosso, "Financial Elite," pp. 80, 82; *Money Trust Investigation, Financial and Monetary Conditions in the United States, H.R.* 1593, 62nd Cong., 3rd Sess., 1913, pt. 23, pp. 1661–71; Redlich, *Molding of American Banking,* 2:386.

29. Carosso, "Financial Elite," pp. 81–82.

30. Albro Martin, *James J. Hill and the Opening of the Northwest* (New York, 1976), p. 345; Adler, *Schiff*, 1:12–13; Carosso, "Financial Elite," pp. 78–81; Roberts, "A Conflict of Loyalties," p. 5; reel 696, CA MSS, p. 935; Thomas C. Cochran and William Miller, *The Age of Enterprise* (New York, 1961), p. 194.

31. Eduard Rosenbaum, "M. M. Warburg & Co.," Leo Baeck Institute, *Year Book* 7 (1962): 137; reel 688, memo by Max Bonn, 29 June 1926.

32. Kurt Grunwald, "'Windsor-Cassel': The Last Court Jew," Leo Baeck Institute, *Year Book* 14 (1969): 119–61; Cecil Roth, "The Court Jews of Edwardian England," *Jewish Social Studies* 5 (Oct. 1943): 362–63; entry for Cassel, *Dictionary of National Biography*, 1912–21, pp. 97–100.

33. Reel 676, CA MSS, 14 May 1884; reel 686, 14 Mar. 1893; reel 688, Schiff to E. Cassel, 23 Sept. 1880; reel 693, CA MSS, Schiff to E. Cassel, 29 Aug. 1880, 15 Apr. 1894; Vincent P. Carosso, *The Morgans* (Cambridge, Mass., 1987), p. 419.

34. Warburg, *Reminiscences*, p. 61; Cyrus Adler Papers (JTS archives), C. Adler to M. Kohler, 26 Nov. 1928; Kobler, *Otto the Magnificent*, p. 22.

35. Adler, *Schiff*, 1: 83.

36. Most of vol. 1 of Adler, *Schiff*, deals with railroad activities; Carosso, *Morgans*, p. 247; Carosso, "Financial Elite," p. 81; Martin, *James J. Hill*, p. 273; *Kuhn, Loeb & Co.: A Century of Investment Banking* (New York, 1967), p. 9; reel 686, Schiff to H. Tatnall, 27 Jan. 1907.

37. Carosso, "Financial Elite," pp. 88–89; Paul B. Trescott, *Financing American Enterprise* (New York, 1963), pp. 125–26; Cochran and Miller, *Age of Enterprise*, pp. 188–92, 196–97; John Chamberlain, *The Enterprising Americans* (New York, 1963), pp. 166–74; Redlich, *Molding of American Banking*, 2:384.

38. Redlich, *Molding of American Banking*, 2:386; *Money Trust Investigation*, pt. 23, pp. 1697–99; Powers, "Schiff"; Chamberlain, *Enterprising Americans*, p. 181; reel 681, CA MSS, p. 290; reel 696, CA MSS, p. 1047.

39. Martin, *James J. Hill*, pp. 284, 345, 378, 394, 406, 436–38; Warburg, *Reminiscences*, pp. 62–63; reel 686, Schiff to S. Rea, 13 Apr. 1903; Kobler, *Otto the Magnificent*, p.21.

40. Adler, *Schiff*, 1:42, 85–87, 91–92, 107–9; reel 680, Schiff to E. Cassel, 14 Aug. 1895; reel 685, Schiff to J. Hill, 28, 31 Dec. 1894; Ben B. Seligman, *Business and Businessmen in American History* (New York, 1971), p. 149; Carosso, *Morgans*, pp. 382–85.

41. Carosso, *Morgans*, pp. 386–88; George Kennan, *E. H. Harriman*, 2 vols. (Boston, 1922), 1:118–20; George Wheeler, *Pierpont Morgan and Friends* (Englewood Cliffs, N.J., 1973), p. 247; Matthew Josephson, *The Robber Barons* (New York, 1934), p. 401; reel 687, Schiff to S. Rea, 23 Sept. 1904.

42. Reel 685, Schiff to E. Cassel, 18 Oct. 1895; reel 689, Schiff to E. Cassel, 25 Nov. 1895; Kennan, *Harriman*, 1:122–26; Chamberlain, *Enterprising Americans*, p. 175; reel 694, CA MSS, memo by Paul Warburg, 20 Nov. 1925.

43. Adler, *Schiff*, 1:117–21; reel 687, Schiff to P. Warburg, 21 Aug. 1906; C. M. Keys, "A 'Corner' in Pacific Railroads," *World's Work* 9 (Feb. 1905): 5818–19; Seligman, *Business and Businessmen*, pp. 153ff; Kennan, *Harriman*, 2:370.

44. Reel 676, Schiff to R. Fleming, 1 Sept. 1897; reel 680, Schiff to L. Gage, 17 Nov. 1897; reel 687, Schiff to E. Cassel, 27 Oct. 1897; reel 688, Schiff to R.

Fleming, 14 July, 1897; reel 689, Schiff to E. Cassel, 6 Aug. 1897, 9 Mar. 1898; Kennan, *Harriman*, 1:127–29.

45. Unless otherwise noted, all material for this and the next four paragraphs is from Kennan, *Harriman*, vol. 1, chap. 11; Martin, *James J. Hill*, 485–509; Carosso, *Morgans*, 474–78.

46. Reel 687, Schiff to R. Fleming, 28 May 1901.

47. Reel 687, Schiff to E. Cassel, 15 May 1901.

48. Ibid.

49. Ibid.; reel 687, Schiff to R. Fleming, 28 May 1901; Chernow, *House of Morgan*, p. 91; Adler, *Schiff*, 1:106.

50. Reel 687, Schiff to E. Cassel, 15 May 1901; Adler, *Schiff*, 1:106.

51. Kennan, *Harriman*, 1:366–67; reel 696, recollections of Otto Kahn [1925], in CA MSS, pp. 1818–24 (Kahn's account differs slightly from Schiff's letters on dates and places); reel 687, Schiff to E. Cassel, 15 May 1901.

52. See for example Martin, *James J. Hill*, 494–504; Carosso, *Morgans*, 474–76; Kennan, *Harriman*, 1:307–17.

53. Reel 696, recollections of Kahn in CA MSS, pp. 1818–24.

54. Reel 687, Schiff to E. Cassel, 15 May 1901; Carosso, *Morgans*, p. 477; Martin, *James J. Hill*, p. 504.

55. "The Wall-Street Smash," *Literary Digest* 22 (18 May 1901): 598–99; Josephson, *Robber Barons*, 441–44; reel 696, recollections of Kahn in CA MSS, p. 1824; reel 687, Schiff to R. Fleming, 28 May 1901; Schiff's letter to Morgan, 16 May 1901, in Adler, *Schiff*, 1:102–7.

56. Kennan, *Harriman*, 1:318–31; Carosso, *Morgans*, p. 478; Martin, *James J. Hill*, pp. 508–10.

57. Reel 687, Schiff to E. Cassel, 11 Nov. 1901.

58. *NYT*, 23 Mar. 1901, 21 Jan. 1915; reel 696, Schiff to G. Kennan, 16 May 1916; *Report of the U.S. Industrial Commission* (Washington, D.C., 1901), 9:769–77.

59. Reel 687, Schiff to L. Littauer, 24 Mar. 1902, to E. Harriman, 15 Apr. 1902; Adler, *Schiff*, 1:45, 111–12.

60. Reel 687, Schiff to H. Schueler, 26 Feb. 1901, to S. Rea, 13 Apr. 1903; reel 676, Schiff to E. Cassel, 16 Apr. 1902; reel 685, Schiff to E. Cassel 24 Apr. 1903.

61. Carosso, *Morgans*, pp. 453–54.

62. Ibid., chap. 15; Martin, *James J. Hill*, pp. 511–30.

63. "Many-Sided Jacob H. Schiff," *New York World Magazine*, 16 Apr. 1905.

64. Reel 685, Schiff to E. Cassel, 24 Apr. 1903; reel 687, to H. Schueler, 26 Feb. 1901, to S. Rea, 13 Apr. 1903; *NYT*, 15 Apr. 1904; Gabriel Kolko, *The Triumph of Conservatism* (Chicago, 1967), pp. 67–68.

65. Kennan, *Harriman*, vol. 2, chaps. 25–26.

66. Reel 687, Schiff to E. Cassel, 1 Mar., 1 Apr., 16 May 1907; Adler, *Schiff*, 1:132–34.

67. Kobler, *Otto the Magnificent*, pp. 46–48; *NYT*, 5, 10 Apr. 1907; Adler, *Schiff*, 1:132–34.

68. Reel 687, Schiff to E. Cassel, 11, 16 May 1907, to R. Fleming, 24 May 1907, to H. Schueler, 24 July 1907; Adler, *Schiff*, 1:114–15, 118–21. The Union Pacific was hit again in 1912, when Taft ordered the railroad to release its stock in the Southern Pacific.

69. Reel 686, Schiff to W. Taft, 19 May 1905; Adler, *Schiff*, 1:43–50; *NYT*, 27, 28 Mar. 1907; Joseph B. Bishop, *Theodore Roosevelt and His Time*, 2 vols. (New York, 1920), 2:40–41.

70. "Many-Sided Jacob H. Schiff," *New York World Magazine*, 16 Apr. 1905; Holland, "Jacob Schiff the New Money King," *Philadelphia Press*, 22 Aug. 1903; Robert N. Burnett, "Captains of Industry" (pt. 12), *Cosmopolitan* 34 (Apr. 1903): 699–701; Keys, "Pacific Railroads," pp. 5818–19; Gilbert Klaperman, *The Story of Yeshiva University* (London, 1969), p. 79. In 1918, *Forbes Magazine* put Schiff's annual income at $2.5 million. His wealth, estimated again at $50 million, placed him among the thirty richest persons in America. B. C. Forbes, "America's Thirty Richest," *Forbes Magazine*, 2 Mar. 1918, pp. 637, 665.

71. Reel 686, Schiff to H. Tatnall, 27 Jan. 1907; reel 689, Schiff to E. Cassel, 16 Apr. 1902; *Money Trust Investigation*, pt. 23, p. 1688; Adler, *Schiff*, 1:175–80; for examples of cooperation between Morgan and Kuhn, Loeb, see Carosso, *Morgans*, pp. 248, 266, 273, 386, 452, 471, 494, 501, 526–27, 773–74, 814–15.

72. Redlich, *Molding of American Banking*, 2:379; Chernow, *House of Morgan*, p. 90; Martin, *James J. Hill*, p. 284; Kolko, *Triumph of Conservatism*, p. 144; Cochran and Miller, *Age of Enterprise*, p. 194; E. Digby Baltzell, *The Protestant Establishment* (New York, 1966), p. 119. (The Morgan Papers were closed to me.) Morgan's son went further; he hired detectives to investigate what he thought was a Jewish conspiracy against him. John D. Forbes, *J. P. Morgan, Jr.* (Charlottesville, Va., 1981), p. 115.

73. Arnsberg, *Schiff*, p. 19; *Kuhn, Loeb*, pp. 13–14; Redlich, *Molding of American Banking*, 2:386; John Davis, *The Guggenheims* (New York, 1978), pp. 102–3, 107; reel 688, Schiff to M. Schiff, 1 May 1905; Adler, *Schiff*, 1:155–60, 170–74.

74. Reel 676, Schiff to E. Cassel, 24 Apr. 1903; Adler, *Schiff*, 1:15, 28–41; *New York Evening Post*, 13 Oct. 1926; *NYT*, 5, 9 Jan. 1906.

75. The most reliable source for Schiff's family life is Frieda Warburg's *Reminiscences*.

76. *Testimony Taken before the Joint Committee of the Senate and Assembly of the State of New York . . . to Investigate . . . the . . . Life Insurance Companies* (Albany, N.Y., 1906), 2:999–1000; R. Carlyle Buley, *The Equitable Life Assurance Society of the United States*, 2 vols. (New York, 1967), vol. 1, chap. 7.

77. For this and the next paragraph, see Buley, *Equitable*, vol. 1, chap. 7; Louis Filler, *Crusaders for American Liberalism* (New York, 1961), chap. 15; *NYT*, 4 April, 6 June 1905; reel 688, Schiff to S. Rea, 3 Mar. 1905, to W. King, 7 June 1905; Adler, *Schiff*, 1:188–89.

78. Reel 677, Schiff to E. Cassel, 4 Apr. 1905; reel 681, Schiff to T. Roosevelt, 26 July 1905, to G. Cleveland, 14 July 1905; reel 693, Schiff to R. Fleming, 13 July 1905; reel 688, Schiff's letters in February 1905 to S. Untermyer, W. Laffan, T. Cuyler, A. Ochs, and E. Root, and Schiff to A. Farquhar, 5 Apr. 1905, to A. Markowitz, 3 Oct. 1905, to H. Schueler, 14 July 1905, to O. Villard, [June or July] 1905, to A. Parker, 29 Mar. 1905, to M. Schiff, 8 May 1905, to L. Wiley, 18 July 1905, to S. Rea, 3 Mar. 1905.

79. Reel 688, Schiff to A. Farquhar, 5 Apr. 1905, to D. Todd, 14 June 1905, to A. Ochs, 28 Feb. 1905, to O. Kahn, 27 July 1905; reel 693, Schiff to R. Fleming, 13 July 1905.

80. Buley, *Equitable*, 1:675–94; Merlo J. Pusey, *Charles Evans Hughes*, 2 vols. (New York, 1951), vol. 1, chap. 15; *Testimony Taken before the Joint Committee*, 3:2438.

81. *Testimony Taken before the Joint Committee*, 2:999–1051; *NYT*, 30 Sept. 1905.

82. *Jewish American*, 6 Oct. 1905; *New York Sun*, 10 Jan. 1907; *Testimony Taken before the Joint Committee*, 3:2437–58; Charles M. Destler, "The Opposition of American Businessmen to Social Control during the 'Gilded Age'," *Mississippi Valley Historical Review* 39 (Mar. 1953): 644.

83. Filler, *Crusaders for American Liberalism*, pp. 189–90; *Testimony Taken before the Joint Committee*, 7:75–119; reel 688, Schiff to J. Wilson, 2 Oct. 1905; to H. Schueler, 27 Oct. 1905.

84. Reel 677, Schiff to E. Clouston, 27 Apr. 1896, to G. Perkins, 2 Sept. 1912; reel 685, Schiff to J. Hill, 9 Nov. 1896; reel 686, Schiff to R. Fleming, 8 Nov. 1912.

85. The references in the Schiff papers to the tariff and the currency are too numerous to list. See Schiff, "Relation of a Central Bank to the Elasticity of the Currency," *Annals of the American Academy of Political and Social Science* 31 (1908): 372–76; Adler, *Schiff*, 1:260–88, 303–7; Matthew Josephson, *The Politicos* (New York, 1968), pp. 530–31, 537; *NYT*, 8 Jan., 2 Feb., 6 Aug. 1906, 12 Nov. 1910.

86. Yonathan Shapiro, "American Jews in Politics," *American Jewish Historical Quarterly* 55 (Dec. 1965): 205; reel 1977, McAdoo file; *NYT*, 27 Oct., 7, 8, 12, 17 Nov., 24 Dec. 1913; Adler, *Schiff*, 1:286–91.

87. Reel 677, Schiff to E. Cassel, 9 June 1903, to S. Low, 14 Dec. 1908, to A. Woods, 19 Aug. 1919; reel 685, Schiff to R. Fleming, 1 Mar. 1897; reel 681, CA MSS, pp. 463–66; reel 1980, Schiff to D. Lyon, 19 Sept. 1916; reel 686, Schiff to E. Cassel, 28 Sept. 1911; *Industrial Relations, Final Report and Testimony . . . [of] the Commission on Industrial Relations*, 64th Cong., 1st sess., 1916, 8:7530–31; Adler, *Schiff*, 1:291–93, 295–98; Lillian Wald, "Jacob H. Schiff," *Survey*, 2 Oct. 1920; *NYT*, 4 Sept. 1916.

88. Reel 676, Schiff to Mr. Japhet, 12 Dec. 1910; reel 677, CA MSS, R. Adamson to M. Schiff, 20 Nov. 1905.

89. Reel 676, Schiff to P. Warburg, 28 June 1906; reel 677, Schiff to J. Mottu, 4 Feb. 1910; reel 686, Schiff to S. Hill, 27 Sept. 1910, to E. Cassel, 28 Sept. 1911; *NYT*, 17 May 1905, 4 June 1911; Adler, *Schiff*, 1:290.

90. Reel 680, Schiff to E. Cassel, 1 Apr. 1907; reel 686, Schiff to E. Cassel, 25 Aug. 1907; reel 687, Schiff to R. Fleming, 18 Apr. 1907; reel 688, Schiff to E. Cassel, 4 Nov. 1907.

91. Thomas C. Cochran, *The American Business System* (New York, 1957), pp. 83–86. Unless otherwise noted, the material for this and the next two paragraphs is from *Money Trust Investigation*, pt. 23, Schiff's testimony, pp. 1660–94, and Carosso, *Morgans*, pp. 624–41.

92. *Money Trust Investigation*, testimony of George Baker in pt. 21, testimony of Henry Davison in pt. 25. Schiff clashed with Untermyer again in hearings before the Industrial Relations Commission of 1915. There he called Untermyer's statement that Morgan and Kuhn, Loeb controlled a large number of railroads "sheer nonsense." *NYT*, 21 Jan. 1915.

93. Carosso, "Financial Elite," p. 83; Louis D. Brandeis, *Other People's Money* (New York, 1932), pp. 170–75.

94. Reel 1977, S. Wolf to Schiff, 13 July 1914.
95. Reel 685, Schiff to P. Warburg, 23 Dec. 1895; *Kuhn, Loeb*, p. 17; *New York Evening Post*, 13 Oct. 1926; Adler, *Schiff*, vol. 1, chap. 6.
96. Gary D. Best, "Jacob Schiff's Early Interest in Japan," *American Jewish History* 69 (Mar. 1980): 355–59.
97. Daniel Gutwein, "Jacob H. Schiff and the Financing of the Russo-Japanese War" (Hebrew)," *Zion* 54 (1989): 321–50; Gary D. Best, "Financing a Foreign War," *American Jewish Historical Quarterly* 61 (June 1972): 313–24; A. J. Sherman, "German Jewish Bankers in World Politics," Leo Baeck Institute, *Year Book* 28 (1983): 69–71; reel 681, memo by Paul Warburg; reel 689, Schiff to E. Cassel, 15 May 1904; *New York Evening Post*, 13 Oct. 1926; Adler, *Schiff*, 1:231–32.
98. "Looking Back 90 Years," *Forward*, 29 Mar. 1996; Jacob H. Schiff, *Our Journey to Japan* (privately printed, New York, 1907); Carosso, *Morgans*, pp. 526–27; Adler, *Schiff*, 1:213–40; Chernow, *Warburgs*, pp. 110–11; David Kranzler, *Japanese, Nazis, and Jews* (New York, 1976), pp. 176, 195–97, 210, 240–41, 276, 330; Margaret Grodinsky, "An American Banker in the Mikado's Capital," *Japan Society Newsletter*, 43 (Apr. 1996): 4–7, courtesy of Robert S. Rifkind.
99. Adler, *Schiff*, 1:237–39; reel 22 (JTS archives), Schiff to Count Okuma, 23 Feb. 1909; reel 677, Schiff to K. Takahashi, 24 Dec. 1908; reels 1977–1986, files of Takahashi correspondence; Jacob H. Schiff, "Japan after the War," *North American Review*, no. 597 (Aug. 1906): 161–68; *NYT*, 22 May 1908, 16 Mar. 1912.
100. Reel 677, CA MSS, p. 20; Kennan, *Harriman*, vol. 2, chap. 18; Tyler Dennett, *Roosevelt and the Russo-Japanese War* (Garden City, N.Y., 1925), pp. 312–13.
101. *NYT*, 16 Mar. 1912; reel 677, Schiff to K. Takahashi, 18 June 1915, to F. Polk, 10 Oct. 1916, to R. Lansing, 12 Mar. 1917; reel 1983, Schiff to J. Wilson, 30 Apr. 1917.
102. Best, "Schiff's Early Interest in Japan," p. 359; reel 677, CA MSS, pp. 3–9, Schiff to J. Wilson, 30 Apr. 1895; reel 685, J. Foster to Schiff, 2 Nov. 1894, Schiff to J. Foster, 5 Nov. 1894, to E. Cassel, 25 Apr. 1895; reel 689, Schiff to E. Cassel, 30 Nov. 1904; Carosso, *Morgans*, pp. 426–27.
103. Reel 677, Schiff to J. Wilson, 5 Feb. 1901; Howard K. Beale, *Theodore Roosevelt and the Rise of America to World Power* (Baltimore, 1956), pp. 200–211; Carosso, *Morgans*, pp. 428–29.
104. Reel 677, Schiff to K. Takahashi, 24, 28 Dec. 1908; Adler, *Schiff*, 1:246–48; reel 694, Schiff to E. Cassel, 15 June 1909; *NYT*, 2 Dec. 1918.
105. Norman A. Graebner, ed., *An Uncertain Tradition* (New York, 1961), pp. 62, 67–73; A. Whitney Griswold, *The Far Eastern Policy of the United States* (New Haven, Conn., 1962), chap. 4; reel 677, Schiff to E. Cassel, 15 June 1909. For the sequence of events in China, see Carosso, *Morgans*, pp. 551–78; a very detailed account is in Walter V. Scholes and Marie V. Scholes, *The Foreign Policies of the Taft Administration* (Columbia, Mo., 1970), chaps. 8–10, 12–13.
106. Reel 677, CA MSS; reel 694, Schiff to E. Cassel, 20 July 1909, 10 Mar. 1910; Carosso, *Morgans*, pp. 551–57.
107. Reel 694, Schiff to E. Cassel, 20 July 1909; reel 677, Schiff to E. Harriman, 3 Aug. 1909, to P. Knox, 24 May 1910.

108. Reel 677, Schiff to W. Straight, 19 Mar. 1909, to O. Kahn, 25 June 1909.
109. Reel 677, Schiff to K. Takahashi, 31 Aug., 24, 28 Dec. 1908, 24 Feb. 1910; Adler, *Schiff*, 1:248–52.
110. Reel 677, Schiff to K. Takahashi, 24 Feb., 8 Mar. 1910; *NYT*, 6, 9 Mar. 1910, 16 Mar. 1912; Adler, *Schiff*, 1:256–57.
111. Carosso, *Morgans*, pp. 558–78; reel 677, CA MSS, Schiff to E. Cassel, 23 Mar., 9 Apr. 1913, reel 687, Schiff to E. Cassel, 29 Dec. 1912.
112. Reel 680, CA MSS, p. 1236; reel 687, William Wolff, "Edward Henry Harriman," *Elks Magazine*, Sept.–Nov. 1927; reel 689, memo by Cyrus Adler, 3 Sept. 1926.
113. Reel 686, statement of H. Tatnall to C. Adler, 3 Sept. 1926.
114. Reel 680, CA MSS, p. 1256; reel 682, CA MSS, p. 1245; reel 1981, Schiff to L. Wiley, 26 June 1916, Schiff's secretary to M. Seidman, 16 Nov. 1916.

2. Leadership and Philanthropy (Notes to Pages 41–81)

1. Jonathan D. Sarna, "Cyrus Adler and the Development of American Jewish Culture," *American Jewish History* 78 (Mar. 1989): 392.
2. Hasia R. Diner, "Jewish Self-Government, American Style," *American Jewish History* 81 (spring–summer 1994): 277–95; Arthur A. Goren, *National Leadership in American Jewish Life*, Ninth Annual . . . Feinberg Memorial Lecture, University of Cincinnati, 8 Apr. 1986.
3. Daniel J. Elazar, ed., *Authority, Power and Leadership in the Jewish Polity* (Lanham, Md., 1991), introduction; Morris D. Waldman, *Nor by Power* (New York, 1953), p. 328; Louis Marshall in *AH*, 5 Jan. 1917.
4. Jeffrey Potter, *Men, Money and Magic* (New York, 1976), pp. 106–7.
5. Reel 697, CA MSS, p. 1099; reel 685, Schiff to E. Cassel, 3 May 1900; Max Heller in *AH*, 3 Jan. 1907; *NYT*, 26 Jan. 1914.
6. Maurice Simon, ed., *Speeches, Articles and Letters of Israel Zangwill* (London, 1937), p. 143.
7. Jonathan S. Woocher, "The Democratization of the American Jewish Polity," in Elazar, *Authority, Power and Leadership*, chap. 6; Goren, *National Leadership*, pp. 3–8; Charles S. Liebman, "Dimensions of Authority in the Contemporary Jewish Community," *Jewish Journal of Sociology* 12 (June 1970): 32ff.
8. AJC archives, "Minutes of the Conference on Organization," 4 Feb. 1906; *AH*, 18 May 1900; *NYT*, 26 Jan. 1917.
9. Reel 691, Schiff to W. Taft, 29 Oct. 1909; Ron Chernow, *The House of Morgan* (New York, 1990), p. 177; Yonathan Shapiro, *Leadership of the American Zionist Organization* (Urbana, Ill., 1971), pp. 63–70; *NYT*, 1 Feb. 1916. Later Brandeis said that he was unaware of Schiff's opposition in 1913. Reel 1978, L. Brandeis to Schiff, 14 Oct. 1915.
10. Charles Reznikoff, ed., *Louis Marshall*, 2 vols. (Philadelphia, 1957), 2:836–38; *AH*, 7 Feb. 1908.
11. Samuel Schulman in *AH*, 5 Jan. 1917.
12. Reel 679, Schiff to M. Sulzberger, 12 May 1908; reel 693, Schiff to L. Stern, 1 June 1908; reel 694, I. Lehman to M. Schiff, 25 Nov. 1925; reel 684, notes by

Morris Waldman, 22 July 1925; *AH*, 21 Feb. 1895. Schiff was also critical of eastern Europeans for not donating to causes earmarked for their group. Reel 1977, A. Liebowitz to Schiff, 27 Feb. 1914.

13. Reel 1978, G. Kohut to Schiff, 28 Apr. 1915; *American Israelite*, 7 Dec. 1905; Waldman, *Nor by Power*, p. 323.

14. Reel 679, Schiff to P. Nathan, 20 Jan. 1914; Judah Magnes Papers (Central Archives for the History of the Jewish People, Jerusalem), P3/407, L. Straus to B. Magnes, 5 Nov. 1912; Baila R. Shargel, *Lost Love* (Philadelphia, 1997), pp. 100, 110–11, 125, 135, 137.

15. *AH*, 21 Oct. 1890; *PAJHS* 6 (1897): 147; *NYT*, 8 May 1904; reel 23 (JTS archives), Schiff to S. Schechter, 28 June 1911.

16. See for example Josef S. Bloch, *Ein Besuch beim Judentum in New York und Umgebung* (Vienna, 1912).

17. For example, reel 691, Schiff to P. Nathan, 22 Jan. 1912.

18. Reel 691, Schiff to A. Dreyfus, 10 Mar. 1919, to L. Wald, 31 Dec. 1897, to J. Riis, 26 Dec. 1906; reel 692, Schiff to E. Cassel, 23 Nov. 1905; reel 1977, Schiff to J. Wilson, 11 Dec. 1914.

19. Reel 691, Schiff to J. Riis, 26 Dec. 1906, to J. Hall, 20 Apr. 1893, to L. Wald, 16, 23 Nov. 1903, to W. King, 20, 31 Jan., 2 Feb. 1905, to J. Asher, 7 Dec. 1906, to A. Ochs, 1 Aug. 1898; reel 690, Schiff to W. Round, 11 July 1887, to M. Stern, 15 Sept. 1893; reel 678, Schiff to H. Rice, 11 Sept. 1891; reel 23, Schiff to R. Grossman, 2 June 1919; Cyrus Adler, *Jacob H. Schiff*, 2 vols. (Garden City, N.Y., 1929), 1:396, 2:60; David M. Eichhorn, *Evangelizing the American Jew* (Middle Village, N.Y., 1978), p. 179.

20. Reel 691, Schiff to J. Riis, 26 Dec. 1906, to E. Jenkins, 16 Dec. 1908, to E. Peabody, 5 May 1891, to C. Adams, 3 Apr. 1891; Samuel Schulman in *AH*, 5 Jan. 1917; Frieda S. Warburg, *Reminiscences of a Long Life* (New York, 1956), p. 82; Jeffrey S. Gurock, "Jacob A. Riis," *American Jewish History* 71 (Sept. 1981): 46.

21. Reel 691, Schiff to S. Wise, 1 Dec. 1910, 25 June 1914; reel 680, CA MSS, p. 730; reel 1982, Schiff to A. Dittenhoefer, 7 Feb. 1917; *NYT*, 2 Dec. 1910.

22. Reel 691, Schiff to S. Coit, 14 Oct. 1902, to H. Moskowitz, 4 Feb. 1907, to I. Singer, 9 July 1908, to I. Seligman, 18 Apr. 1910, to E. Seligman, 1 May 1916; reel 23, Schiff to F. Adler, 17 Mar. 1903, to S. Coit, 25 Dec. 1902; Benny Kraut, *From Reform Judaism to Ethical Culture* (Cincinnati, 1979), chap. 5.

23. Reel 691, Schiff to A. Dreyfus, 10 Mar. 1919; reel 22 (JTS archives), Schiff to E. Cassel, 10 June 1896; reel 1984, Schiff's speech to the Central Committee for the Relief of Jews Suffering through the War, [5 Dec. 1918]; Kurt Grunwald, "'Windsor Cassel': The Last Court Jew," Leo Baeck Institute, *Year Book* 14 (1969):132–33, 157; Todd Endelman, *Radical Assimilation in English Jewish History* (Bloomington, Ind., 1990), p. 76; Theodore Norman, *An Outstretched Arm* (London, 1985), p. 21.

24. Morton Rosenstock, review of *The Many Lives of Otto Kahn*, by Mary Matz, *American Jewish Historical Quarterly* 54 (Mar. 1965): 372; reel 691, Schiff to A. Dreyfus, 10 Mar. 1919; Ron Chernow, *The Warbugs* (New York, 1993), p. 238.

25. Warburg, *Reminiscences*, p. 130.

26. Reel 691, Schiff to W. Dodge, 29 Dec. 1896, to E. Godkin, 23 Sept. 1896; to O. Straus, 18 Apr. 1898.

27. Reel 691, Schiff to A. Orr, 24 Jan. 1895, to H. Bernstein, 29 Sept. 1914, to H. Kallen, 20 Sept. 1918; reel 677, CA MSS; reel 684, Schiff to W. Taft, 12 Dec. 1911; reel 696, Schiff to A. Ochs, 3 Nov. 1902; reel 1978, Schiff to L. Moissiff, 26 Oct. 1915.
28. Fritz Stern, *Gold and Iron* (New York, 1977).
29. Reel 691, Schiff to *AH*, 5 June 1916, to J. Reynolds, 7 Oct. 1895, to W. McKinley, 29 Dec. 1896, to S. Low, 3 Dec. 1901, to J. Mitchel, 12 Dec. 1913; reel 686, Schiff to E. Cassel, 14 May 1914; reel 684, statement by William McAdoo; Naomi W. Cohen, *A Dual Heritage* (Philadelphia, 1969), pp. 146–147.
30. Morton Rosenstock, *Louis Marshall* (Detroit, 1965), pp. 67–68; Wayne A. Wiegand, "'Jew Attack,'" *American Jewish History* 83 (Sept. 1995): 359–79; reel 691, Schiff to L. Marshall, 21 Dec. 1904.
31. Reel 691, Schiff to O. Straus, 25 Aug. 1893; Philip Cowen, *Memories of an American Jew* (New York, 1932), pp. 275–77; Cohen, *Dual Heritage*, pp. 61–62, 318, n16.
32. Reel 1978, C. Eliot to Schiff, 7 May 1915; reel 1981, C. Eliot to Schiff, 13, 15, 22 Mar., 11 Aug. 1917; Schiff to C. Eliot, 14 Mar. 1917; reel 688, Schiff to C. Eliot, 20 Mar. 1917; reel 691, Schiff to C. Eliot, 7 Aug. 1917; *Jewish Messenger*, 28 Oct. 1887.
33. Cowen, *Memories of an American Jew*, p. 324.
34. Reel 685, H. Potter to Schiff, 11 Jan. 1898; reel 676, Schiff to H. Potter, 18 Jan. 1898; *American Israelite*, 2 Apr. 1908. Of a different stripe and less significant to Schiff were the vulgar diatribes of the Populists accusing the "cunning" Jew of controlling the world's banking systems for his own advantage. Richard Hofstadter, *The Age of Reform* (New York, 1955), pp. 77–81; see, for example, James Goode, *The Modern Banker* (Chicago, 1896).
35. Reel 676, Schiff to E. Cassel, 6 Mar. 1888; reel 691, Schiff to T. Fowler, 20 May 1892, T. Fowler to Schiff, 20 May 1892.
36. Frederick Lewis Allen, *The Lords of Creation* (New York, 1966), p. 99; Judith S. Goldstein, *Crossing Lines* (New York, 1992), p. 172, 174–75; reel 691, Schiff to A. Hepburn, 27 Dec. 1909. "Five o'clock shadow," an advertising phrase, was applied to social discrimination by John Slawson, longtime executive director of the AJC.
37. Leonard Dinnerstein, "Leo M. Frank and the American Jewish Community," *Critical Studies in American Jewish History*, 3 vols. (Cincinnati and New York, 1971), 3:34–51, and Dinnerstein, *The Leo Frank Case* (New York, 1968); reel 23, Schiff to J. Slaton, 11, 21 June 1915; reel 1977, Leo Frank file; reel 1978, Schiff to A. Carnegie, 10 May 1915; reel 1979, Slaton file; Schiff papers (JTS archives, Jerusalem), L. Marshall to Schiff, 10 May 1915, Schiff to L. Marshall, 13 May 1915; Rosenstock, *Marshall*, pp. 89–96.
38. Hebrew Union College–Jewish Institute of Religion, news bulletin, July 1963; reel 691, Schiff to H. Berkowitz, 24 Dec. 1917, to A. Elkus, 12 May 1919; reel 1984, H. Berkowitz to Schiff, 17 Jan. 1918.
39. Endelman, *Radical Assimilation*, chap. 4; Ezra Mendelsohn, *On Modern Jewish Politics* (New York, 1993), p.16.
40. B. C. Forbes, "America's Thirty Richest," *Forbes Magazine*, 2 Mar. 1918;

Waldman, *Nor by Power*, p. 326; Alliance Israélite Universelle papers (American Jewish Archives), N. Behar to [N. Leven], 11 Feb. 1901.

41. Herman D. Stein, "Jewish Social Work in the United States," in *The Characteristics of American Jews* (New York, 1965), pp. 147–48, 154; Isaac Markens, *The Hebrews in America* (New York, 1888), p. 309; Boris D. Bogen, *Jewish Philanthropy* (New York, 1917), chap. 9.

42. Reel 22, Schiff and J. Goldman to C. Hallgarten and J. Plotke, 12 Nov. 1901, Schiff to M. de Hirsch, 9 Nov. 1891; reel 688, Schiff to E. Cassel, 24 Dec. 1891; *AH*, 27 May 1887, 10 Feb. 1888; *NYT*, 27 Apr. 1914.

43. Stein, "Jewish Social Work," pp. 152–78, 185–86; Bogen, *Jewish Philanthropy*, pp. 8, 144, 171–79; Paul Boyer, *Urban Masses and Moral Order in America* (Cambridge, Mass., 1978), pp. 144–45.

44. Louis Marshall, *AH*, 5 Jan. 1917.

45. *Jewish Times*, 28 July 1871, 25 Apr. 1873 (Courtesy of Jonathan Sarna); reel 678, CA MSS on Jewish charities; *AH*, 21 Nov. 1879, 8 Oct. 1920; Cowen, *Memories of an American Jew*, pp. 92–93; Adler, *Schiff*, 2:60; Benjamin Rabinowitz, "The Young Men's Hebrew Associations," *PAJHS* 37 (Mar. 1947): 233, 264, 304; Philip Goodman, "The Purim Association of the City of New York," *PAJHS* 40 (Dec. 1950): 158, 162; Bernard Postal in news release of the National Jewish Welfare Board, 7 Feb. 1966.

46. Reel 684, S. Sachs to C. Adler, 3 Oct. 1925; reel 691, Schiff to L. Marshall, 3 June 1902; *PAJHS* 24 (1916): 39; reel 1986, William Goldman, "The Schiff Era in Jewish Philanthropy," 3 Jan. 1920.

47. Reel 677, statement by Henry Potter, Jan. 1899; Markens, *Hebrews in America*, p. 149; reel 677, A. Seligman to B. Loeb, [1899]; Louis Marshall in *AH*, 5 Jan. 1917.

48. *Philadelphia Public Ledger* for both articles, 30 Sept. 1920; unsorted Schiff papers (American Jewish Archives), Schiff to M. Warburg, 19 Jan. 1912.

49. Reel 677, CA MSS, reel 694, Schiff's will; *AH*, 8 Oct. 1920; *Literary Digest*, 16 Oct. 1920; Paul Arnsberg in *Jakob H. Schiff* (Frankfurt, 1969), p. 24, estimates that Schiff gave away $100 million during his lifetime.

50. Reel 694, Schiff to E. Devine, 18 Dec. 1908; reel 23, Schiff to M. Lubetkin, 9 Nov. 1903. Schiff thought that contributions lost their value if they were greeted with much publicity. Reel 689, Schiff to J. Krauskopf, 16 Jan. 1896.

51. Reel 680, Schiff's speech before the Charity Organization Society, 19 Nov. 1907; reel 689, Schiff to A. Cahan, 8 July 1916; Mary Cohen in *AH*, 29 Aug. 1884.

52. Reel 23, Schiff to L. Zinsler, 31 Jan. 1898, to L. Frankel, 20 Mar. 1905; Bogen, *Jewish Philanthropy*, pp. 184–85, 190–91; Morris Waldman in *AH*, 3 July 1908; *NYT*, 22 Oct. 1908.

53. Arnsberg, *Schiff*, pp. 19–23; Yoel Darom to author [July 1993]; Ruth Dresner to author, 4 July 1993; Adler, *Schiff*, 1:355–56; reel 677, Schiff to W. Lippmann, 13 Dec. 1915; reel 688, Schiff to T. James, 24 Aug. 1903; *AH*, 27 May 1887; *NYT*, 26 Jan. 1914; Fritz Morris "The Foremost Jews of Today," *Munsey's Magazine* 30 (Nov. 1903): 230. For similarities to late-nineteenth-century German Jewish philanthropy, see Derek J. Penslar, "Philanthropy, the

'Social Question,' and Jewish Identity in Imperial Germany," Leo Baeck Institute *Year Book* 38 (1993): 51–73.

54. *AH*, 27 May 1887, 22 Dec. 1893; Naomi W. Cohen, *Not Free to Desist* (Philadelphia, 1972), p. 86.

55. Reel 684, notes by Morris Waldman, 22 July 1925; reel 690, Schiff to L. Wald, 3 Sept. 1897, to W. Buck, 30 June 1898; *AH*, 22 Dec. 1893; Boyer, *Urban Masses*, chap. 10.

56. Minnie Louis in *AH*, 8 Oct. 1920; *Boston Herald*, 26 Sept. 1920; Warburg, *Reminiscences*, p. 55; Baron Maurice de Hirsch papers (AJHS archives), Box 59, I-80, Schiff to M. Isaacs, 19 July 1900.

57. Adler, *Schiff*, 1:357, 359–60, 2:10; reel 22, M. Kohler to M. Schiff, 14 Oct. 1925; reel 23, Schiff to H. Rice, 2 Feb. 1892, to N. Rosenau, 1 Feb. 1897; reel 689, Schiff to E. Devine, 8 Feb. 1904, 27 May 1915, notes by Morris Waldman, 22 July 1925; Philip Cowen papers (AJHS archives), Box 2 P-19, "Notes on Jacob Schiff"; *NYT*, 7 Mar. 1905. On new trends in Jewish philanthropy see Bogen, *Jewish Philanthropy*, chaps. 17, 19, 20; Waldman, *Nor by Power*, pt. 3.

58. Schiff's letter to *AH*, 27 Jan. 1905; Max Kohler in *AH*, 8 Oct. 1920; Bogen, *Jewish Philanthropy*, pp. 43–47; Jacob H. Schiff, "Jewish Charity Federation in New York City," *Jewish Charity* 3 (Jan. 1904): 81–82; reel 23, Schiff to editor of *Jewish Charity*, 24 Dec. 1903; reel 682, Schiff to A. Lehman, 14 June 1920; Abraham Cronbach, "Jewish Pioneering in American Social Welfare," *American Jewish Archives* 3 (June 1951): 51–52.

59. Reel 22, Schiff to E. Benjamin, 15 May 1916; reel 1978, Schiff to H. Bernstein, 13 May 1915; Isaac M. Fein, "Israel Zangwill and American Jewry," *American Jewish Historical Quarterly* 60 (Sept. 1970): 33.

60. Reel 689, memo by Robet De Forest; Adler, *Schiff*, 2:34–35; reel 696, CA MSS, p. 1047.

61. Merle Curti, "American Philanthropy and theNational Character," *American Quarterly* 16 (Winter 1958): 420–37; Edward C. Kirkland, *Dream and Thought in the Business Community* (Ithaca, N.Y., 1956), chap. 6; Sarah K. Bolton, *Famous Givers and Their Gifts* (reprint of 1896 edition. Freeport, NY., 1971), pp. 371–80; Allan Nevins, *John D. Rockefeller*, 2 vols. (New York, 1940), 2:644–45.

62. Reel 690, Schiff to C. Eliot, 11 July 1899.

63. *AH*, 26 Jan., 18 May 1900; Andrew Carnegie, "Wealth," *North American Review*, no. 391 (June 1889): 653–64; John Lincoln in *New Republic*, 11 Dec. 1915; reel 677, Schiff to W. Lippmann, 13 Dec. 1915.

64. Albert Shaw, "American Millionaires and Their Public Gifts," *Review of Reviews* 7 (Feb. 1893): 50–51; Jacob H. Schiff, "Social Service and the Free Synagogue," *Free Synagogue Pulpit* 1 (Mar. 1908): 49–51.

65. The Schiff papers abound with references to such matters in the banker's letters to municipal officials. Scattered references are also in *NYT*, for example 1 Feb. 1914, 28 Oct. 1915.

66. Schiff papers (JTS archives, Jerusalem), L. Marshall to Schiff, 9 Feb., 25 May 1915; reel 1978, Schiff to L. Marshall, 8 Feb. 1915; Max Kohler in *AH*, 8 Oct. 1920.

67. Reel 23, Schiff to Montefiore Board, 9 June 1919; reel 684, Schiff to S. Wachsman, 10 Jan. 1917.

68. Dorothy Levenson, *Montefiore* (New York, 1984), p. 3; reel 684, tribute to Schiff from Henry Solomon; Joseph Hirsh and Beka Doherty, *The First Hundred Years of the Mount Sinai Hospital of New York* (New York, 1952), p. 62.

69. Moshe Davis, *America and the Holy Land* (Westport, Conn., 1995), pp. 111–12; *Jewish Messenger*, 25 Sept. 1885. Unless otherwise noted, all material for the entire section is culled from Levenson, *Montefiore*, chaps. 1–6; Adler, *Schiff*, 1:369–81; *AH*, 30 Nov. 1894 (issue celebrating Montefiore's tenth anniversary).

70. *AH*, 29 Oct., 3–24 Dec. 1886.

71. Maurice Fishberg in *AH*, 5 Jan. 1917; reel 23, Schiff to E. Cassel, 8 Dec. 1913; reel 694, Schiff to E. Cassel, 12 Jan. 1914, and Schiff's will.

72. Reel 679, Schiff to M. Sulzberger, 12 May 1908; reel 689, memo by Leopold Stern, 10 Aug. 1925; reel 23, M. Stroock to M. Schiff, 3 Oct. 1925; Barnard Powers, "Jacob H. Schiff: Wall Street's Grand Old Man," *Magazine of Wall Street*, 28 Sept. 1918; Samuel Schulman in *AH*, 5 Jan. 1917.

73. Reel 23, CA MSS; reel 1977, Schiff to L. Wald, 15 June 1914; reel 1978, Schiff to H. Bernstein, 13 Jan. 1915; reel 1981, Schiff to P. Phillips, 15, 23 May 1916; *AH*, 26 Aug. 1898, 3 Nov. 1893, S. Wachsman in *AH*, 5 Jan. 1917.

74. Reel 684, notes by Max Kohler, 14 Oct. 1925.

75. Reel 23, Schiff to F. Warburg, 21 Mar. 1918; reel 681, Schiff to B. Odell, 12 Mar. 1902; reel 1978, Schiff to O. Bannard, 5 May 1915; *AH*, 3 Nov., 29 Dec. 1893, 28 Dec. 1894; *NYT*, 2 Feb. 1913, 8 June 1917.

76. Reel 23, Schiff to L. Wald, 28 May 1914, to S. Lindsay, 19 June 1917; reel 681, Schiff to B. Odell, 12 Mar. 1902; reel 1985, Schiff to H. Bruckner, 16 Oct. 1918, to C. Craig, 15 Oct. 1918; *NYT*, 2 Feb. 1913, 8 June 1917.

77. Reel 1978, Montefiore Home files, esp. Schiff to Mr. Bloch, 8 Nov. 1915, M. Goodman to Schiff, 19 Nov. 1915; reel 689, Schiff to S. Borg, 10 Oct. 1917, to H. Solomon, 22 Jan. 1899; reel 684, M. Stroock to M. Schiff, 3 Oct. 1925; *AH*, 23 Feb. 1894, 8 Oct. 1920. My thanks to Richard Kalmin for locating the Talmud passage for me.

78. Reel 1978, Schiff to L. Shalet, 23 July, 1 Nov. 1915, to Harry Fischel, 15 June 1915; reel 684, notes by Fred Stein.

79. Reel 1978, Schiff to M. Goodman, 25 June 1915; reel 689, Schiff to T. Roosevelt, 31 May 1901, to J. Obermeyer, 15 Feb. 1916; *AH*, 11 Nov. 1887, 21, 28 Dec. 1888.

80. *AH*, 21 Dec. 1888; Milton Goldin, *Why They Give* (New York, 1976), p. 37.

81. Reel 23, Board of Directors to Schiff, 8 May 1918, Schiff to Montefiore board, 9 June 1919, speech by William Goldman, 3 Jan. 1920.

82. Reel 694, Schiff to M. Warburg, 29 Dec. 1913.

83. Jacob R. Marcus, *The Colonial American Jew*, 3 vols. (Detroit, 1970), 3:1219–20; reel 691, Schiff to J. Applegate, 14 Dec. 1892, to C. Dodge, 11 Nov. 1913, to G. Perkins, 14 Jan. 1918; reel 1982, Schiff to L. Fosdick, 9 Oct. 1917; Adler, *Schiff*, 2:49.

84. *NYT*, 26 Jan. 1914; reel 690, Schiff to W. Round, 11 July 1887; reel 691, Schiff to M. Williams, 20 Dec. 1884; reel 1984, Schiff to J. Rogers, 22 Apr. 1918.

85. Adler, *Schiff*, 1:360; reel 23, Schiff to G. Gottheil, 20 Dec. 1887; reel 691, Schiff to Rev. Friedman, 15 May 1902, to I. Seligman, 17 Dec. 1906.

86. Reel 691, Schiff to J. Reynolds, 7 Oct. 1895, to H. Turner, 19 May 1896, to J. Speyer, 15 Jan. 1902; reel 690, Schiff's correspondence with Jacob Riis, Nov. 1906.

87. *NYT*, 22 Oct. 1908; reel 23, Schiff to R. De Forest, 22 May 1916.

88. Reel 682, Schiff to O. Bannard, 7 Dec. 1915, to R. De Forest, 27 Mar. 1916; reel 691, Schiff/De Forest correspondence, esp. for Nov. 1916, O. Bannard to Schiff, 16 Mar. 1916, Schiff to L. Plaut, 17 Dec. 1915, to J. Magnes, 1 May 1916, C. Lowenberg to C. Poskanzer, 28 June 1917; reel 1978, Schiff to E. Breidenbach 13 Dec. 1915; reel 1983, National Employment Exchange files; reel 1984, Schiff to C. Blumenthal, 24 Oct. 1918; Adler, *Schiff*, 1:362–65. On discrimination against Jews by Jews, see Elias Lieberman, "Jewish Anti-Semites," *AH*, 22 Nov. 1918.

89. Adler, *Schiff*, 1:314–17, 360; reel 694, by the terms of Schiff's will, Tuskegee received $10,000; reel 696, Schiff to B. Washington, 16 June 1909; reel 1980, Schiff to L. Marshall, 5 Jan. 1916; *NYT*, 22 Nov. 1915.

90. Reel 676, Schiff to H. Potter, 18 Jan. 1898.

91. Schiff complained, for example, about the quota on Jewish students in the Horace Mann School, reel 691, Schiff to G. Dodge, 27 Sept. 1898, to J. Russell, 20, 24 July 1899. On Harvard: reel 690, Schiff to H. Higginson, 6 June 1902; Goldstein, *Crossing Lines*, pp. 175–77.

92. Reel 1978, F. Boas to Schiff, 19 Feb. 1915, Schiff to F. Boas, 23 Feb. 1915; reel 691, Schiff to J. Schurman, 21 Feb. 1916; Schiff papers (JTS archives, Jerusalem), Schiff to H. Livingston, 8, 10 Mar. 1915; H. Livingston to Schiff, 16 Mar. 1915.

93. Reel 22, Schiff to J. Schmidlap, 9 Oct. 1911; Adler, *Schiff*, 2:38; cf. W. E. Mosse, *The German-Jewish Economic Elite* (Oxford, 1989), p. 319.

94. Reel 23, Schiff to A. Horvitz, 23 Oct. 1911, 26 Dec. 1912, to H. Hurwitz, 6 Dec. 1906; reel 691, Schiff to R. Treman, 30 Apr. 1917.

95. Reel 23, Schiff to S. Low, 19 Feb. 1896, 6 Feb. 1899, to N. Butler, 12 May, 7 Oct. 1902, M. Schiff to J. Nash, 16 Mar. 1899; reel 690, Schiff to S. Low, 2 Mar. 1891, 7 Mar. 1905; Gerald Kurland, *Seth Low* (New York, 1971), p. 57.

96. Reel 23, Schiff to N. Butler, 30 Jan. 1907; reel 690, Adler's memo of interview with George Plimpton, 11 Dec. 1925; Thomas Bender, *New York Intellect* (Baltimore, 1987), pp. 287–90; E. Digby Baltzell, *The Protestant Establishment* (New York, 1966).

97. Reel 23, Schiff to N. Butler, 30 Jan. 1907; reel 1979, Schiff to J. Billikopf, 13 Oct. 1916; Harold S. Wechsler, *The Qualified Student* (New York, 1977), pp. 136–39.

98. Reel 23, Schiff to J. Schurman, 2 Jan. 1912; unsorted Schiff papers (American Jewish Archives), Schiff to M. Warburg, 19 Jan. 1912; reel 690, Schiff to G. Plimpton, 3 June 1915; *NYT*, 11, 12 Feb. 1913; Wechsler, *Qualified Student*, p. 176.

99. Adler, *Schiff*, 2:11–17; reel 690, G. Plimpton to Schiff, 2 June 1915; reel 23, Schiff to N. Butler, 3 Sept. 1915; reel 684, notes by Annie Meyer, [May 1926], notes by Virginia Gildersleeve; Virginia Gildersleeve in *AH*, 5 Oct. 1920; *NYT*, 7 Oct. 1915.

100. Adler, *Schiff,* 2:39, 43; reel 691, Schiff to L. Marshall, 7 Dec. 1908; AJC archives, "Minutes of the Executive Committee," 1 Jan. 1909; cf. Rosenstock, *Marshall,* p. 69.
101. Wechsler, *Qualified Student,* p. 176; reel 691, Schiff to J. Funk, 9 Feb. 1905.
102. Paul Ritterband and Harold S. Wechsler, *Jewish Learning in American Universities* (Bloomington, Ind., 1994), pp. 15–16.
103. Cohen, *Dual Heritage,* pp. 14–15; Naomi W. Cohen, *Encounter with Emancipation* (Philadelphia, 1984), p. 207; Jeffrey Gurock, "From *Publications* to *American Jewish History,*" *American Jewish History* 81 (winter, 1993–94): 155, 158. Years later, a university in Kentucky used the same reasoning (i.e. Jewish studies as a means of countering prejudice) when it appealed to Schiff for funds. Reel 1978, W. Amriger to Schiff, 18 Oct. 1915.
104. Reel 23, Schiff to C. Adler, 1 Apr. 1912. Schiff also donated large sums for the same purpose to the New York Public Library. Reel 678, Schiff to G. Rives, 10 Dec. 1897; Adler, *Schiff,* 2:34–37; Philip Goodman, "American Jewish Bookplates," *PAJHS* 45 (Mar. 1956): 151–52.
105. The following account is based primarily on the manuscript of David Gordon Lyon, "Relations of Jacob H. Schiff to Harvard University" (courtesy of Harvard University library). Schiff also contributed to the American School of Oriental Research in Jerusalem. Adler, *Schiff,* 2:37.
106. Lyon MS, pp. 2, 4, 10, 39–40; reel 690, Schiff to D. Lyon, 8 Jan. 1890; reel 23, Schiff to S. Rosendale, 27 Feb. 1890; Ritterband and Wechsler, *Jewish Learning,* pp. 101–7; Charles W. Eliot, "Jacob H. Schiff," *Menorah Journal* 7 (1921): 19.
107. Reel 23, C. Eliot to Schiff, 10 Feb. 1903; reel 680, C. Eliot to Schiff, 3 Jan. 1906.
108. Charles Eliot in *AH,* 5 Jan. 1917; Lyon MS, pp. 43–47; reel 23, Schiff to C. Eliot, 10 May 1905, to M. Sulzberger, 12 Dec. 1910; reel 690, M. Sulzberger to Schiff, 11 Dec. 1910; Cowen, *Memories of an American Jew,* p. 124; Eliot, "Jacob H. Schiff," p. 20.
109. *The Semitic Museum of Harvard University: Addresses . . . at the Formal Opening . . . on Feb. 5, 1903* (Cambridge, Mass., 1903). See also Barbara M. Solomon, *Ancestors and Immigrants* (New York, 1956), pp. 181–86; Baltzell, *Protestant Establishment,* pp. 144–48; reel 23, Schiff to C. Eliot, 2 Jan. 1906, C. Eliot to Schiff, 3 Jan. 1906; reel 22, M. Kohler to M. Schiff, 14 Oct. 1925. On the 250th anniversary of Jewish settlement in America, Eliot publicly noted civilization's debt to the Jews (Edmund J. James, *The Immigrant Jew in America* [New York, 1907], p. 4), and he wrote a laudatory account of Jews in his introduction to Samuel W. McCall, *Patriotism of the American Jew* (New York, 1922).
110. Eliot, "Jacob H. Schiff," pp. 17, 19–20; reel 694, C. Eliot to Schiff, 3 Apr. 1914; reel 23, Schiff to C. Eliot, 25 June 1906, to A. Faust, 15 Oct. 1912.
111. Adler, *Schiff,* 2:30–33; Lyon MS, pp. 51–53; reel 23, Schiff to A. Lowell, 15 Dec. 1910, 5, 14 Nov. 1913, CA MSS; Cohen, *Encounter with Emancipation,* p. 208; Ritterband and Wechsler, *Jewish Learning,* pp. 106–7.
112. Lyon MS, pp. 48–49; Ritterband and Wechsler, *Jewish Learning,* p. 286, n76; reel 690, Schiff to D. Lyon, 2 May 1910.

113. Reel 690, Schiff to M. Sulzberger, 6 May 1891; reel 1981, F. Chadwick to Schiff, 7 Mar. 1917; reel 694, M. Kohler to M. Schiff, 14 Oct. 1925; reel 1984, K. Kohler to Schiff, 19 Aug. 1918; AJC archives, Schiff file, H. Friedenwald to J. Finley, 28 May 1908; "The Two Hundred and Fiftieth Anniversary of the Settlement of the Jews in the United States," *PAJHS* 14 (1906).

114. Reel 23, Schiff to H. Berkowitz, 26 Oct. 1900; Henry Berkowitz in *AH*, 12 Nov. 1920; *NYT*, 9 Feb., 28 Apr. 1914.

115. Reel 23, CA MSS; reel 678, CA MSS on Jewish scholarship; reel 691, Schiff to S. Schechter, 17 July 1907, to S. Rabinowitz, 1 Dec. 1915; Adler papers (JTS archives), C. Adler to Schiff, 16 May 1914; Adler, *Schiff*, 2:55–56, 62–65; Shuly R. Schwartz, *The Emergence of Jewish Scholarship in America* (Cincinnati, 1991), pp. 102–4; Jonathan D. Sarna, *JPS: The Americanization of Jewish Culture* (Philadelphia, 1989), pp. 108, 120; *NYT*, 11 Feb. 1914.

116. Cyrus Adler in *AH*, 5 Jan. 1917; reel 23, Schiff to I. Hershfeld, 14 Jan. 1910, C. Adler to Schiff, 5, 25 June 1905; reel 691, Schiff to E. Cohen, 6 Dec. 1909.

117. *AH*, 27 May 1898.

3. The New Immigrants (Notes to Pages 83–123)

1. Reel 691, Schiff to M. de Hirsch, 23 Oct. 1891; reel 22 (JTS archives), Schiff and J. Goldman to C. Hallgarten and J. Plotke, 12 Nov. 1901; Zosa Szajkowski, "The *Yahudi* and the Immigrant," *American Jewish Historical Quarterly* 63 (Sept. 1973): 15; Esther L. Panitz, "The Polarity of American Jewish Attitudes towards Immigration," in *The Jewish Experience in America*, ed. Abraham J. Karp, 5 vols. (Waltham, Mass. and New York, 1969), 4:36–50; Naomi W. Cohen, *Encounter with Emancipation* (Philadelphia, 1984), pp. 301–3, 380, n26.

2. Mark Wischnitzer, *To Dwell in Safety* (Philadelphia, 1948), chaps. 3, 4; *Judge*, 23 Jan. 1892.

3. Reel 678, Schiff to E. Cassel, 4 Dec. 1888; Alliance Israélite Universelle papers (American Jewish Archives), N. Behar to [N. Leven], 5 June 1901; *AH*, 31 July 1907; Cohen, *Encounter with Emancipation*, p. 305.

4. Reel 22, Schiff and J. Goldman to C. Hallgarten and J. Plotke, 12 Nov. 1901; reel 23 (JTS archives), Schiff to A. S. Levy. 30 Mar. 1903; Cohen, *Encounter with Emancipation*, pp. 299–308, 319 for this and the next two paragraphs.

5. See annual *Proceedings* of the Union of American Hebrew Congregations, esp. 1890–1914; Egal Feldman, "Prostitution, the Alien Woman and the Progressive Imagination," *American Quarterly* 19 (summer 1967): 203.

6. Paul Boyer, *Urban Masses and Moral Order in America* (Cambridge, Mass., 1978), chaps. 7–8; reel 23, Schiff to M. de Hirsch, 23 Oct. 1891; *AH*, 27 May 1887.

7. *AH*, 21 Oct., 2 Dec. 1881, 20 Jan., 10 Mar., 14 July 1882; Gilbert Osofsky, "The Hebrew Emigrant Aid Society of the United States," *PAJHS* 49 (Mar. 1960): 175–76, 186; Philip Cowen, *Memories of an American Jew* (New York, 1932), pp. 96–97; Ronald Sanders, *Shores of Refuge* (New York, 1988), pp. 105–9.

8. Naomi W. Cohen, *A Dual Heritage* (Philadelphia, 1969), pp. 67–70; Samuel Joseph, *History of the Baron de Hirsch Fund* (Fairfield, N.J., 1978), pp. 6–22.

9. Joseph, *Baron de Hirsch Fund*, pp. 12–13, 21; Zosa Szajkowski, "Emigration to America or Reconstruction in Europe," in *The Jewish Experience in America*, ed. Abraham J. Karp, 5 vols. (Waltham, Mass., and New York, 1969), 4:22–27.

10. Joseph, *Baron de Hirsch Fund*, chap. 2; reel 22, Schiff to Dr. Blau, 27 Jan. 1909.

11. Reel 22, Schiff to M. de Hirsch, 10 May 1892, to J. Scrymser, 10 May 1892, to S. Reinach, 16 Nov. 1909, to F. Philippson, 23 Dec. 1909, J. Goldman to M. Schiff, 29 Oct. 1925; reel 688, Schiff to E. Cassel, 24 Dec. 1891.

12. Reel 691, Schiff to H. Blum, 14 Oct. 1889. Reacting to the English attitude, Schiff boycotted a dinner in honor of Sir Julian Goldsmid, president of the Anglo-Jewish Association.

13. Reel 22, Schiff and J. Goldman to C. Hallgarten and J. Plotke, 12 Nov. 1901; reel 691, Schiff to P. Nathan 20 June 1912; unsorted Schiff papers (American Jewish Archives), Schiff to M. Warburg, 29 Dec. 1913; Alliance Israélite Universelle papers, N. Behar to [N. Leven], 11 Feb. 1901; Zosa Szajkowski, "The Alliance Israélite Universelle in the United States," *PAJHS* 39 (June 1950): 418–19, 431.

14. Baron Maurice de Hirsch papers (AJHS archives), Schiff to M. Isaacs, 14 Aug. 1901; reel 692, Schiff to N. Leven, 5 Nov. 1902. The Schiff papers abound with letters on the European/American rift.

15. *Industrial Relations, Final Report and Testimony . . . [of] the Commission on Industrial Relations*, 64th Cong., 1st sess., 1916, 8:7526–30; *NYT*, 21 Jan. 1915.

16. *AH*, 21 Feb. 1895.

17. Cohen, *Encounter with Emancipation*, pp. 310–11.

18. Reel 690, Schiff to H. Leipziger, 26 Nov. 1894, to R. Maclay, 2 July 1895, to A. Hewitt, 2 Dec. 1897.

19. Reel 689, Schiff to R. De Forest, 16 May 1902, to F. Brooks, 1 July 1912; Cowen, *Memories of an American Jew*, p. 107; *Chicago Daily Tribune* in *American Israelite*, 20 Oct. 1910.

20: Reel 690, Schiff to L. Zinsler, 25 Aug. 1896, 1 Feb. 1897, 30 June 1899, 21 Mar. 1907, to J. Dukas, 1910–17 contributions; *AH*, 16 May 1890, 26 Jan. 1900, 8 Oct. 1920; Shelley Tenenbaum, *A Credit to Their Community* (Detroit, 1993), pp. 32–33, 75, 78–79, 82; Cowen, *Memories of an American Jew*, 107–9; *NYT*, 26 Jan. 1914, 1 May 1983, see also *NYT*'s coverage of annual meetings every January: *American Banker*, 28 Oct. 1983.

21. Tenenbaum, *Credit to Their Community*, pp. 82, 97–98; Cyrus Adler, *Jacob H. Schiff*, 2 vols. (Garden City, N.Y., 1929), 1:365–66; *NYT*, 26 Jan. 1914.

22. Reel 22, Schiff to S. Reinach, 16 Nov. 1909; Jacob H. Schiff, "Technical Education among Jews," *Menorah* 3 (July 1887): 36–38; Joseph, *Baron de Hirsch Fund*, pp. 25, 27–28; *AH*, 27 May 1887; Abraham J. Karp, "The Making of Americans," in *Contemporary Jewry, Studies in Honor of Moshe Davis*, ed. Geoffrey Wigedor (Jerusalem, 1984), p. 54.

23. Joseph, *Baron de Hirsch Fund*, pp. 24–31, chap. 6; reel 22, Schiff to S. Reinach, 16 Nov. 1909, to J. Simon, 16 Nov. 1909; *AH*, 27 May 1887; *NYT*, 28 Feb. 1916.

24. Philip Cowen papers (AJHS archives), Box 2 P-19, "Notes on Jacob Schiff."

25. Reel 690, numerous letters from Schiff to L. Wald, 1893–1918, are the basis for this and the next four paragraphs on the founding of the settlement, its activities, and Schiff's advice and contributions. See also reel 690, H. Potter to

Schiff, 29 July 1895; reel 677, Schiff to H. Rice, 7 Nov. 1889; Lillian D. Wald, *The House on Henry Street* (New York, 1915); Adler, *Schiff*, 1:382–92; Allen F. Davis, *Spearheads for Reform* (New York, 1967), chap. 1.

26. Reel 1982, Schiff to F. Clark, 27 June 1917, to J. Mitchel, 12 Apr. 1917, to W. Prendergast, 24 Mar., 21 Sept. 1917; Adler, *Schiff*, 1:385–89; *NYT*, 1, 2 Feb. 1914. At the celebration of the twentieth anniversary of the settlement, Mitchel spoke in favor of the extension of settlement work.

27. Clare Coss, ed., *Lillian D. Wald* (New York, 1989), pp. 43–44.

28. Schiff letters to Wald from 1915 to 1917 in the Lillian Wald papers (New York Public Library) attest to a deep friendship.

29. Doris G. Daniels, *Always a Sister* (New York, 1989), pp. 37–38; Boyer, *Urban Masses and Moral Order*, chap. 16.

30. Reel 690, Schiff to L. Wald, 6 Dec. 1917; Lillian Wald in *Survey*, 2 Oct. 1920; Daniels, *Always a Sister*, pp. 95–96.

31. Reel 690, Schiff to L. Wald, 15 Jan. 1906, 6 Jan. 1916; reel 691, to J. Asher, 7 Dec. 1906; Wald, *House on Henry Street*, passim.

32. Reel 691, Schiff to L. Wald, 28, 31 Dec. 1897, 20, 22 Dec. 1914; Coss, *Wald*, pp. 46–47; Jeffrey Gurock, "Jacob A. Riis," *American Jewish History* 71 (Sept. 1981): 38–46.

33. Boyer, *Urban Reform and Moral Order*, pp. 179–81; Adler, *Schiff*, 1:292–96, 351–53; *NYT*, 1 Feb. 1914.

34. Reel 22, Schiff and J. Goldman to C. Hallgarten and J. Plotke, 12 Nov. 1901; Charles Reznikoff, ed., *Louis Marshall*, 2 vols. (Philadelphia, 1957), 2:977. Unless otherwise noted, all material for this and the next four paragraphs comes from a fuller account in Cohen, *Encounter with Emancipation*, pp. 331–41.

35. Naomi W. Cohen, "The Ethnic Catalyst," in *The Legacy of Jewish Migration*, ed. David Berger (New York, 1983), pp. 143–45.

36. *American Israelite*, 2 Feb. 1905; Charlotte Baum, Paula Hyman, and Sonya Michel, *The Jewish Woman in America* (New York, 1975), pp. 170–75.

37. Schiff hinted darkly in one letter that the real purpose for a seminary was to avoid an imminent scandal, but he didn't explain what it was. Reel 691, Schiff to M. Ottinger, 19 Dec. 1902.

38. *NYT*, 9 Feb. 1914, 28 Feb. 1916; Rebekah Kohut in *AH*, 8 Oct. 1920; Cohen, *Encounter with Emancipation*, p. 313.

39. Reel 693, Schiff to J. Barondess, 21 Oct. 1912.

40. *AH*, 25 May 1900; reel 691, Schiff to S. Schechter, 11 Feb. 1904, to L. Marshall, 28 Sept. 1908.

41. Reel 22, Schiff to A. Solomons, 24 Oct. 1900; reel 23, Schiff to A. Kohut, 26 May 1892, CA MSS on JTS; reel 691, Schiff to H. Mendes, 2 Feb. 1888, to M. Ottinger, 19 Dec. 1902, to M. Sulzberger, 9 Oct. 1899, 2 July 1901, to L. Marshall, 13 Nov. 1901, to A. Solomons, 15, 17, 23 May 1901; *AH*, 19 Nov. 1886, 17 Feb. 1888; Abraham J. Karp, "Solomon Schechter Comes to America," *American Jewish Historical Quarterly* 53 (Sept. 1963): 54; Robert E. Fierstein, *A Different Spirit* (New York, 1990), pp. 99, 115–17, 133–34; Cohen, *Encounter with Emancipation*, p. 314.

42. JTS miscellaneous archives, reel 46, speech by Cyrus Adler at memorial meeting for Therese Schiff, 31 Mar. 1933; Reznikoff, *Marshall*, 2:863; *AH*, 27 Dec.

1889; *Proceedings* of the Union of American Hebrew Congregations, 1909, p. 6241; *American Israelite*, 9 Jan. 1902.

43. *Menorah* 33 (July 1902): 62; *NYT*, 6 May, 3 June 1912, 10 Feb. 1913; reel 691. Schiff to B. Bettman, 3 Apr. 1893; reel 23, Schiff to editor, *AH*, 11 Mar. 1919; reel 1984, Schiff's speech to the Centeral Committee for the Relief of Jews Suffering through the War [5 Dec. 1918].

44. Reel 23, Schiff to B. Bettman [Apr. 1900], 18 July 1904, to H. Mendes, 14 Mar. 1902, to editor, *AH*, 11 Mar. 1919; *NYT*, 6 May 1912; Michael A. Meyer, "A Centennial History," in *Hebrew Union College-Jewish Institute of Religion at One Hundred Years*, ed. Samuel E. Karff (Cincinnati, 1976), pp. 42–43.

45. Reel 679, Schiff to I. Zangwill, 17 Oct. 1905; reel 1984, Schiff's speech to the Central Committee for the Relief of Jews Suffering through the War [5 Dec. 1918]; Jacob H. Schiff, "Social Service and the Free Synagogue," *Free Synagogue Pulpit* 1 (Mar. 1908): 49; Solomon Schechter papers (JTS archives), S. Schechter to M. Sulzberger, 15 Aug. 1899; Adler, *Schiff*, 2:45; Cyrus Adler, "Jacob Henry Schiff," *American Jewish Year Book* 23 (1921–22): 37.

46. Reel 691, Schiff to D. Philipson, 20 Jan. 1905.

47. Samuel Schulman in *AH*, 5 Jan. 1917, 8 Oct. 1920; reel 678, CA MSS on chap.13; reel 684, M. Boardman to C. Adler, 29 July 1925; reel 691, statement by Max Bonn, 29 June 1926; reel 1979, Schiff to E. Herz, 13 Dec. 1915; Adler, *Schiff*, 2:44–46; Adler, "J. H. Schiff," pp. 37–38; James P. Warburg, *The Long Road Home* (Garden City, N.Y., 1964), p. 19; Ron Chernow, *The Warburgs* (New York, 1993), pp. 91, 314. Frieda S. Warburg (*Reminiscences of a Long Life* [New York, 1956], p. 43) wrote that her father composed his own prayer for grace at meals. Testifying to vestiges of his rigid observance, she also recalled a severe scolding from her adoring father for having picked a flower on the Sabbath. Jessica Feingold to author, 24 May 1993. (Variations of the story tell how a different child, not Frieda, was scolded.)

48. *AH*, 27 May 1898; *American Israelite*, 4 Jan. 1917; Robert Liberles, *Religious Conflict in Social Context* (Westport, Conn., 1985), p. 109; Adler, *Schiff*, 2:45.

49. Reel 691, Schiff to L. May, 6 May 1892, I. Lehman to M. Schiff, 25 Nov. 1925; reel 694, E. Friedman to C. Adler, 28 Oct. 1926; reel 1977, Schiff to L. Marshall, 1 Oct. 1914. On the outreach program of the Brotherhood of Emanu-El to the Lower East Side and on Schiff's support, see reel 691, Schiff to J. Silverman, 23 Nov. 1903, and Myron Berman, "A New Spirit on the East Side," *American Jewish Historical Quarterly* 54 (Sept. 1964): 60–79.

50. Warburg, *Reminiscences*, pp. 78–79; Adler, *Schiff*, 2:47.

51. *AH*, 25 May 1900; Herbert Rosenblum, "The Founding of the United Synagogue of America," (Ph. D. diss., Brandeis University, 1970), pp. 39–41.

52. Cyrus Adler, *I Have Considered the Days* (Philadelphia, 1945), p. 243; Rosenblum, "Founding of the United Synagogue," p. 84; cf. Fierstein, *A Different Spirit*, pp. 133–34.

53. Reznikoff, *Marshall*, 2:874; Schechter papers, L. Marshall to S. Schechter, 25 Aug. 1908; Cyrus Adler papers (JTS archives), C. Adler to L. Marshall, 21 July 1922.

54. Reel 691, Schiff to B. Drachman, 9 July 1902; reel 695, Schiff to K. Kohler, 14 Aug. 1900; reel 23, M. Sulzberger to Schiff, 27 Apr. 1903, CA MSS on JTS;

Adler, "J. H. Schiff," p. 34; JTS, *Students' Annual*, 1916, p. 161; Moshe Davis, *The Emergence of Conservative Judaism* (Philadelphia, 1963), p. 324.

55. Solomon Schechter, *Seminary Addresses and Other Papers* (New York, 1915), pp. 9–30; Michael Greenbaum, "Mission Conflict in Religiously Affiliated Institutions of Higher Education" (D. Ed. diss., Teachers College, Coumbia University, 1994), p. 20; Rosenblum, "Founding of the United Synagogue," pp. 92–105; reel 23, Schiff to K. Kohler, 10 Oct. 1904, to S. Schechter, 18 Oct. 1904; reel 691, Schiff to H. Mendes, 4 July 1904.

56. Reel 691, Schiff to C. Adler, 16 Nov. 1903; Adler, "J. H. Schiff," p. 34; Mordecai M. Kaplan diary (JTS archives), 31 Oct. 1915; Alexander Marx to Gerson D. Cohen [1948]; JTS, *Students' Annual*, 1915, pp. 43–45.

57. Reel 691, Schiff to C. Adler, 3 Nov. 1903, to S. Schechter, 27 Jan. 1909; *Menorah* 40 (June 1906): 336; Schechter, *Seminary Addresses*, pp. 48–50; Cohen, *Encounter with Emancipation*, pp. 315–17.

58. Jewish Theological Seminary, *Semi-Centennial Volume*, ed. Cyrus Adler (New York, 1939), pp. 124–25; "*NYT*, 5 Apr. 1914. For several years, Schiff actively supported the Jewish Teachers' College Fund, a joint venture of the seminary and HUC that aimed at preparing teachers for areas both east and west of the Mississippi. Schiff papers (JTS archives, Jerusalem), numerous letters and reports relating to the fund, 1917–1920.

59. JTS, *Semi-Centennial Volume*, pp. 92, 95–96; Schechter papers, I. Friedlaender to Schiff, 11 Jan. 1911; Solomon Grayzel, "Jacob H. Schiff and Jewish Books," *Jewish Book Annual* 5 (1946–47): 78–80; reel 693, Schiff to L. Marshall, 8 Aug. 1919; reel 694, I. Lehman to M. Schiff, 25 Nov. 1925; Louis Marshall papers (JTS archives), file 79–1; Adler, *Schiff*, 2:58.

60. Reel 681, Schiff to M. Sulzberger, 6 Feb. 1906; Rosenblum, "Founding of the United Synagogue," pp. 100, 106–8; Ira Robinson, ed., *Cyrus Adler: Selected Letters*, 2 vols. (Philadelphia, 1985), 1:128, 398; *American Israelite*, 27 June, 11 July 1907, 12 Mar. 1908.

61. Baila R. Shargel, *Lost Love* (Philadelphia, 1997), pp. 100, 128.

62. Arthur A. Goren, *National Leadership in American Jewish Life*, Ninth Annual . . . Feinberg Memorial Lecture, University of Cincinnati, 8 Apr. 1986, pp. 4–9; Moses Rischin, *The Promised City* (New York, 1964), pp. 104–6.

63. Sanders, *Shores of Refuge*, pp. 185–86; Leo N. Levi, "The Modern Dispersion," *Menorah* 34 (June 1903): 331–32.

64. Henry Gersoni, *Jew against Jew* (Chicago, 1881); Cohen, *Encounter with Emancipation*, pp. 308–14, 328–29.

65. Jacob Gordin, *The Benefactors of the East Side* (Yiddish), in Yakov Gordin, *Eynakters* (New York, 1917); *AH*, 6, 20, 27 Mar. 1903.

66. *AH*, 17 July–25 Sept. 1903; Isaac M. Rubinow, "The Jewish Question in New York City," *PAJHS* 49 (Dec. 1959): 90–136.

67. Annette Kohn, "Break Down the Barriers," *Jewish Charity* 3 (Mar. 1904): 140–41; *American Israelite*, 13 June 1901 (*Tageblatt*), 2 Feb. 1905, 10 Nov. 1910; *Menorah* 3 (Dec. 1902): 435; *AH*, 15 Nov. 1895; Cohen, *Encounter with Emancipation*, p. 326; Cyrus Adler papers (AJC archives), L. Marshall to H. Morgenthau, 1 June 1914.

68. See, for example, George Price, "The Russian Jews in America," in *The Jewish*

Experience in America, ed. Abraham J. Karp, 5 vols. (Waltham, Mass. and New York, 1969), 4:336–45.

69. Jenna W. Joselit, *Our Gang* (Bloomington, Ind., 1983), pp. 8–9, 16; *NYT,* 27 Sept. 1895; reel 690, Schiff to L. Marshall, 14 Apr. 1902, to M. Schiff, 26 July 1915.

70. Louis Finkelstein in *AH,* 2 Oct. 1936; Cowen, *Memories of an American Jew,* pp. 91–92; Arthur A. Goren, "Sacred and Secular," *Jewish History* 8, nos. 1–2 (1994): 277, 288; reel 1978, Schiff to T. Shonts, 15 Sept. 1915; Judah Magnes papers (Central Archives for the History of the Jewish People, Jerusalem), P 3/828, Schiff to J. Magnes, 11 Nov. 1908; *AH,* 16 Feb. 1906; Zosa Szajkowski, "Paul Nathan, Lucien Wolf, Jacob H. Schiff and the Jewish Revolutionary Movements in Eastern Europe," *Jewish Social Studies* 29 (Apr. 1967): 80–83.

71. Lloyd Gartner to author, June [8] 1993.

72. Arthur A. Goren, "Pageants of Sorrow, Celebration and Protest," *Studies in Contemporary Jewry* 12 (1996): 211–14.

73. Robinson, *Cyrus Adler,* 1:123–24; *AH,* 17 Nov. 1905; 5 Jan., 2 Feb. 1906; *Maccabaean* 10 (Jan. 1906): 29; Arthur A. Goren, *Dissenter in Zion* (Cambridge, Mass., 1982), pp. 14–15.

74. AJC archives, "Minutes of the Conference on Organization," 3–4 Feb. 1906, remarks by A. Kraus, E. Hirsch, O. Wise; Schiff papers (JTS archives, Jerusalem), Schiff to C. Adler, 3 Nov. 1916; *AH,* 22 Dec. 1905.

75. *AH,* 2 Feb. 1906.

76. Reznikoff, *Marshall,* 1:19–24; *Maccabaean* 10 (Feb. 1906): 76; AJC archives, "Minutes of the Conference on Organization," 3–4 Feb. 1906; reel 693, Schiff to editor, *Jewish Daily News,* 11 Feb. 1906; Zosa Szajkowski, "The Impact of the Russian Revolution of 1905 on American Jewish Life," *YIVO Annual of Jewish Social Science* 17 (1978): 93.

77. *AH,* 16 Feb. 1906.

78. Naomi W. Cohen, *Not Free to Desist* (Philadelphia, 1972), p. 15, chap. 2; *Proceedings* of the Union of American Hebrew Congregations, 1909, pp. 6254–61; Arthur A. Goren, *New York Jews and the Quest for Community* (New York, 1970), pp. 44–45.

79. Reel 693, Schiff to M. Sulzberger, 12 May, 29 June 1908, to Dr. Blau, 10, 30 July, 28 Aug. 1908, to N. Leven, 23 June 1909; Adler, *Schiff,* 2:160.

80. Reel 693, Schiff to C. Adler, 7 Sept. 1908; Arthur Gorenstein, "The Commissioner and the Community," *YIVO Annual of Jewish Social Science* 13 (1965): 187–212. It is interesting that, at the same time, new Italian immigrants, smarting under the existence of crime in their neighborhoods, organized a self-defense organization, the White Hand, to resist the notorious Black Hand. Humbert S. Nelli, *Italians in Chicago* (New York, 1970), pp. 134–35.

81. Reel 23, letter by Schiff, 22 Mar. 190[9]; Goren, *New York Jews,* chaps. 2–3; Reznikoff, *Marshall,* 1:36.

82. AJC archives, "Transcript of the Annual Meeting of the AJC," 8 Nov. 1908.

83. Goren, *New York Jews,* chap. 3; *AH,* 5 Mar. 1909; reel 23, letter by Schiff, 22 Mar. 190[9].

84. Reel 1978, J. Magnes to Schiff, 14 July 1915; Goren, *New York Jews,* chap. 5, pp. 61, 125–26, 144, 182, 184.

85. Adler, *Schiff*, 1:292–93; Goren, *New York Jews*, pp. 196–98; Will Herberg, "The Jewish Labor Movement in the United States," *American Jewish Year Book* 53 (1952): 20.

86. Reel 1978, J. Magnes to B. Schlesinger, 29 June 1915, C. Heineman to Schiff, 2 July 1915; Magnes papers, P 3/1593, J. Magnes to Schiff, 25 May 1915, Schiff to J. Magnes, 26 May, 3 June 1915, to R. Easley, 3 June 1915; *NYT*, 2 July 1915.

87. Magnes papers, P 3/1593, Schiff to J. Magnes, 4 July 1915, J. Magnes to Schiff, 7 July 1915.

88. Reel 1979, Cloak Manufacturers Association file, 1916; *NYT*, 29, 30 Apr., 10 May, 28 June 1916; Melech Epstein, *Jewish Labor in U.S.A.*, 2 vols. (New York, 1969), 2:28–33.

89. *Dearborn Independent, The International Jew*, vol 2 (Dearborn, Mich., 1921), pp. 137–48; Reznikoff, *Marshall*, 1:38–43; Goren, *New York Jews*, chap. 10.

90. Reel 22, Schiff and J. Goldman to C. Hallgarten and J. Plotke, 12 Nov. 1901; Cohen, *Encounter with Emancipation*, pp. 34–39.

91. In *AH*, 22 July 1904.

92. Reel 22, Schiff to J. Goldman, 13 Jan. 1892, to M. Isaacs, 25 Oct. 1888, to D. Lubin, 20 Apr. 1891; Osofsky, "Hebrew Emigrant Aid Society," p. 175; *Proceedings* of the Union of American Hebrew Congregations, 1883,' p. 1417, 1884, p. 1453; Joseph, *Baron de Hirsch Fund*, pp. 49, 127–29; Irving A. Mandel, "The Attitude of the American Jewish Community toward East European Immigration," *American Jewish Archives* 3 (June 1950): 13–16, 24. Privately, Schiff made contributions and paid visits to individual colonies—see, for example, Joseph Brandes, *Immigrants to Freedom* (Philadelphia, 1971), p. 83. For the improvement of traffic facilities and freight rates to Woodbine, he used his connections with the Pennsylvania Railroad. Reel 22, Schiff to S. Rea, 17 May 1916, M. Kohler to M. Schiff, 14 Oct. 1925; reel 692, Schiff to F. Thomson, 10 Nov. 1893.

93. *American Israelite*, 8 Dec. 1910; Cohen, *Encounter with Emancipation*, p. 320.

94. Reel 22, Schiff to J. Hill, 25 Aug., 5 Oct. 1891, 3 June 1892; reel 23, Schiff to J. Hill, 20 July, 12 Aug., 12 Sept. 1891; Adler, *Schiff*, 2:87–88; Albro Martin, *James J. Hill and the Opening of the Northwest* (New York, 1976), pp. 438–39.

95. Reel 22, J. Rosenwald to Schiff, 11 Sept. 1916; reel 23, Schiff to C. Spivak, 27 Nov. 1905; reel 692, Schiff to J. Krauskopf, 14 June 1918; reel 1978, Schiff to G. Deutsch, 12 May 1915; Brandes, *Immigrants to Freedom*, chaps. 4–6; Joseph, *Baron de Hirsch Fund*, pp. 71–82; *NYT*, 6 Dec. 1915, 30 Nov. 1916.

96. *AH*, 31 Oct. 1890; reel 683, Schiff to M. de Hirsch, 23 Oct. 1891. In 1891, Schiff became involved in the Russian Transportation Fund, a new agency for the removal of immigrants from the cities. Reel 22, Schiff to K. Haas, 5 Nov. 1891; Joseph, *Baron de Hirsch Fund*, p. 39.

97. Reel 23, Schiff to S. Wolf, 29 Dec. 1890; *AH*, 17, 31 Oct. 1890; Joseph, *Baron de Hirsch Fund*, p. 184.

98. Reel 683, Schiff to M. de Hirsch, 23 Oct. 1891; reel 693, Schiff to E. Cassel, 14 Oct. 1891; Sheldon M. Neuringer, "American Jewry and the United States Immigration Policy" (Ph.D. diss., University of Wisconsin, 1969), pp. 20–26.

99. Joseph, *Baron de Hirsch Fund*, p. 71; reel 23, Schiff to M. Sulzberger, 27 Sept. 1906.

100. Janine M. Perry, "The Idea of Immigrant Distribution in the United States, 1890–1915" (master's thesis, Hunter College, 1975), chaps. 1–3; Joseph, *Baron de Hirsch Fund*, pp. 184–205; Cohen, *Encounter with Emancipation*, pp. 317–18, 320–22; reel 22, Schiff to F. Underwood, 22 Oct. 1903; IRO papers (AJHS archives), Box 91, I-91, Schiff file. For pre-IRO dispersion projects see Zosa Szajkowski, "The Attitude of American Jews to East European Jewish Immigration," *PAJHS* 40 (Mar. 1951): 235–41.

101. Joseph, *Baron de Hirsch Fund*, pp. 184–205; IRO papers, D. Bressler to Schiff, 25 Feb. 1910; Kate Claghorn in *Jewish Charity* 3 (Nov. 1903): 30–33. Schiff also blamed the Yiddish press, charging that the papers opposed distribution in order to preserve their readership. Reel 22, Schiff to H. Sabsovich, 7 Feb. 1911.

102. *AH*, 17 July–21 Aug., 25 Sept. 1903; National Liberal Immigration League papers (New York Public Library), P. Hall to M. Beals, 14 Feb. 1910; Cohen, *Encounter with Emancipation*, pp. 322–25.

103. *AH*, 22 July 1909; reel 23, Schiff to C. Sulzberger, 12 July 1909. In 1915, his eyes fixed on Jews made homeless by the war, Schiff confidently asserted that the West would welcome Jewish immigrants and that it could absorb about two million. *NYT*, 4 May 1915.

104. *American Israelite*, 22 July–5 Aug., 2 Sept. 1909; *NYT*, 7, 24 Jan. 1910, 23 Jan. 1911, 16 Feb. 1914.

4. Captivity and Redemption (Notes to Pages 124–152)

1. Reel 22 (JTS archives), Schiff to J. Goldman, 10 May 1898, to H. Guenzberg, 23 Jan. 1907; reel 679, Schiff to I. Zangwill, 21 Nov. 1905; Schiff address in *AH*, 8 Oct. 1920.

2. Reel 22, Schiff to M. Blumenthal, 13 Sept. 1899, to S. Kahn, 12 Oct. 1899; Egal Feldman, *The Dreyfus Affair and the American Conscience* (Detroit, 1981), chap. 10; Naomi W. Cohen, "American Jewish Reactions to Anti-Semitism in Western Europe," *Proceedings* of the American Academy for Jewish Research, 45 (1978): 29–65.

3. Reel 22, J. Marcus to S. Wolf, 10 Oct. 1920.

4. Reel 692, Schiff to N. Katzenelsohn, 21 June, 31 July 1904.

5. Reel 22, Schiff to I. Loeb, 22 Dec. 1890, to E. Cassel, 9 June 1891, to J. Seligman, 29 June 1891, to P. Schiff, 8 July 1891; *AH*, 17, 31 Oct. 1890; Naomi W. Cohen, *A Dual Heritage* (Philadelphia, 1969), pp. 57–60.

6. Cyrus Adler and Aaron M. Margalith, *With Firmness in the Right* (New York, 1946), pp. 218–21; Cohen, *Dual Heritage*, pp. 60–62; Philip Cowen, *Memories of an American Jew* (New York, 1932), p. 273; reel 22, Schiff to A. White, 1 Aug. 1892; reel 1977, L. Marshall to Schiff, 28 Aug. 1914.

7. Cohen, "American Jewish Reactions to Anti-Semitism," pp. 32–33, 35; Cohen, *Dual Heritage*, p. 62.

8. Reel 22, Schiff to H. White, 10 Dec. 1890, to O. Villard, 19 June 1905, to P. Nathan, 3 June 1907, to C. Hallgarten, 14 Dec. 1914; reel 679, Schiff to G. Jones, 15 Sept. 1891; Cyrus Adler, *Jacob H. Schiff*, 2 vols. (Garden City, N.Y.,

1929), 2:115. For alerting Americans to Russian atrocities, Schiff contributed to the publication of the memoirs of Russian Minister Urusov.

9. Reel 22, Schiff to J. Pulitzer, 13 July 1891, to O. Straus, 18 June 1891, 31 May 1902; Adler, *Schiff*, 2:116; Cohen, *Dual Heritage*, p. 63; Ira Robinson, ed., *Cyrus Adler: Selected Letters*, 2 vols. (Philadelphia, 1985), 2:39; on Kennan, see Max M. Laserson, *The American Impact on Russia* (New York, 1962), pp. 372–80.

10. Reel 22, Schiff to P. Cowen, 16 July 1892, to C. Stover, 3 Feb. 1892, Schiff's speech to the Chamber of Commerce, 4 Feb. 1892; *AH*, 12 Feb. 1892; Cohen, *Dual Heritage*, p. 65; Cowen, *Memories of an American Jew*, p. 319.

11. For example, reel 22, Schiff to P. Nathan, 21 July 1903.

12. Reel 22, Schiff to E. Cassel, 20 Jan. 1891, to P. Warburg, 25 Oct. 1900; reel 685, Schiff to P. Warburg, 23 Dec. 1895; Adler, *Schiff*, 2:122.

13. Adler, *Schiff*, 2:122–23; reel 679, Schiff to G. Wilenkin, 8 Oct. 1908.

14. Elting E. Morison, ed., *The Letters of Theodore Roosevelt*, 8 vols. (Cambridge, Mass., 1951–54, 2:885, 3:524–25, 657.

15. Reel 679, T. Roosevelt to Schiff, 27 Oct. 1902; Cohen, *Dual Heritage*, pp. 123–26.

16. Reel 694, Schiff to E. Cassel, 11 Nov. 1908; reel 1985, Schiff to S. Wolf, 30 Aug. 1918; Cohen, *Dual Heritage*, pp. 123, 131–32, 147–48; Morison, *Letters of Roosevelt*, 7:471; Adler, *Schiff*, 2:71–72.

17. Reel 679, Schiff to P. Nathan, 10 Oct. 1902, 26 Jan. 1904; reel 681, Schiff to N. Leven, 28 Oct. 1902; Morison, *Letters of Roosevelt*, 4:859; *AH*, 4 Nov. 1904; Cohen, "American Jewish Reactions to Anti-Semitism," p. 35; E. Digby Baltzell, *The Protestant Establishment* (New York, 1964), pp. 151, 153.

18. For example, reel 679, Schiff to P. Nathan, 26 Jan. 1904.

19. NCRSRM papers (AJHS archives), Box 3 I-5: N. Joseph to C. Sulzberger, 26 Apr. 1906; reel 679, Schiff to J. Hay, 19, 21 May 1903; reel 680, Schiff to T. Roosevelt, 7 June 1903; reel 22, Schiff to I. Straus, 5 May 1903, to P. Nathan, 2 June 1903, to T. Roosevelt, 6 Aug. 1903.

20. Reel 22, Schiff to H. Sabsovich, 13 May 1903; Taylor Stults, "Roosevelt, Russian Persecution of Jews, and American Public Opinion," *Jewish Social Studies* 33 (Jan. 1971): 13–22.

21. Cohen, *Dual Heritage*, pp. 127–30; Stults, "Roosevelt, Russian Persecution of Jews," pp. 17–19; reel 22, Schiff to S. Low, 18 May 1903, to P. Nathan, 2 June, 21 July 1903, to N. Leven, 26 June 1903, to C. Adler, 21 July 1903; *American Israelite*, 10 Feb. 1892.

22. Isidore Singer, ed., *Russia at the Bar of the American People* (New York, 1904), pp. 142–61; Arnold White, "The Jewish Question: How to Solve It," *North American Review*, no. 178 (Jan. 1904): 10–24.

23. Reel 684, Schiff to L. Wiley, 9 Aug. 1903; reel 22, Schiff to T. Roosevelt, 6 Aug. 1903, T. Roosevelt to Schiff, 13 Aug. 1903; Singer, *Russia at the Bar*, pp. 161–64; *American Israelite*, 23 July 1903, 4 Feb. 1904; *AH* 7, 14 Aug. 1903.

24. *American Israelite*, 6 Aug. 1903; reel 22, Schiff to C. Adler, 4 June 1903, T. Roosevelt to Schiff, 13 Aug. 1903.

25. Reel 681, Schiff to K. Kaneko, 10 Feb. 1905; Robinson, *Cyrus Adler*, 2:38; Herman Bernstein in *AH*, 8 Oct. 1920; Naomi W. Cohen, *Encounter with Emancipation* (Philadelphia, 1984), p. 236.

26. Reel 22, Schiff to P. Nathan, 29 Mar., 19 July, 11 Oct. 1905, to C. Hallgarten, 14 December 1904.
27. Reel 676, Schiff to H. Schueler, 27 Oct. 1905; reel 679, Schiff to G. Wilenkin, 27 Mar. 1905, to J. Stillman, 29 Aug. 1905; reel 688, Schiff to E. Cassel, 18 Oct. 1905; Cowen, *Memories of an American Jew*, p. 278; Adler, *Schiff*, 2:133.
28. Cowen, *Memories of an American Jew*, chap. 10; reel 22, N. Rothschild to Schiff, 7 Apr. 1904; reel 691, Schiff to P. Nathan, 28 Dec. 1904. Contrary to Lord Rothschild's opinion, the French Rothschilds backed loans to Russia during the Russo-Japanese War. A. J. Sherman, "German Jewish Bankers in World Politics," Leo Baeck Institute *Year Book* 28 (1983): 69.
29. Cowen, *Memories of an American Jew*, chap. 10; *NYT*, 9 Apr. 1911; Mark Levene, *War, Jews, and the New Europe* (Oxford, 1992), pp. 56–59.
30. Reel 22, Schiff to N. Katzenelsohn, 21 June 1904, 31 July 1904; reel 679, CA MSS, Schiff to V. von Plehve [1904]; Adler, *Schiff*, 2:123–28, 146; Naomi W. Cohen, "The Abrogation of the Russo-American Treaty of 1832," *Jewish Social Studies* 25 (Jan. 1963): 7–8.
31. Reel 22, Schiff to G. Wilenkin, 22 Aug. 1904; reel 677, Schiff to K. Takahashi, 24 Dec. 1908; reel 679, Schiff to G. Wilenkin, 27 Mar. 1905; reel 687, Schiff to E. Cassel, 11 Oct. 1908; Adler, *Schiff*, 2:128, 142–43; Walter V. Scholes and Marie V. Scholes, *The Foreign Policies of the Taft Administration* (Columbia, Mo., 1970), p. 123.
32. Reel 22, G. Kennan to Schiff, 11 Apr. 1917; reel 692, Schiff to W. Short, 6 Apr. 1917, to G. Kennan, 11 Apr. 1917; *NYT*, 24 Mar. 1917; Laserson, *American Impact on Russia*, pp. 387–89.
33. Reel 22, Schiff to P. Cowen, 7 Aug. 1905.
34. *Jewish Comment*, 18 Aug. 1905.
35. Ibid., Abraham Ascher, *The Revolution of 1905* (Stanford, Calif., 1988), pp. 18–19, 300–301; NCRSRM papers, S. Wolf to M. Heller, 11 Dec. 1905.
36. Adolf Kraus, *Reminiscences and Comments* (Chicago, 1925), pp. 156–57; Cowen, *Memories of an American Jew*, pp. 328–30; Cohen, *Dual Heritage*, pp. 132–35; Adler, *Schiff*, 2:128–33; *The Memoirs of Count Witte*, trans. and ed. Abraham Yarmolinsky (New York, 1967), pp. 163–64; Herman Bernstein, in *AH*, 8 Oct. 1920.
37. Reel 22, Schiff to P. Cowen, 16 Aug. 1905, to P. Nathan, 15 Sept., 6 Nov. 1905; reel 681, S. Witte to Schiff, 11 Sept. 1905; Morison, *Letters of Roosevelt*, 5:207; *AH*, 15 Sept. 1905.
38. Judith S. Goldstein, *The Politics of Ethnic Pressure* (New York, 1990), p. 42. For this and next paragraph, see *AH*, 18 Aug., 1, 29 Sept. 1905; *Jewish Comment*, 18 Aug.–15 Sept. 1905; *Maccabaean* 9 (Sept. 1905): 161–62; *Jewish American*, 18, 25 Aug., 8 Sept. 1905.
39. Reel 22, Schiff to P. Nathan, 15 Sept. 1905.
40. Ascher, *Revolution of 1905*, p. 255; reel 679, Schiff to I. Zangwill, 21 Nov. 1905, to N. Katzenelsohn, 29 Nov. 1905, to Henry Higginson, 5 July 1906, to R. Noetzlin, 9 Sept. 1906; reel 692, Schiff to C. Adler, 10 Nov. 1905, to E. Cassel, 23 Nov. 1905.
41. Reel 22, Schiff to L. Wald, 22 Jan. 1906; reel 679, Schiff to E. Root in CA MSS, p. 140; Morris D. Waldman, *Nor by Power* (New York, 1953), pp. 325–26; *AH*,

10 Nov. 1905; Zosa Szajkowski, "The Impact of the Russian Revolution of 1905 on American Jewish Life," *YIVO Annual of Jewish Social Science* 17 (1978): 55–56.

42. The summary in this and the next two paragraphs, unless otherwise documented, is based on the files of the NCRSRM, I-5, boxes 1–3. Included but too numerous to cite individually are the communications between the committee and its European counterparts and all of the committee's correspondence. Especially important for this section were the files entitled "Financial and Executive Committee Reports," "Reports: Financial, Fact-finding, Orphans, etc.," and "Jacob Henry Schiff." The activities of the NCRSRM were also reported weekly in *AH*, 10 Nov. 1905–5 Jan. 1906.

43. Szajkowski, "Impact of the Russian Revolution," pp. 54–87; *AH*, 24 Nov. 1905; support of Jewish Defense Association in Zionist journal, *Maccabaean* 9 (Nov.–Dec. 1905): 252, 263–66, 300–1, 317–18.

44. Naomi W. Cohen, *Not Free to Desist* (Philadelphia, 1972), p. 22.

45. *AH*, 10 Nov. 1905; reel 22, Schiff to D. Wolffsohn, 28 Dec. 1905, to Dr. Blau, 30 July 1908; reel 679, Schiff to N. Rothschild, 7 Dec. 1905; reel 676, Schiff to O. Schiff, 19 Dec. 1905; reel 691, Schiff to P. Nathan, 29 Dec. 1905, 15 Feb. 1906; Szajkowski, "Impact of the Russian Revolution," pp. 104–5.

46. NCRSRM papers, "Report of the Executive Committee," Dec. 28, 1905; reel 22, T. Roosevelt to Schiff, 14 Dec. 1905; Stephen Gwynn, ed., *The Letters and Friendships of Sir Cecil Spring-Rice*, 2 vols. (Boston, 1929), 2:12–13, 27–29; Adler, *Schiff*, 2:136–38; Cohen, *Dual Heritage*, p. 134.

47. Reel 22, Schiff to P. Nathan. 10 Oct. 1906; reel 679, Schiff to I. Zangwill, 21 Nov. 1905, to N. Katzenelsohn, 29 Nov. 1905; reel 691, Schiff to P. Nathan, 29 Dec. 1905; Adler, *Schiff*, 2:133–36.

48. Reel 22, Schiff to T. Roosevelt, 27 June, 23, 26 July 1906, to I. Zangwill, 5 July 1906, to S. Jaros, 20 June 1906, to P. Nathan, 26 July 1906, to C. Adler, 25 July 1906, to N. Katzenelsohn, 19 Oct. 1906; Goldstein, *Politics of Ethnic Pressure*, pp. 45–51; Szajkowski, "Impact of the Russian Revolution," pp. 83, 85.

49. Reel 22, Schiff to R. Noetzlin, 9 Sept. 1906, to M. Stone, 30 Dec. 1903, 30 Dec. 1908, to P. Nathan, 19 May 1905, to P. Warburg, 22 July 1906, E. Cassel to Schiff, 3 Jan. 1907; reel 23 (JTS archives), Schiff to I. Zangwill, 25 Oct. 1906; reel 679, Schiff to E. Cassel, 17 Jan. 1907; Cohen, *Dual Heritage*, pp. 146–47.

50. Reel 22, Schiff to S. Jaros, 20 June 1906, to A. Kraus, 21 June 1906; reel 679, Schiff to E. Root, 9 Oct. 1906, to E. Cassel, 17 Jan. 1907; Adler, *Schiff*, 2:141–42.

51. Reel 694, E. Cassel to Schiff, 3 Jan. 1907, 21 Oct., 15 Dec. 1908, Schiff to E. Cassel, 11 Oct., 11 Nov. 1908; reel 22, Schiff to E. Cassel, 17 Jan. 1907.

52. Reel 22, Schiff to C. Montefiore, 17 Nov. 1910, to I. Zangwill, 2 Feb. 1912, G. Wilenkin to Schiff, 22 Nov. 1908; reel 679, Schiff to G. Wilenkin, 8 Oct., 4 Dec. 1908.

53. Reel 22, Schiff to H. Taft, 2 Aug. 1909, L. Wolf to C. Adler, 27 July 1926; Zosa Szajkowski, "Paul Nathan, Lucien Wolf, Jacob H. Schiff and the Jewish Revolutionary Movements in Eastern Europe," *Jewish Social Studies* 29 (Apr. 1967): 91. A variation of the story appears in an interview with Schiff in *AH*, 25 June

1909. There the banker told of a famous "journalist," a Jew by birth only, who, when raising the question of the Jewish condition directly to the czar, was royally snubbed.

54. Unless otherwise noted, all material in this section is drawn from my article, "Abrogation" (see n. 30), which gives a fuller analysis and documentation of the abrogation campaign.

55. Cohen, *Encounter with Emancipation*, p. 236.

56. Reel 22, Schiff to S. Wise, 17 Nov. 1910, to Mr. Feinberg, 2 Dec. 1910; *AH*, 25 June 1909.

57. Reel 22, Schiff to W. Taft, 24 July, 3 Aug. 1908, to O. Straus, 4 Dec. 1908; Cohen, *Encounter with Emancipation*, p. 237.

58. Reel 691, Schiff to W. Taft, 29 Oct. 1909; Adler, *Schiff*, 2:150; AJC archives, "Minutes of the Executive Committee," 20 Feb., 29 May 1910; Cohen, *Encounter with Emancipation*, p. 237; Morton Rosenstock, *Louis Marshall* (Detroit, 1965), p. 55.

59. AJC archives, "Minutes of the Executive Committee," 29 May, 26 Sept. 1910; reel 22, Schiff to C. Adler, 16 Aug. 1910; reel 679, Schiff to A. Ochs, 28 Apr. 1911; Laserson, *American Impact on Russia*, pp. 434–37; Charles Reznikoff, ed., *Louis Marshall*, 2 vols. (Philadelphia, 1957), 1:88; *NYT*, 27 Nov. 1911.

60. Reel 22, Schiff to C. Adler, 16 Aug. 1910, to M. Sulzberger, 23 Dec. 1910; Reznikoff, *Marshall*, 1:59n.

61. Reel 681, W. Taft to Schiff, 23 Feb. 1911; AJC archives, "Minutes of the Executive Committee," 19 Feb. 1911; Simon Wolf, *The Presidents I Have Known* (Washington, D.C., 1918), pp. 294–310; Reznikoff, *Marshall*, 1:78–87. Schiff later denied that he had purposely refused to shake hands with Taft. Reel 1985, Schiff to S. Wolf, 24 May 1918.

62. Reel 22, Schiff to C. Adler, 27 Jan. 1911. Afraid of a charge that they were dominated by the Jews, the organization tied the passport issue to the case for Jan Pouren.

63. AJC archives, "Minutes of the Executive Committee," 20 Feb. 1910; *NYT*, 1, 6 Dec. 1911.

64. Wolf, *Presidents I Have Known*, pp. 310–17; Archibald Butt, *Taft and Roosevelt*, 2 vols. (Garden City, N.Y, 1930), 2:625; William Howard Taft papers (Library of Congress), W. Taft to W. Barnes, 11 Feb. 1911, to Hart Lyman [8 Apr. 1911], to O. Bannard, 17 June 1911, to H. Taft, 25 Nov., 3 Dec. 1911, O. Bannard to Taft, 5 Nov. 1911; reel 22, Schiff to J. Mack, 16 Oct. 1911.

65. House Committee on Foreign Affairs, *Termination of the Treaty of 1832 With Russia*, 62nd Cong., 2nd Sess., 1911, pp. 66–67.

66. Reel 692, Schiff to W. Taft, 7 Dec. 1911; reel 684, 12 Dec. 1911; Butt, *Roosevelt and Taft*, 2:796; Taft papers, W. Taft to C. Taft, 2 Dec. 1912.

67. AJC archives, "Minutes of the Executive Committee," 25 Dec. 1911; reel 22, M. Warburg to Schiff, 1 May 1910; reel 697, Schiff to W. Wilson, 25 Mar. 1915; Schiff papers (JTS, Jerusalem), Schiff to C. Adler, 14 Jan., 25 July 1916, C. Adler to Schiff, 24 July 1916, F. Brylawski to C. Adler, 4 Aug. 1916; *Dearborn Independent, The International Jew*, vol. 2 (Dearborn, Mich., 1921), pp. 206–7.

68. Reel 677, Schiff to L. Marshall, 11, 15 Aug. 1912; Cyrus Adler papers (AJC archives), W. Wilson to C. Adler, 21 Oct. 1912; Reznikoff, *Marshall*, 2:1152–55.

69. Reel 677, Schiff to G. Perkins, 2 Sept. 1912.
70. Reel 679, Schiff to C. Adler, 15 Dec. 1911; Judah Magnes papers (Central Archives for the History of the Jewish People, Jerusalem), P3/407, L. Straus to B. Magnes, 5 Nov. 1912; Cohen, *Dual Heritage*, pp. 219-21; *NYT*, 30, 31 July, 25, 26 Sept. 1913.
71. Reel 22, Schiff to S. Wolf, 9 Oct. 1916.

5. In Search of a Refuge (Notes to Pages 154-188)

1. AJC archives, Immigration file, L. Marshall to L. Lipsky, 17 Dec. 1912; Arthur Gorenstein, "A Portrait of Ethnic Politics," *PAJHS* 50 (Mar. 1961): 202-38; Henry B. Leonard, "Louis Marshall and Immigration Restriction," *American Jewish Archives* 24 (Apr. 1972): 11-23; Naomi W. Cohen, *Not Free to Desist* (Philadelphia, 1972), pp. 47-48, 50.
2. Sheldon M. Neuringer, "American Jewry and United States Immigration Policy, 1881-1953," (Ph. D. diss., University of Wisconsin, 1969), chaps. 1-3; John Higham, *Strangers in the Land* (New York, 1973), chap. 7; Esther L. Panitz, "The Polarity of American Jewish Attitudes towards Immigration," and "In Defense of the Jewish Immigrant," in *The Jewish Experience in America*, ed. Abraham J. Karp, 5 vols. (New York and Waltham, Mass., 1969), 4:31-62, 5:23-63.
3. *Proceedings* of the Union of American Hebrew Congregations, 1911, p. 6635; reel 22 (JTS archives), Schiff and J. Goldman to C. Hallgarten and J. Plotke, 12 Nov. 1901, M. Kohler to M. Schiff, 14 Oct. 1925; reel 678, Schiff to S. Wolf, 29 Dec. 1890, to J. Billikopf, 2 May 1910; reel 691, Schiff to I. Loeb, 19 Sept. 1890, to A. Nettleton, 17 Mar. 1892, to N. Bijur, 10 Mar. 1902, to T. Roosevelt, 11 Mar., 1902, 7 Jan. 1909, to P. Nathan, 15 Feb. 1906; Cyrus Adler, *Jacob H. Schiff*, 2 vols. (Garden City, N.Y., 1929), 2:76-80.
4. Reel 22, M. Kohler to M. Schiff, 14 Oct. 1925; reel 680, Schiff to H. Osborn, 15 Mar. 1912; reel 691, 18 Dec. 1912; *American Israelite*, 25 Aug. 1904.
5. Lillian Wald papers (New York Public Library), Schiff to L. Wald, 31 Dec. 1912; reel 678, Schiff to M. Sulzberger, 27 Dec. 1906; reel 693, Schiff to P. Nathan, 12 Aug. 1904; Zosa Szajkowski, "Paul Nathan, Lucien Wolf, Jacob H. Schiff and the Jewish Revolutionary Movements in Eastern Europe," *Jewish Social Studies* 29 (Jan. 1967): 23-25; Neuringer, "American Jewry and United States Immigration Policy," p. 77.
6. Reel 691, Schiff to L. Marshall, 8 Feb. 1907; *Menorah* 35 (Sept. 1903): 160; *NYT*, 17, 24 Jan. 1910.
7. Reel 23 (JTS archives), Schiff to J. Finley, 3 May 1912; reel 677, Schiff to H. Rice, 7 Nov. 1889, to A. Herbst, 10 June 1912; reel 680, CA MSS; Adler, *Schiff*, 1:395-96; *NYT*, 16 Feb. 1914; "In Defense of the Immigrant," *American Jewish Year Book* 12 (1910-11); Cohen, *Not Free to Desist*, pp. 49, 52.
8. Reel 23, Schiff to L. Wald, 11 Feb. 1911, to E. Devine, 7 Feb. 1911, to J. Finley, 3 May 1912; Cyrus Adler papers (AJC archives), H. Friedenwald to C. Adler, 3 May 1912.
9. Cohen, *Not Free to Desist*, chap. 3; reel 691, Schiff to T. Roosevelt, 7 Jan. 1909,

to P. Nathan, 16 July 1907, 12 Dec. 1911, 22 Jan. 1912, to R. Watchorn, 3 Mar. 1909; Ira Robinson, ed., *Cyrus Adler: Selected Letters*, 2 vols. (Philadelphia, 1985), 1:132; *American Israelite*, 2 July 1908.

10. Leonard, "Louis Marshall and Immigration Restriction," pp. 15–23; Charles Reznikoff, ed., *Louis Marshall*, 2 vols. (Philadelphia, 1957), 1:115–59; reel 22, M. Kohler to M. Schiff, 14 Oct. 1925; reel 23, Schiff to J. Finley, 3 May 1912; reel 1978, N. Behar to Schiff, 2 July 1915; *NYT*, 14 Jan., 9 Apr. 1911, 18 Feb. 1914.

11. Devine wrote the editorial, "The Selection of Immigrants" *Survey*, 4 Feb. 1911; reel 23, Schiff to E. Devine, 7 Feb. 1911, to L. Wald, 11, 14, 24 Feb., 3 Mar. 1911, to N. Butler, 3 Apr. 1911.

12. Reel 22, Schiff to A. Ballin, 13 Jan. 1914; reel 23, Schiff to W. Wilson, 15 Jan. 1915, to J. Wadsworth, 22 Jan. 1917; reel 679, Schiff to S. Wolf, 31 Jan. 1919; Cohen, *Not Free to Desist*, pp. 48, 51–53.

13. Reel 692, I. Zangwill to A. Meyerowitz, 21 Oct. 1920. The best study of the Galveston movement is Bernard Marinbach, *Galveston* (Albany, N.Y., 1983).

14. Zosa Szajkowski, "The Attitude of American Jews to East European Jewish Immigration," *PAJHS* 40 (Mar. 1951): 238; reel 23, Schiff to N. Leven, 16 Sept. 1907; reel 692, Schiff to P. Nathan, 28 Dec. 1904; Janine M. Perry, "The Idea of Immigrant Distribution in the United States, 1890–1915" (master's thesis, Hunter College, 1975), pp. 50–51.

15. Reel 22, Schiff to N. Katzenelsohn, 19 Oct. 1906, to P. Nathan, 27 July 1906; reel 23, Schiff to M. Sulzberger, 27 Sept. 1906. On Mesopotamia and Zionism, see below.

16. Higham, *Strangers in the Land*, pp. 128–30, chap. 6; Cyrus Adler papers (AJC archives), C. Adler to H. Friedenwald, 21 Feb. 1907; reel 22, Schiff to P. Nathan, 25 Feb. 1907, to O. Straus, 22 Jan., 15 Feb. 1907; reel 692, Schiff to C. Hallgarten, 24 June 1907, to P. Nathan, 24 June 1907; *Menorah* 35 (Sept. 1903): 160.

17. *AH*, 20 June 1913.

18. Adler, *Schiff*, 2:96–99; reel 22, Schiff to I. Zangwill, 30 Aug. 1909; reel 23, Schiff to C. Sulzberger, 12 July 1909; reel 692, Schiff to P. Nathan, 27 Aug. 1906; Marinbach, *Galveston*, p. 12; *NYT* 19 Oct. 1909.

19. Marinbach, *Galveston*, esp. chap. 1; Isaac M. Fein, "Israel Zangwill and American Jewry," *American Jewish Historical Quarterly* 60 (Sept. 1970): 31–33; reel 22, Schiff to P. Nathan, 21 Sept. 1906, to I. Zangwill, 16 October, 1906, 14 Sept. 1913, to C. Sulzberger, 18 Dec. 1906; reel 678, statement by Jacob Billikopf on Galveston; *Proceedings of the Sixth National Conference of Jewish Charities*, 1910, pp. 125–27.

20. Reel 22, Schiff to M. Gries, 1 Mar. 1910; reel 692, Schiff to M. Gries, 23 Feb. 1910. Attempting to build up support from local communities, Schiff also spoke at an assembly of the Jewish Chautauqua. *NYT*, 19 July 1909.

21. *Proceedings of the Sixth National Conference of Jewish Charities*, 1910, pp. 124–25.

22. Reel 22, Schiff to C. Sulzberger, 25 Feb., 15 July 1907, to C. Hallgargen, 19 July 1907, to F. Philippson, 13 Feb. 1913; reel 692, Schiff to D. Bressler, 5 July 1907; Joseph Leftwich, *Israel Zangwill* (New York 1957), chap. 7; Joseph H. Udelson, *Dreamer of the Ghetto* (Tuscaloosa, Ala., 1990), pp. 184–85, 198;

Maurice Simon, ed., *Speeches, Articles and Letters of Israel Zangwill* (London, 1937), pp. 290-91; "Jewish Territorial Organization: in *Encyclopedia of Zionism and Israel*, ed. Raphael Patai, 2 vols. (New York, 1971), 2:636-37; for this and the next three paragraphs see Marinbach, *Galveston*, pp. 6-22.

23. Reel 679, Schiff to I. Zangwill, 17 Oct., 21 Nov. 1905; reel 692, Schiff to I. Zangwill, 7 July, 11 Nov. 1909; reel 694, Schiff to G. Meyer, 1 May 1914; reel 23, Schiff to M. Sulzberger, 26 Sept. 1906; Schiff to C. Sulzberger, 12 July 1909; Naomi W. Cohen, *A Dual Heritage* (Philadelphia, 1969), pp. 139-41.

24. Ronald Sanders, *Shores of Refuge* (New York, 1988), p. 247; Simon, *Speeches of Zangwill*, p. 290; *NYT*, 27 Oct. 1907; Fein, "Israel Zangwill and American Jewry," p. 29; reel 23,Schiff to I Zangwill, 28 May 1908.

25. Reel 22, Schiff to P. Nathan, 27 Aug., 5, 20 Dec. 1906, 3 Jan. 1907; Henry Cohen, *The Galveston Immigration Movement, 1907-1910* (n.p. [1910]), courtesy of Abraham Karp.

26. Ibid., pp. 8-9; Marinbach, *Galveston*, chap. 3; reel 678, Schiff to J. Billikopf, 2 May 1910; reel 22, Schiff to I. Zangwill, 29 Aug. 1912.

27. Reel 692, I. Zangwill to A. Meyerowitz, 21 Oct. 1920. The summary of Schiff's activities as administrator is culled from Marinbach, *Galveston*, and from numerous letters in the Schiff papers. The quotation is from reel 693, Schiff to I. Zangwill, 1 Feb. 1910.

28. Reel 22, Schiff to D. Bressler, 5 July 1907; reel 684, Schiff to I. Zangwill, 20 Mar. 1913; reel 692, Schiff to C. Sulzberger, 15 July 1907; Fein, "Israel Zangwill and American Jewry," p. 23.

29. Reel 22, Schiff to I. Zangwill, 16 Oct. 1906, to P. Nathan, 5, 20 Dec. 1906; Fein, "Israel Zangwill and American Jewry," p. 33; Joseph Brandes, *Immigrants to Freedom* (Philadelphia, 1971), pp. 256-58.

30. Reel 22, Schiff to I. Zangwill, 18 Oct. 1907, 23 Aug. 1910, 13 Oct., 21 Nov., 1911, 20 Feb, 7 May, 22 July 1912; reel 678, statement by Jacob Billikopf on Galveston.

31. Marinbach, *Galveston*, pp. 45-49, 53-55, 128-29, 149-55; reel 22, Schiff to O. Straus, 8 Dec. 1908, to F. Philippson, 13 Feb. 1913, to I. Zangwill, 13 Feb., 13 May 1913.

32. Marinbach, *Galveston*, chap. 4; AJC archives, Immigration/Galveston file, B. Cable to W. Bennet, 28 July 1910; Cohen, *Galveston Immigration Movement*, p. 7.

33. Reel 22, Schiff to I. Zangwill, 23 Aug. 1910, 22 July 1912, to S. Wolf, 30 Aug. 1910, to C. Norton, 29 Aug. 1910; Cohen, *Dual Heritage*, pp. 178-80; Morton Rosenstock, *Louis Marshall* (Detroit, 1965), p. 55; Marinbach, *Galveston*, pp. 65-67, 87-90, 109.

34. Reel 22, Schiff to D. Bressler, 30 Aug. 1910, to M. Kohler, 19 Oct. 1910, to I. Zangwill, 11 Jan. 1911, M. Kohler to M. Schiff, 14 Oct. 1925; reel 683, Schiff to C. Norton, 16 Dec. 1910; *Proceedings* of the Union of American Hebrew Congregations, 1911, pp. 6617-34; Marinbach, *Galveston*, pp. 110-12; *NYT*, 19 Oct. 1910.

35. Marinbach, *Galveston*, chaps. 6-9; reel 692, Schiff to I. Zangwill, 30 Aug. 1909; Galveston Immigration Plan papers (AJHS archives), Box 1, Schiff to D. Bressler, 1 Apr. 1914, to S. Wolf, 22 Apr. 1914, D. Bressler to Schiff, 15 June

1914; Jacob H. Schiff, "The Galveston Movement," *Jewish Charities* 4 (June 1914): 5–6.

36. David M. Bressler in *Jewish Comment*, 31 July 1914; Henry Berman in *AH*, 19 June 1914; reel 684, Schiff to I. Zangwill, 9 Apr. 1915; reel 692, Schiff to C. Sulzberger, 2 Nov. 1914; reel 1978, Schiff to L. Sanders, 25 Aug. 1915; Marinbach, *Galveston*, pp. 173, 178–79.

37. Marinbach, *Galveston*, pp. 181–84.

38. Theodore Norman, *An Outstretched Arm* (London, 1985), pp. 16–18, 21–22, chaps. 4–6; Gilbert Osofsky, "The Hebrew Emigrant Aid Society of the United States," in *The Jewish Experience in America*, ed. Abraham J. Karp, 5 vols. (New York and Waltham, Mass., 1969), 4:77; Alex Bein, *Theodore Herzl* (New York, 1970), chap. 13.

39. Reel 678, Schiff to I. Zangwill, 2 Dec. 1909.

40. Reel 22, Schiff to E. Cassel, 9 June 1891; reel 681, CA MSS, Oct. 1891; reel 686, Schiff to E. Cassel, 22 Aug. 1892; reel 692, Schiff to M. de Hirsch, 8 Jan. 1892.

41. Reel 22, Schiff to E. Cassel, 9 June, 16 Sept. 1891, to A. Solomons, 20 July 1891; Kurt Grunwald, "'Windsor-Cassel': The Last Court Jew," Leo Baeck Institute, *Year Book* 14 (1969): 128; Corinne A. Krause, "Mexico—Another Promised Land?" *American Jewish Historical Quarterly* 61 (June 1972): 325–29, 332; Adler, *Schiff*, 1:199–203.

42. Reel 22, Schiff to M. de Hirsch, 9 Nov. 1891, 8 Jan. 1892, to E. Cassel, 16 Sept., 14 Oct. 1891; reel 692, Schiff to E. Cassel, 17 Dec. 1891, to M. de Hirsch, 24 Nov. 1891; Adler, *Schiff*, 2:91–93; Krause, "Mexico," pp. 331–34; Samuel Joseph, *History of the Baron de Hirsch Fund* (Fairfield, N.J., 1978), pp. 40–42. Again in 1907, Mexico indicated to Jewish leaders its desire to encourage immigration. Oscar Straus papers (Library of Congress), O. Straus to Schiff, 24 June 1907.

43. Moshe Perlmann, "Paul Haupt and the Mesopotamian Project," *PAJHS* 47 (Mar. 1958): 154–64; Cohen, *Dual Heritage*, pp. 66–67, 88–90; Mayer Sulzberger in *AH*, 21 May 1909.

44. Cohen, *Dual Heritage*, p. 89; Perlmann, "Paul Haupt and the Mesopotamian Project," p. 161; Simon Schama, *Two Rothschilds and the Land of Israel* (New York, 1978), chaps. 3–5; *AH*, 14 May 1909.

45. Reel 679, T. Herzl to Schiff, 27 Apr. 1904; reel 693, Schiff to O. Schiff, 5 May 1903, to O. Straus, 13 Apr., 6 May 1903, to M. Sulzberger, 17 Apr. 1903; reel 695, Schiff to E. Cassel, 24 Apr. 1903; Grunwald, "'Windsor-Cassel,'" pp. 142–44.

46. Reel 22, Schiff to E. Cassel, 9 June 1903; reel 693, Schiff to O. Schiff, 5 May 1903; Adler, *Schiff*, 2:93–94; Grunwald, "'Windsor Cassel,'" pp. 142–44; Marnin Feinstein, *American Zionism* (New York, 1965), pp. 236–37.

47. Michael Heymann, "The Zionist Movement and the Schemes for Jewish Settlement in Mesopotamia after the Death of Herzl," *Herzl Year Book* 7 (1971): 129–61; *American Jewish Year Book* 11 (1909–10): 97–98; Simon, *Speeches of Zangwill*, p. 321; Cohen, *Dual Heritage*, pp. 140–43.

48. Reel 693, Schiff to I. Zangwill, 3 Feb., 8 Apr., 11 Nov. 1909, 7 Jan., 1 Feb., 29 Mar. 1910, to L. Cohen, 8 July 1909; reel 678, Schiff to I. Zangwill, 2 Dec.

1909; *AH*, 4 June 1909; Heymann, "Zionist Movement," pp. 146–49, 152, 159, 167–68. Schiff was only mildly interested in Zangwill's suggestion of Cyrenaica, but again he made the same conditions. Reel 684, Schiff to I. Zangwill, 8 Apr. 1909.

49. Reel 23, Schiff to E. Cassel, 17 Aug. 1909; reel 678, Schiff to I. Zangwill, 2 Dec. 1909; reel 693, Schiff to I. Zangwill, 3 Feb., 11 Mar., 8 Apr. 1909, 7 Jan., 1 Feb., 29 Mar. 1910, to M. Warburg, 16 May 1910; *NYT*, 9, 26, 30 May 1909; *AH*, 4, 25 June 1909; Heymann, "Zionist Movement," p. 149.

50. Reel 693, Schiff to I. Zangwill, 7 Jan., 1 Feb. 1910; Cohen, *Dual Heritage*, pp. 143–44.

51. Reel 693, Schiff to S. Mexin, 16 July 1915; AJC archives, "Minutes of the Executive Committee," 12 May 1912; Cohen, *Dual Heritage*, p. 144.

52. Selig Adler, "Backgrounds of American Policy toward Zion," in *Israel: Its Role in Civilization*, ed. Moshe Davis (New York, 1956), pp. 255–57; Rudolf Glanz, *Studies in Judaica Americana* (New York, 1970), p. 380; Egal Feldman, *Dual Destinies* (Urbana, Ill., 1990), chap.8. Cyrus Adler later reported to Schiff that in 1891 Solomon Hirsch, then minister to Turkey, discussed the matter with Secretary of State John Sherman. When Sherman said that the United States was willing to join an agreement of the Great Powers guaranteeing Palestine to the Jews on "some basis equitable [read money] to the Turkish Government," Hirsch replied that only a show of armed force would influence the Turks to part with a land with places holy to both Muslims and Christians. Schiff papers (JTS, Jerusalem), C. Adler to Schiff, 25 June 1916; Adler, *Schiff*, 2:161–62; Robinson, *Cyrus Adler*, 1:50.

53. Feinstein, *American Zionism*, chap. 3; reel 693, Schiff to H. White, 17 Mar. 1891.

54. Reel 23, CA MSS; reel 679, CA MSS; reel 691, Schiff to A. Dittenhoefer, 11 Dec. 1905, to J. Hollander, 6 Feb. 1911; reel 693, Schiff to K. Sarasohn, 5 Apr. 1898, to N. Katzenelsohn, 19 May 1904; Reznikoff, *Marshall*, 2:797–98; Naomi W. Cohen, "The Reaction of Reform Judaism in America to Political-Zionism," in *The Jewish Experience in America*, ed. Abraham J. Karp, 5 vols. (Waltham, Mass., and New York, 1969), 5:149–82.

55. Reel 693, Schiff to H. Friedenwald, 18 Nov. 1907.

56. Reel 693, Schiff to K. Sarasohn, 5 Apr. 1898; *NYT*, 4 Apr. 1911; Richard Gottheil in *Jewish Criterion*, 27 Nov. 1903.

57. Aaron S. Klieman and Adrian L. Klieman, eds., *Zionism: A Documentary History*, vol. 2 (New York, 1990), pp. 83–84; Moshe Davis, *With Eyes toward Zion*, vol. 4 (Westport, Conn., 1995), pp. 56–57; *AH*, 22 July 1909 (Schiff at the Jewish Chautauqua); reel 693, Schiff to B. Richards, 4 Oct. 1907; *NYT*, 30 May 1909.

58. Reel 22, Schiff to N. Katzenelsohn, 31 July, 19 Oct. 1906; reel 693, Schiff to N. Katzenelsohn, 19 May 1904, to H. Rosenthal, 23 Nov. 1904, to L. Marshall, 6 Oct. 1908.

59. *AH*, 5 Jan. 1917; reel 693, Schiff to Mr. Cohen, 17 June 1915; Norman Hapgood, "The Future of the Jews in America," *Harper's Weekly*, 27 Nov. 1915. Schiff's young friend Judah Magnes also criticized leadership by the stewards. Reel 1978, J. Magnes to Schiff, 10 Aug. 1915. To undercut Zionist influence

over the masses, Schiff toyed with the idea of making the *Day*, a Yiddish paper he supported, pledge an anti-Zionist stand. Reel 1977, J. Magnes to Schiff, 8 Apr. 1914.

60. Robert Gordis, *Understanding Conservative Judaism* (New York, 1978), p. 122; Richard Gottheil papers (Zionist archives, formerly in New York), R. Gottheil to T. Herzl, 4 June 1903; Adler, *Schiff*, 2:162–64; Cohen, *Dual Heritage*, pp. 88–90; reel 679, T. Herzl to Schiff, 10 Apr. 1904; reel 695, Schiff to O. Schiff, 5 May 1903.

61. Raphael Patai, ed., *The Complete Diaries of Theodor Herzl*, 5 vols. (New York, 1960), 4:1501, 1620–33, 1628, 1631; reel 22, Schiff to N. Katzenelsohn, 31 July 1904; reel 23, Schiff to N. Katzenelsohn, 7 July 1904; reel 693, Schiff to K. Kohler, 6 May 1907; reel 695, Schiff to N. Katzenelsohn, 19 May, 21 June 1904.

62. Reel 679, Schiff to S. Schechter, 12 July 1904; reel 693, Schiff to H. Rosenthal, 23 Nov. 1904, to N. Rothschild, 7 Dec. 1905, to B. Bettman, 8 Feb. 1907; Evyatar Friesel, "Jacob H. Schiff Becomes a Zionist," *Studies in Zionism*, no. 5 (Apr. 1982): 60–61.

63. Reel 679, Schiff to S. Schechter, 12 July 1904; reel 693, Schiff to Schechter, undated, to K. Kohler, 6 May 1907; Solomon Schechter papers (JTS archives), S. Schechter to H. Bentwich, 7 July 1904; Norman Bentwich, *Solomon Schechter* (New York, 1938), p. 316.

64. Reel 691, Schiff to M. Margolis, 7 May 1907; reel 693, Schiff to K. Kohler, 6 May 1907, to S. Schechter, 23 Sept. 1907; Herbert Parzen, "The Purge of the Dissidents," *Jewish Social Studies* 37 (summer–fall 1975): 291–315; Naomi W. Cohen, *Encounter with Emancipation* (Philadelphia, 1984), pp. 294–96.

65. *NYT*, 29 July 1907; Adler, *Schiff*, 2:164–66.

66. Comments by individuals and newspapers are too numerous to cite. For the remainder of the paragraph, see reel 693, Schiff to S. Schechter, 23 Sept. 1907, to A. Isaacs, 3 Oct. 1907; Adler, *Schiff*, 2:166–69; Cohen, *Encounter With Emancipation*, pp. 296–97; *AH*, 20, 27 Sept. 1907; *NYT*, 15 Sept. 1907; Baila R. Shargel, *Lost Love* (Philadelphia, 1997), p. 133; Harry Friedenwald, *The Attitude of the American Zionist* (Baltimore, 1907).

67. L. Marshall, *AH*, 20 Sept. 1907; Straus papers: O. Straus to Schiff, 25 Sept. 1907, Schiff to O. Straus, 26, 29 Sept., 4 Oct., 19 Nov. 1907.

68. Reel 693, Schiff to S. Schechter, 24 Jan. 1909, to B. Richards, 4 Oct. 1907, to H. Friedenwald, 18 Nov. 1907, to J. Magnes, 10 Feb. 1909; reel 691, Schiff to J. Frankel, 6 Jan. 1910.

69. Reel 679, Schiff to P. Nathan, 24 Dec. 1908; reel 693, Schiff to C. Adler, 9 Apr. 1908, to L. Marshall, 6 Oct. 1908; Judah Magnes papers (Central Archives for the History of the Jewish People, Jerusalem), P3/828, Schiff to J. Magnes, 24, 26 Apr. 1911; Schechter papers, L. Marshall to S. Schechter, 24 Mar. 1908; *American Israelite*, 14 May 1908.

70. Reel 693, Schiff to I. Levi, 5 Jan. 1910; *American Israelite*, 29 July 1909.

71. Reel 679, Schiff to N. Katzenelsohn, 24 Oct. 1913; reel 693, Schiff to I. Zangwill, 29 Aug. 1912; Bentwich, *Schechter*, pp. 322–31; *AH*, 20 June 1913.

72. Reel 693, Schiff to I. Zangwill, 29 Aug. 1912, to J. Rosenwald, 4 Dec. 1914; Schiff in *AH*, 20 June 1913; *Maccabaean* 24 (Jan. 1914): 6–7.

73. Reel 679, Schiff to N. Katzenelsohn, 24 Oct. 1913, to N. Straus, 27 Mar. 1912; reel 693, Schiff to J. Magnes, 24 Apr. 1911; reel 1985, Schiff to M. Wertheim, 11 Oct. 1915; Jacob R. Marcus, *United States Jewry*, vol. 4 (Detroit, 1993), pp. 475–76.

74. Reel 693, Schiff to J. Rosenwald, 21 Nov. 1912, 27 Jan. 1913, to L. Marshall, 21, 28 Mar. 1910, J. Rosenwald to Schiff, 1 Dec. 1914; Reznikoff, *Marshall*, 2:705–6; Nathan Efrati, *American Jewry and the Yishuv* (Lecture. Jerusalem, 1993), pp. 6–7, 24; Gabriel Davidson and Max J. Kohler, "Aaron Aaronsohn," *PAJHS* 31 (1928): 202–3.

75. For the background of the Technikum, see Carl Alpert, *Technion* (New York, 1982), pp. 1–17, and Schiff in *AH*, 3 July 1914. Magnes papers, P3/828, Schiff to J. Mack, 4 Feb. 1909, to J. Magnes, 15 Feb. 1909; reel 693, Schiff to P. Nathan, 24 Dec. 1908, to I. Zangwill, 3 Feb. 1909, to L. Marshall, 21, 28 Mar. 1910; Reznikoff, *Marshall*, 2:704.

76. Of the numerous letters dealing with the matter, see esp. reel 693, Schiff to J. Magnes, 10, 15 Feb. 1909, to P. Nathan, 8 July, 9 Oct., 13 Nov., 2 Dec. 1908, 3 Jan. 1909, to J. Mack, 13 Jan. 1909, to I. Zangwill, 3 Feb. 1909; reel 691, Schiff to P. Nathan, 12 Dec. 1911; reel 681, CA MSS, pp. 957–58.

77. Alpert, *Technion*, pp. 36–59, and "Language War" in *Encyclopedia of Zionism and Israel*, 2:702–3, for background material on the language war; *AH*, 16, 30 Jan., 6, 20 Feb. 1914; *American Israelite*, 8, 14 Jan. 1914; see also coverage for 1914 in the American Zionist monthly, *Maccabaean*.

78. For example, see Nahum Sokolow in *AH*, 28 Nov. 1913, Max Heller in *American Israelite*, 15 Jan. 1914; reel 1977, J. Mack to Schiff, 5 Feb. 1914. Nathan's pamphlet, *Der Kampf um die Hebraische Sprache in Palestina*, caused an unusual split between Schiff and Louis Marshall at an AJC meeting. Pained by what he considered Marshall's unwarranted attack on Nathan, the banker threatened to resign from the AJC. Reel 1978, Schiff to L. Marshall, 19 Jan. 1914; Reznikoff, *Marshall*, 2:707–9.

79. Schiff supported a modern Hebrew periodical in America as well as the teaching of Hebrew through the *kehillah*. Marcus, *United States Jewry*, 4:362, 576–77.

80. Reel 693, Schiff to L. Marshall, 17 Nov. 1913, 6 Apr. 1914, to P. Nathan, 10 Sept., 15, 28 Oct., 4, 7 Nov., 28 Dec. 1913, 27 Feb., 10 Apr. 21 July 1914, to S. Levin, 13 Nov. 1913, to A. Kraus, 7 Nov. 1913, to J. Magnes, 3 Feb. 1914, to J. Mack, 7 May 1914, to E. Lewin-Epstein, 6 Apr., 20 Nov. 1914; reel 684, Schiff to I. Zangwill, 11 Feb. 1914; reel 694, Schiff to S. Wolf, 8 July 1914; reel 1977, Schiff to E. Lewin-Epstein, 8, 20 Apr. 1914, to L. Marshall, 31 Oct. 1914; *AH*, 24 Nov. 1914; *NYT*, 6 July 1914; Magnes papers, P/3 832, entire file deals with Technikum; *American Israelite*, 22 Jan. 1914; Bentwich, *Schechter*, pp. 325–28.

81. *AH*, 12 Dec. 1913, 27 Feb. 1914; *American Israelite*, 22 Jan. 1914; *Maccabaean* 24 (Feb. 1914): 55–57; *NYT*, 27 Jan., 1 Feb. 1914; reel 1977, J. Mack to Schiff, 26 Feb. 1914, J. Magnes to Schiff, 9 Jan. 1914, M. Sulzberger to Schiff, 25 Feb. 1914.

82. On developments that followed the compromise, see references in n. 80 to 1914 correspondence; *American Israelite*, 28 May 1914; reel 679, Schiff to P. Nathan, 20 Jan. 1914.

83. Reel 693, Schiff to L. Marshall, 11 June 1914, to S. Wise, 18 June 1914; reel 1977, Schiff to J. Mack, 2 Feb. 1914, L. Marshall to Schiff, 21 Apr., 10 June 1914.

84. Cyrus Adler papers (JTS archives), C. Adler to L. Marshall, 20 July 1914; *AH*, 3 July 1914; *NYT*, 6 July 1914; Robinson, *Cyrus Adler*, 1:252–53; Efrati, *American Jewry and the Yishuv*, p. 12. It is interesting that Zionist leader Chaim Weizmann was also unwilling to alienate the Hilfsverein. Jehuda Reinharz, *Chaim Weizmann* (New York, 1985), pp. 391–92.

85. *AH*, 10 July 1914; *Maccabaean* 25 (July 1914): 2–7. The Zionist periodical *Maccabaean* had affirmed even earlier that Zionists would not trade control of the *yishuv* for money. *Maccabaean* 24 (Jan. 1914): 3–4.

86. *AH*, 17 July 1914; *American Israelite*, 27 Aug. 1914; reel 1977, S. Wolf to Schiff, 7 July 1914.

87. Reel 693, Schiff to P. Nathan, 21 July 1914, to J. Mack, 5 Jan. 1920; reel 1977, Schiff to L. Marshall, 31 Oct. 1914; reel 1978, Schiff to editor, *AH*, 24 Nov. 1915; Adler, *Schiff*, 2:175–76; Naomi W. Cohen, *American Jews and the Zionist Idea* (New York, 1975), p. 23.

88. Reel 693, Schiff to J. Rosenwald, 4 Dec. 1914; reel 1977, Schiff to G. Selikovitch, 22 Dec. 1914; reel 1978, Schiff to C. Melchior, 25 Jan. 1915; *Maccabaean* 26 (May 1915): 84; reel 1978, Schiff to L. Abbott, 3, 6, 29 Dec. 1915, to J. Magnes, 3, 15 Aug. 1915, L. Abbott to Schiff, 4, 28 Dec. 1915; reel 1979, S. Schulman to Schiff, 30 Nov., 1, 3 Dec. 1915, Schiff to S. Schulman, 6, 13 Dec. 1915; Louis Brandeis and Samuel Schulman in *Outlook*, 5 Jan. 1916.

89. Ephrati, *American Jewry and the Yishuv*, p. 8.

6. The World at War (Notes to Pages 189–237)

1. See, for example, *Tageblatt*, 7 Jan. 1917, *Independent*, 15 Jan. 1917, issue of *AH* celebrating Schiff's birthday, 5 Jan. 1917; reel 689, Schiff to E. Arnstein, 19 Sept. 1918; reel 694, R. Fleming to Schiff, 7 Feb. 1917; reel 1985, Schiff to L. Marshall, 20 Sept. 1918. Schiff explained that since his hearing loss made it impossible for him to participate in discussions, his attendance at meetings was both a "farce" and "painful."

2. Chaim Weizmann, *Trial and Error*, 2 vols. (Philadelphia, 1949), 1:62; Naomi W. Cohen, *Encounter with Emancipation* (Philadelphia, 1984), p. 63; *NYT*, 11 Feb. 1913.

3. Reel 689, Schiff to M. Boardman, 11 Aug. 1914; *NYT*, 30 July 1911, 22 Nov. 1914. See also reel 1977, Schiff to L. Wiley, 1 Oct. 1914; reel 1982, Schiff to L. Greenberg, 29 Jan. 1917, to editor *Jewish World*, 2 Feb. 1917. The interview in the *Times* gave rise to numerous comments by readers. *NYT*, 25 Nov., 6, 26 Dec. 1914.

4. Charles W. Eliot, *The Road to Peace* (Boston, 1915), chap. 10; *NYT*, 20, 23, 25, 26 Nov. 1914; Mark Levene, *War, Jews, and the New Europe* (Oxford, 1992), p. 28.

5. *NYT*, 4 Dec. 1914; unsorted Schiff papers (American Jewish Archives), Schiff to M. Warburg, 28 Jan., 16 Feb. 1915, M. Warburg to Schiff, 12 Feb. 1915.

6. Reel 680, CA MSS, pp. 996–97; *NYT*, 26 Nov., 1 Dec. 1916; *AH*, 1 Dec. 1916; reel 1977, Schiff to M. Thomason, 4 Jan. 1915, to K. Takahashi, 6 Jan. 1915, to M. Schiff, 9 Oct. 1914; reel 681, CA MSS, pp. 996–99; reel 684, Schiff to C. Eliot [Apr. 1916]; reel 1981, Schiff to K. Takahashi, 21 June 1916; Priscilla M. Roberts, "A Conflict of Loyalties," in *Studies in the American Jewish Experience*, vol. 2, ed. Jacob R. Marcus and Abraham J. Peck (Lanham, Md., 1984), p. 9.

7. Reel 679, Schiff to E. Cassel, 9 Mar. 1898; reel 680, Schiff to M. Bonn [Dec. 1914]; reel 1977, S. Levinson file; reel 1981, Schiff to W. Bryan, 28 Aug. 1914, to N. Toy, 30 Dec. 1914, to W. Wilson, 19 Nov. 1914, to R. Schiff, 3 May 1916; reel 1978, New York Peace Society file, Schiff to R. Thompson, 3 Dec. 1915, to E. Marshall, 15 Feb. 1915; reels 1980 and 1984, League to Enforce Peace files; Merle Curti, *Peace or War* (New York, 1936), pp. 212–14; New York Peace Society *Yearbook*, 1911–18; *NYT*, 1 Nov. 1914, 9 Feb., 26 Mar., 18 June, 25 July, 27 Dec. 1915, 28 May, 27 Nov. 1916, 26 Jan. 1917; *AH*, 1 Dec. 1916; Cyrus Adler, *Jacob H. Schiff*, 2 vols. (Garden City, N.Y., 1929), 2:178.

8. Reel 1977, Schiff to K. Takahashi, 7 Oct. 1914; reel 1979, Schiff to K. Takahashi, 18 June 1915; reel 685, Schiff to B. Fleisher, 19 Dec. 1916.

9. Reel 1977, F. Chadwick, C. Bernheimer, and S. Levinson files; reel 1978, M. Malevinsky to Schiff, 11 Nov. 1915; reel 1982, W. Short to Schiff, 3 Apr. 1917.

10. Reel 23 (JTS archives), Schiff to S. Schechter, 28 June 1911; reel 679, Schiff to W. Guthrie, 6 Oct. 1915, to A. Zimmerman, 19 Oct. 1914; reel 690, Schiff to W. Hewitt, 7 Feb. 1912, to A. White, 8 Jan. 1912; reel 1977, Schiff to L. Marshall, 26 Oct. 1914, to L. Wolf, 14 June 1915, L. Marshall to Schiff, 30 Oct. 1914; Paul Arnsberg, *Jakob H. Schiff* (Frankfurt, 1969), pp. 51–54; Adler, *Schiff*, 2:17–18, 33, 37–38, 180, 293–95, 325–26; Naomi W. Cohen, *A Dual Heritage* (Philadelphia, 1969), p. 4.

11. Reel 1977, Schiff to J. Noeggerath, 1 Sept. 1914, T. Harris to Schiff, 4 Dec. 1914; reel 22 (JTS archives), Schiff to M. Warburg, 22 Sept. 1915; reel 679, Schiff to P. Nathan, 14 Oct. 1914; Roberts, "Conflict of Loyalties," p. 7.

12. Reel 1977, Schiff to J. Wilson, 17 Sept. 1914; reel 1978, correspondence with J. von Bernstorff, Sept. 1915; reel 689, Schiff to M. Boardman, 28, 31 Aug. 1914; Senate Subcommittee of the Committee on the Judiciary, *Brewing and Liquor Interests and German Propaganda*, 65th Cong., 3rd sess., 1919, 2:1448.

13. When Dernburg indulged in public remarks that sounded too callous, Marshall and others recommended that Schiff call off a scheduled appearance by the German at the YMHA. Reel 1977, L. Marshall to Schiff, 14 Oct., 14 Dec. 1914; Adler, *Schiff*, 2:189–90; reel 1978, Schiff (a) file, Feb. 1915; reel 679, Schiff to A. Zimmermann, 19 Oct. 1914; Joseph Rappaport, "Jewish Immigrants and World War I" (Ph.D. diss., Columbia University, 1951), p. 144n.

14. Frederick C. Luebke, *Bonds of Loyalty* (De Kalb, Ill., 1974), pp. 90–91, 122, 161–62, 128, 229; reel 1977, Schiff to H. Muensterberg, 11 Nov. 1914, H. Muensterberg to Schiff, 18 Nov. 1914, M. Jastrow to Schiff, 15 Dec. 1915; reel 690, Schiff to G. Viereck, 28 Dec. 1916; Leo P. Ribuffo, *The Old Christian Right* (Philadelphia, 1983), pp. 21, 187.

15. Reel 679, Schiff to A. Zimmermann, 19 Oct. 1914; reel 1978, Schiff to G. Viereck, 26 May 1915; reel 1980, Schiff to J. Magnes, 13 June 1916.

16. Reel 1977, Schiff to J. Noeggerath, 1 Sept. 1914, to H. Muensterberg, 11 Nov.

1914; reel 679, Schiff to A. Zimmermann, 19 Oct. 1914, to P. Nathan, 14 Oct. 1914; Adler, *Schiff*, 2:192. Schiff also voiced his opposition to a German Jewish desire to close the border to fugitive Jews from the east. Reel 1980, Schiff to M. Warburg, 19 May 1916.

17. Senate Subcommittee, *Brewing and Liquor Interests*, 1:3–6, 2:1388–89, 1986–90, 1993–97; unsorted Schiff papers (American Jewish Archives), Schiff to M. Warburg, 9 Oct., 25 Nov., 15 Dec. 1914, 28 Jan., 16 Feb., 22 Sept. 1915; reel 697, Schiff to M. Warburg, 2 May 1916; Roberts, "Conflict of Loyalties," pp. 10–14, 21; John Kobler, *Otto the Magnificent* (New York, 1988), pp. 86–89; *NYT*, 26 Mar. 1915; Ron Chernow, *The Warburgs* (New York, 1993), p. 166. The firm also turned down a request by the Hamburg-American line to buy some of its ships stranded in American ports. *NYT*, 19 Feb. 1915.

18. Unsorted Schiff papers, Schiff to M. Warburg, 5 Nov. 1915; reel 694, M. Warburg to Schiff, 12 Feb., 10 Oct. 1915; reel 1980, Schiff to J. Magnes, 13 June 1916.

19. Unsorted Schiff papers, Schiff to M. Warburg, 5 Nov. 1915, to P. Nathan, 16 Feb. 1915.

20. Joseph Rappaport, "The American Yiddish Press and the European Conflict in 1914," *Jewish Social Studies* 19 (July–Oct. 1957): 113–19; reel 1977, L. Marshall to Schiff, 14 Oct., 14 Dec. 1914; Charles Reznikoff, ed., *Louis Marshall*, 2 vols. (Philadelphia, 1957), 2:511. Louis Marshall, then president of the AJC, took issue with the Jewish posture. Urging strict neutrality, he claimed that only strict nonpartisanship could gain a hearing for the rights of Jews in post-war Europe.

21. Reel 1981, Schiff to C. Eliot, 14 Mar. 1917.

22. Reel 689, Schiff to E. Wadsworth, 10 Jan. 1917, to M. Warburg, 25 Nov. 1914; Ron Chernow, *The House of Morgan* (New York, 1990), pp. 195–200; Kobler, *Otto the Magnificent*, p. 88; *NYT*, 25, 26, 27, 30 Nov., 1 Dec. 1916; Adler, *Schiff*, 2:193–201.

23. Levene, *War, Jews, and the New Europe*, pp. 56–59; Stephen Gwynn, ed., *The Letters and Friendships of Sir Cecil Spring-Rice*, 2 vols. (Boston, 1929), 2:148, 201, 242, 245, 286, 309, 312, 373; Jacob H. Schiff, "The Jewish Problem Today," *Menorah Journal* 1 (Apr. 1915): 77.

24. Reel 1977, B. Richards to Schiff, 5 Nov. 1915; Cohen, *Dual Heritage*, pp. 236–37; Naomi W. Cohen, *Not Free to Desist* (Philadelphia, 1972), pp. 89–90; Reznikoff, *Marshall*, 2:674, 900–903.

25. Judith Goldstein, "Ethnic Politics," *American Jewish Historical Quarterly* 65 (Sept. 1975): 40–41.

26. Unsorted Schiff papers, Schiff to M. Warburg, 22 Sept., 10 Oct. 1914; Adler, *Schiff*, 2:250–54; Roberts, "Conflict of Loyalties," pp. 18–21; Chernow, *The Warburgs*, pp. 167–69; *NYT*, 29 Sept., 2 Oct. 1915; Kobler, *Otto the Magnificent*, p. 88; Levene, *War, Jews, and the New Europe*, p. 61; *NYT*, 29 Feb. 1916. In 1916, Kuhn, Loeb floated a municipal loan for the municipality of Paris. Schiff attempted to match this with similar loans to Germany, but the U-boat crisis made that plan impossible. Reel 694, Schiff to M. Warburg, 11 Oct. 1916.

27. Carl H. Voss, ed., *Stephen S. Wise* (Philadelphia, 1969), p. 71; reel 684, Schiff to I. Zangwill, 9 Apr. 1915; *Day*, 3 Oct. 1915.

28. Reel 1977, G. Wilenkin to Schiff, 6 Sept., 11 Oct., 4 Dec. 1914, Schiff to G. Wilenkin, 13 Sept., 14 Dec. 1914; reel 679, Schiff to P. Nathan, 23 Sept. 1914; reel 697, Schiff to G. Wilenkin, 23 Sept. 1914.

29. Reel 22, Schiff to H. Bernstein, 1 Mar. 1916, to L. Wiley, 14 Apr. 1916; *NYT,* 26 Nov. 1915, 29 Feb. 1916; reel 679, Schiff to Warburg, 23 Nov. 1915; reel 697, CA MSS, p. 579; Schiff papers (JTS archives, Jerusalem), Schiff to L. Marshall, 15 Jan. 1915; AJC archives, "Minutes of the Executive Committee," 17 Mar., 20 Sept. 1915; *American Jewish Year Book* 18 (1916–17): 300–301; Reznikoff, *Marshall,* 2:649; Chernow, *House of Morgan,* p. 196; Rappaport, "Jewish Immgrants and World War I," p. 143.

30. Reel 679, Schiff to W. Wilson, 25 Mar. 1915; reel 689, Schiff to J. Kean, 19 July 1916; reel 1977, L. Marshall to Schiff, 28 Aug. 1914; Schiff papers (JTS archives, Jerusalem), Schiff to C. Adler, 14 Jan., 25 July 1916, C. Adler to Schiff, 24 July, 7 Aug. 1916, L. Marshall to Schiff, 14 Jan. 1915; AJC archives, Schiff file, Schiff to H. Bernstein, 7 July 1914; *American Jewish Year Book* 19 (1917–18): 458–61.

31. Adler, *Schiff,* 2:68, 192; *NYT,* 29, 31 Oct. 1915; reel 691, Schiff to B. Richards, 8 Feb. 1919.

32. Reel 677, Schiff to J. Beck, 13 Jan. 1913; Adler, *Schiff,* 1:38–41, vol. 2, chap. 12, passim. According to a report in the *New York Times* (1921), Schiff once offered to buy Monticello and present it as a gift to the country. Charles B. Hosmer, Jr., "The Levys and the Restoration of Monticello," *American Jewish Historical Quarterly* 53 (Mar. 1964): 247.

33. Reel 23, CA MSS; Adler, *Schiff,* 1:326–27; *New York Sun,* 13 Dec. 1904; *Jewish Comment,* 16 Dec. 1904; *American Israelite,* 5 Jan. 1905; "Many-Sided Jacob H. Schiff," *New York World Magazine,* 16 Apr. 1905; reel 689, Schiff to A. Gwinner, 9 Jan. 1905.

34. Reel 1981, Schiff to J. Bass, 1 Nov. 1916, to H. Morgenthau, 22 Sept. 1916; *NYT,* 19 June 1916, 24 Jan. 1917.

35. Reel 680, CA MSS; reel 1984, Schiff to M. Jastrow, 28 May 1918; reel 1985, Schiff to F. Warburg, 18 Mar. 1918; Judah Magnes papers (Central Archives for the History of the Jewish People), P3/118, Schiff to J. Magnes, 27 Mar. 1917; Adler, *Schiff,* 2:203–4.

36. Reel 686, Schiff to E. Cassel, 10 Apr., 14 May 1914; reel 689, Schiff to M. Boardman, 26 Feb. 1915; reel 694, Schiff to S. Wolf, 10 July 1914; *NYT,* 11 July 1914, 16 Feb. 1915, 2 Apr. 1914. Warburg's appointment generated rumors of a link between Kuhn, Loeb and the government, obliging Warburg to emphasize his dissociation from the firm.

37. Priscilla M. Roberts, "The American 'Eastern Establishment' and World War I" (Ph.D. diss., University of Cambridge, 1981), pp. 207–8; Frieda S. Warburg, *Reminiscences of a Long Life* (New York, 1956), p. 76; reel 684, M. Strook to M. Schiff, 3 Oct. 1925; reel 697, Schiff to J. Schurman, 3, 17 June 1918; David G. Singer, "The Prelude to Nazism," *American Jewish Historical Quarterly* 66 (Mar. 1977): 419.

38. References in the Schiff papers to the banker's consultations on financial issues with Wilson and the Treasury Department (1914–19), his participation in liberty loan rallies, and his service on ad hoc committees are too numerous to cite

individually. Some of the material is in Adler, *Schiff*, 2:201, 205–6, 210–25, 235–46, 273–76, 287; see also *NYT*, 10 Sept. 1914, 5, 12, 25 May 1917, 12 Apr., 13 Dec. 1918. For his personal contributions and service in patriotic organizations: reel 1985, Schiff to D. Duval, 8 Apr. 1918, to J. Wilson, 9 May 1918, R. Easley to Schiff, 25 Apr. 1918; reel 1981, Schiff to G. Creel, 30 Nov. 1917, to E. Anderson, 28 June 1917; reel 1983, J. Koettgen to Schiff, 25 Sept. 1918; reel 1984, Schiff to E. Bernays, 7 June 1918, to A. Rothstein, 28 Oct. 1918; James R. Mock and Cedric Lawson, *Words That Won the War* (Princeton, N.J., 1939), pp. 217–19; *NYT*, 19 Jan., 17 Feb. 1918.

39. *NYT*, 4 May 1917.

40. John Higham, *Strangers in the Land* (New York, 1973), pp. 195, 204–7; Zosa Szajkowski, *Jews, Wars, and Communism*, vol. 1 (New York, 1972), pp. 75–76, 135; Harry Barnard, *The Forging of an American Jew* (New York, 1974), p. 208. An anti-Semitic atmosphere kept the government from utilizing the services of Jews.

41. Rappaport, "Jewish Immigrants and World War I," pp. 278–81; Ronald Sanders, *Shores of Refuge* (New York, 1988), p. 297; Szajkowski, *Jews, Wars, and Communism*, 1:115–18, chap. 10; reel 691, Schiff to R. Morris, 15 Apr. 1918; reel 1982, Schiff to E. Friedman, 5 July 1917, to H. Kallen, 25 July 1917, L. Marshall to Schiff, 20 Apr. 1917; *NYT*, 10 Nov. 1915, 4 May 1917.

42. *American Jewish Year Book* 20 (1918–19): 391, 21 (1919–20): 627–29; AJC archives, "Minutes of the Executive Committee," 23 Sept., 11 Nov., 9 Dec. 1917, 13 Jan. 1918; Morton Rosenstock, *Louis Marshall* (Detroit, 1965), pp. 103, 106; reel 1985, Schiff to C. Rosebault, 9 Oct. 1918; reel 1986, L. Lashman to Schiff, 23 Feb. 1918.

43. Reel 691, Schiff to S. Untermyer, 1 Apr. 1917, to H. P. Mendes, 7 May 1918; reel 1983, Schiff to J. Wilson, 6 Apr. 1917; *NYT*, letter to editor, 3 Apr. 1917; Samuel Joseph, *History of the Baron de Hirsch Fund* (Fairfield, N.J., 1978), p. 225; Szajkowski, *Jews, Wars, and Communism*, p. 135.

44. Adler, "Schiff, 1:366–69, 2:225–27, 229–31; reel 689, Schiff to L. Arnstein, 2 Apr. 1917, to E. Brown, 4 Apr. 1918, to Mrs. Osborn, 1 July 1918; reel 1986, American Red Cross file; *NYT*, 31 Oct. 1913; Foster R. Dulles, *The American Red Cross* (New York, 1950), p. 99.

45. Reel 689, Schiff to A. Lucas, 24 Aug. 1917, to H. Davison, 12 July 1917; Dulles, *American Red Cross*, p. 143.

46. Shortly before Schiff's death, Marshall complained to Davison about Red Cross discrimination against Jews in postwar Poland. Reznikoff, *Marshall*, 1:290–94.

47. Reel 689, Schiff to A. Lucas, 24 Aug. 1917.

48. Adler, *Schiff*, 2:227–29; reel 689, Schiff to T. Roosevelt, 27 June 1917; reel 1982, Schiff to L. Marshall, 28 June 1917; reel 1983, Louis Wiley folder, S. Wolf to Schiff, 18 July 1917; Oscar Straus papers (American Jewish Archives), O. Straus to Schiff, 22 June 1917; Rosenstock, *Marshall*, pp. 108–9; *NYT*, 27, 30 June 1917; *American Jewish Year Book* 21 (1919–20): 646–47.

49. Reel 23, Schiff to W. Wilson, 15 Jan. 1915; reel 1981, Schiff to L. Marshall, 22 Jan. 1917; Cohen, *Not Free to Desist*, pp. 52–53.

50. Reel 691, Schiff to H. Moskowitz, 20 Apr. 1917; *NYT*, 29 Oct. 1917.

51. Thomas M. Henderson, *Tammany Hall and the New Immigrants* (New York, 1976), pp. 177–79, 224, 217–19; Rappaport, "Jewish Immigrants and World War I," p. 289; Will Herberg, "The Jewish Labor Movement in the United States," *American Jewish Year Book* 53 (1952): 32–33; *NYT*, 24 Mar. 1917.

52. Rappaport, "Jewish Immigrants and World War I," pp. 282–90; Henderson, *Tammany Hall*, p. 228; Szajkowski, *Jews, Wars, and Communism*, pp. 145–47, 515; *NYT*, 1 Nov. 1917; reel 1982, Fusion Committee file.

53. Szajkowski, *Jews, Wars, and Communism*, chap. 6; reel 1982, Schiff to W. Edidin, 14 Sept. 1917, J. Newman to Schiff, 15 Sept. 1917; reel 1978, J. Magnes to Schiff, 23 Aug. 1915; Arthur A. Goren, ed., *Dissenter in Zion* (Cambridge, 1982), pp. 160, 162; Henderson, *Tammany Hall and the New Immigrants*, p. 235; *New York Tribune*, 20 Oct. 1917. Another pacifist whom Schiff tolerated was Lillian Wald.

54. Reel 679, Schiff to B. Kamenka, 23 Apr. 1917; reel 1981, P. Cravath to Schiff, [Apr. 1917]; reel 1982, L. Marshall to Schiff, 8 June 1917. The editor of the *Forward* wrote the *Times* questioning the popular notion that the names of the Bolshevik leaders proved that they were Jewish. *NYT*, 13 June 1917.

55. Reel 1981, CA MSS, wire signed by Oscar Straus et al., [Apr. 1917]; reel 1982, A. Guenzberg to Schiff, 24 Apr. 1917, L. Marshall to Schiff, 25 Apr. 1917; AJC archives, "Minutes of the Executive Committee," 16 May 1917; *American Jewish Year Book* 20 (1918–19): 371–73; *NYT*, 29 Apr. 1917; Arthur A. Goren, *New York Jews and the Quest for Community* (New York, 1970), p. 229.

56. Reel 1981, E. Root to Schiff, 4 May 1917; Szajkowski, *Jews, Wars, and Communism*, chap. 18; Cohen, *Not Free to Desist*, p. 99, *NYT*, 4 May 1917.

57. Reel 22, Schiff to L. Wald, 25 Apr. 1917, to I. Tolstoy, 9 May 1917; reel 679, Schiff to O. and E. Schiff, 1 May 1917; *NYT*, 18, 25, 26 Mar., 10, 13, 29 Apr. 1917; Adler, *Schiff*, 2:256–57.

58. *NYT*, 26 Mar., 13, 29 Apr., 11 May, 8, 18 July 1917; reel 22, Schiff to S. Asch, 8 May 1917; reel 692, Schiff to B. Kamenka, 15 May, 7 June, 11 July 1917; reel 1981, L. Marshall to E. Paul, 5 Apr. 1917. Schiff did not recoup the loans to the Lvov government. Reel 1984, Schiff to S. Mason, 22 Nov. 1918.

59. *NYT*, 13 Apr., 11 May, 18 July 1917; reel 22, Schiff to T. Rousseau, 5 July 1917, to L. Wald, 11 July 1917.

60. Reel 1982, Schiff to L. Marshall, 2 July 1917; *American Jewish Year Book* 20 (1918–19): 374.

61. "Jewish War Relief Work," *American Jewish Year Book* 19 (1917–18): 194–226; Merle Curti, *American Philanthropy Abroad* (New Brunswick, N.J., 1988), pp. 241–45; reel 1978, C. Dumba to Schiff, 12 Feb. 1915, Schiff to J. Stolper, 1 June 1915; unsorted Schiff papers (American Jewish Archives), Schiff to M. Warburg, 28 Jan., 16 Feb. 1915. During the war, Schiff continued to defend Jewish immigration to the United States. He announced in 1915 after a trip to states west of the Mississippi that at least two million Jews could be absorbed there. Undertaken in part to ascertain American sentiment toward Jews, his journey convinced him, he said, that they would be welcomed. On the same trip the banker reportedly suggested that the United States purchase lower California from Mexico. If the story was true—and indeed he had rejected the idea when first broached by Oscar Straus—it stemmed from the desire to prepare

safe havens for those made homeless by the war. *NYT,* 4, 9 May, 6 Dec. 1915; Schiff papers (JTS archives, Jerusalem), L. Marshall to Schiff, 20 Feb. 1915.

62. AJC archives, "Minutes of the Executive Committee," 31 Aug., 7 Nov. 1914; Cyrus Adler papers (JTS archives), L. Marshall to C. Adler, 2 Sept. 1914; reel 1977, Schiff to D. Bressler, 4 Oct. 1915, L. Marshall to Schiff, 9 Oct. 1915; *NYT,* 16 Nov. 1914.

63. Zosa Szajkowski, "Concord and Discord in American Jewish Overseas Relief," *YIVO Annual of Jewish Social Science* 14 (1969): 99–142; Melvin I. Urofsky, *American Zionism from Herzl to the Holocaust* (Garden City, N.Y., 1975), pp. 168–69; Oscar Handlin, *A Continuing Task* (New York, 1964), ch. 2.

64. *NYT,* 22 Dec. 1915; reel 694, Schiff to S. Wolf, 24 Dec. 1915.

65. Reel 680, CA MSS, pp. 1122–23; reel 691, Schiff to J. Magnes, 8 Mar. 1918; reel 1978, Schiff to H. Bernstein, 8 June 1915, to M. Schiff, 15 Mar. 1915, H. Bernstein to Schiff, 8 July 1915; reel 1979, C. Adler to Schiff, 23 June 1916; reel 1984, Schiff to L. Harrison, 1 Feb. 1918; Schiff papers (JTS archives, Jerusalem), L. Marshall to Schiff, 15 Mar. 1915; *NYT,* 30 Oct. 1914.

66. *American Jewish Year Book* 18 (1916–17): 9, 19 (1917–18): 202–4; reel 1977, AJRC files; reel 1978, Schiff to M. Guggenheim, 13 Dec. 1915, J. Rosenwald files; reel 1981, AJRC files; reel 1982, Jewish War Relief files, Jewish Welfare Board files; reel 1985, J. Rosenwald file; *NYT,* 22 Dec. 1916, 16 Apr., 21 Nov., 3, 6, 13, 16 Dec. 1917; Jacob R. Marcus, *United States Jewry,* vol. 4 (Detroit, 1993), pp. 621–22.

67. Adler, *Schiff,* 2:281–83; the voluminous correspondence relating to relief and the Jewish Welfare Board is found in reels 1977–84, files on AJRC, Jewish Welfare Board, and Joint Distribution Committee for 1914–18. See also reel 1977, Schiff to C. Bernheimer, 27 May 1915, to J. Billikopf, 13 July 1915; reel 1978, Schiff to D. Goldberg, 18 Aug. 1915; reel 1981, Schiff to J. Billikopf, 16 July 1917; *NYT,* 30 Oct. 1914, 22, 23 Nov. 1915, 19 Nov. 1917.

68. Schiff papers (JTS archives, Jerusalem), Schiff to L. Marshall, 5 Feb. 1915; *American Jewish Year Book* 19 (1917–18): 451–58; reel 1978, L. Marshall to Schiff, 30 Dec. 1915; *NYT,* 29 Oct., 7 Dec. 1917; Adler, *Schiff,* 2:282. At one meeting of the relief campaign, Jews also asked Wilson, albeit in vain, to broaden the scope of the Belgian Relief Committee to include Poland and Lithuania.

69. *American Jewish Year Book* 19 (1917–18): 202; reel 697, statement by Schiff on Jewish Relief Day, 20 Jan. 1916; reel 1977, Schiff to B. Richards, 18 Sept. 1914; *AH,* Nov. 10–Dec. 29, 1917; Curti, *American Philanthropy Abroad,* pp. 243–44; *NYT,* 18 Feb. 1918; Arthur A. Goren, *National Leadership in American Jewish Life,* Ninth Annual . . . Feinberg Memorial Lecture, University of Cincinnati, 8 Apr. 1986, pp. 19–20.

70. Urofsky, *American Zionism,* pp. 168–71; Melvin I. Urofsky and David W. Levy, eds., *Letters of Louis D. Brandeis,* vol. 4 (Albany, 1975), pp. 205, 211–13, 234; reel 693, Schiff to L. Marshall, 28 Aug. 1914; reel 1977, W. Bryan to Schiff, 28 Aug. 1914, Schiff to J. Magnes, 1 Nov. 1915; reel 1978, Schiff to J. Rosenwald, 8 Feb. 1915; reel 1979, Schiff to C. Adler, 22 June 1916, to J. Magnes, 24 Feb. 1916; Schiff papers (JTS archives, Jerusalem), L. Marshall to Schiff, 3 Feb., 8 Mar. 1915, to W. Bryan, 8 Mar. 1915, Schiff to L. Marshall, 3

Feb. 1915; Magnes papers, P3/1594, Schiff to J. Magnes, 8 Mar. 1916; Norman Bentwich, *For Zion's Sake* (Philadelphia, 1954), pp. 99–101; Boris D. Bogen, *Born a Jew* (New York, 1930), chap. 9; Frank E. Manuel, *The Realities of American-Palestine Relations* (Washington, D.C., 1949), pp. 140–42.

71. On Palestine see Reel 679, Schiff to J. Goldman, 4 June 1915, to E. Bicknell, 20 Jan. 1916; reel 693, Schiff to A. Kraus, 9 Oct. 1914, to H. Morgenthau, 2 Sept. 1914, to M. Warburg, 25 Feb. 1916, to A. Murray, 10 Jan., 16 May 1916, to R. Lansing, 16 Nov. 1916; reel 1977, H. Morgenthau to Schiff, 17 July, 26 Sept., 22 Nov. 1917, to R. Tinsley, 17 Oct. 1914, L. Marshall to Schiff, 30 Oct. 1914; reel 1981, Schiff to C. Adler, 26 Jan. 1917, to Dr. Sobernheim, 25 Sept. 1916, A. Elkus file, A. Ruppin to Schiff, 16 June 1915; reel 1985, Palestine file; Schiff papers (JTS archives, Jerusalem), C. Adler to Schiff, 25, 26 June 1916; Magnes papers, P3/1593, Schiff to J. Magnes, 1 Nov. 1915; Henry Morgenthau, *Ambassador Morgenthau's Story* (Garden City, N.Y., 1918), pp. 378–79; *NYT,* 28 Oct. 1914, 10 May, 31 Oct. 1915.

72. Reel 1977, Schiff to J. Magnes, 1 Nov. 1915, to L. Marshall, 31 Oct. 1914; reel 1978, Schiff to C. Melchior, 25 Jan. 1915, to J. Magnes, 3 Aug. 1915; reel 1979, Schiff to J. Magnes, 8 Mar. 1916; reel 1980, Schiff to J. Saffier, 5 Jan. 1916; AJC archives, "Minutes of the Executive Committee," 16 May 1917; *American Jewish Year Book* 20 (1918–19): 374–75.

73. See, for example, Urofsky, *American Zionism*, chap. 5; Yonathan Shapiro, *Leadership of the American Zionist Organization* (Urbana, Ill., 1971), chap. 4; Reznikoff, *Marshall*, 2:511–12.

74. Reel 1977, H. Schneiderman to Schiff, 6 May 1915; Schiff papers (JTS archives, Jerusalem), L. Marshall to Schiff, 19 Feb. 1915; Goren, *New York Jews*, p. 222.

75. Reel 1978, J. Magnes to Schiff, 10 Aug. 1915; *Maccabaean* 26 (Apr. 1915): 58; Urofsky and Levy, *Letters of Brandeis*, 4:237; Goren, *New York Jews*, pp. 219–22; Cohen, *Not Free to Desist*, p. 92.

76. Reel 1977, Schiff to C. Adler, 7 May, 21 Oct. 1915; reel 1978, Schiff to G. Selikowitsch, 5 Oct. 1915, to J. Magnes, 21 May, 3 Aug. 1915, to K. Sarasohn, 28 Oct. 1915; reel 1979, Schiff to C. Adler, 23 July 1916; Schiff papers (JTS archives, Jerusalem), Schiff to C. Adler, 8 Mar., 23 June 1916; *NYT,* 11 Mar. 1916; Ira Robinson, ed., *Cyrus Adler: Selected Letters,* 2 vols. (Philadelphia, 1985), 1:292–93.

77. AJC archives, "Minutes of the Executive Committee," 9 May 1915; see also Magnes papers, P3/1594, Schiff to J. Magnes, 22 Mar. 1916; see references in n. 76.

78. AJC archives, "Minutes of the Executive Committee," 14 Aug. 1914; reel 1977, L. Miller to Schiff, 19 Aug. 1914; reel 1978, Schiff to E. Kaufman, 23 June 1915.

79. *AH,* 3 Mar. 1916; Goren, *National Leadership*, pp. 11–17; AJC archives, "Minutes of the Executive Committee," 9 May 1915, Schiff file, Schiff to L. Marshall, 10 Mar. 1916, to C. Adler, 8 Mar. 1916; Cohen, *Not Free to Desist*, p. 96.

80. Goren, *National Leadership*, pp. 1, 15; Justine W. Polier and James W. Wise, eds., *The Personal Letters of Stephen Wise* (Boston, 1956), p. 152.

81. Magnes papers, P3/1593, J. Magnes to Schiff, 10 Aug. 1915, P3/1594, J. Magnes to Schiff, 3 July 1916.

82. Goren, *National Leadership*, p. 13; *Dos Yiddishe Folk*, 13 Aug. 1915; *Tageblatt*, 5 May 1915; reel 691, Schiff to J. Magnes, 5 May 1916, to H. Kallen, 20 Sept. 1918; reel 1977, H. Schneiderman to Schiff, 6 May 1915, C. Adler to Schiff, 18 May 1915; reel 1978, H. Bernstein to Schiff, 4 Nov. 1915, Schiff to H. Bernstein, 13 May 1915; Schiff papers (JTS archives, Jerusalem), L. Marshall to Schiff, 15 Nov. 1915, C. Adler to Schiff, 28 May 1916; Magnes papers, P2/118, Schiff to J. Magnes, 5 July 1918, P3/1594, Schiff to J. Magnes, 19 Dec. 1916; AJC archives, Friedenwald file, H. Friedenwald to AJC, 12 June 1916; Alexandra A. Levin, *Vision* (Philadelphia, 1964), pp. 224, 228–31; Robinson, *Cyrus Adler*, 1:273–74.

83. Cyrus Adler, *I Have Considered the Days* (Philadelphia, 1945), p. 307; reel 1978, C. Eliot to Schiff, 7 May 1915, 30 Aug. 1915; reel 1981, C. Eliot to Schiff, 15, 22 Mar. 1917, Schiff to C. Eliot, 14 Mar. 1917.

84. Reel 679, Schiff to C. Adler, 17 May 1915; reel 691, Schiff to P. Nathan, 10 Aug. 1914; reel 1977, Schiff to H. Schneiderman, 6 May 1915; reel 1978, Schiff to H. Bernstein, 5 Mar. 1915; reel 1979, Schiff to C. Adler, 31 May, 23 July 1916; Schiff papers (JTS archives, Jerusalem), L. Marshall to Schiff, 15 Nov. 1915; AJC archives, Schiff file, Schiff to C. Adler 14 Aug. 1915, 8 Mar. 1916, to L. Marshall, 10 Mar. 1916, "Minutes of the Executive Committee," 7 Mar. 1915, 12 Mar. 1916; Magnes papers, P3/1594, Schiff to J. Magnes, 30 Mar. 1916; Robinson, *Cyrus Adler*, 1:323–24.

85. Reel 691, Schiff to *AH*, 5 June 1916; reel 693, Schiff to J. Rosenwald, 4 Dec. 1914, 10 Feb. [1916], J. Rosenwald to Schiff, 1 Dec. 1914; reel 1978, Schiff to L. Sanders, 25 Aug. 1915, to L. Brandeis, 13 Oct. 1915; reel 1980, Schiff to T. Gregory, 7 Feb. 1916; *NYT*, 1. Feb. 1916; Robinson, *Cyrus Adler*, 1:392; Yonathan Shapiro, "American Jews in Politics," *American Jewish Historical Quarterly* 55 (Dec. 1965): 204–10.

86. Reel 1979, Schiff to L. Brandeis, 29 Feb. 1916, L. Brandeis to Schiff, 3 Mar. 1916.

87. Reel 1977, H. Schneiderman to Schiff, 6 May 1915; *Tageblatt*, 15 May 1915; *AH*, 3 Mar. 1916.

88. *NYT*, 11 Mar. 1916; Urofsky and Levy, *Letters of Brandeis*, 4:116–17.

89. *Zukunft* 21 (Apr. 1916): 288–90; reel 1979, Schiff to C. Adler, 25 May 1916; *American Jewish Year Book* 18 (1916–17): 423–25; Adler, *Schiff*, 2:301; Robinson, *Cyrus Adler*, 1:302–5; *American Jewish Chronicle*, 19 May 1916.

90. Reel 1979, Sholom Asch file.

91. Reel 1979, Schiff to C. Adler, 25 May 1916, 2, 12 June 1916; *AH*, 26 May 1916; Adler, *Schiff*, 2:300–1.

92. Reel 679, Schiff to C. Adler, 26 May 1916; reel 1979, J. Barondess to Schiff, 1 June 1916, Schiff to S. Wolf, 6 June 1916, H. Bernstein file; reel 1980, Central Jewish Institute file, Schiff to J. Magnes, 5 July 1916; reel 1981, Schiff to J. Rosenwald, 5 June 1916, I. Singer to Schiff, 6 June 1916; Urofsky and Levy, *Letters of Brandeis*, 4:202–5; *NYT*, 22 May, 2 June 1916; *AH*, 26 May, 2 June 1916; *American Jewish Chronicle*, 26 May, 2 June 1916; *The Big Stick* (Yiddish), 2, 9 June 1916 (my thanks to David Roskies for calling this journal to my attention); *Maccabaean* 28 (June 1916): 123; M. Olgin in *Forward*, 23 May 1916; A. Liessin, *Zukunft* 21 (June 1916): 468.

93. Reel 1979, Schiff to C. Adler, 25 May, 2 June 1916, C. Adler to Schiff, 1 June 1916, P. Warburg to Schiff, 6 June 1916, S. Wolf to Schiff, 15 June 1916.

94. Reel 1980, Schiff to J. Magnes, 25 May 1916, to A. Cahan 8 July 1916; reel 1981, Schiff to J. Rosenwald, 5 June 1916; *NYT*, 5 June 1916; *AH*, 9 June 1916; Adler, *Schiff*, 2:303–4.

95. Reel 1980, Kehillah files, Schiff to A. Cahan, 8 July 1916; Schiff papers (JTS archives, Jerusalem), C. Adler to Schiff, 9 June 1916; *NYT*, 6, 10, 15 June 1916; *AH*, 9, 23 June 1916; *American Israelite*, 15 June 1916; *Day*, 15 June 1916; *Current Opinion*, 61 (July 1916): 19; *Hebrew Standard*, 9 June 1916.

96. Cohen, *Not Free to Desist*, pp. 93–97; AJC archives, "Minutes of the Executive Committee," 9 Apr. 1916.

97. AJC archives, "Minutes of the Executive Committee," 9 May 1915; reel 679, Schiff to C. Adler, 23 July 1916, CA MSS, p. 304f; reel 1978, L. Marshall to Schiff, 10 Nov. 1915; reel 1980, Schiff to L. Marshall, 21 July 1916; reel 1981, Schiff to C. Adler, 11 July 1917, to B. Richards, 6 July 1917, to H. Cutler, 23 Apr. 1917; Cyrus Adler papers (JTS archives), Schiff to C. Adler, 16 July 1917; Robinson, *Cyrus Adler*, 1:328; Cohen, *Not Free to Desist*, pp. 96–98, 112.

98. Reel 679, Schiff to L. Marshall, 2 Jan. 1919; reel 1981, Schiff to H. Cutler, 29 Jan. 1917; Cohen, *Not Free to Desist*, pp. 112–13.

99. For example, reel 1977, Schiff to L. Sanders, 28 Jan. 1914.

100. Urofsky, *American Zionism*, chap. 4, pp. 202–20.

101. Evyatar Friesel, "Jacob H. Schiff Becomes a Zionist," *Studies in Zionism*, no. 5 (Apr. 1982), pp. 56–69; Shapiro, *Leadership of the American Zionist Organization*, pp. 111–17; *AH*, 27 Apr. 1917.

102. *NYT*, 4 Apr. 1911, 8 Jan. 1914; Schiff, "Zionism and Nationalism," *AH*, 16 Jan. 1914.

103. *NYT*, 23 Apr. 1917; reel 678, statement by Jacob Billikopf on the Galveston movement; Friesel, "Schiff Becomes a Zionist," p. 73.

104. Reel 1982, H. Kallen to Schiff 24 July 1917; reel 1984, H. Kallen to Schiff, 7 July 1918.

105. Friesel, "Schiff Becomes a Zionist," pp. 62–63; reel 1979, Schiff to L. Brandeis, 29 Feb. 1916; reel 1981, E. Ben Yehudah to Schiff, 20 July 1917; reel 1983, C. Adler to Schiff, 2 Jan. 1918; Adler, *Schiff*, 2:308.

106. Reel 1978, Schiff to J. Magnes, 3 Aug. 1915; reel 1984, Schiff to D. Lubin, 30 Apr. 1918; Schiff papers (JTS archives, Jerusalem), Schiff to C. Adler, 21 Jan. 1918; Magnes papers, P3/1594, Schiff to J. Magnes, 22 Mar. 1916; *AH*, 3 Mar. 1917.

107. Reel 1979, Schiff to J. Magnes, 24 Feb. 1916, to L. Brandeis, 29 Feb. 1916; reel 1981, Schiff to R. Waley-Cohen, 3 Oct. 1917; Louis Brandeis papers (University of Louisville archives), reel 78, Schiff to L. Brandeis, 8 Mar. 1916; Magnes papers, P3/1594, Schiff to J. Magnes, 24 Feb., 22 Mar. 1916; Urofsky and Levy, *Letters of Brandeis*, 4:103–4; *AH*, 3 Mar. 1916.

108. Reel 1980, J. Magnes to Schiff, 25 Feb. 1916; AJC archives, "Minutes of Executive Committee," 15 Apr. 1917; Magnes papers, P3/1594, correspondence in April 1917 between J. Magnes and Schiff, C. Adler, L. Marshall, J. Mack, see also J. Magnes to Schiff, 22 Jan. 1918.

109. *NYT*, 23 Apr. 1917; *AH*, 27 Apr. 1917; reel 679, Schiff to O. and E. Schiff, 1

May 1917; reel 1982, Schiff to H. Jackson, 26 Apr. 1917; reel 1984, Schiff to
D. Lubin, 30 Apr. 1918; Adler, *Schiff*, 2:308; Stuart E. Knee, *The Concept of
Zionist Dissent in the American Mind* (New York, 1979), pp. 90–91. The purpose of the League of Jewish Youth, to combat indifference to Judaism on the
part of the young people, was readily endorsed by Schiff and Marshall.

110. Reel 1982, Schiff to D. Philipson, 11 May 1917; reel 1983, D. Philipson to
Schiff, 1, 18 May 1917; reel 1985, Schiff to J. Mack, 4 Apr. 1918.

111 Reel 1982, Schiff to D. Philipson, 11 May 1917; reel 1983, D. Philipson to
Schiff, 18 May 1917; *NYT*, 21 May 1917; *AH*, 18 May 1917.

112. Reel 1979, Schiff to S. Schulman, 6 Dec. 1915; reel 1980, Schiff to H. Hur-
witz, 17 May 1915; reel 1981, Schiff to E. Friedman, 15 May 1917; reel 1982,
Schiff to H. Enelow, 16 May 1917; *AH*, 3 Mar. 1916, 4 May 1917; Central
Zionist Archives (Jerusalem), A405/230, Schiff to D. Philipson, 11 May 1917.

113. Reel 1981, E. Friedman to Schiff, 10 May, 5, 14 Aug. 1917, Schiff to E. Fried-
man, 15 May 1917; reel 1982, E. Friedman to Schiff, 23 May 1917, Schiff to E.
Friedman, 5 July 1917. Friesel, "Schiff Becomes a Zionist," passim; Adler,
Schiff, 2:308–12. See also *NYT*, 30 Dec. 1917; Elisha Friedman, "Zionism and
Hebrew Idealism," *AH*, 29 June 1917, *AH*, 4 Jan. 1918.

114. *AH*, 4 Jan. 1918.

115. Except where noted, for this and the next two paragraphs, see reel 679, Schiff
to E. Friedman, 25 Sept., 26 Oct. 1917, to I. Zangwill, 17 Oct. 1917, E. Friedman to Schiff, 21, 28 Sept., 25 Oct. 1917; reel 1982, Schiff to E. Friedman, 9,
29 Oct. 1917, E. Friedman to Schiff, 27 Oct., 2, 23 Nov. 1917. For this paragraph, see also reel 1982, Schiff to L. Marshall, 14 Nov. 1917, L. Marshall to
Schiff, 14 Nov. 1917; Urofsky, *American Zionism*, p. 251; Friesel, "Schiff Becomes a Zionist," pp. 74–75. Marshall had announced his support of Palestine
as a religious and cultural center to the cheers of the *kehillah* convention in
April 1917. "I do not know whether I am talking Zionism," he said, "but I have
always been such a Zionist." *NYT*, 29 Apr. 1917.

116. Reel 679, Schiff to I. Zangwill, 17 Oct. 1917; reel 1982, Schiff to L. Marshall, 14
Nov. 1917, L. Marshall to Schiff, 14 Nov. 1917; Central Zionist Archives,
A405/230, Schiff-Mack correspondence for November and December 1917;
Urofsky and Levy, *Letters of Brandeis*, 4:435; Knee, *Concept of Zionist Dissent*, p. 95.

117. Reel 679, Schiff to J. Mack, 4 Apr. 1918; reel 693, Schiff to I. Zangwill, 5 Mar.
1918; reel 1984, Schiff to D. Lubin, 30 Apr. 1918; Schiff papers (JTS archives,
Jerusalem), Schiff to C. Adler 15 Jan. 1918; Central Zionist Archives,
A406/229, S. Wise to J. Mack, 6 Dec. 1917, J. de Haas to J. Mack, 8 Dec. 1917;
Barnard, *Forging of an American Jew*, p. 198; Friesel, "Schiff Becomes a Zion-
ist," pp. 66–80, 87–92; Adler, *Schiff*, 2:312–17.

118. Reel 1984, I. Friedlaender to Schiff, 6 Jan. 1918, H. Kallen to Schiff, 11 Jan.
1918; reel 1985, ZOA file, J. Mack–Schiff correspondence March-April 1918;
Central Zionist Archives, A405/230 and A405/193, letters of J. Mack to Schiff,
esp. January–February, April 1918.

119. For a few examples of Schiff's numerous contributions, see reel 697, Schiff to
J. Mack, 4 Jan., 30 July, 26 Dec. 1918. Schiff was also consulted by Sir Herbert
Samuel, first British high commissioner for Palestine, reel 693, H. Samuel to
Schiff, 16 Aug. 1920. In addition to references listed below, material for this

paragraph comes from the voluminous Schiff-Mack correspondence for 1918–20 in Central Zionist Archives, A405/230 and A405/193. Reel 682, CA MSS, pp. 1199–1201; *NYT*, 10 Mar. 1919; *AH*, 2 Jan. 1920; Urofsky and Levy, *Letters of Brandeis*, 4:323.

120. Jacob H. Schiff, "Let American Jewry Unite for the Up-Building of Palestine," *New Palestine*, 16 Jan. 1920; reel 693, Schiff to P. Nathan, 16 Jan. 1920, to J. Rosenwald, 18 Dec. 1919; reel 1981, Schiff to E. Friedman, 26 Oct. 1917; Central Zionist Archives, A405/230, interview of Schiff with Zionist leaders, 13 June 1919.

121. Reel 679, Schiff to P. Nathan, 16 Jan. 1920, to editor *Jewish Morning Journal*, 5 May 1920; reel 684, Schiff to I. Zangwill, 14 Aug., 10 Sept. 1919; reel 693, Schiff to C. Eliot, 2 Feb. 1920.

122. Jacob H. Schiff, "The Need for a Jewish Homeland," *Nation*, 26 Apr. 1919; reel 1986, Schiff to S. Bass, 11 Mar. 1919; *NYT*, 9 Feb., 10 Mar. 1919.

123. Reel 679, Schiff to editor *Jewish Morning Journal*, 5 May 1920; reel 682, CA MSS, pp. 1199–1201; reel 684, Schiff to I. Zangwill, 14 Aug. 1919; reel 1986, Schiff to S. Bass, 11 Mar. 1919, to M. Jastrow, 10 July 1919, special bulletin of ZOA, 2 Feb. 1920; AJC archives, Schiff file, Schiff to H. Schneiderman, 17 Mar. 1919; Reznikoff, *Marshall*, 2:539.

124. Levene, *War, Jews, and the New Europe*, pp. 96–98; Gwynn, *Sir Cecil Spring Rice*, 2:420–22; AJC archives, "Minutes of the Executive Committee," 2 Feb 1918; Charles I. Goldblatt, "The Impact of the Balfour Declaration in America," *American Jewish Historical Quarterly* 57 (June 1968): 455–515.

125. Reel 1982, Schiff to H. Bernstein, 20 Nov. 1917; Schiff papers (JTS archives, Jerusalem), Schiff to C. Adler, 21 Jan. 1918; *AH*, 23 Nov. 1917, 4 Jan. 1918; *NYT*, 2 June 1918. One Yiddish journalist, without any evidence, suggested that Schiff, like the Rothschilds, approved of the declaration for the purpose of economic exploitation. Goldblatt, "Impact of the Balfour Declaration," p. 481.

126. AJC archives, "Minutes of the Executive Committee," 2 Feb., 7, 10 Apr. 1918.

127. Reel 1985, ZOA file, Schiff-Mack correspondence for Mar.–Apr. 1918; Cohen, *Not Free to Desist*, pp. 109–10; Friesel, "Schiff Becomes a Zionist," p. 81; Knee, *Concept of Zionist Dissent*, pp. 95–98.

128. Aaron S. Klieman and Adrian L. Klieman, eds., *Zionism: A Documentary History*, vol. 4 (New York, 1990), pp. 114–27; *NYT*, 12, 14 Sept. 1918; Friesel, "Schiff Becomes a Zionist," pp. 82–83.

129. Reel 679, Schiff to editor *Jewish Morning Journal*, 5 May 1920.

130. For example, *AH*, 9 Apr. 1920, London *Jewish Chronicle*, 5 Mar. 1920.

7. The End of an Era (Notes to Pages 238–250)

1. Reel 22 (JTS archives), Schiff to E. Benjamin, 17 June 1919; reel 684, Schiff to I. Zangwill, 10 Sept. 1919; reel 694, Schiff to S. Wolf, 7 Nov. 1918; reel 1978, Schiff to S. Fleischer, 19 Feb. 1915; reel 1981, Schiff to J. Rosenwald, 12 May 1916; reel 1984, Schiff to G. Blumenthal, 24 Oct. 1918; reel 1985, Jewish War Relief and Foreign Affairs files for 1919–20; reel 1986, Schiff to H. Schneiderman, 22 Sept. 1919; *NYT*, 4 May 1920.

2. *NYT,* 23 Oct. 1918, 6 Jan., 10 June 1919; reel 1985, Schiff to J. Cushman, 30 Mar. 1920, to S. Tyng, 17 May 1920; reel 680, Schiff to J. Wadsworth, 22 Sept. 1919, to I. Zangwill, 27 Sept. 1918; reel 689, Schiff to M. Warburg, 19 Jan. 1920; Cyrus Adler, *Jacob H. Schiff,* 2 vols. (Garden City, N.Y., 1929), 2:206–7.

3. Reel 689, Schiff to J. Rosenwald, 21 Nov. 1918, J. Rosenwald to Schiff, 25 Nov. 1918; reel 1985, Schiff to J. Rosenwald, 6 Dec. 1918, J. Rosenwald to Schiff, 9 Dec. 1918; entry for Schiff in *Encyclopedia of American Biography* (1974).

4. Reel 1978, Schiff to C. Eliot, 4 May 1915; reel 1984, Schiff to T. Masaryk, 4 Nov. 1918, to M. Smith, 29 Nov., 3 Dec. 1918.

5. Reel 1985, Schiff to L. Marshall, 4 Nov. 1918; reel 1986, Schiff to I. Landman, 10 July 1919; AJC archives, "Minutes of the Executive Committee," Sept. 1918–Dec. 1918, 6 Mar., 12 Oct., 16 Nov., 14 Dec. 1919, 10 Oct. 1920; Central Zionist Archives (Jerusalem), Schiff to J. Mack, 21 July 1919; Charles Reznikoff, ed., *Louis Marshall,* 2 vols. (Philadelphia, 1957), 1:290–94, 2:530–33, 585–93, 601–21; *NYT,* 22 May 1919.

6. Reel 1986, Schiff to H. Schneiderman 17, 18 June 1919; *NYT,* 12 Dec. 1918; Cyrus Adler and Aaron M. Margalith, *With Firmness in the Right* (New York, 1946), pp. 152–53.

7. AJC archives, "Minutes of the Executive Committee," Oct. 1918–Dec. 1919; annual surveys in *American Jewish Year Book* for 1918-21, esp. vols. 21, 22; reel 1986, C. Adler to Schiff, 13 Aug. 1919, Schiff to S. Melamed, 11 June 1919, to H. Schneiderman, 17 Mar., 17 June 1919, B. Richards to Schiff, 8 Dec. 1918, 31 May 1919.

8. Reel 684, Schiff to I. Zangwill, 23 Oct. 1919; Ira Robinson, ed., *Cyrus Adler: Selected Letters,* 2 vols. (Philadelphia, 1985), 1:384; Naomi W. Cohen, *Not Free to Desist* (Philadelphia, 1972), pp. 110–21.

9. Jacob R. Marcus, *United States Jewry,* vol. 4 (Detroit, 1993), p. 623; reel 684, Schiff to I. Zangwill, 14 Aug. 1919; reel 1985, Schiff to J. Tumulty, 12 Dec. 1918, Schiff's secretary to W. Graves, 30 Sept. 1918, Louis Marshall file a; reel 1986, AJC files a-b.

10. *American Jewish Year Book* 21 (1919–1920): 169–70, 279–82, 286–89, 22 (1920–1921): 266–68; reel 1985, Schiff to A. Sack, 11 Oct. 1918.

11. Cohen, *Not Free to Desist,* pp. 121, 127; AJC archives, "Minutes of the Executive Committee," 9 Nov. 1918, 14 Dec. 1919. The State Department reported that it had asked Denmark to ascertain the actual state of affairs.

12. Reel 1981, Schiff to L. Marshall, 9 Apr., 12 Nov. 1917; reel 1984, Schiff to S. Mason, 18, 22 Nov. 1918; reel 1985, Schiff to Lord Swaythling, 30 Sept. 1918, Russia file, L. Marshall to Schiff, 11 Sept. 1918; reel 1986, Russian Information Bureau file, 1920; AJC archives, "Minutes of the Executive Committee," 16 Nov. 1919; Adler, *Schiff,* 2:258–59.

13. AJC archives, "Minutes of the Executive Committee," 16 Nov., 9 Dec. 1919, 14 Mar. 1920; Cohen, *Not Free to Desist,* p. 127; Morton Rosenstock, *Louis Marshall* (Detroit, 1965), pp. 113–14; Willaim E. Leuchtenburg, *The Perils of Prosperity* (Chicago, 1958), pp. 68–69.

14. AJC archives, "Minutes of the Executive Committee," 20 Oct. 1918, 16 Feb. 1919.

15. AJC archives, "Minutes of the Executive Committee," 24 Sept. 1918; reel 1985, A. Sack to Schiff, 12, 14 Sept. 1918, Schiff to A. Sack, 2 Dec. 1918; Adler, *Schiff*, 2:257–59.

16. Cohen, *Not Free to Desist*, pp. 124–25; Leo P. Ribuffo, *The Old Christian Right* (Philadelphia, 1983), p. 9; *NYT*, 15, 17 Feb. 1919.

17. AJC archives, "Minutes of the Executive Committee," 10 Oct. 1920; Ribuffo, *Old Christian Right*, pp. 9–13; John Higham, *Strangers in the Land* (New York, 1973), pp. 277–86; Leonard Dinnerstein, *Antisemitism in America* (New York, 1994), pp. 78–83; Schiff papers (AJC archives), Schiff to L. Marshall, 9 June 1920; Cohen, *Not Free to Desist*, pp. 129–36.

18. *Dearborn Independent, The International Jew*, 4 vols. (Dearborn, Mich., 1921–22), esp. 2:34, 44–47; 3:198–216, 249–56, chap. 60; vol. 4: chap. 77. One account of Ford reveals how the *Dearborn Independent* employed detectives to keep Schiff and the people he saw socially under surveillance. Albert Lee, *Henry Ford and the Jews* (New York, 1980), pp. 23–24.

19. Denis Fahey, *The Mystical Body of Christ in the Modern World* (Waterford, Ireland, 1935), pp. 89–93, 170–71; Comte de Saint-Aulaire, *Geneva versus Peace* (New York, 1937), pp. 90–93; *Key to the Mystery* (Montreal, 1937), pp. 7–11; Pat Robertson, *The New World Order* (Dallas, Tex., 1991), pp. 65, 73, 123, 178; Ribuffo, *Old Christian Right*, pp. 59, 113.

20. Adler, *Schiff*, 2:357–61.

21. Unless otherwise noted, all material for this and the next five paragraphs comes from scrapbooks entitled "Press Tributes to Jacob Henry Schiff" (JTS archives).

22. *AH*, 8–22 Oct. 1920; Adler, *Schiff*, 2:362.

23. Reel 22, M. Kohler to M. Schiff, 14 Oct. 1925; reel 23 (JTS archives), speech by William Goldman, 3 Jan. 1920.

24. Gerson D. Cohen, "Jewish Identity and Jewish Collective Will in America," paper presented at the General Assembly of Jewish Federations and Welfare Funds, Nov. 10, 1973, p. 9.

25. On the 1920s, see Henry L. Feingold, *A Time for Searching*, vol. 4 of *The Jewish People in America*, 5 vols. (Baltimore, 1992); Melvin I. Urofsky, "American Jewish Leadership," *American Jewish History* 70 (June 1981): 401–17; Morris D. Waldman, *Nor by Power* (New York, 1953), chap. 30; Jonathan S. Woocher, "The Democratization of the American Jewish Polity," in *Authority, Power and Leadership in the Jewish Polity*, ed. Daniel J. Elazar (Lanham, Md., 1991), pp. 169–70.

26. See references to Feingold and Waldman in n. 25.

27. A term for the 1920s used by E. Digby Baltzell, *The Protestant Establishment* (New York, 1966), chap. 9.

28. Reel 1985, L. Marshall to Schiff, 24 Apr., 18 Sept. 1920; Cyrus Adler, *I Have Considered the Days* (Philadelphia, 1945), pp. 328–29.

Index

Aaronsohn, Aaron, 183
Adamson Act of 1916, 30
Addams, Jane, 93
Adler, Cyrus: as adviser to Schiff, 43; and American Jewish Committee, 112; in American Jewish Congress debate, 109, 216, 221, 222–23; on an American Jewish historical society, 76; on Asch's depiction of Schiff, 220; on the Balfour Declaration, 235; and Friedenwald's resignation from AJC, 218; on government response to proposed Palestine purchase, 283n.52; on Haifa Technikum board, 184; and Haupt, 171; immigration restriction opposed by, 157; invited to become a shekel-payer, 226; *Jacob H. Schiff: His Life and Letters*, xiii; on Jewish support for Japan against Russia, 134; in Jewish Theological Seminary reorganization, 102; on minority rights, 241; at 1919 strategy meeting with Schiff, 250; in Russian treaty abrogation campaign, 145; on Schiff as hero worshiper, 42; at Schiff's funeral, 246; on Schiff's Hebrew, 2; on Schiff's opposition to Allied loans, 197; on Schiff's religious behavior, 100; on Schiff's role in the "language war," 185–86; at Versailles, 241
Adler, Felix, 49
Agadir Crisis, 190
Agricultural colonization, 117–19
Ahlwardt, Hermann, 131
AJC. *See* American Jewish Committee
AJRC (American Jewish Relief Committee), 211, 212

Alexander, James, 26
Allen, Frederick Lewis, 8, 54
Alliance Israélite Universelle: on needy Jews in New York, 84; Schiff and American Jewish Committee cooperation with, 112; Schiff preferring German Hilfsverein to, 47; and Schiff's crusade for Russian Jews, 125, 142; on Schiff's international role, 56; and Schiff's Mexican settlement plan, 170; Schiff suggests sending immigrants to San Francisco, 159; as seeking to control emigration process, 87
American China Development Company, 36
American Friends of German Democracy, 201
American Hebrew (newspaper), 127
American Israelite (newspaper), 182
Americanization: and Christianity, 94; elitism as inconsistent with, 249; ghettos as impervious to, 86, 117; Hebrew Technical Institute in, 91; Jewish leaders demanding, 50, 89, 98; Jewish Theological Seminary in, 96, 97, 98, 99, 102, 104; and the *kehillah*, 116; prewar crusade hardening prejudice against Jews, 70; Schiff in Americanization of Jewish immigrants, xiii; wartime crusade for, 200, 201, 203
American Jewish Chronicle (periodical), 192, 194, 221
American Jewish Committee (AJC): in American Jewish Congress debate, 215–24; on the Balfour Declaration, 235–36; and the Bolshevik